Peckinpah: A Portrait in Montage
The Definitive Edition

50 years after "The Wild Bunch"
From the Writer Who Knew Him Best

by
Garner Simmons

David Samuel Peckinpah
February 21, 1925-December 28, 1984

Peckinpah: A Portrait in Montage
The Definitive Edition

50 years after "The Wild Bunch"
From the Writer Who Knew Him Best

by
Garner Simmons

Equuleus

ISBN: 9781079792331

Library of Congress Cataloging-in-Publication Data

Simmons, Garner, 1943—
Peckinpah: a portrait in montage the definitive edition / by
Garner Simmons, p. cm.

ISBN: 9781079792331
    1.   Peckinpah, Sam, 1925-1984. 2. Motion Picture
       producers and directors—United States--Biography

"A richly entertaining book. Sam Peckinpah is… a director who needs adversity to get the juices flowing. Fortified by booze and shots of vitamin B12, [he] rides the whirlwind… firing the incompetents beneath him, baiting the ones over him and bullying and testing and goading the rest… [This book reveals] the complex interplay of power and art or movie and mythmaking as practiced by Peckinpah, an idiosyncratic but skillful manipulator."

~ Molly Haskell, *The New York Times Book Review*

"Simmons'… anecdotal approach to Peckinpah's life and work… takes off and soars into a very interesting overview of one of our more brilliant and 'difficult' directors, and of the system in which he works…"

~ G. William Jones, *The Southwestern Review*

"Excellent study of the director, exhaustively researched, thoroughly detailed."

~ Quarterly Review of Film Studies

"The first book of substance on Sam Peckinpah's life's work. Widely quoted around the world."

~ Max Evans-Author: *Goin' Crazy with Sam Peckinpah*

In memory of Nick Redman

Contents

To Begin

Having devoted so much to watching, thinking and writing about the extraordinary life and films of Sam Peckinpah, I feel the time has come to gather and publish them under a single cover. A kind of coda to the inspired madness that was Sam Peckinpah's life by design.

In doing so, it is my intention to bring focus and clarity to one of the most talented, complicated and self-destructive men I have ever known. A true American original. A visionary artist, who had that rare ability to stare unblinking into the crucible of life and see what others could not, then capture it on film.

I first met Sam Peckinpah in the summer of 1973 in Mexico City as I was beginning to research a book on his life and films. He was just beginning preproduction on *Bring Me the Head of Alfredo Garcia*, his ninth feature and the sixth in five years. Sam was 48. I was 30. The details of how that meeting came about as well as its aftermath can be found within these pages in the Preface and beyond the 1998 edition of *PECKINPAH: A Portrait in Montage*, the work that stands at the core of this endeavor.

I will always be in Sam's debt for his openness and candor in allowing me access to the unapologetic and uncensored details of his life. I would also like to thank all those –family and friends, cohorts and enemies – who took the time to speak frankly with me about their experiences working with the director. As is recorded throughout these pages, for better or worse, Sam Peckinpah courted controversy and was never afraid of exposing the unvarnished truth.

Along the way, I have written and published a number of other pieces on the director and his work. They are also gathered here in an attempt to better understand both the man and his work: a total of only fourteen films produced over a little more than two decades.

Given time off for bad behavior, the fact that Peckinpah was actually able to produce anything of value stands as a testament to his remarkable talents and the obsessive-compulsive nature of his personality.

For many years, his first feature, *The Deadly Companions*, was discredited and dismissed in part because of Peckinpah's own dissatisfaction with the final film. In the essay titled "*The Deadly Companions* Revisited" I have attempted to rectify that misconception.

The Wild Bunch, of course, has received the lion's share of both the praise and vilification in the fifty years since its initial release in the summer of 1969. While other books and articles have been written in an attempt to understand the director's stunning achievement, in the essay "Through a Glass Darkly: Sam Peckinpah's *The Wild Bunch*" I have attempted to move past the superficial details and minutia to explore the reality of Peckinpah's unique directorial style. While many have attempted to duplicate his achievement, all his imitators lack the passion that continues to make that film resonate with all who see it, a classic in every sense of the word.

Over the years, Warner Brothers has sought to remake the film without success. As I write this, it is reported that Mel Gibson is planning to take it on. But as I point out in "*Straw Dogs,* Then and Now," when it comes to Peckinpah, it isn't a matter of retelling a story but of somehow capturing the nuances, the honesty and the depth of a troubling masterwork. Peckinpah's best films may be imitated but never surpassed. To attempt to do so is a fool's errand.

As indicated above, I first encountered Sam Peckinpah on *Bring Me the Head of Alfredo Garcia*. Included here is the essay published by *Sight & Sound* in conjunction with the retrospective of Sam's work screened at the Locarno International Film Festival in the summer of 2015, where I was a principal speaker. In it, I have attempted to take a fresh look at another of Peckinpah's most demanding films. Panned by critics at the time of its release in 1974, few save the late Roger Ebert recognized the brilliance of Peckinpah's dark and troubling tale. Dismissed by most as another violent, blood-soaked shoot-em-up, the film survives today as a cult classic. In truth, it is Peckinpah's most personal work, an extraordinary love story of obsession, madness, betrayal, and loss in which Warren Oates delivers his finest, most complex performance.

And finally, "Two Lions on the Edge of Winter," which first appeared in *Cultural Weekly*, is an extraordinary moment away from the cameras when two old friends, Sam Peckinpah and Peter O'Toole, who unfortunately never managed to find a picture to work on together, took time to share a glass and reminisce one afternoon at the legendary Formosa Café. A candid look at two kindred spirits, who both left indelible marks upon the cinema.

Taken together, these six very different pieces hopefully will provide a sense of who Sam Peckinpah was. A towering talent who sacrificed everything for his art. Unflinching, his films captured the raw passions, ironies, and contradictions of human emotion. And like Jason Robards' character in *The Ballad of Cable Hogue*, he *found it where it wasn't...* and we are all the richer for it.

Garner Simmons
Woodland Hills, California
May 2019

Photo by Garner Simmons:
On the set of *Bring Me the Head of Alfredo Garcia*

Acknowledgments

In addition to the many who helped bring about the initial version of this book back in 1982 and whose names can be found under the acknowledgments in that edition, I need to recognize a number of others. First, the late Mel Zerman, publisher of Limelight Editions of New York, who recognized the value of what I had written and stepped forward to acquire the rights and republish the book with additional material in 1998. Prior to his death at age 79 in 2010, Mel secured Limelight's future by merging with Amadeus Press which continued to publish *Peckinpah: A Portrait in Montage* through Proscenium Publishers of New York following 2003. Eventually, Hal Leonard Books would acquire Amadeus / Limelight and continue to keep the book in print until eventually spinning off Hal Leonard's trade book division to Rowman & Littlefield, its present publisher. Deserving special thanks in all this is John Cerullo, Senior Executive Editor of R&L, whose help in making this present edition possible has been invaluable.

Similarly, I want to thank Michael Bliss, editor for both *"The Deadly Companions Revisited"* which appeared in *New Essays on the Films of Sam Peckinpah* and *"Through a Glass Darkly: Sam Peckinpah's The Wild Bunch"* which appeared in *The Wild Bunch at 50: Golden Anniversary Essays on Sam Peckinpah's Greatest Film,* for his continued encouragement and support. Also I need to thank Adam Leipzig, editor and publisher of *Cultural Weekly*, whose friendship and unflagging championing of the arts over the years continues to brighten the landscape of literary Los Angeles.

To my wife Sheila, whose comments, willingness to proofread, and constant support make all things possible. And as always, I remain indebted to my fellow Dog Brothers Paul

Seydor, David Weddle, Jesse Graham, Ron Shelton, and the late Nick Redman, to whom this book is dedicated.

Finally, to Robert McCullough, who convinced me of the need to bring together all of my writings on the life and films of Sam Peckinpah under one cover. This book would simply not be possible without his persistent and insightful guidance.

My thanks to all.

(Photo courtesy of Metro-Goldwyn-Mayer)

A Portrait in Montage

PECKINPAH

With a new Preface and a new Postscript

by Garner Simmons

LIMELIGHT EDITIONS, New York

1998

Acknowledgments

A project of this proportion requires time as well as the support and cooperation of a great many people. In the nearly ten years this book has taken, I have been exceptionally fortunate and wish to thank those individuals, institutions, and organizations that have helped to make it possible.

Foremost among those is Stuart Kaminsky, who initially put me in contact with Sam Peckinpah. As both my friend and advisor at Northwestern University, he offered continued encouragement and an example that always provided me with a touchstone, the quality of which I hope is reflected in this text. For this and much more, I will always be grateful.

Also at Northwestern, Jack Ellis and the late Paddy Whannel, who helped to develop in me an appreciation for objective criticism and the American film, deserve my thanks.

To my good friend George Wead at the University of Texas I wish to extend my lasting gratitude. His patience and persistence with me finally flowered with the publication of this book. I must also thank Suzanne Comer of the University of Texas Press for her time and consideration in bringing this project to fruition, as well as Beth Allen, who so carefully attended to the copy editing.
And to Paul Seydor, whose book *Peckinpah: The Western Films* provides invaluable insights, I will always be indebted for his constructive criticism and support.

I should further wish to thank individually Dan Faris, Charles Titone, and Joseph Hill, each of whom contributed to this project out of a genuine affection for the films of Peckinpah.

My gratitude as well goes to the now defunct publications *Film Heritage* and *The Velvet Light-trap* for publishing portions of the material found herein, albeit in a different form, during the course of my research and writing. I am also grateful to Gil Iverson of Four Star International (Beverly Hills, California) for allowing me to screen Peckinpah's television work, Doug Lemza of Films Incorporated (Wilmette, Illinois), and the Northwestern University Film Division for the use of its facilities.

Of the many people who graciously consented to take the time to be interviewed by tape, longhand, or telephone, none was more cooperative than Sam Peckinpah. Indeed, his only concern through-out was that he be portrayed without flattery, a concern that both improved this text and cemented our friendship, for which I will always be grateful.

Always helpful and direct, Denver and Betty Peckinpah, Sam's brother and sister-in-law, were invaluable in helping me unearth the Peckinpah family history, as was Sam and Denver's sister, Fern Lea Peckinpah Peter. They not only opened their homes to me, but also made it possible for me to interview Sam's mother, Fern Church Peckinpah; his uncle, Mortimer Peckinpah; and his irrepressible aunt, Jane Visher, whose memory at 87 was as clear as the mountain streams she still fished. I also gained numerous insights from two other points of view, those of my good friends David E. Peckinpah, Peckinpah's nephew, and Walter Peter, his brother-in-law. My thanks to them all.

Among others, several are deserving of special note. First is the late composer Jerry Fielding to whom this book is dedicated in part. Outspoken, articulate, talented, and fiercely loyal, Jerry Fielding was one of those rare individuals who could be counted on, in the words of Robert Culp's moving eulogy, "to go back-to-back in the alley with you when the chips were down." Of all the people I have met both within and without the motion picture industry, few can compare. The same may be said of his wife, Camille, who so frequently kept track of us all. Thanks are simply not enough.

Next, Katy Haber, Peckinpah's erstwhile secretary who has since proved herself on other battlefields as well, must be thanked for both coordinating my efforts and helping me understand Sam Peckinpah's manic lifestyle.

And of course, I would be remiss if I did not acknowledge my great appreciation for the late character actor Strother Martin, who made time to speak with me at length on Peckinpah when we first met in Chicago, and whose friendship I shall always miss.

As for others who were kind enough to share their memories, insights, and impressions of Peckinpah, both pro and con, I shall always be indebted for their candor and generosity: Kenneth Andreen, R. G. Armstrong, Newt Arnold, Lucien Ballard, Martin Baum, Ernest Borgnine, Jerry Bresler, James Caan, Joe Canutt, Gordon Carroll, Aurora Clavel, James Coburn, Cliff Coleman, Gary Combs, Garth Craven, Jackie Craven, Helmut Dantine, William Davidson, Gordon Dawson, Kip Dellinger, Jack Elam, Max Evans, Emilio Fernandez, Charles B. FitzSimons, David Foster, Donny Fritz, David Zelag Goodman, Joie Gould, Walon Green, Betty Gunn, Jerry Harvey, Ted Haworth, Charlton Heston, Dustin Hoffman, William Holden, Bo Hopkins, Whitey Hughes, Carol James, Kent James, Ben Johnson, L. Q. Jones, Walter Kelley, Burt Kennedy, Frank Kowalski,

Kris Kristofferson, Philip Lathrop, Arthur Lewis, Lou Lombardo, Ida Lupino, Richard Lyons, Joel McCrea, Ali MacGraw, Steve McQueen, Daniel Mainwaring, Daniel Melnick, Warren Oates, Begonia Palacios, Kristen Peckinpah, Marie Selland Peckinpah, Matthew Peckinpah, Melissa Peckinpah, Sharon Peckinpah, Alf Fegley, Al Pettitt, Blain Pettitt, Alex Phillips, Jr., Slim Pickens, Jason Robards, Jeb Rosebrook, Frank Santillo, Randolph Scott, Donald Siegel, James Silke, Stella Stevens, Carlos Teran, Casey Tibbs, Chano Urueta, Robert Visciglia, Robert Webber, Chuck Wilborn, Joe Wizan, Bitsy Wright, Ron Wright, and Burt Young.

This book is in partial repayment to the late Eric Ryan, who first opened my eyes, and David Sellin, who filled them with an understanding of significant form, and to Michael Bethke and Scott Gibbs, who in leaner times kept me alive, for which I shall always be grateful.

And finally let me thank Toby Barthoff, who typed this manuscript when it was very rough, and Sheila McHugh Simmons, who helped me polish it.

Preface

The last time I saw Sam Peckinpah he was fifty-nine. Whitehaired and wizened, he barely resembled the man I had first met in Mexico City more than a decade before. Back then he arguably had been the most feared director in the film industry. But on this night in early December 1984, he seemed more fragile, like some ancient prizefighter past his prime, still at ringside awaiting the sound of the bell. We met at the bullet-scarred trailer he owned in Paradise Cove, a small beach community in Malibu, California, to discuss a screenplay I had written called *The Last Western*.

When Sam had phoned to ask what I was doing with the script, I had told him that I was trying to find the money to produce it. "We need to talk. Maybe tomorrow night." I hesitated. As one of the writer-producers of a struggling television series at Warner Brothers that year, I had been trying to balance an eighty-hour workweek against time for my family. "Matthew's here," he said, referring to his only son and last child with his first wife, Marie Selland. Like Sam—perhaps because of him, Matthew had joined the Marines right out of high school. Having done a tour of duty in the Far East, he had recently been discharged and was living with Sam while he sorted out his life. "He's turned into a hell of a kid. You ought to see him," Sam added. "Besides, we've got to talk about your script." I promised to be there.

The next evening after work, as I drove down to the beach along the two-lane highway that runs through Malibu Canyon, I can remember thinking back to where it all had begun. Back to a time when I was what my father used to call "the best educated bartender in Chicago."

*   *   *

5

It was a hot, muggy July night in 1969. I had ridden the El down to the Loop to meet my brother, John, who wanted to see a film that had just opened there called *The Wild Bunch*. As we bought our tickets and moved into the airconditioned darkness, I had no way of knowing that the next two-and-a-half hours would profoundly change my life.

When the lights finally dimmed and the curtain rose, I can still remember the rush of excitement as Jerry Fielding's edgy, elegiac score began. Watching the film unspool, spilling its complex images across the screen, I was swept away into another time. A dusty West Texas town circa 1913. Soldiers on horseback. A Temperance meeting. Gunmen on a rooftop. Then without warning, every expectation I had brought into the theater was turned upside-down as Pike Bishop played by William Holden slammed the station master against a post and commanded: "If they move, kill 'em!" An instant later the final credit filled the screen: "Directed by Sam Peckinpah."

Completely caught up in the juxtaposition of appearance and reality, I was unprepared for the sudden eruption of violence as the town became a battlefield where death was graphic, intense and arbitrary. It seems to me now to be the defining moment in which the American cinema lost its innocence.

Fascinated by Peckinpah's complex vision of humanity, I watched as he consciously blurred the line between good and evil for protagonist and antagonist alike. A tale of honor, loyalty and existential commitment propelled to a cathartic climax as four men take on an army, it left me both exhilarated and stunned. Indeed, as the strains of "La Golondrina" filled the theater and I watched Peckinpah reprise the Bunch's poignant ride out of the small Mexican village where they had sought refuge from both their past and present, I found myself confronted by a strange sense of loss.

Stepping from the cool theater into the heat of the Chicago night, three things became clear. First, I knew what I had just experienced was extraordinary—a film so unique that it could only have been made by an American artist with a singular vision. Second, I wanted to know more—to understand how such a film could come to be produced. And finally, I knew I had to see the film again.

The following night I returned with friends, insisting they experience it for themselves. Here, I thought, was an important cinematic masterpiece that could not be ignored. They hated it. I loved it even more. Although I knew nothing about Sam Peckinpah except his name, I marveled at his ability to stare unblinking into life's crucible and record the images he found there. In the weeks that followed, I returned to see the film a half-dozen times bringing with me anyone who would come. Some were as moved by it as I was. Still others loathed it. The controversy confirmed my suspicions: here was a filmmaker whose acute observations exposed truth at the expense of comfort. Compelled to look deeper, I applied to film school.

Over the next four years, I saw every film Sam Peckinpah had ever made. The more I saw, the more convinced I was that he was an original American artist working in the medium of motion pictures. I decided to write a book.

Through Stuart Kaminsky, whose biography on film director Don Siegel contained an afterword by Peckinpah, I secured two phone numbers that purportedly would put me in touch with the director. Dialing the first, I waited while the phone rang a dozen times. On the thirteenth ring Sam answered. It was a little before noon California time, but Sam was just waking up. His voice sounded like he was gargling broken glass. Our conversation was decidedly one-sided—almost entirely mine. As I awkwardly introduced myself he held up his end of the conversation with silence. Attempting to fill the void I explained the kind of book I hoped to write. The silence on the other end lengthened. I kept talking. Eventually I ran out of words. Peckinpah still said nothing. Finally I offered to fly to wherever his next film location might be so we could meet, and he could decide for himself whether or not he was interested. Still no reply. Thirty seconds ... forty ... fifty. At last he cleared his throat. "Okay," he said. "Send me whatever you think I should read, and I'll let you know." And he hung up.

Left with a promise but no address, I called the second number. It turned out to be Camille Fielding, wife of composer Jerry Fielding, and one of Sam's few real friends. She immediately recognized my dilemma and told me she would make certain Sam got whatever I sent her.

A week went by without response. Finally, on the tenth day the phone rang. On the other end was the decidedly British accent of Peckinpah's assistant, Katy Haber. She asked me to hold for Sam. He growled something that passed for a greeting, then said: "Read what you sent. Not bad ... not good either. But not bad. If you're still serious, you can meet me in Mexico. Next month. Maybe six weeks. Keep in touch. We'll let you know." The film was *Bring Me The Head of Alfredo Garcia*. He didn't have to ask twice.

In August 1973, armed with a tape recorder, a camera and a smattering of Spanish, I flew to Mexico City to meet him. Having checked into a small, out-of-the-way hotel, I took a taxi to the Aristos where Peckinpah and his preproduction team had supposedly taken up residence. From the lobby, I called the Presidential Suite.

Katy Haber answered. It was a little before ten in the morning. They were planning to start looking for locations as soon as Peckinpah was ready. I said I would wait.

Over the next few hours, I managed to identify and introduce myself to Gordon Dawson, Peckinpah's cowriter and producer on the film, and Bill Davidson, his unit production manager. Finding them wasn't hard. We were the only three Americans watching the elevators rise and fall. Seeing me as a potential complication to an already overburdened day, Dawson laid out the ground rules: whatever else might happen, the film, not my book, was the priority here. He explained that he had two cars waiting outside. When Peckinpah finally came down, he and his assistant would travel in the lead car. I would follow with everyone else in the second. I agreed. We continued our vigil.

A little after four in the afternoon, the elevator door finally opened and Sam Peckinpah stepped out accompanied by his assistant, Katy Haber. Dawson and Davidson looked relieved. As they started toward the door, I introduced myself to Katy Haber who turned to Peckinpah: "Sam, this is your biographer." We shook hands and moved out through the sliding glass doors to the waiting cars.

Nodding to Dawson, Sam pointed me towards the first car: "He comes with me." And for the next three weeks we rode together through Mexico City and the surrounding countryside discussing life and art and films, his in particular.

It is impossible for me to separate my memories of Sam Peckinpah from my memories of Mexico. Especially that first trip as we searched for common ground. Of prowling the streets of sun-baked, half forgotten towns. Of a Mexico City patrolled by policemen armed with automatic weapons who saluted as we passed through the gates of a restaurant on the way to lunch with a general's son. Of drinking and talking and pissing (both figuratively and literally) on the studio.

Among the potential locations were the ruins of a 16th Century Church, its walls scarred with decades of graffiti. Standing in what had once been the sacristy, Peckinpah studied the names carved into the adobe and wondered aloud how anyone could commit such desecration. When reminded that the poet Byron had carved his name into a marble column at Delphi during his first visit to Greece, he fixed me with a look. "Got a knife" he deadpanned, but never acted

8

on the impulse.

Prior to arriving in Mexico, I had taken an address book and filled it with the names of all those credited in his films as well as his immediate family. As we got to know each other, I explained to Peckinpah that in order to write a book worth reading, I was going to have to interview more than just him. To accomplish this I would need him to provide me with phone numbers for the names in the book. Peckinpah agreed, but did nothing. Days drifted into weeks. The address book remained unfilled.

Three days before I was scheduled to fly on to California and continue my research, I was standing with Dawson and Haber in Peckinpah's room. Telling a self-deprecating story about himself and his father, who had been a judge in the Superior Court of California, Peckinpah laughed: "It's been like that my whole life—I've always been known as David Peckinpah's son." Sharing his laughter, Dawson, whose own father had been head of the wardrobe department at Columbia Pictures, nodded: "That's my trouble, too, Sam. I've always been known as Tom Dawson's son." Then it was Haber's turn as she confessed to always being known as her father's daughter. As they turned to me, an uncomfortable silence infested the room. I stared at Peckinpah without speaking. Despite my feelings for my father, I found myself unable to say that I had always lived in his shadow because it was not true. Dawson glanced at Haber. Breaking the silence, Peckinpah nodded: "Give me that address book," he said at last. I handed it to him. He flipped through the still empty pages then tossed it to Haber: "Go through my Rolodex and fill in the phone numbers. He's got work to do."

From Mexico City to Los Angeles to Fresno, I tracked down and interviewed all who knew him and were willing to share their impressions. His brother Denver, then a Superior Court Judge, spoke freely. His mother, Fern, who still lived alone at eighty, was more guarded, meeting me with a lever action .30.30 before inviting me inside to talk. By the time I flew back to Chicago, I had recorded over fifty hours of interviews. Friends, enemies, cohorts, family. Everyone had an opinion. Frequently they disagreed. Which was just the way Sam liked it. Life was conflict, filled with half-truths and innuendo. Like Akira Kurosawa's classic *Rashomon,* a film Peckinpah had seen many times, truth existed between opposing points of view.

By December, having transcribed the tapes and begun writing, I was back in Mexico for the final weeks of shooting. Peckinpah had moved into a house in the San Angel District of Mexico City. Again, all I had was a phone number. Arriving at my hotel, I picked up the phone and dialed. A woman speaking only Spanish answered. Thinking I had perhaps dialed the wrong number, I attempted, in faltering Spanish, to ask to speak to *Senior* Peckinpah. Her rapid reply left me stumbling badly and about to hang up when Peckinpah's laughter, low, dark and merciless, crackled over the line. "Really had you going, didn't I?" he exulted. For Peckinpah, everything was a test.

As the days rolled on towards Christmas, *Bring Me the Head of Alfredo Garcia* continued to shoot at a series of locations outside Mexico City. Working by day and drinking by night, Peckinpah invited me to join him. To ask whatever questions remained unanswered and draw my own conclusions. It was a six-day workweek. On Sundays we watched the Spanish-dubbed telecasts of American football, betting on the teams purely on the basis of the color of their jerseys.

With regard to the drinking, itself, while some have suggested Peckinpah was continuously drunk while directing this picture, I can only testify to what I saw. It is true that he drank daily, usually at night after the company had wrapped for the day. Yet he never failed to complete a day's scheduled shooting. At the same time, the images Peckinpah committed to film were sufficiently impressive that producer Martin Baum, who was present during much of the filming, took care to secure Peckinpah's services as director of the next picture he intended to produce.

By the Feast of the Virgin, when the company made its final move to a hacienda near Teotihuacan, Peckinpah suggested we forgo the hotel and get a jump on the following day's work by camping out at location. I agreed. What I failed to realize was that for Peckinpah, "camping out" did not include much sleeping. As pilgrims chanted prayers to the Virgin while making their way to the pyramids, Peckinpah broke out the brandy. We drank till dawn debating life, death and filmmaking. As the sun broke over the horizon, he stared across the table. "Unless it comes from experience," he said, raising his glass, "Writing isn't worth a shit." We drank a toast to good writing. "Which is why" he added with a cryptic smile, "I think I'll shoot you."

Not quite awake, I was sent to the wardrobe truck where a Mexican dresser gave me a serape, a couple of crossed bandoleers and a sombrero that looked like it had soldiered with Pancho Villa. Unsettled by what I saw, I stared into the mirror as Gordon Dawson entered. "What the fuck are you supposed to be?" he asked. "You look like a goddamned sight gag." Having begun his career in the wardrobe department, Dawson immediately began swapping one item for another. At last, he sent me back to Peckinpah for approval.

Looking me over, Peckinpah turned to Dawson. "We have doubles on the coat?" he asked. Dawson nodded. "Good," Peckinpah replied. Then cocking a thumb in my direction, he added: "Squib him."

Squibs, as I was about to learn, were blood packets backed with explosive charges used to create the appearance of bullet hits during filming. Cast as a bodyguard to a Mexican land baron played by Emilio Fernandez, I was placed at the far end of a room and handed a rifle. Over the better part of the next week, Peckinpah filmed both the beginning and end of his picture. In the finale, I was one of the gunmen who die in a gunfight with Warren Oates. Blown apart in slow motion, Peckinpah insisted I lie there for two days while others stepped over me and he completed shooting his scene. As Peckinpah had foreseen, the experience sharpened my perspective.

Back home, I read through my notes, transcribed the rest of my tapes, and wrote a rough draft of the first six chapters. Knowing they needed work but uncertain exactly how to proceed, I sent copies of the chapters to both Sam and his brother Denver, then a judge in the Superior Court at Fresno.

While Sam remained silent, Denver responded immediately, inviting me to come out to California so that we could go over the text together. When I took him up on his offer, he cut straight to the heart of the matter: "To begin with," he said, "You're being entirely too kind to the man"

Returning to Chicago, I tossed out what I'd written. Began anew. It was some time later that I finally heard from Peckinpah. On June 18, 1974, he wrote me the following letter:

Dear Gar:

First things first. I consider you a personal friend, and even more than that someone I respect.

The second thing is, your book is basically dull.

With due respect to your efforts, I suggest you get a collaborator namely William Murray [who had done the interview with Peckinpah that appeared in *Playboy* magazine] ...

What I am trying to say is, my friend, that you are missing the point of whatever I am living for, [and] that of course is the one omission I cannot tolerate.

You need a kick in the ass, and that's [a kick] only deliverable by you. Comments in detail will follow.

I wish I could be more positive, as you know my affection for you and your intent.

The only thing I can say about my life is that I have a will to survive, and in my business you need a sense of irony no, a sense of humor that goes beyond irony.

I suggest you walk away from the project, go catch some fish, get drunk in a reasonably bad whorehouse and then come back and confess your sins to whoever [sic] will listen, and only then will [you] realize [sic] where I am really at ...

I respect your efforts and your friendship but sincerely dislike what I have read.

Kindest regards, Sam Peckinpah

PS If this cannot be accomplished I suggest you pull the project. These are words I do not like to say. But I will not tolerate the book as is.

PPS I had one bad experience with Max Evans [a book on the making of *The Ballad Of Cable Hogue* entitled *Sam Peckinpah, Master of Violence* that only told the details Evans' wife wouldn't find objectionable] but for a reason I could understand. I respect you too much to let that happen again.

The letter arrived on June 21. Angry, I wrote back the same day.

Dear Sam:

First things first: I consider the kick in the ass you gave me in your letter of June 18th basically justified. Too bad you weren't quicker. I had already reached the point of self-ass-kicking a few weeks earlier ...

As far as your suggestion of a collaborator goes, BULLSHIT!!! I started this [and] I will finish it alone. Tell Mr. Murray he can write his own book with my blessing and yours, too, if that's what you want. I have spent too much time, sweat, blood and booze on your goddam life to allow somebody else to start fucking around with it now. I appreciate the sentiment, but no thank you ...

You are not a hero. . . You're an antihero, a part-time drunk working on fulltime status, and at times an asshole.

I have already grabbed your life by its anal sphincter with a pair of white-hot pliers since returning to Chicago and am currently in the process of ripping what I have written from frontal lobe to scrotum. I intend to leave you as clearly naked as I can get you. I will make you only one promise: I will not make you into anything I do not honestly feel you are. This will not necessarily be a child's book ...

At the same time, if in the end [you and I] find that we honestly cannot agree on the difference between piss and spit in a high wind, then you damn sure better be prepared for a book on the life of Sam Peckinpah as I see it ...
Kindest regards, Gar Simmons

On July 1, the following Mailgram reached me via Western Union:

JUST GOT YOUR LETTER SUGGEST YOU GET IN TOUCH WITH MAX EVANS AS SOON AS POSSIBLE

PS. LOVED THE LETTER SUGGEST YOU WRITE THE BOOK THAT WAY LOVE

SP

From Peckinpah's point of view, it was tough love. But it worked. Fueled by the furies he unleashed, I attempted to find the real Sam Peckinpah beneath the masks. To separate the heat and light from the fire. In truth, the book became better because Sam refused to allow it to be less than honest. In all I witnessed and wrote about, I left out nothing save one thing: Sam's addiction to cocaine.

~ ~ ~

To my knowledge, prior to the filming of *The Killer Elite,* Sam Peckinpah was addicted to only one substance: alcohol. This is not to say he had not indulged himself in all manner of vices. A practicing hypochondriac, his medicine cabinet looked like it belonged to a medieval apothecary. Yet aside from booze and cigarettes, his main addiction prior to *The Killer Elite* was a daily injection of Vitamin B12 that he dropped his pants to receive each morning regardless of who was in the room.

But starting with that picture he was seduced by the popular mythology of that time into taking the drug that was being trumpeted as "safe"—the "in" drug of the Seventies. Should someone offer you a line of coke, the prevailing wisdom went, you should indulge the same way you would if it were a glass of fine champagne. Never one to pass up an experience, Sam indulged himself and was hooked.

Given what I had set out to do, I attempted to come to terms with Sam and cocaine as honestly as I could. But given the fact that I was writing the biography of a man whose work I respected and admired and wanted to see continue, it seemed impossible to expose his involvement with cocaine without destroying his career. In the midst of this, an opportunity presented itself that seemed the perfect solution.

During the course of the filming of *The Killer Elite* the star of the picture, James Caan, agreed to an interview during which he said to me: " ... What do I think of Sam Peckinpah? If I get two more signatures I'm going to have the man put away... The man is definitely deranged. I mean in a marvelous way, you understand. But they are going to put him away. First, they're going to put his liver at UCLA Medical Center. It will never rot ... it's going to be like one of them fossils. A thousand years from now they're going to be saying, 'There's Sam Peckinpah's liver still bouncing around, having a coke and wearing dark glasses.'"

"Having a coke. "What Caan had meant could not have been clearer. When I transcribed the interview I intentionally wrote the word with a lower case "c" so that it wouldn't be mistaken for the soft drink. For those perceptive enough to see it, it said what needed to be said without doing any more damage to his career than Peckinpah was doing himself. Pleased with the compromise, I sent the manuscript off to my then publisher. But somewhere along the line, seeing it set in galleys, some well-meaning soul decided to correct the oversight by capitalizing the word into "Coke" (a mistake rectified in this new edition). So much for trying to skirt the truth.

Since then of course, Peckinpah has died and others have taken it upon themselves to recount, sometimes in minute detail, his transgressions with respect to drugs and especially cocaine. In reality, his addiction to it was his undoing. Despite moments of brilliance in his films beginning with *The Killer Elite,* he never again managed to attain the greatness he achieved before it.

However, as I drove down to see Peckinpah back on that early December evening in 1984, he was still very much alive and on my mind. Turning off the coast highway at Paradise Cove, I could not help

14

feeling a sense of irony. The screenplay I had come to discuss was a Western I had written nearly ten years earlier. In many ways it had both been influenced by and was a tribute to Peckinpah's vision as a filmmaker. Having watched his decline, I found myself hoping that perhaps this film, assuming we could find a way to mount a production, might allow him a chance to start over. That in returning to where he had begun, Peckinpah might find a kind of redemption and once again prove his critics wrong. It was a gamble. But it was a gamble I was prepared to make if he was.

Reaching the trailer, I parked my car as Peckinpah emerged. It was good to see him. We greeted each other with a handshake and a bear hug. Matthew joined us as we moved inside. Sam offered me a bottle of Calistoga water. We began to talk. About where we each had been and what the future might hold. Openly proud of Matthew, Peckinpah was clearly attempting to rebuild their relationship.

When we finally got around to discussing the screenplay, I asked Peckinpah what he thought. "It's good," he said. "Reminds me of *Ride the High County.*" It was his highest compliment.

Weighing the moment, I hesitated. "So you'd consider directing it," I offered at last. The words hung in the air between us as all they implied tumbled through my mind.

"The script needs work," he said dryly. "A lot of work. We'd really have to dig into it ... tear it apart. That is, if you think you're up to it."

"Sounds like you're looking for a fight," I answered, wondering how much tearing he had in mind.

He grinned. "The script's good. We can make it better." I nodded. "I guess there's only one way to find out."

"Actually, I've got a couple of projects right now," he finished his Calistoga. "I'm going down to Mexico over Christmas. When I get back, we'll talk."

That sounded fine, I said, rising to go. He walked me out to my car. We shook hands. Promised to get together in the new year. Driving off, I glanced into the rearview mirror. He was standing alone, hands jammed into the pockets of his chinos, the body language of a bantamweight. Three weeks later he was dead.

~ ~ ~

Looking back one may wonder why Sam put us all through so much pain? The answer, of course, is because he was searching for the truth. And to find it required the destruction of all pretenses.

As someone once said of Miles Davis, he was both selfish and selfless. He was selfish because he robbed those who loved him most of the time he could have spent with them and gave it to his music. And he was selfless for the same reason. The same was true of Sam Peckinpah. If Sam made everyone who cared about him pay a price, none paid more than his family or himself.

Having spent a lifetime exploring the meaning of life and death, in the end Sam had raged "against the dying of the light" with pace-makers and pure oxygen. But nothing could hold back the night. Perhaps owing to the violent way in which he had lived his life, some thought that in dying Sam was fulfilling some sort of personal death wish. But that's not true. Sam's only wish was for life. He simply lived himself to death. It was an irony he would have appreciated. An existential solution to the absurdity he understood so well.

He had lived hard and died before his time. But then, he had crammed more into the six decades he had been given than most men could have managed in twice the time. Echoing the words of Pike Bishop, the aging gunfighter played by William Holden in *The Wild Bunch,* Peckinpah wouldn't have had it any other way.

Once, twenty-five years ago, as we rode through the mountains surrounding Mexico City, Peckinpah asked me why I had chosen to write a book about him. In reply, I told him about the first time I had seen *The Wild Bunch.* Of how it had caused me to seek out the rest of his work. Few films can stand the test of time. But I told him that I thought several of his would still be shown as long as there was a way to project images on a screen. Self-deprecating to end, Peckinpah shook his head: "Bullshit. I'm just a good whore. I go where I'm kicked." It was a line he had used before. Widely quoted, it was also a lie.

As this book reaches publication for a second time, evidence continues to mount in support of Peckinpah's unique place in American film history. In 1988, Peckinpah's *Pat Garrett and Billy the Kid* was restored to the director's cut and presented in a special screening at the Directors Guild Theater. In 1992, *Ride the High Country* was selected for preservation in the National Film Registry of the Library of Congress, an honor that has been bestowed upon only 25 films a year since 1989. 1995 saw curator Kathleen Murphy mount a comprehensive retrospective of Peckinpah's work at Lincoln Center in New York. In addition, a number of books [most notably

16

Paul Seydor's *Peckinpah, The Western Films: A Reconsideration* and David Weddle's *"If They Move, Kill 'Em: The Life and Times of Sam Peckinpah"* have critically examined his life and work. And following Warner Brothers' restoration and rerelease of the director's cut of *The Wild Bunch,* Paul Seydor and Nick Redman collaborated on a documentary chronicling the making of that film that was nominated for an Academy Award in 1997.

To place this in perspective, Peckinpah's entire feature output is comprised of only fourteen films. But then, to paraphrase the actor Robert Culp, who spoke at the posthumous memorial honoring Peckinpah at the Directors Guild in 1985: what is surprising is not that Sam only made fourteen pictures, but that given the way he went about it, he managed to make any at all.

Most of what you are about to read is a recounting of the things I saw and heard over twenty-five years ago, when I did the bulk of the research for the original edition. In truth, given the publishing prejudices of the time (the manuscript was turned down by virtually every New York publishing house, some more than once), nine years would pass between that first phone conversation with Peckinpah and the book finally reaching print. Such a project cannot be done for money. It is an act of faith. An uncompromising belief that others will want to read what you have to share. As a friend of mine, the novelist Bill Barich, once pointed out, the way to read this book is a chapter at a time, watching each film in its turn. Since we live in an age when most films are readily found on videotape or disc, such an approach will maximize the experience. I recommend it.

Here then is a portrait of Sam Peckinpah as I found him: a film-maker as inseparable from his films as a dancer from the dance.

Garner Simmons
Westlake Village, California
May 1998

Introduction

On the evening of February 21, 1975, on a quiet street high in the Hollywood hills overlooking what was once Grauman's Chinese Theater, a lone Dodge station wagon bearing a Goldwyn Studios gate pass pulled to a stop before a walled, two-story Spanish mansion that had once belonged to Max Reinhardt, the flamboyant Austrian entrepreneur who had come to Hollywood in the thirties to transform his stage production of *A Midsummer Night's Dream* for the screen. Four men climbed out: American film director Sam Peckinpah; his older brother, Denver, then a judge with the Superior Court of California at Fresno; Kip Dellinger, the director's business manager at the time; and Don Waters, his personal driver.

By chance, it was Sam Peckinpah's fiftieth birthday, and they had come to the house at the invitation of its owners, composer and arranger Jerry Fielding and his wife, Camille, for a drink. Not quite by chance, some 250 guests were already inside in anticipation of surprising the director. Unwittingly, Peckinpah struck first.

Bypassing the front door, the director moved toward the bushes to answer nature's call with his brother close behind. Unfortunately, the bushes they selected grew beneath the darkened library windows behind which stood roughly 100 waiting well-wishers.

Instantly recognizing what they were about to do, Kip Dellinger, a conspirator in the birthday celebration plot, nervously cleared his throat and suggested loudly, "Why don't you just go in and use the john?"

"I can't just walk in on the lady and say, 'Show me where your bathroom is,'" the judge replied as he and his brother took their stand.

The quantity of beverage already consumed then took its toll as the Peckinpah boys performed a duet under the stars. A hundred pairs of eyes widened as the steam rose from the hibiscus into the cool night air. Then, to the mutual satisfaction and relief of all concerned, the virtuoso performance ended and the party began. Clearly, even at fifty; Sam Peckinpah remained an impulsive little boy.

To say the least, Peckinpah was surprised that night. One of the most controversial directors in the American cinema, he had wondered at times whether he had two friends left in the whole world, much less 250, willing to help him celebrate a birthday. And in truth, among the family and friends, associates and enemies, wives and lovers gathered that night, the feelings were somewhat mixed. But then, it could not have been otherwise, for no two people perceive Peckinpah in the same way.

Denver Peckinpah, who prefers being called "Denny" and has

known Sam longer than any other man alive, rolled a cigarette and reflected on his brother: "Sam's strong on the truth. But he's also ready to con anybody that isn't careful. A lot of people have been taken in. All that business about being a 'good whore'—that's just plain con. He tells these interviewers what they want to hear. But in the end, he generally gets whatever he's gone after."

At the same time, actor-director L. Q. Jones, who portrayed the bounty hunter T. C. in *The Wild Bunch* and the evil Taggart in *The Ballad of Cable Hogue,* recalled twenty years of friendship, enmity; and association: "There are three or four or five directors who are sheer genius in what they do, and Sam is certainly one of those. But he also relies a great deal on the people around him. And as much as I think Sam's a genius, I also think he's a fucking idiot. But then, it takes a genius to fuck up in the idiotic ways he does. Everybody hates Sam; everybody loves Sam. Sam intentionally makes everybody on the set uncertain in order to get what he wants. He'll figure out which way you're headed and then keep at you until he's got you thinking 180 degrees from where you were. Then, just when you think you've got it licked, he'll start in on you and force you another 180 degrees so you're back where you started only you can't recognize it. He wants you off balance because that's the way he sees the world—nothing is certain."

On the set of *Bring Me the Head of Alfredo Garcia,* the producer of the picture, Martin Baum, talked about his director: "I find Sam to be an original thinker. He's irascible at times. He's a guy who doesn't fool anybody about the fact that he likes to drink. Take him on that basis, or leave him on that basis. To paraphrase President Lincoln: "If more directors would drink the same brand, it would be good for the industry.' I love him. I can't wait to make another picture with him. I think the pain that he goes through and puts his cast and crew through is difficult but necessary. Everything worthwhile is difficult, and Sam is always reaching for something better than what he has to start with. He is successful about eighty percent of the time by my estimation, and that's a pretty good average." By the start of shooting on their next film together, *The Killer Elite,* Baum and Peckinpah would no longer be on speaking terms.

Like his films, Peckinpah openly courts contradiction and conflict, for it is out of this conflict that he is able to create. At the same time, there is about him an aura of fragile vulnerability. Openly emotional and therefore sensitive to the point of susceptibility, he would be at the mercy of all who moved him were he not a fighter. Instead, he instinctively strips all those he meets of their pretenses, leaving them more vulnerable than he is.

20

He does the same thing to his audiences when they view his films. Creation for Peckinpah is not an act of sensationalism, but an act of self-preservation. As one associate put it, "Take Sam two feet away from his work and his life is emotional chaos. He works everything out in his films." The man and his work are inseparably locked together in a struggle for creation. It is impossible to attempt to understand one without dealing with the other.

This relationship is complicated by the fact that Sam Peckinpah has managed to surround himself with a legend that needs to be purged. It is part fact and part whiskeyed fiction all strained through the consciousness of a habitual romantic liar who is partial to telling the truth. A contradiction in terms? Perhaps. But what you must understand is that Sam Peckinpah has spent a lifetime becoming just that by design.

Little boy ... con artist ... genius ... idiot ... original thinker. He is all of these and more. It depends on to whom you are talking and when. To a degree, each is accurate, but none can stand alone. Therefore, this study should not be construed as a biography.

Rather it is a *montage,* a composite picture of both the director and his work from multiple perspectives. Drawn together, these various insights and impressions will provide the reader with a valid portrait of a man amid his complexities. A creative sensibility in conflict with a commercial medium. The filmmaker—Sam Peckinpah.

"I am seriously thinking of writing a play for the screen. I have a subject for it. It is a terrible and bloody theme. I am not afraid of bloody themes. Take Homer or the Bible, for instance. How many bloodthirsty passages there are in them—murders, wars. And yet these are the sacred books, and they ennoble and uplift the people. It is not the subject itself that is so terrible. It is the propagation of bloodshed, and the justification for it, that is really terrible!"

~Leo Tolstoy on his eightieth birthday in 1908 as recorded by I. Teneromo and translated by David Bernstein, *New York Times,* January 31, 1937; reprinted in Jay Leyda, *Kina: A History of Russian and Soviet Film* (New York: Collier, 1973), p. 4ro.

1 A California Heritage

"Start the ball."

David Samuel Peckinpah was born on the twenty-first of February 1925. Legend has it that this event took place on—or at least in the shadow of—Peckinpah Mountain. The unromantic truth is that both Sam and his older brother, Denver, were born in a Fresno hospital. Their ancestry, however, is firmly rooted in California pioneer history.

Peckinpah's father was David Edward Peckinpah; his mother, Fern Louise Church. By coincidence, both the Peckinpahs and the Churches had come their separate routes across the mountains by ox team and prairie schooner to settle in California in the early 1850s. The Peckinpahs settled near Bodega Bay, north of San Francisco, and the Churches made their home at Folsom beside the American River.

Charles Mortimer Peckinpah was Sam's grandfather. The family had changed its name from "Peckinpaugh" before leaving Illinois because they felt it "used too much ink." Charles was the twelfth of fourteen children born to Thadius Rice Peckinpah and his wife, Elizabeth.

By the age of eighteen, Charles Peckinpah stood six feet two inches and was an accomplished carpenter with an interest in lumbering. Following an unsuccessful venture in the timber business in the early 1870s, he apprenticed himself to the wagonmaking trade. After saving enough money to buy a mule team, he built himself a pair of wagons and headed for Death Valley to work in the borax mines. It took several years, but he eventually accrued enough capital to return to lumbering.

Along with six of his brothers and sisters, Charles purchased a total of 1,200 acres of timberland rich in yellow and sugar pine in 1883 on a mountain north of Coarsegold, California, near what is now Yosemite National Park. By 1885, the Peckinpah mill was turning out roughly a million board feet a year.

In 1890, Charles married Isabelle Toner, an Irish Catholic girl from the County Tyrone. He was 42. She was 20. Jane Visher, an Indian girl they later adopted, still lives near Peckinpah Mountain and occasionally still visits the high mountain meadow where the mill once stood. At the age of 87 she recalled her adopted parents' courtship: "Charlie and Belle were married in San Francisco. They met in Sonoma County. He was a fiddler at dances, and the Toner girls would go to them. And that's how they met. She had known Charlie since she was a little girl. He had brought her a doll and told her he would marry her when she grew up. And he did."

The marriage was a successful one. Belle bore three sons, all delivered on Peckinpah Mountain without the services of a doctor: Mortimer, born in 1893; David, born in 1895; and Lincoln, born in 1897. In addition to Jane Visher, they also adopted a second girl, Lena Long. Both girls were Sierra Mono Indians.

The Peckinpah sawmill stood on the bluffs high above the south fork of Willow Creek. It took a full day to make the 3,000 foot climb up the steep incline in a wagon pulled by a twelve-mule team. Stewart Edward White, whose cabin stood above the Peckinpah mill for many years, wrote of "Uncle Charlie" Peckinpah and his family in his book *The Cabin,* first published in 1909. He recalled Sam Peckinpah's grandfather in the following description:

> He has property, and a family, and slow benevolent patience that has taken care of every forlorn and incompetent relative, in direct defiance of his own interests and those of his boys. In repose, his face has a Lincolnian sadness, but when he smiles it twinkles all over like sun on broken water. He possesses a fiddle on which he plays jiggy, foot-tapping things. His home is down the mountain at the Forks. There he often furnishes music for some of the dances. The quadrilles are especially grand, for then the musician, both eyes closed, calls out. No one knows what he says, or what it all has to do with the figures; no one cares. Each remark is jerked out with an accompanying strong sweep of the bow and swaying of the body. It is all about "honey!" "Pig'n a corn!" "Politeness!" "Swing 'round," "Go down, Mosses!" "Coon up a plum tree!" and various inarticulate but inspiring sounds.

The Peckinpahs were a musical family. In addition to Charlie's fiddle playing, Belle played the organ, and each of the three boys was taught to play an instrument: Mort, the violin; Dave, the clarinet; and Link, the piano. Charlie and Belle would play at country dances, traveling as many as twenty miles and playing all night long.

After more than twenty years of lumbering on Peckinpah Mountain, "Uncle Charlie" was forced to sell his mill to the Pierce Lumber Company during a recession in the first decade of the twentieth century. He built a general store and way station at South Fork below the mountain and brought his family down it for good.

Sam Peckinpah's father and uncles received "book learning" until the age of twelve at a one-room schoolhouse in North Fork, Madera County. But when the time came for the boys to go to high school, Charlie hauled lumber all the way to Fresno, a two-day ride by wagon. There he built a small house on Van Ness Street north of Olive. It was in high school that the boys first spread the rumors of Indian blood in their veins.

Mort Peckinpah, who became the family historian before his death in 1977, recalled: "There is no Indian blood in the Peckinpah family to my knowledge, although my brothers and I always told everybody we were Indians. The three of us were raised with Indians. When we started to school, we were the only white kids in school with thirty Indians. We learned to talk Indian and fight Indian. So when people saw how we spelled our name, they automat- ically assumed we were part Indian. No truth to it at all. The name 'Peckinpaugh' is really German-Dutch from the lower Rhine Valley."

Sam Peckinpah's maternal grandfather was Denver Samuel Church. He was born December 11, 1862, in Folsom, California, the third son of Emory J. Church, a blacksmith. In celebration of the news of the first Union victory of the Civil War at Antietam Creek, he was named after James William Denver, a former congressman from California then serving as a general in the Union Army.

In the drought of 1863, Denver Church's uncle, Moses J. Church, who had become a sheep man in Napa County, drove his herd of sheep south into the San Joaquin Valley in search of water. The ensuing battle between Moses Church and the riders for the Centerville Cattlemen's Association headed by a man named Yank Hazleton reads like something out of Zane Grey or Luke Short. Church was a tough, persistent fighter, however, and eventually defeated the cattle interests. He became known as the "father of Fresno irrigation" for the 1,000 mile canal system he built. When the irrigated land brought settlers, Moses Church, a Seventh Day Adventist, set up the Temperance Colony in Fresno. It was to help with the land survey for the Temperance Colony that Moses sent for his nephew Denver to come to Fresno in 1875 at the age of thirteen.

Denver Church attended Healdsburgh College in Sonoma County, California, in 1881. Among the subjects he studied were the Bible, public speaking, and shorthand. A great outdoorsman, he helped pay his way by supplying meat and fish to the school. A handsome man at five foot ten inches with black hair and blue eyes, he met and fell in love with a girl named Louise Derrek, who had come to the school from Carson City, Nevada, when Denver was in his senior year. He graduated from Healdsburgh in 1885 and returned to Fresno but continued to court his "Luttie" for four more years. They were married December 31, 1889.

With the financial support of Moses Church, who was building a tuberculosis clinic in Fresno, both Denver Church and his bride began studying medicine at California Medical School in San Francisco. But when Louise became pregnant with their first child, Earle, born in 1890, Denver decided to switch to law. In 1893, he passed the bar in Fresno. That same year, their second child was born, a daughter named Fern Louise.

Denver practiced law in Fresno for the next four years, eventually becoming assistant district attorney. But when he ran for district attorney in 1896, he was defeated. With the birth that year of their third child, Denver Lilbern, Denver Church found himself out of a job.

He drifted to Salt Lake City looking for work, selling potato peelers he had made to pay his way. Luttie and the children eventually joined him. But the baby was seriously ill with tuberculosis and died the following winter at the age of eighteen months.

The Churches left Salt Lake City in the spring of 1898 and spent most of the next year and a half traveling around the western United States by covered wagon, almost settling down near Big Hole, Montana, to raise cattle. Still jobless, however, Denver brought his family back to Fresno in the fall of 1899.

In a letter written some years later to her then grown son, Earle, Louise Church recalled how difficult it had been for his father during this period. Always the adventurer, Denver had heard about the gold rush near Nome shortly after their return to Fresno. "Everyone was talking Alaskan gold," Louise remembered. "And [Denver] bought a dozen or so dogs, a dentist's set, etc., paid his fare and was on the boat to sail [from San Francisco] ...when [a friend] came [aboard] at midnight with a letter from me saying, D. W. Cartwright will take you in the County Clerk's office as [assistant] district attorney.' I waited with the man at the window [of the railway station] when I thought [Denver] was on his way."

It was a time of prosperity. By 1905, the Churches were able to purchase the Angel homestead in Crane Valley below Peckinpah Mountain. The following year saw the birth of their fourth child, a daughter named Nedra. It was the same year that Denver was elected to his first term as district attorney of Fresno County. He had finally established himself in the legal profession.

26

All of his life, however, Denver preferred to think of himself more as a cattle rancher than a lawyer. It was with this in mind that he purchased an additional 160 acres from an Indian named Dunlap in 1909. It lay just south of Crane Valley along Finegold Creek. Over the next several decades, Denver would add to this cattle ranch until he owned more than 4,000 acres.

Running for reelection as district attorney in 1910, Denver wrote the following memo to himself in his personal diary: "Go to see your friends immediately after election. Let them know that you are as enthusiastic about them as you were before the election." He became the first district attorney in Fresno history to gain a second term. In 1912 the Democratic Party nominated him to run for representative to Congress. Politically wise and extremely popular, Denver easily won the election and moved with his family to Washington, D.C.

As the daughter of a freshman congressman, twenty-year-old Fern Church was presented to Washington society as a debutante. Her portrait was sketched for the society page of the *Washington Post,* and she was tutored in painting. However, she was in love with a young man back home of whom her father disapproved. Denver informed Fern's suitor to keep away from his daughter. To Fern's dismay, her suitor vanished.

During the 1914-15 winter, Fern remained at the ranch in California while her parents returned to Washington. It was then that she met David Peckinpah. Without money to go to law school, David, a lanky six feet two inches, had gone to work as a cowboy on the Church ranch. Attracted to Fern, he courted her throughout the next year. Mid-December 1915, they were married at South Fork by Superior Court Judge George E. Church (an uncle) who had ridden up from Fresno especially for the occasion. Denver Church gave the couple "seven dollars and a leg of lamb" as a wedding present and put his new son-in-law in charge of the ranch.

Because of their different social positions and Fern's original hopes of marrying another man, the marriage was not ideal. David Peckinpah's aspirations to become a lawyer, however, pleased his new father-in-law, who set about making arrangements for him to attend law school. On September 23, 1916, Fern Peckinpah gave birth to a son. He was named Denver Charles Peckinpah after his grandfathers.

Elected to his third term in office on an antiwar platform, Denver stood to vote with fifty congressmen who opposed the United States's entry into the First World War in the spring of 1917. It was a bitter defeat. He vowed not to run for reelection.

The following September he brought David, Fern, and his grandson to Washington so that David could begin his studies at National University Law School. He also procured a job for his son-in-law as a doorman at the House of Representatives.

True to his word, Denver did not seek reelection in 1918, choosing instead to return to private law practice with his son, Earle, now also a lawyer. It is worth noting that among his last acts as a congressman was a vote against Prohibition. He was an abstainer.

David Peckinpah graduated from law school in 1919 and, following his admission to the California bar, joined his father-in-law in practice. The firm of Church, Church and Peckinpah lasted five years. Then, in 1924, with Denver's election to the Superior Court at Fresno, the partnership was dissolved, and David took up offices with another lawyer named Raymond Carter in Fresno's Brix Building.

In America the following year, 1925, along with three major mine disasters, a tornado, a train wreck, and the Scopes Monkey Trial, David Peckinpah's second son, David Samuel, was born.

2 Growing Up

"We all dream of being a child again."

It was ten days before Christmas 1973. Sam Peckinpah sat in his trailer, which was parked before a massive Mexican hacienda, the final location for the feature film *Bring Me the Head of Alfredo Garcia*. He poured himself another glass of Mexican brandy and leaned back.

"When I was five or six years old," he began, "I remember riding my horse up around the pines in Crane Valley. Her name was Nellie, and I'd only have a rope around her nose for a rein—handmade hackamore. It was where my grandfather, Denver Church, ran his cattle. And a couple of miles away, my Grandfather Peckinpah had built his sawmill. It was the finest time of my life. There will never be another time like that again."

Even today, if you travel into the Sierra foothills around Bass Lake in California and ask the local residents about the high country above South Fork, they talk to you about Peckinpah Mountain. And if you spend any time in that area, you cannot help but be impressed by what you learn of its colorful past.

Coarsegold, a nearby mining town of more than 10,000 people in the 1880s, now has a population of less than 500. But the vanished miners, cattlemen, and lumberjacks had a flair for the descriptive: Slick Rock and Round Rock, Bear Butte and Badger Flats, Hookers Cove, Whiskey Creek, Deadman's Gulch, Shuteye, Bootjack, Dogtooth, and Rattlesnake Lake. From the grass-covered mounds of Boneyard Meadow to the pines on Horsecamp Mountain above Bailey Flats there is a wealth of material for a thousand stories. And more than forty years ago, when Sam Peckinpah was a boy, it was an area closer to the nineteenth century than the twentieth.

Slim Pickens, the well-known Western character actor whose career includes such memorable roles as the evil deputy in *One-Eyed Jacks* and the bomb-riding pilot in *Dr. Strangelove,* has worked with Peckinpah on many occasions creating colorful roles like the grizzled cowboy who drives Steve McQueen and Ali MacGraw to Mexico at the close of *The Getaway*. Six years older than the director, Pickens was also reared in and around Crane Valley, having gotten his start in show business as a rodeo clown at the nearby Pines Rodeo.

"You know, up in that part of the country," Pickens recalled, "up around Coarsegold and Bass Lake ...when I was a kid, by golly, it was a rough damn place, more like the turn of the century than the twenties or thirties. I remember somebody shot our next-door neighbor, but we never did find out who. And I can remember my folks driving cattle right through the middle of town.

"A lot of the people up in that part of the country were throw-backs to what the West used to be. Coarsegold had been mining country, and old boys like Elam who was a miner up there that I recall, went to school with his kids—he'd been diggin' in that one goddamn mine all his life, the Texas Flat Mine.

"And I remember another old boy, Tom Baysore, that was half Indian up there. Now that was a flat character! I remember one time, by golly, I stopped by his place there, and he had this water barrel. And he'd dip his water out with an old dipper there, and he'd drink what he wanted from the dipper and put the rest back in the barrel. Well, this time there was this old gal that seen him do it, and she got all unstrung and said she didn't think that was very 'sanitorium'!

"Yes sir, there was a lot of old characters like that, but they're all gone now, and most people nowadays don't have the slightest clue as to what it was really like. It was a hell of a good old time, but you had to live through it to understand it." Like Slim Pickens, Sam Peckinpah grew up watching that "hell of a good old time" die off.

When her first child was born, Fern Peckinpah was not interested in being a mother. As a result, she left the rearing of her first son to his grandparents, the Churches. Because Fern also had certain ideas about class distinctions, she rarely allowed the boy to visit his father's family. It was nine years before Fern consented to have a second child.

In 1925, the year Sam was born, his Grandfather Peckinpah died. Despite the fact that Charlie's widow, Belle, lived on until 1948, Fern Peckinpah refused to allow her any part in the bringing up of Denny and Sam. Neither of the boys learned much about the Peckinpah side of the family.

Because he shared a common first name with his father, Sam was known at home as "D. Sam." Fern tended to dote on the boy but nevertheless made him Denny's responsibility. Therefore, when Denny went to visit his grandparents, he always took his younger brother along.

More than one old timer from around Bass Lake remembers D. Sam as a spoiled child.

At an early age D. Sam began showing signs of a strongly independent character. Denny recalls: "Up at the cabin in Crane Valley we used to have to rake pine needles every year. Our grandfather Denver Church was a great tease. Sam was about three years old then, and I remember Denver picking on him about something or other. Well, he finally got Sam so mad that Sam grabbed up a pitchfork that stood nearby—which he could hardly handle because he was so small—and took off after Denver and ran him around the pile of pine needles and eventually treed him. I remember Denver looking down and laughing. So I guess you'd have to say that Sam was always inclined to have considerable self-confidence and integrity of purpose! Nobody conned him very much."

By the time Sam began school in Fresno in 1931, the Great Depression was making itself felt. Nevertheless, that same year the Peckinpahs adopted a baby girl whom they named Fern Lea. David Peckinpah's law practice operated as much on the barter system as it did on cash. Provided they had a just cause, no clients were refused regardless of how little they could pay. Instead of cash, it was often fresh milk or several month's laundry that stood the fee.

Above all else, David Peckinpah expressed a desire to be able "to enter [his] house justified" in the knowledge that he had always tried to do the right thing. And he attempted to instill a sensitivity for humanitarian causes in his sons.

In 1930, Denver Church had retired from the bench in order to devote all of his energies to his cattle ranch. Within two years he went broke. It was not the first time nor would it be the last. As a rancher, Church went broke thirteen times. He was more successful as a politician.

In 1932, he ran again for Congress in order to get money to plow back into his cattle business. His grandson Denny remembers: "You'd be walking down the street with Denver and one of his constituents would say, 'Well, hello, Denver!' And Denver would say, 'Well, hello there. How've you been? How's the family?' Then you'd walk on, and Denver'd say, 'Who the hell was that?'" He easily won the election.

Though a lifelong Democrat, Church despised Franklin D. Roosevelt. He felt so strongly about the matter that he refused to run for reelection in 1934. He saw excessive governmental control as the greatest danger facing the nation. He retired from public office for the last time and returned to the cattle business even though he was unopposed and sure of reelection.

At that time a young friend of Denny's named Blain Pettitt was hired to work cattle for Church. He stayed only one year before going on with Denny to become a lawyer and a judge, but he still recalls his work on the Church ranch: "Denver Church was an incredible man. Just as plain as an old shoe and everybody liked him. I remember he had false teeth, but he never liked to eat with them. At the dinner table he used to take them out and put them in his shirt pocket. Then after dinner he'd put them back in, and they'd be covered with foxtails and whatever else was loose in his pocket. He was a real character.

"He had two old packers who worked for him on the ranch—Bill Dillon and Bill Baker. They were the last of a dying breed. Bill Dillon had one glass eye that he was always misplacing, and he always carried a gun with no front sight. He'd wear it hidden beneath his overalls. He was an alcoholic. Fought a lot and swore even more. But somehow he managed never to swear around a woman. He'd just change his wording in the last second and scare everybody half to death because they were so used to what he normally said.

"Wild Bill Baker, on the other hand, had absolutely no discretion. He'd stand there, women or no women, and in this roaring voice say whatever came into his head. He drank a lot but somehow wasn't the alcoholic Dillon was. He had been both a prizefighter and a wrestler in his day—they always said he'd wrestled Strangler Lewis. I remember he had cauliflower ears. The amazing thing about him was he was a terrific dancer! Working on the Church ranch was quite an experience."

Apparently Church's greatest flaw as a rancher was the fact that he didn't give his cattle enough to eat. Al Pettitt, Blain's younger brother who worked for Church for a number of years, remembers: "I used to have these long arguments with old Denver about feeding the cattle more, and I'd always lose. But I knew I was right, so I'd have to get up in the middle of the night and go out and feed them again. But old Denver was really one of a kind. Nothing fazed him. Later on, I remember him wearing a piece of sash cord because he didn't have a belt. One day he was standing there and his pants just dropped down around his ankles. Didn't bother him a bit. He pulled them up and kept right on talking. He was as down to earth as any man could be. Everybody just naturally liked him."

Although it was during the Depression, the Churches and the Peckinpahs rarely went without meat on the table. Both families had lived off the land before there existed such conventions as hunting or

32

fishing *seasons*. Fern Lea remembers: "The killing of a deer out of season never occurred to my Grandfather Church or my father, whom I always called 'Deda,' or anyone else in the family as being illegal. It was simply meat for the table, and that was it. We never killed what we didn't eat.

"I remember once Sam caught a lot of trout, and my Granddad said to Sam, 'I see you've got quite a bunch of trout there.' And Sam smiled and said that he did. And Granddad smiled back and said, 'Well, I hope you like to eat them.' And he prepared them for Sam, and Sam had to eat all of the thirteen or fourteen trout he'd caught. My Granddad simply refused to allow Sam to waste what he considered to be 'God's bounty.' I don't think Sam ever forgot that lesson."

If hunting for food was a family tradition, survival was seen as an important part of that tradition. Before young Sam was ever allowed to go hunting with the other men of the family, he had to learn the art of observation. Sam still recalls his grandfather's constant questioning: "I remember my grandfather always forcing me to be observant. 'Where did you go? What did you see? Where did you cross the fence? Describe what you saw there ... ' He made me tell him all these things because when you were hunting by yourself in the high country that was the difference between making it back to camp and starving in the woods. He made me tell him everything, and if I couldn't he'd give me a kick in the ass. One good boot from the judge was all you needed."

In order to teach him the need for accuracy with every shot, Denver Church would send Sam out with a shotgun, two shells, and the order: "Come back with two quail, or don't bother to come back." Sam remembered his grandfather's admonition: "So I never learned to shoot a bird on the wing when I was a kid. But you really learn how to hunt when you only have one shell per bird. I 'ground sluiced' them—I'd sneak in amongst 'em and knock off two with one shot while they were still on the ground and then try one wing shot. I never hit a goddamn thing in the air. But then that wasn't the point: meat was the point."

When it finally came time for Sam to go on his first hunting trip, it was his brother, Denny, then a student at Fresno State, who took him. Denny remembers: "We used to take trips into the high mountains with considerable regularity, and this particular one was before I was married. Sam was about twelve, perhaps a little younger, and we went in below Knobloch's cabin. We camped in the old Chetwood place, and this was Sam's first hunting trip in the high country. This was back when there was really good hunting up there. So we went out, and I jumped a big buck late in the afternoon of the first day and shot at him but missed, and he cut back toward Sam. So I started over, and I was feeling kind of bad for him because this was his first time deer hunting and he hadn't had a shot at anything. When I got there Sam was all excited. He had almost been run over by the buck and in his excitement had simply levered every cartridge out of the rifle without firing a shot so that, of course, the deer had gotten away. That was only Sam's first time out; however, by his second trip, we had to take Sam's ammunition away because he had already killed three deer and two were the limit!"

Sam still speaks of hunting in the same terms today that his grandfather did prior to the turn of the century: "In my family there is no hunting for sport; it's killing for meat. You don't waste anything: the meat, the hide, the horns—everything. If you wound a deer, you follow him until you kill him—until he drops or you do. I've had to stay out all night four times. There is nothing of importance while hunting except for the commitment you have to the animal—you must respect him.

"One year I remember shooting my third deer. He was at the edge of a bluff, maybe a hundred yards off. It was snowing. I was walking. I snuck around a tamarack and shot him in the neck. When I circled around to where he was, he was hanging half over the edge but still alive. As I approached him he watched me with this mixture of fear and resignation, and I wanted to say 'I'm sorry' because I really didn't mean to kill him. I got caught up in the chase. But there was nothing I could do except pull his hindquarters away from the edge and put a bullet through his head to end his suffering. When that was done, I knelt beside the carcass in the snow to gut it and found myself unable to control my tears. I had had such incredible communication with that animal. I would have done anything to have seen him run again. But when you're really hunting there is a relationship between a man and what he kills to eat that is absolutely locked. It's hard to explain to people who think that meat comes from their local grocery store or to these cats who come out and shoot anything that moves for trophies. But I cried for that deer with more anguish than any other time in my life. It was dusk, and the snow was coming down harder. It was one of the most extraordinarily moving moments in my life."

This kind of commitment also shaped the Peckinpahs' attitudes toward their domestic animals. David Peckinpah had founded the humane society in Fresno. When their family dog, Shag, grew so feeble at the age of eighteen that he was in constant pain, David took him out and, as the dog finished his last morsel of ground sirloin, put a bullet through the old dog's head. If you could love a pet for eighteen years, he thought, you had no right to take him to some sterile place to be put to sleep by strangers. David Peckinpah was so upset by what he had had to do that he was despondent for a week, refusing to eat.

As a good example of the kind of respect for firearms that Denver Church attempted to instill in his grandsons, the following story is told by several people who knew the old man: When he was in his seventies, he became concerned that he was no longer the marksman he had always felt himself to be. Therefore, one day he took his rifle, set up a target, and paced off 100 feet. Then he fired a single round at the target. When he went to examine it, he found that he had missed the bull's-eye by one inch. He simply remarked on the fact that he could not do it anymore and never fired a gun again.

Because it was at least in part a chance to live a boyhood dream, both Denny and Sam learned how to "cowboy" on their grandfather's ranch. Sam remembers: "It wasn't a game; my grandfather expected you to earn your keep. I learned that you didn't ride for pleasure. My dad had been a cowboy, and he taught both me and Denny ahead of me the tricks of the trade. I got bucked off, stomped on, rolled over, but I learned to work cattle.

"Everybody rode. My Grandmother Church—we all called her 'Mudgie'—she could ride with the best of them. She was a sensational woman. She had a recipe for campfire coffee in the *Congressional Record Cookbook*. What a lady—only five feet tall but capable of doing anything that had to be done.

"I remember riding with her for cattle in those foothills at Dunlap. Boy, it was hotter than hell, and I felt like I was going to pass out. I must have been twelve or thirteen at the time. And she reined up and said to me, 'Rest awhile.' I rested and she went on!

"She had a horse named 'Patches'—a paint. And I remember at one point it reared up and she just sat him out and then took her quirt and hit him with the butt end—'thwack'—right between the ears. And he went down on his knees! Then she turned to me and said, 'A horse is something you ride!' But when we looked up ahead on the trail, we saw a rattlesnake just coming across the road. So I jumped off my horse and got a stick, but by then it was too late; the snake was already into the brush on the far side of the road so I stopped. But Mudgie climbed down from her horse and took the stick and just walked in amongst 'em. When she found the snake she went 'thwack' again, and that was all there was to it. With all her love for them, she took very little shit off of animals."

By 1938, as the Depression had worn on, Denver Church once again found it necessary to sell off his entire herd. This meant that in the spring of the year, they had to round up the cattle and cut out the calves for branding and earmarking. Denny came home from law school with his young wife, Betty. David and Fern drove up from Fresno bringing Sam and Fern Lea. Everybody who could ride helped the hired cowboys in the last go round. Fern Lea remembers as a girl watching from the corral fence: "It was the last roundup, and they were earmarking the calves and branding them. This meant they cut the ears, and the blood would spurt in the air. And I remember my grandfather standing there, and I asked him if they had to hurt them so much. And he looked at me sternly and said, 'If you've got any tears, you'd better get out of here right now!' It was something that had to be done, and as far as he was concerned, tears had no place in it. It was a very sad time for Denver because he really loved that ranch." Church was seventy-five years old.

That summer Sam, at thirteen, entered the Junior Rodeo at The Pines across Bass Lake. He remembers he did not win any prizes: "There are certain things I don't do—bull-dogging is one of them and bull-riding is another. Now the people who are really tough cats are the boys on the rodeo circuit. I mean I ain't that tough. I've tried it, but I just got the shit kicked out of me. I did it twice. When I was about thirteen I was really into it, and I rode this one bull calf who dumped me on my ass but good. So I got up and said, 'Well, fuck you!' And I was just bullheaded enough to try another. Well, that son of a bitch turned right around and did the same thing to me, and I hit on the same spot the same way. So I got up and said, 'Okay, I got the message!' But it really taught me to respect the rodeo hands who do it for a living. That is some kind of life!"

While Sam naturally took to learning everything he could about the outdoor life, he was a restless though capable student in school. Because his basic reading habits had begun with his family's practice of reading and appreciating the Bible, Sam read it cover to cover. Certain passages of the Book of Judges and Song of Solomon he read often enough to commit to memory. Besides the Bible, Sam read for pleasure everything from the so-called escapist literature of Edgar Rice Burroughs to more serious works like Moby Dick.

In Fresno, Sam had attended elementary school with a mixture of races. There were Orientals, Indians, Chicanos, blacks, whites-all within the same school working and playing together. Yet, as nearly as he can remember, he never experienced racial bigotry in his youth. It was simply a matter of priorities: what was important was how *well* you could Indian wrestle, not whether you were one.

In the Peckinpah tradition both Denny and Sam were expected to learn to play a musical instrument. Denny was given violin lessons, and Sam tried first the piano and later the trumpet. When both boys showed an exceptional talent for noise but little for music, the whole notion of having other musicians in the family was dropped.

In 1940 Denver graduated from Hastings College of Law near San Francisco and went to work for the district attorney's office in

Fresno as had his grandfather before him. At the same time, Sam, a wiry 118 pounds, entered Fresno High School. Despite his size, he went out for the football team. What he lacked in weight he made up for in spirit and hustle. Unfortunately, Sam's aggressive character was not limited to football practice; he managed to get into as many scrimmages off the playing field as on it. At the end of his freshman year, his parents decided to remove Sam from Fresno and enroll him in nearby Clovis High School for his sophomore year.

Now with Denny entering the legal profession along with the other men in the family, more often than not the dinner table conversation would work its way around to law. Consequently, Sam had a firsthand opportunity to witness just how ambiguous the truth really was, even for men who devoted their lives to its discovery. He recalls: "There's an old Biblical saying that goes 'When you make a judgment it all depends upon whose ox is being gored.' My whole family—my father, grandfather, brother, and uncle—all were lawyers, and all became judges. From the constant contact with them as I grew up, I realized that there was no such thing as *simple* truth.

"My father felt that the law had a responsibility to teach rather than to punish. He was concerned with the reduction of juvenile delinquency. Therefore, after he became a judge, he refused to put a kid who'd been convicted of a felony or a misdemeanor in jail. Instead he'd set them loose; but the boy would have to show up every Saturday to work for the state in the San Joaquin Valley. And that's the way he disciplined me. When I'd fuck up, which was constantly, I was out there in the goddamn sun. When I was sixteen, he made me sit through a statutory rape trial because he thought I would better understand the complexities of trying to establish the truth and keep out of trouble.

"My father was of the opinion that you earned what you got. Nothing was ever given to you. Then all of a sudden, out of nowhere, something would happen—something nice, something special. He was the 'Boss,' and that's what Denny and I called him. Even when we grew up, he was still tough, and he'd knock you on your ass if you were out of line; but he never held a grudge. That term 'Boss' was used with such affection. You called him 'Boss,' but he was more than that. He was your friend. He was always behind you, helping you."

Sam's sophomore year at Clovis proved to be no better in terms of discipline than his freshman year had been. As a result, he was taken out of Clovis and reenrolled in Fresno for his junior year. He made the first-string junior varsity as a linebacker and quarterback for the single wing in football. He remembers the team's greatest moment as when it soundly defeated the second-string varsity team.

Along with his usual conflicts that year, Sam managed to win a part in the school play, which by chance was aptly titled *Out of the Frying Pan into the Fire!* He acted well but fought better, so his parents decided to send him to military school for his final year of high school.

He spent his senior year, 1942-43, attending San Rafael Military Academy located just above San Francisco on the San Pablo Bay. Although he was hardly subdued by the military atmosphere at San Rafael, it did manage to focus his attention on his studies by eliminating most other distractions. He would have graduated *cum laude* for his academic achievement, but he also had earned more demerits in that single year than anyone else had in the history of the school.

With the bombing of Pearl Harbor, Denver Peckinpah received an ensign's commission in the Naval Reserve. He then transferred into air combat intelligence and was assigned to a patrol bombing squadron. On February 19, 1943, just two days before his 18th birthday, Sam enlisted in the Marine Corps to report for duty upon graduation from San Rafael. At home that year, David and Fern Peckinpah had adopted another child, a daughter whom they named Susan, thus giving Fern Lea a sister to watch over.

Sam was assigned to Flagstaff, Arizona, Marine Program 3D. From there he was sent to Lafayette, Louisiana. At both of these bases, Sam took advantage of the wartime policy of allowing eligible servicemen to enroll in college courses whenever a campus was close and courses did not interfere with military duties. He was able to take a number of courses at Arizona State College and Louisiana State Teachers College and seemed to be heading for a degree in mathematics or engineering. He took winter boot camp at Camp Pendleton.

Because he had scored well on his military tests and because he had a military school background, Sam was sent to Officer Candidate School at Camp Lejeune, North Carolina. "The first time Sam and I got together during the war," Denny recalls, "was when I was stationed with an air combat intelligence unit in the Navy at Quonset Point and Sam was at Camp Lejeune in Marine OCS. I got a pass and hitched a ride down there on a Military Air Transport plane, and we spent a weekend together. There were no rooms in the one hotel in town and a long line, but Sam and I were persistent. We'd work our way through the line to the desk and be told there were no rooms available and then go to the end of the line. About the fifteenth time through the line, the clerk must have gotten tired of seeing our faces and somehow found us a room to sleep in.

"Fortunately, we got together one more time as well, and that was in New York City. In celebrating that reunion we were having such a good time that Sam missed his train back to Lejeune and as a result washed out of OCS. As it happened, that class that Sam would have graduated with had a seventy percent casualty rate, so we always thought that perhaps it was a good thing that it happened that way."

In the summer of 1945, Sam received orders to go to China in the war's Pacific Theater. On August 6, however, the United States dropped the first atomic bomb on Hiroshima, Japan. August 9 a second bomb at Nagasaki quickly concluded the war.

As a consequence, Sam saw virtually no combat action in his eighteen-month tour of duty in the Far East. However, when the troop train in which he rode from Tientsin to Peking was shot at sporadically by the communists, he watched a coolie die from a sniper's bullet—a moment that Sam still remembers as "one of the longest split seconds" of his life.

Sam spent the better part of the year in Peking. He visited the Winter Palace. He learned enough Mandarin to get along and became interested in Zen. And he fell in love with the Orient—its children, its countryside, its pace, its women. He claims to have even requested discharge in Peking to marry a Chinese girl but was eventually turned down. He was returned stateside for final release from the Marines.

When he arrived in Los Angeles, he was still in uniform and went to the airport bar. "I was standing there about to order a drink," he remembers, "when I heard this voice behind me say; 'Shove over.' So I turned around, and as I did I cocked my leg back and cocked both my arms, ready for a fight when this somewhat stocky guy who was standing there said, 'Hey; you don't have to do that. I just wanted to buy a serviceman a drink!' And that was Orson Welles—the only time I've ever met him. And at the time I had no thought of entering the theater or movies or anything like that. He just bought me a drink, and I think I bought him one, and we went our separate ways."

One war had ended for Sam Peckinpah, but it would be neither the last nor the most difficult.

3 Learning a Trade

"...and knowledge rather than choice gold."

Upon his return from the service in the Marine Corps, Sam Peckinpah enrolled in Fresno State College, receiving advanced standing for the course work he had completed while on duty. In 1947, he met and married Marie Selland, an aspiring actress majoring in drama. When she introduced him to the theater department, Peckinpah, who had been majoring in history, was completely captivated by what he saw. For the first time he really knew what he wanted to do—become a director. Among his most prized accomplishments at Fresno State was a one-hour version of Tennessee Williams's *The Glass Menagerie,* which he adapted and directed for his senior project.

Following his graduation from Fresno State in 1948, Peckinpah enrolled in graduate studies in drama at the University of Southern California. By the following year, he had completed most of his course work toward a master's degree, but after the birth of his first child, daughter Sharon, Peckinpah left school without writing his thesis and began looking for work.

On the recommendation of his advisor at USC, Peckinpah applied to the Huntington Park Civic Theatre near Los Angeles, which was looking for a director in residence. The person hired could expect to select his own plays, do his own casting, build his own sets, aim his own lights, and generally put in a normal sixteen-to-eighteen-hour day. He could not expect a large salary. In short, it was an ideal job for someone with an appetite for everything but food. By his own estimation, Peckinpah beat out forty-one other applicants, including several from Harvard and Yale. It was a real coup.

During the two seasons he spent at Huntington Park, Peckinpah proved to be a diverse and imaginative director with productions of such varied fare as Thornton Wilder's *Our Town,* Kaufman and Hart's *The Man Who Came to Dinner,* and Rodgers and Hammerstein's *South Pacific.* At the same time, he conducted an ongoing actor's workshop using plays by Congreve, Moliere, Ibsen, and Pirandello. He also had a fondness for the works of William Saroyan who had also come from

Fresno, California, to make a name for himself. During the intervening summer, Peckinpah directed summer stock in Albuquerque, New Mexico. Always strapped for cash, Peckinpah recalled hardly making enough money in these years "to reach the level of utter poverty." He explained: "I stayed alive because my dad and brother lent me money. Let's say I didn't have to worry about income tax in those days."

Sam's brother, Denny, who had gone into law partnership with his father in the firm of Peckinpah and Peckinpah after the war, recalled: "Both my Dad and I had tried to talk Sam into going to law school because we thought it would make an even better firm if we called it 'Peckinpah, Peckinpah and Peckinpah.' But Sam was always interested in drama, and no amount of talking could persuade him differently. After college he got himself a job as director at the Huntington Park Theatre.

"Sam did very well for himself at Huntington Park; so well, in fact, that they offered him a raise if he'd stay on there another year. Both the Boss and I thought he should take it, but Sam had other ideas. The next thing I knew, Sam was going to work for a television station as a janitor or stagehand or something. I remember talking at length with my dad about it, and we tried to talk Sam out of quitting the theater. The way Sam saw it, however, he thought he had a better chance to make films by going at it through television. He felt that he'd learned all that he could from the theater. When Sam made up his mind, there was no stopping him."

So Peckinpah went to work for KLAC-TV in Los Angeles as a stagehand. In that same year, 1952, he returned to USC to complete his master's studies. It was in searching for an acceptable thesis project that Peckinpah hit upon a way to take advantage of his access to KLAC-TV's studio facilities. His thesis, entitled "An Analysis of the Method Used in Producing and Directing a One Act Play for the Stage and for a Closed Circuit Television Broadcast," was an attempt to examine the practical relationships between directing live theater and directing live television.

The play he selected was Tennessee Williams's one act *Portrait of a Madonna* in which he cast his wife, Marie, in the leading role of Lucretia Collins. It was performed on stage at USC's Stop Gap Theatre, July 8, 1953. Then, over the next several weeks, Peckinpah modified his production for television. On July 27, having dressed the set at one o'clock in the morning following the completion of the station's previous day's scheduled programming, Peckinpah mounted his television production of the play beginning at 8 A.M. After roughly three and one-half hours of intense rehearsal, the play was performed for closed circuit broadcast between 11: 35 A.M. and 12:06 P.M. using three fixed-position cameras. A simultaneous 35mm kinescope recording of the production was also done for submission with his thesis.

While this amounted to a learning exercise for the young director, it was also a prophetic one. In commenting upon the success of the television production, Peckinpah noted in his thesis: "In general, each shot was effective, but the intimacy of the television screen with its tremendously reduced viewing space, called for a more varied and imaginative use of the camera." It was a lesson he would not forget.

While actually writing his thesis, Peckinpah continued to work at KLAC-TV, although not without controversy. He claims to have been banned from the set of *The Liberace Show* after he offended the star by appearing on the set in jeans and a work shirt instead of a suit and tie. Eventually, he managed to get promoted to prop man on *The Betty White Show.*

Determined to gain more experience despite his lowly position, Peckinpah, on his own, rented the necessary equipment, including a special camera mount that allowed him to place a 16mm motion picture camera on a television dolly to shoot a segment of the show. He shot forty minutes of film, much of it with sound. Then he rented a Moviola editing machine and began to assemble the footage. Because he knew nothing about operating a Moviola at the time, he spent the entire first night completing two cuts. He was determined, however, and when he showed the finished product to the production heads at KLAC, they were suitably impressed. As a reward, Peckinpah was promoted to head of the properties department for allowing KLAC to appropriate his ideas for handling prerecorded shows.

Unfortunately, Peckinpah found himself in an argument with a studio executive soon afterward in which he was told by the executive that he was not being paid to think but to do as he was told. "So I told him," Peckinpah recalled, "that if that was the case, he could take the goddamn job and shove it up his ass!" As a reward for his tact, Peckinpah was told by KLAC that he was free to broaden his experience elsewhere.

In 1953, Peckinpah was offered an opportunity to join the Editors Union, when, after viewing the things he had done, a friend managed to secure him a position as an assistant editor at CBS. "I began working at CBS as an assistant, which is an eight-year apprenticeship gig, just at the time my wife went into labor [with their second daughter, Kristen], and I was supposed to show up for work. Obviously, I couldn't leave. I rushed her to the hospital, waited, and finally called CBS to tell them I wouldn't be in, and they fired me because I hadn't given them enough notice. It seems that to work for CBS you had to program childbirth to fit into the commercial breaks. So I've always had a soft spot in my heart for that network." As 1953 ground to a close, Sam sold his rifle and a mounted deer head for enough money to buy a Christmas tree and presents for his kids and decided it was time to try to break into the motion picture industry.

"I knew Pat Brown, who was then attorney general," Denny Peckinpah remembered, "and so I told Sam that when he felt he was ready, to let me know and I'd talk to Pat about the possibility of getting him in to talk to somebody in the film industry. This wouldn't guarantee Sam anything, but I thought it might give him a chance to show the right people what he could do.

"When Sam said he thought he was ready, I drove...to Santa Barbara where Pat was attending a district attorney's convention. And Sam drove up from Los Angeles. I introduced them, and they went over Sam's portfolio for about forty-five minutes. Then Pat called Wanger." Walter Wanger was an independent producer for Allied Artists at the time and a rough customer in his own right, having served a short prison term for shooting a man in a domestic quarrel.

"I was given an opportunity to get into Wanger's office," Peckinpah remembered. "And there I had to wait—for three days, eight hours a day. I think he hoped I'd go away. I finally outwaited him because I was determined to get a job in film. Fortunately, Wanger was doing a prison picture called *Riot in Cell Block 11* and figured that somebody who came from a family of lawyers and judges might have some weight with the warden. So he assigned me to the picture as something like the third assistant casting director at $100 per week for two weeks and three days. That may not sound like much today, but then it was more than I'd made in quite a while. Don Siegel was directing the picture, and he taught me a lot. I did a good job for him, I guess, because he kept me on for four more pictures."

In writing about *Riot,* Stuart Kaminsky, in *Don Siegel: Director(© 1974 by Film Fan Monthly, p. 85), records:

When Don Siegel and the crew were first ushered into the office of the warden [of Folsom Prison] before starting the picture, there was an air of guarded hostility. Siegel recalls that when he was introduced as the director, the warden, without looking up from his desk, said: "How long are you going to be here?"

Siegel: Sixteen days. Warden: You're full of shit.
Siegel: Maybe you have a point there, but with your cooperation
we can get the picture done in sixteen days.

The next person introduced to the grunting warden, who still
didn't look up from his work, was Siegel's personal assistant, Sam
Peckinpah. This was the first picture Peckinpah had worked on ...
When Peckinpah was introduced, the warden looked up for the
first time and asked if he was a member of the Peckinpah family from
Fresno. Peckinpah said he was and the warden, who knew
Peckinpah's father, an attorney, stood up, put his arm around the
assistant to the director, smiled and became cooperative.

Riot, because of its use of an actual location rather than a studio
set, made a great impression on Peckinpah. He would remember the
atmosphere of realism provided by Folsom Prison as well as the way
Siegel employed actual prisoners as extras.

Peckinpah worked on four other pictures for Siegel while Siegel
was under contract to Allied Artists: *Private Hell 36* (Siegel, on
loan to the independent producers group, The Filmakers, requested
Peckinpah as his "dialogue director," a Hollywood euphemism for a
director's personal assistant, 1954); *Annapolis Story* (1955); *Invasion of the Body Snatchers* (1956); and *Crime in the Streets* (1956).

Siegel, an action director with a strong cult following prior to
achieving greater notoriety with films like *Coogan's Bluff* and *Dirty
Harry,* remembered his onetime assistant very well: "I thought
Peckinpah was very bright and that he had a great deal of insight. So I
used to trap him into doing things that I knew would cause him
problems because I knew he would learn by having to find his way
out. And it never took him very long. Then I told him to read the
script and figure out how he would do it, then watch what I did. I
told him that at first he would think that my way was better but
that pretty soon just the reverse would happen. It was very good
training, and Sam, of course, has always been a very talented
person despite his shortcomings at liars' poker."

In consideration of the ongoing popular appeal of *Invasion of
the Body Snatchers* (the film was remade in 1979), something
should be said about Peckinpah's work on the original production.
Peckinpah acted in his usual capacity on the picture as Siegel's
dialogue director. He also played a small speaking part as Charlie
Buckholtz, the town meter reader, who, like most of the town,
becomes one of the pod people. However, there remains a
persistent rumor that Peckinpah did a rewrite on the screenplay as

well, a rumor still abetted by Peckinpah himself: "I did, and was paid for, a one week 'polish.' I rewrote one scene and cleaned up some dialogue."

"As far as I'm concerned," recalled director Siegel, "Sam rewrote none of *Invasion of the Body Snatchers*. It's something that really should be cleared up. At one time, I'm certain that it served his purpose to be able to say that he had done a rewrite on *Invasion*. But considering he is now both an established writer and director—and extraordinary in both areas, I might add—credit for the script of *Invasion* should go to the man who was really responsible, Danny Mainwaring. Now as my dialogue director Sam no doubt changed a word here and there, but under no circumstances do I think he rewrote enough to be even remotely considered as doing a substantial rewrite."

Siegel was not the only director who employed Peckinpah as dialogue director during his two and one-half years at Allied Artists. "I think I did twelve or thirteen pictures there," Peckinpah recalled. "I became sort of a resident dialogue director. I did those five pictures with Don [Siegel] and a couple with a director named Jacques Tourneur, another fine cat. I remember two in particular: a thing called *Wichita* that starred Joel McCrea, a truly great actor with a fine sense of humor, and another film, which starred Bob Stack and Raymond Burr, *Great Day in the Morning.*"

Joel McCrea, whose long and distinguished acting career would eventually be crowned by his appearance in Peckinpah's *Ride the High Country,* remembered working with Peckinpah on *Wichita,* a film in which Peckinpah appeared as a bank clerk and on which he served Tourneur as dialogue director.

"Sam was very quiet and very nice," McCrea stated. "He'd come over and rehearse the stuff, y'know. But he didn't speak out or do anything to make you say 'This guy is going to go somewhere' the way some guys do. Sam was very reticent, very reserved, which, I should say, is very unusual for Sam today."

In 1955, Siegel was approached to produce and direct a new television series called *Gunsmoke*. "The reason that I turned it down" laughed Siegel at the memory of refusing to get in on the ground floor of one of the longest running shows in the history of television, "and this shows you my ignorance—was that I thought in casting Jim Arness as Matt Dillon you would have an unbeatable giant that nobody would have a chance against. I also did not want to get tied down to a TV series, and I still feel I made the right choice." He did give several of the scripts submitted to him to Peckinpah to look over, however. Peckinpah liked what he saw and began to write a script for the show.

"It took me three months to write my first *Gunsmoke,*" Peckinpah remembered. "It was back when the show was still a half hour, and Charles Marquis Warren was producing. I did twelve or thirteen of them—I can't remember which—and by the end I was able to knock one out in about eight hours—eight hours, that is, after twenty straight hours of lying awake getting my ideas together. But writing is something I have always found to be a painful and exhausting process. That's why I've always written at such odd hours. Once I get going, I just don't stop until it's finished or I collapse, whichever comes first. And if I collapse before the finish, I start to work again as soon as I come off the floor. It's cost me more than a few secretaries. I do not write or live from nine to five."

Most of Peckinpah's writing for *Gunsmoke* consisted of adapting the radio plays of John Meston for television. One of these was produced employing a then little known character actor named Strother Martin who went on to become a fine supporting actor, before his untimely death in 1980, with roles like the evil overseer in *Cool Hand Luke* and Coffer in Peckinpah's *The Wild Bunch.* "The first time that I met Sam," Martin recalled, "was after he had written a half-hour *Gunsmoke* in which I played Cooter Smith, a fragile little man who didn't know day from night—a delicate little person, scared to death of the world and just trying to get along, a child who had never grown up. Cooter was retarded. I thought he was a very sacred character, and he got more responsibility than he could handle, eventually shooting some people who had been unkind to him. The story had been done on the radio version of *Gunsmoke,* but Sam did the screenplay for it. It was one of the best roles I had in the early days, and I thought so much of it that I own a print of the film.

"Shortly afterward I got a call from Sam who asked me to meet him out at the Quonset hut he owned in the Malibu Hills. He introduced me to his wife and kids, and we had dinner. I remember him then as a very shy man. I think he learned later that in order to be a director and get things done the way you want them, you have to develop some sort of marine drill sergeant front."

Sam's third daughter, Melissa, was born in 1956. Within the next year Sam had a growing list of writing credits for television. *Broken Arrow, Blood Brother, Tales of Wells Fargo,* and *Have Gun, Will Travel* all bought Peckinpah scripts. It was then that he was approached to write his first feature film.

Peckinpah remembered: "I was writing a lot of things for television at the time, and the word was going around that I was a pretty hot writer. So Frank Rosenberg, a very good friend of mine and an enormously talented guy himself, gave me this book to read, *The Authentic Death of Hendry Jones,* by a writer named Charles Neider. I loved the book and was then approached to write the screenplay. I did and they paid me, I think, $3,000, which was scale at that time. It took me six months to write it. Most of the time was just getting the thing together. I wrote the last ninety pages in nine days. That, of course, became *One-Eyed Jacks,* which Brando finally directed. I think they had something like seven other writers work on it after I finished it. Later, as producer of the film, Rosenberg called me up and asked me to come back and work on the script, but by that time I was directing television so I told him I was sorry but I couldn't do it."

The screenplay for *The Authentic Death of Hendry Jones* was completed, typed, and delivered to Rosenberg by early October 1957. It was a story based loosely on *The Authentic Life of Billy the Kid* by Pat F. Garrett, the man who killed him. One of the reasons it took Peckinpah almost six months to complete the project was the amount of time he put into researching the events leading up to and surrounding the death of Billy the Kid, work done in order to give his script an air of authenticity. Although Brando would drastically alter the story's conclusion (to the point of having the Kid, played by Brando, kill the sheriff and win the girl), Peckinpah's research would eventually serve as a basis for a film he would direct on the same subject some fifteen years later.

As 1958 opened, the break Peckinpah had been waiting for finally arrived. "I had written five episodes for *Broken Arrow* and as a result had become friends with Elliott Arnold, one of the producers on the show. One day, out of left field, he said to me, 'Would you like to direct?' Christ, they knew I was dying to direct. They didn't have to ask a second time." He directed an episode entitled "The Knife Fighter."

Frank Kowalski, a script supervisor, screenwriter, and longtime friend, remembered another script Peckinpah wrote that same year: "Sam brought me this script to read. We were both in the process of learning the ropes, working as script supervisors and dialogue directors and good shit like that. He had written the script for *Gunsmoke,* and he wanted my opinion. Now, I read a lot of scripts at that time, most of them the greatest heaps of horseshit you ever set your eye in, but this one was incredibly good. In fact, it was one of the best things I've ever read. Well, damned if *Gunsmoke* didn't turn it down because they felt it wasn't in keeping with their format or some such nonsense. Anyway,

Sam took that same script and reworked it, and it became the pilot for *The Rifleman.*

"I did this one script for *Gunsmoke,*" Peckinpah recalled, "that Charles Marquis Warren turned down—said it was a piece of shit! I knew it was one of the best things I'd written, so I took it back and reworked it, and Dick Powell at Four Star bought it as the pilot for *The Rifleman.* I went along with the property as part of the bargain. Dick Powell was a really fine gentleman and the eagle behind Four Star's success. He helped me a great deal."

This pilot for *The Rifleman* was produced at Four Star by Arthur Gardner and Jules Levy and was originally aired as "The Sharpshooter" on *Dick Powell's Zane Grey Theater* during the spring of 1958. It was a story drawn by Peckinpah from what he knew best: growing up in the California foothills. Even the settings recall the Crane Valley that Sam knew as a boy with names like the Dunlap Ranch and North Fork. Because of the popular response it received, a sponsor was readily found and the series set for the fall of 1958. Among the contract stipulations was one that guaranteed Peckinpah a chance to direct. Each episode was shot on a three-day schedule. Over the next year, Peckinpah directed four episodes of *Rifleman:* "The Marshal" (August 1958), "The Boarding House" (December 1958), "The Money Gun" (April 1959), and "The Babysitter" (August 1959).

R. G. Armstrong, the fine character actor whose roles for Peckinpah have included the Bible-quoting father in *Ride the High Country,* the shotgun-toting preacher in *Major Dundee,* and the maniacal deputy, Bob Ollinger, in *Pat Garrett and Billy the Kid,* remembered: "I came out to Hollywood in 1958 after doing three or four shows on Broadway as an actor. That was to play the part of the father in Henry Hathaway's *From Hell to Texas.* It wasn't long after that I was cast in the pilot for *The Rifleman* as the sheriff.

Well, I had begun as a writer at the University of North Carolina and had a play I'd written produced there starring Andy Griffith. From there I'd finally gone to Broadway. So at the time they wanted me for *The Rifleman* as a regular, I was full of New York and wasn't about to stay here and play a Westerner. So in the fourth episode when they couldn't make a deal with me, Sam wrote me out—killed me—and he directed that episode himself. It was called 'The Marshal' and introduced Paul Fix to the series. James Drury was in it and Warren Oates. It was kind of the beginning of Sam's stock company, so to speak."

Although *The Rifleman* ran for five seasons on television, Peckinpah left the show in 1959. He recalled: "I walked from the series because Jules Levy and that group had taken over my initial concept and perverted it into pap. They wouldn't let Johnny grow up. They refused to let it be the story of a boy who grows to manhood learning what it's all about. They sent me a memo which was a classic. I had it framed and hung it in my office for a long time to remind myself of what I had to deal with. It read, 'Remember, we're doing this for children.' I got the message. Boy, did I get the message! I sent them a memo back which said, 'I am not doing this for children; I'm doing this for me.' Then I quit."

It was at this time that Peckinpah worked on two other projects that he hoped to make into feature films as writer-director. The first was a script on a subject that had personally interested him for a long time: Pancho Villa. This script would eventually be reworked into a screenplay called *Villa Rides* and sold later in his career. The second was a book he became enthusiastic over called *Hound Dog Man,* which dealt with a twelve-year-old Texas farm boy's initiation into manhood through his experience on a hunting trip with a backwoodsman named Blackie Scantling. It was a book that reflected all of the concerns Peckinpah had hoped to emphasize in *The Rifleman* but that had been frustrated by its producers. The book had been written by Fred Gipson, the author of *Old Yeller,* a Walt Disney film of a few years earlier. Peckinpah made only one mistake: he told producer Collier Young about the book. Young bought the property and hired Don Siegel to direct it. Unfortunately, the project subsequently developed into a vehicle for the new teenage rock idol Fabian. In Kaminsky's biography, Siegel is quoted as saying: "Sam Peckinpah wanted to do a picture from the book...I'm sorry he didn't do it. He would have done it the way it should have been done—small." Peckinpah remained in television.

One of the most important facets of *Dick Powell's Zane Grey Theater* was the fact that it was an anthology rather than a series. This allowed Powell to use the program to showcase the pilot projects produced at Four Star. In early 1959, Powell commissioned Peckinpah to write and direct a half-hour pilot that if successful would be promoted as a series under the title *Winchester.* Given a free hand, Peckinpah began immediately to work on a script. The main character, Dave Blassingame, was conceived by Peckinpah as a self-sufficient drifter and named for his father and a ranching family from his youth. Blassingame rode an Appaloosa, had a large mixed-breed dog named "Brown," and, to justify the title, carried a Winchester .32 Special, equipped with a four-power, crosshair scope sight modeled after one used by Theodore Roosevelt to hunt big game. The pilot, starring Brian Keith as Dave Blassingame and Neville Brand as the heavy, was called "Trouble at Tres Cruces." It was shot mid-February and telecast on *Zane Grey Theater* March 26, 1959. Although it was very well received, no immediate takers offered to sponsor the series.

Shortly after completing "Trouble at Tres Cruces," Peckinpah was hired by ZIV Productions to direct a pilot project that ZIV owned called *Klondike,* which was to be based upon the bestseller *Klondike Fever* by Pierre Berton. Although the project seemed to have great potential, especially considering Alaska's recent entry into the Union, Peckinpah found the production situation at ZIV unworkable. After completing the pilot he left ZIV and returned to Four Star. In the course of the experience on *Klondike,* however, Peckinpah met the head of NBC-TV at the time, David Levy.

"Dave Levy was a great man, a damn good writer in his own right," remembered Peckinpah, "and for whatever reason, he really liked the things I was writing. He told me that if I could put a series together, he would see what he could do about getting it on NBC. Well, *Klondike* was set for NBC, but that sure as hell wasn't going to make it for me. So I went to Dick Powell and suggested that he approach Levy with *Winchester.* Levy liked what he saw, and they found a sponsor. As it turned out, of course, Four Star really didn't have the rights to the name *Winchester,* so we had to change the name to *The Westerner.* And Dave Levy and NBC picked it up for the fall of '60. Don Siegel, Dick Powell, and Dave Levy—those were the three gentlemen who really made it possible for me to get the background I needed to make the move into features."

Between December of 1959 and October 1960, Peckinpah over-saw the production of thirteen episodes of *The Westerner.* Of these, he directed five, employing seven other directors on the remaining eight. Because Peckinpah acted as producer for the series, he found himself involved in all facets of production; this experience helped to flesh out his basic understanding of the various areas of film production.

"For *The Westerner,* I had a writer who worked with me named Bruce Geller, an exceptionally talented man who had a great poten- tial. He had also written for *The Rifleman.* We did several *Westerners* together: I directed them, and Bruce wrote some great scripts. He wrote two exceptional comedies for the series that I directed: 'Brown' and 'The Courting of Libby.' And then we did one called 'Hand on the Gun,' which I did with Brian and Michael Ansara and a young actor named Ben Cooper. They were all superb. It's a story about a kid who thinks that being fast is all there is to gunfighting. Bruce had a really incredible sense of story; it was really well written. That was also the first time I had a really great cutter—Ted Kent, who's retired now. I remember coming into the cutting room and he was just finishing up, and he said to me, 'We're about twenty seconds over.' So I looked at what he'd done—it was the only thing I directed but hadn't been involved with the editing—and I asked him, 'You know where to take the twenty seconds?' He said, 'I do,' and I said, 'Thank you very much.' He had it all; there was nothing to change. *The Westerner* was a great experience because I had really sensational people to work with."

The new series was scheduled to premiere Friday, September 30, 1960, at 8:30 in the evening on NBC television. The other network competition was ABC's new half-hour animated situation comedy *The Flintstones,* a novelty at the time, and CBS's hour-long *Route* 66, also new that season.

As a series, *The Westerner* involved the full spectrum from comedy to serious drama. For the opening show Peckinpah selected an episode he had directed entitled "Jeff," which he had cowritten with writer Robert Heverly. Peckinpah, who claimed he first had heard the story from a seventy-five-year-old former prostitute recalling her first love, remembered the episode as causing something of a stir.

"Some *Westerners* were pretty rough for that time," the director recalled. "In fact, some of the network affiliates didn't want to telecast the first show we had. It was about a guy who goes to take this young whore, whom he knew as a kid, home. They absolutely refused to air it. At least until David Levy and Dick Powell got to them and worked it out."

On the Monday following the telecast, James Powers reviewed the first episode for *The Hollywood Reporter* (p. 9), calling it "breathless theatre" and "a standout series whose strongest competition in the weeks ahead will be its own standards." The review went on: "The opening show has Brian Keith, the running character, concerned with prostitution, sadism and pimping. One man in the show came right out and said 'damn.' It was, you may be surprised to know, a moving poetic drama (not melodrama, drama), written with expert economy and directed and acted the same."

Despite this high praise, *The Westerner* was canceled after only thirteen shows. This was at least partially due to the controversial subject matter that still found resistance, especially among affiliates serving rural areas. The decisive blow, however, came from a phenomenon that occurred that year in the television industry that became known in the trade papers as the "hour hop." This was the year that suddenly found the American viewing audience showing a decided preference for hour shows over half-hour ones. As evidence of the trouble this trend caused Four Star, twelve of its fourteen primetime shows were canceled as soon as their contracts permitted. For *The Westerner,* cancelation occurred with only half of its scheduled twenty-six shows on film.

Speaking of those thirteen episodes in an interview with a *Los Angeles Times* reporter in 1975, Brian Keith noted that he had watched the reruns of the series recently. "It was fifteen years since I had seen it," Keith remarked. "I watched every one. We always remember things as being better than they were, and only four or five of these were really good. But those four or five were as good as anything anybody has ever done."

It was a series that made its mark, establishing Peckinpah as a talent to be reckoned with. As time passed, *The Westerner* would attain an almost legendary place in television history. In December 1980, two decades after the series' initial run, Cecil Smith, the *Los Angeles Times's* first-string television critic recalled *The Westerner* in an article entitled "I Love Losers: The Best of TV Invariably Flopped": "The late Bruce Geller, who produced winners like *Mission: Impossible* and *Mannix,* and I used to swap tales about what we thought was the Greatest Loser of them all, maybe the best weekly show that ever was loosed on the mundane air—*The Westerner.* Sam Peckinpah made it for Dick Powell's Four Star organization. It starred Brian Keith and was maybe the only honest portrait of a cowboy that ever got onto film."

But *The Westerner* was a personal victory for Sam Peckinpah as well. It allowed him to prove his capabilities both to the industry and to his family. "The Boss came down to Los Angeles with Ken Andreen, who is now a judge," Peckinpah recalled, "and I invited him over to see a screening we were having of *The Westerner* for the censors over at NBC. At that time, it was really a different ball game, because we not only had the censors but about sixty people who were hooked on *The Westerner* as well. After it was all over, the Boss came up to me and said, 'A little rough, but.' And he gave me a nod and a smile, and I knew that I had made it." Later that year *The Westerner* would win Sam Peckinpah a Producers Guild nomination for Best Filmed Series.

In the late 1950s, Sam Peckinpah's father had been appointed to fill a vacancy in the Superior Court of California at Madera. Accepting the appointment had been a difficult decision because it required him to give up his residence in Fresno and move back to rural Madera County, something his wife, Fern, refused to do. Despite his wife's threat of divorce, David Peckinpah not only returned to Madera alone to accept the judgeship, but campaigned for reelection in the fall of 1960. A colorful and flamboyant speaker, he easily won against a much younger opponent.

On November 30, 1961, however, David Peckinpah died from a heart attack. His death was sudden and unexpected. Daughter Fern Lea still remembers what followed the call that her father was on the critical list: "I had a difficult time getting ahold of Sam, who was separated from Marie at that time. When I finally did get him, he didn't have a car, and my husband and I had to drive over and pick him up. By the time we got to the airport we had missed our plane. Well, Sam was furious. His jaw was clenched and he was talking to the reservation clerk through his teeth, but there was nothing we could do. So while Sam went and called Denny, I changed our reservations to the next available flight.

"I saw Sam picking up the change and leaving the telephone booth, and he was very quiet. But when he got to me he kind of brightened and said: 'Well, let's go get a drink and something to eat. Got any money?' And I said, 'No.' And he said, 'Cash a check.' I said, 'It'll bounce.' He just looked at me and kind of half smiled and shrugged, so I cashed a check for twenty dollars.

"Then we went to the restaurant and I said to Sam that I didn't know what to order, and he said, 'Have a lobster salad.' Then he said, 'Come on. Drink your drink.' And I thought, 'Gee, he's hurrying me.' So I ate my lobster salad and finished my drink and Sam said, 'Have another drink.' And I said, 'I've already had one drink.' And Sam insisted, 'Have another.' And he ordered us each another drink. Then he said very quietly, 'He didn't make it.' And I sat there and I couldn't imagine a world without my father, but I didn't want to cry in front of all those people. Then Sam grabbed my arm very firmly and said, 'But it's okay.' Sam had known about Deda's death since getting off the phone with Denny, but he had waited to make it easier on me. Then we got on the plane and Sam said, 'I'm glad we didn't make that flight.' And so was I because neither Sam nor I wanted to remember our father any way but strong and alive."

In Fresno, Fern Peckinpah requested a small private service for her husband. Her children disagreed. They felt their father's friends should be invited as well. The day of his funeral three thousand people showed up to pay "the Boss" their last respects. David E. Peckinpah had entered his house justified.

4 The Deadly Companions

"I left my teeth marks in his scalpin' hand."

Following the cancelation of *The Westerner,* Brian Keith was cast as the male lead in a feature film entitled *The Deadly Companions* being produced independently by a company called Carousel with financing through Pathe-America. Because a director had not yet been selected, Keith suggested Sam Peckinpah. (According to Peckinpah, so did director John Ford.) Because it was a very low-budget feature, producer Charles B. FitzSimons considered the suggestion and made Peckinpah an offer. Out of work and anxious to break into directing feature films, Peckinpah accepted.

FitzSimons had worked on *The Deadly Companions* with screenwriter A. S. Fleishman for more than two years. During this period, Fleishman reworked his screenplay as a novel, publishing it under the title *Yellowleg* in 1960. Then together they had formed Carousel along with FitzSimons's sister, actress Maureen O'Hara, for the purpose of making the picture without outside interference. O'Hara would play the female lead opposite Keith in this tale of revenge and redemption.

The story is of a former Union soldier who attempts revenge on the man who scalped him on a Civil War battlefield. In the course of this attempt, he accidently kills the son of a saloon girl and then helps her to transport the boy's body across the desert for burial beside the father's grave.

Peckinpah recalled: "Up until that time almost all my awards had been Writers Guild Awards, and Brian and I had just completed a series that had only gone thirteen shows—but not because they were poorly written.... And I thought they [Carousel] were hiring me to fix that shitty script!"

FitzSimons, formerly a producer for Edward L. Alperson at National Pictures, stated: "After all that Fleishman and I had been through with this script, Sam came to me with some suggested

55

rewrites which I properly disposed of in the wastepaper basket. And I think that may have started the conflict."

There were a number of plot elements that Peckinpah found unacceptable: the scalping scar that causes Yellowleg to never take his hat off, the bullet lodged in his shoulder that makes his aim uncontrollable, and the need to carry a corpse across the desert for days in intense heat. He also felt that the dialogue was awkward and needed revision.

"Peckinpah never had anything whatsoever to do with the story structure itself," FitzSimons stated, "except in the few ways he directed the picture which did not bring it up to my expectation. I don't think that Sam understood—or, if he did, he was not in agreement with the premise of the picture: the problem of revenge for a man of moral fiber is the moment he catches up with it. It was a morality play in Western clothing which we had constructed around the quotation 'Revenge is mine saith the Lord.'"

In addition to Brian Keith and Maureen O'Hara, the cast for the picture included Chill Wills, Steve Cochran, and Strother Martin. Filming began in Old Tucson, Arizona, in late January 1961.

"I met with the producer, Mr. Charles B. FitzSimons," remembered Peckinpah, "and he had this thing about his script. So I went with it anyway, thinking that I would be able to work things out on the set, but FitzSimons didn't want a single word changed and, of course, his sister was in the goddamn thing so that tended to complicate matters even more. So Brian and I worked it out in such a way that we would be able to alter lines on the spot without letting anyone know and managed to get about twenty percent of the most awful bullshit out of the film. We had to shoot both day and night. We'd shoot exteriors during the day and interiors during the night. On top of that, we had twelve days of inclement weather. It was a fucking disaster. I did have a great cameraman, however, named Bill Clothier, and for his help I will always be grateful."

"Bill Clothier did a fabulous job as cameraman," stated FitzSimons. "He's one of the best outdoor cameramen in the business. We shot in incredible conditions. When we went down there to make the picture, we expected nothing but sunshine. In fact, there was a recurring theme of drought throughout the picture. But when we got down there, we hit nothing but rain. But then we only had so much money, so we didn't have the luxury of waiting. I had

56

scheduled the picture for twenty-one days, and we shot it in twenty-one days. But we did not shoot at night. Sam did not want to stop when we did, but I told him we were stopping because I was responsible for the money. It is probably the shortest shooting schedule on a feature that he's shot in his life."

Aside from Brian Keith, whose performance as Yellowleg was equal to his fine work on *The Westerner,* only Clothier was in a position to help Peckinpah. Clothier, who has specialized in directing photography for Westerns, spoke of Peckinpah in an interview with Tim Hunter for *On Film* magazine a decade later: "Sam Peckinpah has a great deal of talent, and he proved it on a picture or two that he has made lately. I made a picture with him called *The Deadly Companions.* He had some problems with the producers. In fact, I got the impression they didn't want me to help the director. But I worked with him. I told them at a meeting one night, 'Look! You hired me to make this picture, and you hired him to make this picture. And as long as he is making it, I am going to ... help him.'" With Clothier as an ally, Peckinpah was able to bring at least some of his perceptions to bear upon the story.

By mid-February, the filming of *The Deadly Companions* had been completed, and Peckinpah began to work with the film's editor, Stanley Rabjohn, on his "cut" of the film. In an interview with Ernest Callenbach (published in *Film Quarterly,* Winter 1963-64) during the director's preproduction work on *Major Dundee,* Peckinpah commented on the cutting of the picture: "Well, after making my first cut I left the organization very abruptly. I didn't like it. I had nothing to do with that. In fact, the whole point of the story was screwed up by the cutting. For example, at the end, where Brian Keith is marching to kill Turkey [Wills], the character played by Steve Cochran steps up in front of him with his particular kind of little boy bravado, which he does quite well, and Brian pulls his gun and kills him, a brutal, realistic act. But it was cut in such a way that it appears as if the shot came from Turkey, which changed the whole focus of the thing—we really had everyone riding off into the sunset, which wasn't my touch."

The ending was a problem for FitzSimons as well. "Among other things," he recalled, "Sam shot an ending for the picture that I couldn't use. He had Brian Keith walk up and shoot Steve Cochran in the belly. That was the Peckinpah version. That was not what I wanted in a million years. The character of Yellowleg would never do that. It simply showed a complete misunderstanding of the character. I was trying to show a moral man who somebody had done something dastardly to a drunken reb—had scalped him on the battlefield—and despite his morality, he was going to find the son of a bitch and kill him. But he wasn't going to kill other people. We finally had to have Turkey appear to shoot Billy in the back because it was the only way to overcome the problem which Sam left me. In the original script, it was to be an old-fashioned gunfight between Yellowleg and Billy in which you didn't know who was going to win, and if anything the hero was at a disadvantage because of his old shoulder wound. This, of course, would keep the audience on the edge of their seats as the tension of the gunfight built. But the way Peckinpah shot it made absolutely no sense. How can you have a man shoot another against whom he bears no grudge and then turn around and be unable to kill the man he's hated for years?

"In his *Playboy* interview [August 1972], Sam was fairly accurate. He said that all I was interested in was pushing him around. But you have to understand what's meant by that. I am a great believer in the auteur theory as it applies to a producer. In my opinion, the producer and particularly the independent producer is responsible to the people through whom he has raised the money, and he is responsible to all of the combined creative elements in the production. I also believe that there has to be a boss. Sam made the initial cut, but I rejected it. Under the Directors Guild agreement, the director is entitled to first cut, but there is nothing that says the producer has to stay with it. The picture was released as close to what I wanted as possible. I was never able to get what I wanted completely because Peckinpah did not supply me with the film. It was a running battle. The final cut was about seventy percent of what I wanted and probably ten percent of what he was looking for. But this is a business of compromise, a business of egos and erratic talents."

"The one thing I learned [on *The Deadly Companions*]," Peckinpah maintained, "was never to agree to direct a picture unless you have script control. Since then, I've learned that sometimes even that is not enough."

Pathe-America, the company distributing the film, went out of business soon after the film was released. But *The Deadly Companions* managed to do reasonably well despite mixed reviews. Ironically, Peckinpah's notices were frequently better than the picture's. James Powers wrote in *The Hollywood Reporter* (June 6, 1961): "Peckinpah sets himself a difficult problem in character adjustment [but] ... handles all this beautifully, except for the technical question noted [the putrefaction of the boy's corpse in the desert heat].... In his handling of the story, he displays a genuine feel for drama and film." *Variety* ("Tube," June 7, 1961) reported:

58

"Fleishman's screenplay is pretty farfetched and relies heavily on coincidence but, for the most part, it plays. This thanks to superior emoting by the four principals and an auspicious debut as a director by Sam Peckinpah, a fine TV helmsman."

While this was the beginning of Peckinpah's career as a feature film director, it was also the end of his thirteen-year marriage to Marie, despite the birth that year of their fourth child and only son, Matthew. As one observer of the time put it: "Sam loved Marie. But he wanted a storybook marriage, and they [ideal marriages] just don't exist."

It is equally true that the motion picture industry is very demanding. Long hours and extended time away from home often have led to infidelity, marital strife, and divorce. Temptation is not easily resisted.

An incurable romantic who has been married five times to three women, and who frequently has fallen in love with prostitutes on a "pay-as-you-go" basis, Peckinpah summed up the end of his first marriage: "You clothe the object of your own needs in the vestments of your own desires. When you wake up to the fact that it just ain't there, that's when you've got to go."

5 Ride the High Country

"Good fight ...I enjoyed it."

There is a rumor that *Ride the High Country* was first offered to film director Budd Boetticher who had directed a number of Randolph Scott Westerns in the late fifties and early sixties. When he turned it down, the rumor continues, it was offered to Burt Kennedy, Boetticher's scriptwriter, who had recently directed his first feature, *The Canadians*. When Kennedy finally turned it down, the rumor concludes, Sam Peckinpah was offered the job. Another rumor credits John Ford, the renowned Western director with recommending Peckinpah for the picture. The truth is that Peckinpah got the assignment on his own merit.

Richard Lyons, the film's producer, recalled: "I've heard several stories through the years that a number of other directors were considered for *Ride the High Country,* but that's a lot of crap. I was the producer, and I'd know. The way Sam got the picture was that he and I were both at the William Morris Agency in those days, and Silvia Hirsch, who was with the agency, heard that I was looking for a director for this Western and asked me if I'd ever heard of Sam Peckinpah. I said no and she convinced me to look at a couple of the segments of *The Westerner* that Sam had directed. So I did, and they really impressed me.

"Now you have to understand that this picture was to be made at Metro and they were very class conscious. I mean they just didn't even consider hiring television directors. But I called Sol Siegel who was head of production at the studio at the time and told him that I had this director who'd worked in television, and I'd seen four segments that he'd done and I thought they were outstanding. Well, Siegel was coming in over the weekend and said he'd have a look at one. So he came in, and we ran one, and then he did just what I'd done. He said, 'You got any more?' So we looked at them all, and when we finished Siegel turned to me and said, 'Hire him.'"

Ride the High Country was Dick Lyons's first major picture as a producer. He had received his training at what was known as the "B" unit at Twentieth Century-Fox under Robert L. Lippert. While working there a $200,000 feature he had produced called *The Sad Horse* caught the attention of Siegel who then brought him to Metro-Goldwyn-Mayer.

Specifically, Lyons was hired to produce a small budget Western—roughly around $800,000—primarily for release in European markets to offset expensive productions, which were then being made by MGM, like Lewis Milestone's *Mutiny on the Bounty* starring Marlon Brando. The story Lyons finally decided to film dealt with two over-the-hill gunfighters who get one last chance at glory when they are hired to escort a gold shipment from a High Sierra mining camp back to civilization.

Joel McCrea recalled: "It's always been known as Peckinpah's picture, but Dick Lyons really put the whole thing together. He was the one who dug Sam up and got me out of a kind of retirement and got Randy [Scott]. In this business, it seems that performers and directors have artistic integrity towards everything but the bank. Well, Dick had to do that. He had to face the Metro people, and he backed Sam right down the line. He's never gotten the credit he's deserved. There's no question that Sam was the magic ingredient that made the thing go, but we were all brought together by Dick Lyons."

Lyons's first concern was in finding a script with potential. He remembered: "Actually the fellow who wrote *Ride the High Country* didn't get credit for writing it. N. B. Stone, Jr., who is no longer alive, got credit for it. But another writer named William S. Roberts—Bill Roberts, a writer who shared a suite with me at the studio—and Sam, who did what I call a dialogue rewrite, really de- served the credit.

"The way it came about was one day I happened to mention my need for a good property to Roberts who told me about this friend of his, N. B. Stone, Jr., who had this screenplay he'd written years before about two old guys who were through but got one more chance in life. Well, it sounded like a pretty good idea, and Roberts put me in touch with Stone.

"Now the strange thing about Stone was that he would not work anywhere but his apartment. I finally found out why. He was something of an alcoholic, and he could never remember where he was writing or what he was writing or anything. I used to have to go over to his apartment, and we would hunt for pages together. And this went on for seven or eight weeks until the studio started putting pressure on me for a script.

"Well, I finally got this 145-page first draft out of Stone and read it. It was awful. I couldn't believe anything could be that bad. So I went to Bill Roberts and asked him to read it, because I knew I was in big trouble. Well, Roberts felt terrible about the whole thing and offered to do an uncredited rewrite. So we worked nights and weekends on it out at Roberts's house, and he virtually rewrote the whole damn thing. But he wouldn't put his name on it because he wanted to do something for Stone who really needed a break.

"Unfortunately, it didn't help Stone, however, because other people would call him up after *Ride the High Country* was out and ask him to write for them, but he could never produce. And I'd get these calls from producers who would say, 'How the hell did you ever get that great script out of N. B. Stone?' And I'd have to say, 'Well, it wasn't easy.'"

After completing what he considered a workable draft of the script, Lyons went about signing his two stars, McCrea and Scott. Joel McCrea was a personal friend of Lyons, and after reading the script he agreed to play the part of the former marshal who has gone bad. Then Burt Kennedy, a mutual friend of both Lyons and Scott, acted as an intermediary in getting Scott to play the role of the old marshal whose chief concern was doing his job.

Then a strange thing happened. "Dick Lyons called me one day," stated Kennedy, "and says, 'I think I'm in trouble. Joel doesn't want to play the bad guy. You're a friend of Randy's. Do you suppose you could talk to him?' So I said I'd try and hung up the phone only to get this call from Randy who said he had a problem he wanted to talk over with me. So Randy came up to the house, and he said to me: 'Burt, do you suppose there's any chance that I could switch parts with Joel?' So of course I immediately told Randy that I thought I could handle it and called Dick Lyons back. So I straightened the whole thing out, but really I had nothing to do with it!"

After signing his stars, Lyons finally got in touch with Peckinpah. "I went out to where Sam was living at the time," Lyons remembered. "I think he was between divorces and living on the beach. Anyway, I gave him a copy of the script and explained the deal to him. He called me back after he'd read the thing and said it was the finest script he'd ever read and that he definitely wanted to direct it.

"Now Sam was handed the basic format for *Ride the High Country* which, as I've indicated, was excellent. But at least he knew what to do with it once he got it. He was handed a gem, but he knew how to cut it to really bring out its brilliance. Strange as it may seem, most people don't know what to do with a diamond in the rough.

"What Sam did was a tremendous three-to-four-week dialogue rewrite. And he made possibly the single most important structural change. In the original Stone-Roberts script, Randy, the 'black hat' character, dies at the end. Sam switched it so that the good guy died. And that, I think, really gave the film its tremendous impact, because it worked against the tradition of the bad guy 'paying his debt.'"

"The thing we didn't know when Lyons hired him," recalled Joel McCrea, "was that Sam was such a good writer. He improved the script immensely. We had this publicity meeting at the Beverly Brown Derby to flip a coin to see who would get first billing. Randy won the flip. Sam was there, but he was very quiet. He was totally in agreement with whatever we wanted to do, and I complimented him on his writing. You just didn't get any inclination that he was going to be anything but very easy to get along with. But then, he didn't bend over backward to try to charm anybody either."

As the director, Peckinpah was instrumental in casting the balance of the picture. Both Ron Starr who played Heck Longtree and Mariette Hartley who played Elsa had virtually no film acting experience. "Ron Starr had been a used car salesman," recalled Lyons, "and Mariette Hartley was an actress without any screen experience. That was because both Sam and I agreed that we wanted two young people who were more fresh and natural than the ones the studio wanted us to use.

"But it was with the Hammond brothers that Sam really showed what he could do. He knew how to control those heavies and how to make them effective. He cast all five of them—James Drury, Warren Oates, L. Q. Jones, John Davis Chandler, and John Anderson. And when he wardrobed them he said to them: 'Now you guys are a unit. I want you to stay away from the rest of the cast. You are the Hammond brothers. You eat by yourselves, you live in the motel by yourselves. You hate everybody here!' And he kept them all as a unit and it worked."

The original area selected for filming was the Mammoth Lakes region of the High Sierras near Bishop, California, on the far side of the mountains from Crane Valley and the real Coarsegold. Whereas another director might have chosen to shoot the entire picture on the back lot, Peckinpah insisted that the background terrain had to change as the party climbed and descended in elevation. Mammoth was ideal.

The cinematographer contracted to shoot the film was Lucien Ballard, who had worked with Peckinpah on several of the early *Westerner* episodes at Four Star. Peckinpah discussed with Ballard the kinds of problems they would have in shooting the film, and Ballard included in their list of equipment a Chapman Crane.

Of the many memorable shots involving the Chapman there is one that begins at a river bank by a stand of aspen trees as Steve Judd mounts his horse and rides on ahead, leaving Heck and Gil to exchange comments on the likelihood of Steve joining them to steal the gold. As Heck and Gil mount up, the camera begins to crane some thirty feet into the air allowing us to look beyond the aspens, golden in the autumn sunlight, to where Steve is joined by his companions. Uniquely coupled with the beauty of this shot is its impact from the way it visually parallels the relationship between these three men: Steve rides ahead, alone and pointing the way, while Gil and Heck must pass over the same ground in order to reach him.

Unfortunately, the production company had only four days of beautiful weather. Then it snowed—unusual for mid-October— even for Mammoth. Due to the limited budget, MGM told Lyons to move the company. L. Q. Jones who played Sylvus Hammond in the film still remembered that day: "We had gotten snowed out of Mammoth, but the problem wasn't that. The problem was that they had pulled the plug and moved the company without telling Sam. They didn't even bother to consult with him. So the first thing he knew about it was that morning when he got up, and instead of going to work, he was moving. Well, he was like a chicken with a broken neck. He got so mad that he finally wound up riding back in the bus with us rather than in the car the studio had provided for him.

"I'll never forget that trip 'cause he and I were sitting side by side and we were playing poker. And I had put my hat between us to keep my money in, and the next thing I knew Sam's keeping his money in it, too. Well, that's all right, but Sam is a horrendous poker player—especially when he's mad—and he really had a burr up his nose that day. So we played all the way from Mammoth to L.A., which is about a five- or six-hour trip by bus. And I won a fortune. I mean it was my day. And when I got through, I had like a dollar and a half in the hat because Sam had bet my winnings! Later, to get even with them for this move, Sam moved the company out to Bronson Canyon, and he made them 'snow' the whole damn thing. And they were screamin' cause we had soapsuds out the ass!"

Bronson Canyon is, of course, in the middle of Griffith Park in Hollywood and therefore never sees snow. So in order to reproduce the look of a mining camp high in the Sierras, Peckinpah insisted on snow for the tents that art director LeRoy Coleman had made out of sailcloth, filched from *Mutiny on the Bounty,* as well as for the surrounding area. To accomplish this scene, Lucien Ballard suggested liquid soap under pressure that produced a foam that clung to the sloping sides of the tents. It worked beautifully. But it would only stand up under the intense heat in the Canyon for several minutes, which meant that they had to frequently "resnow" the set.

In addition to Bronson Canyon, a number of other locations were employed in order to match the variety of backgrounds and striking visuals shot in the first four days. Among these were Frenchmen's Flat, the Conejo Valley, Malibu Canyon, the Twentieth Century-Fox ranch, and the MGM back lot. To complicate matters even more, a serious fire was raging in nearby Topanga Canyon and Bel Air, and the smoke from this fire darkened the skies over much of the surrounding area. These conditions placed an extra burden on Lucien Ballard and his crew to get the effects they wanted. The look of the finished film is a tribute to their abilities.

"Lucien Ballard did a magnificent job," stated Joel McCrea. "He was very smart. He knew Sam better than any of the rest of us, and he had a very tactful way of saying, 'What would you think of it if we shot it from over here?' And of course, it would look twice as good. He never took any credit for that. He's a very talented fella."

McCrea's costar, Randolph Scott, retired from the motion picture business following the completion of his work on *Ride the High Country,* leaving behind a distinguished career. He is now a private businessman in Southern California and declines to give interviews or "talk about old movies." In a phone conversation, he did, however, make the following statement about his experience with Peckinpah: "Sam, in my estimation, is one of the top directors the upper echelon of directors. I would have liked to have worked on other films with him. I wish that he had come along earlier in my career, which is not to say that I was not satisfied with the many men I did work with. But Sam is a great troubleshooter on a film. He has an innate instinct and talent for dealing with a script that many others just do not have. Sometimes, you know, a scene doesn't play well as it's written, and Sam had the ability to take something that didn't work and alter it in such a way that it would work."

"There is a scene in the film as it now stands," recalled Warren Oates, "where I am forced by my brothers to take a bath. That scene came about in a strange way. It originally involved my reaching into a hole and pulling out a rattlesnake by the tail. So they had this pipe they were going to put down in the ground and put the rattlesnake down the pipe head first so that his tail would be sticking out for me to grab. Then I was to throw the snake into my brother's tent. So the guy who had the rattlesnake said that the snake would be milked, but because Sam insisted that it's mouth be open, there was a chance that I would be bitten. If that happened, milked or not, I was going to be sick.

"So I said, 'Oh, shit!' and I went over to the assistant director and asked him to have a medical attendant and an ambulance standing by so I could be rushed out of there and pumped out if I got bit. And when he asked me why I told him that if that snake bit me, I wasn't going to be around for a while, and they might have to shoot around me. So he immediately went to Sam, and they hashed it around for awhile.

"Then after lunch, Sam came up to me and said they had talked it over and decided to do something else. He looked at me, and I looked a little ripe, and he said: 'They're going to try to give you a bath, and you don't let 'em. Take out your knife. Cut 'em. Kill 'em. But don't let 'em give you a bath.' And that's how the scene worked out."

"Sam and I don't always agree," stated L. Q. Jones. "On *Ride the High Country,* we damn near fell to blows over the scene where we all ride into town—all the brothers—with Elsa, the girl, in the lead—and we're singing 'When the Roll Is Called Up Yonder I'll Be There.' I said to Sam: 'You've got t'be outta your fuckin' skull! You mean to tell me that this group of heavies is gonna ride into that town singing a hymn? I'll kiss your ass, but I'm not gonna do it!' Well, anyway it ended up that we did it, and he was right, and I was dead wrong. It worked."

R. G. Armstrong, who plays Joshua, the Bible-quoting farmer, whose complex relationship to his daughter is laced with repressed incestuous desire channeled into overprotection, recalled: "It was a small budget picture, so Sam had to fight for everything he wanted and got most of it. Let me give you an example. For about a week they had a chicken wrangler [someone who tends chickens on a movie set] out there, and they had to pay him $150 per day. Well, they hadn't gotten around to shootin' what the chickens were required for, so finally, on the day Sam needed the chickens, the chicken wrangler and his stock weren't there. Apparently, the production manager decided that Sam wasn't going to use them and sent them away. Well, Sam refused to shoot anything until the chickens were brought back. And they went around on it for about an hour, and finally they sent out and brought back the chicken wrangler, and Sam set up the shot where the camera starts on the chickens—a very tranquil scene—then he comes up to my face and the blood dripping out of it, and—boom—the audience is shocked into an awareness of what is going on.

"When Sam finished that shot, he set up the shot where Warren Oates is so frustrated he starts shooting at the chickens, taking it out on them. Then he sets up the shot of Warren's bird menacing the chickens. These were some of the touches that made the movie great, and Sam had to fight for them. There weren't any chickens in the script. Sam added all that." As with Peckinpah's addition of the hymn sung by the Hammonds, the use of the chickens helped to add a texture to the sequence.

"I found as I worked with Sam," stated Joel McCrea, "and I'd worked with some pretty good ones—Stevens, Wellman, Hitchcock, Sturgis—that we got along just fine. Sam contributed a lot. You could just tell you were going to get something a little better because he really knew what he was doing. I'd watch him direct the other people like the boy and girl we had. They didn't know what to do. He made them good.

"Then about the middle of the shooting, Sam became critical of the crew—not the whole crew, but when something would go wrong, he'd jump on whoever seemed to be at fault with: 'What the hell do you think you're doing? How long have you been at MGM?' And some of these guys had been around a long time, so things were none too pleasant. Now he was never hard on the cast. He wouldn't pick a patsy like Otto Preminger would do. But he was tough on the crew, and that created just a little more tension on the set than you would feel with a George Stevens, for example. I did know other directors who used to do the same thing—John Ford used to do it—but I never approved of it."

"Sam started his syndrome of firing people on *Ride the High Country*," recalled Dick Lyons. "He got after this sound boom operator we had. He was a young guy, and he'd allow the boom to come into the frame, and Sam got pretty hard on him. We finally had to fire him. But then, Sam can be pretty rough on a crew. I've got a picture of Sam in my office which is signed "To Dick Lyons, 'Get rid of 'em' Sam Peckinpah." But Sam was always a dedicated guy—a fighter. You have to be in this business to get anywhere."

Principal photography for the picture was completed on November 22nd, 1961. Then Peckinpah's luck took over. Sol Siegel, the production head of the studio, had broken into an open feud with Joseph R. Vogel, who was the head of MGM's parent organization, Loew's Incorporated, and the man who had appointed Siegel to his position. Because of this power struggle, Siegel felt it imperative that he make his own decisions and make them stick. Peckinpah was told to report to Siegel's office the following day.

MGM employed a fulltime staff of cutters under the direction of Margaret Booth, MGM's editor in chief, who had begun her career as an editor working for D. W. Griffith before MGM had even been formed. As a consequence, MGM could easily have decided to take the film as shot and turn it over to Booth for routine editing by a staff editor with minimal interference from Peckinpah on the "director's cut." There was one complication, however. Margaret Booth disliked the daily rushes that had come in from location and had virtually said that the film would be impossible to cut. Siegel, on the other hand, had been impressed by what he had seen. This circumstance, coupled with the fact that Siegel was a fighter and had liked Peckinpah from their first meeting, caused him to offer Peckinpah a legitimate chance to make the first cut on the picture.

"Sam and I were just a couple of young guys at a major studio, and everybody was always looking down their noses at us," stated Lyons. "But Sam was smart. He was learning in those days. We had a marvelous little editor named Frank Santillo, and Sam spent fourteen weeks with Frank in the cutting room editing the picture until they threw him off the lot. But in those fourteen weeks, Santillo taught him how to edit."

Santillo had begun his editing career as an assistant to the montage specialist Slavko Vorkapich when Vorkapich had worked at MGM in the thirties on such films as *Viva Villa!* and *The Good Earth.* Santillo has since worked extensively as an editor, winning an Academy Award for *Grand Prix* in 1965. He recalls: "At first, Sam didn't tell me what to do. He just looked at the film he'd shot and said, 'That's a hell of a lot of film!' So I told him that I would make a rough cut of each sequence as I thought it should look using Sam's script as a guide. Then he could tell me what he wanted me to change. Sam agreed to this and I went ahead.

"I had a couple of assistants working with me, and they would

assemble particular scenes, and I would work with the most difficult ones and assemble the major sequences of action so that Sam
could see better what he had. Because they had set a time limit on
when the first cut of the picture had to be completed, we would work
far into the night. Sam would sit there with a pad of paper sketching
us as we worked. As we progressed, Sam gained a lot of confidence
in me.

"Sam had an uncanny feeling for editing. One night while we
were cutting the picture I said to him, 'You're going to be one of
the really great directors in this business because you're really
sharp on detail.'

"Let me give you an example of what I mean. There were a lot of
dialogue sequences that I had cut together, and I felt that they were
really well balanced. When we screened them, Sam liked them. But
when we got back to the editing room, he started to make changes
in those very same sequences that he had said were so good. He
would change things around so that we'd be substituting reaction
shots for dialogue shots. He was constantly striving to bring out
nuances in his characters, and not just the good guys but the bad guys
as well. He'd start in with 'Trim this. Cut that. Change that,' until we
really got what we wanted. And that's why Sam is so much better
than so many other directors. They'll just look at a sequence, and
they'll say 'That's fine,' but they'll never really bring out the
potential of what's on film.

"The thing that's really difficult in cutting for Sam is that he
shoots a lot of film, but it's all good. That makes it difficult to
decide what to keep and what to throw away. With other directors,
you start to assemble a scene and about half of the stuff is no good,
so you can throw it away. You have no problem in deciding what to
use. Sam's footage is just the opposite. And Sam knows every inch
of that film. You'll almost be finished with a picture, and Sam will
look at it, and he'll say there was such and such a shot and to cut it
in. And Sam doesn't care how long it takes. You've got to find it
because it is essential to Sam's conception of that character.

"But probably the best illustration of what Sam was able to do
with *Ride the High Country* is in the final shootout sequence at the
end of the film. Margaret Booth had seen the dailies and said: 'This is
the worst footage I've ever seen. It's impossible. Two old guys who
have been trapped by three young ones. Nobody will ever believe
they could possibly win. And the number of shots they all fire when
they're standing there in the open. It's ridiculous!'

"At any rate, I had done montage for Metro for years, and during the Second World War I had worked for the military censors at

the Pentagon. We'd get the footage shot by the Army, and we'd have to cut it quickly, making a little story out of it, and then turn it over to the newsreels. So when we came to this final sequence in the picture, Sam was upset because he really didn't want to cut any of it. I mean it was all good footage. So as always, I took it and made a rough cut. But because of my work with Vorkapich, I knew that even with a one-frame cut the audience could retain something of what was on the screen, and because of my war experience, I knew how exciting a battle sequence could be made by cutting it to a fast pace. When a guy is shooting, you don't have to show him first standing there, then aiming, then firing. You've got to imply a lot. Boom!—he fires. Boom!—somebody's hit. Boom!—somebody else is hit. You make the sequence move by allowing the audience to fill in the gaps. Consequently, I cut the sequence and some of the shots were only six frames long [one-quarter of a second on the screen], and I said to Sam that even at that length some of them would appear to be too long on the screen. And he said, 'Oh, no.' I could tell that he was afraid that maybe I'd cut them too short already.

"So we went to the screening room and looked at what I'd cut, and after the sequence was over Sam looked at me, smiled, and said, 'You know, you're right.' And then we went back, trimmed the sequence down until it was exactly the way Sam wanted it, and some of the shots were only two frames long. Sam has always given me credit for teaching him how to 'flash cut' like that.

"Yet the things which really make the scene work for me are the little touches that Sam was able to add. I remember Margaret Booth saying that she just couldn't understand why Sam had taken those pictures of the chickens. Nobody in the middle of a gunfight was going to take time out to shoot at chickens. But that's what is so wonderful about Sam—those little touches that help the audience see into a character's personality. Margaret just couldn't understand that."

In the first week of January 1962, the initial cut of *Ride the High Country* was shown to Sol Siegel. Peckinpah remembered: "When it was over he called me up—I was in the editing room—and he said: 'You've gambled and you've won! Would you like to put this in final cut?' And I said, 'Yes sir, I would.' And he said, 'Then do it.' Later he called me to his office and said: 'They'll be on you every minute, and when it gets bad, call me. Everything else you handle yourself. And Margaret Booth—if you want her around, fine; if not, kick her ass out!' Well, all in all, Margaret was a good old hide. We generally got along because she was rougher than hell with me, and I was the same way with her. We had kind of an hones relationship. But Sol Siegel, there was a real gentleman!"

Unfortunately, Joseph R. Vogel removed Siegel as head of production at MGM shortly thereafter, assuming the duties himself. It was then that Peckinpah was barred from the studio.

"After they threw Sam off the lot," remembered Lyons, "Frank Santillo and I had to finish the dubbing ourselves. Dubbing is very important, because it is the one chance you have to rerecord any sound you aren't satisfied with. Well, I'd have to call Sam after each sound reel was approved and play it for him over the phone. It must have sounded awful. I was also responsible for the music for the picture.

"Anyway, we finally got the first answer print, and Joe Vogel comes in to screen it with Sam, myself, and Frank Santillo. It was right after lunch, and Vogel falls asleep right after the first reel and begins to snore heavily. Now you have to remember that Sam had really not been around for any of the postproduction sound work. So as soon as he heard Vogel's snoring he jabs me in the ribs, breaking about three, and says in a loud whisper: 'What the hell is that noise? I knew I couldn't leave you alone in that dubbing room!' And I said: 'Sam, there's nothing I can do. That's the president of the company snoring!' And Sam said even louder, 'I'll be a son of a bitch!' But nothing could wake Vogel except the lights going on. When that happened, Vogel stopped snoring, stood up, and said, 'That's the worst picture I've ever seen!'"

"Vogel called it 'the worst thing he'd ever seen,'" Peckinpah remembered, "after sleeping through it! After he was through, I stood up and said: 'Mr. Vogel, let me tell you something. You give me three days with that picture in first-run houses, and you'll have your cost back along with a percentage of the profit!' ... and I might have added, 'You son of a bitch!'"

This, of course, did little to reestablish Peckinpah's image at MGM. Fortunately, however, the film was cut the way Peckinpah had wanted it cut, and Vogel, who under different circumstances might have recut it to suit his own whims, decided instead not to waste any more money on it. The film was released as the bottom half of a double bill, coupled with either *The Tartars* or *Boys' Night Out.*

"*Ride the High Country* went out and did horrendously bad," L. Q. Jones recalled. "But that was because they had saddled it as the bill filler to *Boys' Night Out,* which possibly lays claim to be the second, if not the first, worst picture ever made. Then they discovered that *Ride the High Country* was making the money, and nobody was staying around for the other picture. So they finally got smart and pulled it back and rereleased it."

Among those calling for the film's rerelease was Jim Silke, a young commercial artist and writer who at that time had founded a magazine called *Cinema* and has since become an instructor at the American Film Institute. He saw *Ride the High Country* for the first time at a drive-in. Impressed, he decided to interview Peckin-pah for *Cinema.*

"I cornered him out at CBS studios," Silke recalled." I don't know whether anybody had ever done a story on him up to that point. Sam still had black hair then and smoked from a Franklin Delano Roosevelt cigarette holder. We talked and he was just as outspoken then as he is now, but we got along well. And I wrote up some questions for him to answer. He took them home and an-swered them in his own write-rewrite-think-rewrite again style. It took him weeks. It was on the basis of those questions that I wrote my interview in *Cinema.*

"I remember I asked him to cast ten different roles which in-cluded the Dragon Lady, Little Orphan Annie, Sam Houston, Hotspur. But the first one on the list was the Apache chief Victorio. And Sam said he spent about three hours with the casting books trying to cast Victoria, but he couldn't do it so he refused to answer that one. What impressed me was that he would spend that much time on it.

"So, anyway, I put the article out, and it created some interest locally. At the same time, some Belgian writer gave the picture a big writeup. Then I got a call from the Los Feliz Theater in L.A., and they wanted to play it. That was extraordinary because they played prestige foreign pictures almost exclusively. I think Bergman's *Wild Strawberries* had its American premiere there. For *Ride the High Country* that was its first real chance."

On rerelease *Ride the High Country* became the "sleeper of the year" as the critics began to discover it:

A superior Western. . .Although it has its lapses, Sam Peckin-pah's colorful tale of two superannuated cowboys gives evidence of careful craftsmanship. It is a resourceful young director's attempt to create something original within a fairly rigid framework of tradition.

> *~Joseph Morgenstern, New York Herald-Tribune*

A perfectly dandy little Western [that] is a downright pleasure to watch....Take two cornbelt veterans like Mr. McCrea and Mr. Scott, give them a taut, tangy script, a trim supporting cast and a good director, and you have the most disarming horse opera in months. From the opening scene, the film projects a steady, natural blend of wisdom and humor, excellently photographed in color against some lovely vistas.

~Howard Thompson, New York Times

This story could have been sheer slumgullion, but under Sam Peckinpah's tasteful direction, it is a minor chef d'oeuvre among westerns.

~Time

As a consequence of all this, the film began being discussed as a possible dark horse nomination for an Academy Award in two categories, best direction and best original screenplay. When Peckinpah learned of this, he called both Metro and the Academy and told them flatly not to bother, "If this film is nominated for best screenplay without my name on it as writer, I will sue every one of you!" *Ride the High Country* received no nominations for an Academy Award that year.

Released for foreign distribution in 1963, the film, called by a variety of names abroad (most notably by its working title, *Guns in the Afternoon),* won the Belgium International Film Festival Grand Prix (beating out Federico Fellini's *8 ½* among others), Mexico's Diosa de Plata (Silver Goddess) for Best Foreign Film, as well as high praise from France's *Le Conseil des Dix.*

More important to Peckinpah, however, was the personal victory bound to this film. His sister, Fern Lea, recalls: "We went to see *Ride the High Country* at a sneak preview, and when it was over, I went into the ladies' room and cried and cried because the character played by Joel McCrea reminded me so much of my father who had just died the year before. My father liked to quote the Bible and could. The line 'All I want to do is enter my house justified' was a saying I often heard my father say." This was Peckinpah's tribute to "the Boss."

Peckinpah's real vindication as a director, however, came from his former employer, Sol Siegel, who upon seeing the film in a theater wrote Sam a letter that began, "Who the fuck do you think you are ... John Ford?"!

74

"D. Sam" sits on his grandfather Denver Church's knee at the age of one.
(Photo courtesy of Fern Church Peckinpah)

Sam Peckinpah poses with his father, David, "the Boss," outside their home in Fresno (ca. 1942). *(Photo courtesy of Fern Church Peckinpah)*

Sam Peckinpah as a cadet at San Rafael Military Academy, 1943. *(Photo courtesy of Fern Church Peckinpah)*

76

Sam Peckinpah (with beard) in happier times stands beside his first wife, Marie, and their three children, Melissa (in Marie's arms), Sharon, and Kristen, in his Quonset hut at Malibu (ca. 1956); his sister, Fern Lea, stands with her husband, Walter Peter (holding daughter Suzanne), while Peckinpah's then typist, Nancy Galloway; stands in the middle with her two children, Steven (in front of Fern Lea) and Cathy. *(Photo courtesy of Fern Lea Peckinpah Peter)*

Sam and Denver Peckinpah hunting deer in Nevada (ca. 1959).
(Photo courtesy of David E. Peckinpah)

Brian Keith as Dave Blassingame and John Dehner as Burgundy
Smith in *The Westerner*, 1960. *(Photo courtesy of Four Star
Enterprises)*

Brian Keith as Yellowleg attempts to help Kit (Maureen O'Hara) despite her resistance in *The Deadly Companions. (Photo courtesy of Pathe-America)*

Billy (Steve Cochran, back to camera), Yellowleg (Brian Keith), Kit (Maureen O'Hara), and Turk (Chill Wills) share a campfire in *The Deadly Companions. (Photo courtesy of Pathe-America)*

Randolph Scott and Joel McCrea stage a mock gunfight on the set of
Ride the High Country. (Photo courtesy of Metro-Goldwyn-Mayer)

Ron Starr (mounted) as Heck Longtree confronts the four
Hammond brothers—left, L. Q. Jones, James Drury, John
Anderson, and John Davis Chandler—in the mining camp at
Coarsegold in *Ride the High Country;* note the "snow" made from
soapsuds. *(Photo courtesy of Metro-Goldwyn-Mayer)*

Charlton Heston as Major Dundee pours a drink for James Coburn as Sam Potts while Michael Anderson, Jr., as the bugler Ryan looks on. *(Photo courtesy of Columbia Pictures)*

Richard Harris receives help cutting a birthday pinata on location in Mexico during the filming of *Major Dundee: foreground left to right,* Jim Hutton, Sam Peckinpah, Charlton Heston, James Coburn, and Michael Anderson, Jr. *(Photo courtesy of Columbia Pictures)*

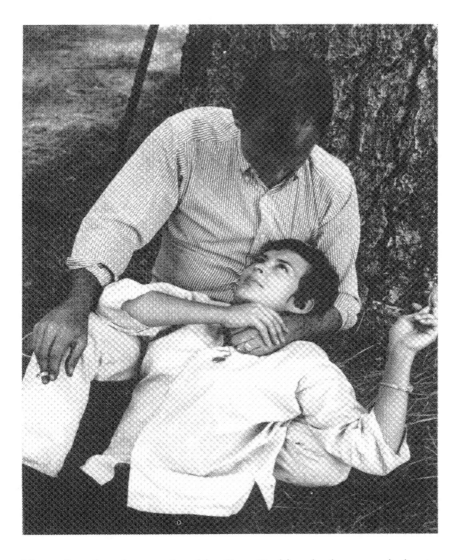

Unemployed and unemployable, Sam Peckinpah shares an intimate moment with his second wife, actress Begonia Palacios (ca. 1965). *(Photo by Denver Peckinpah)*

METROGOLDWYNMAYER p,eseots
A MARTIN RANSOHOFF P,odoctioo

SPENCER TRACY • STEVE McQUEEN
KARL MALDEN

in

THE
CINCINNATI
KID

Directed by SAM PECKINPAH
A Filmways Picture

This preproduction ad was run by MGM in *The Hollywood Reporter* in 1964. Spencer Tracy left the project before filming began and Peckinpah was removed as director less than a week into shooting by producer Martin Ransohoff "for shooting unauthorized nudes at night."

Sam Peckinpah (on camera dolly) checks the final framing through the viewfinder as Pike Bishop (William Holden) and the Bunch escort a lady across the street at the opening of *The Wild Bunch;* Lucien Ballard stands in white Stetson with his hands in his back pockets watching Peckinpah. *(Photo by Paul Harper)*

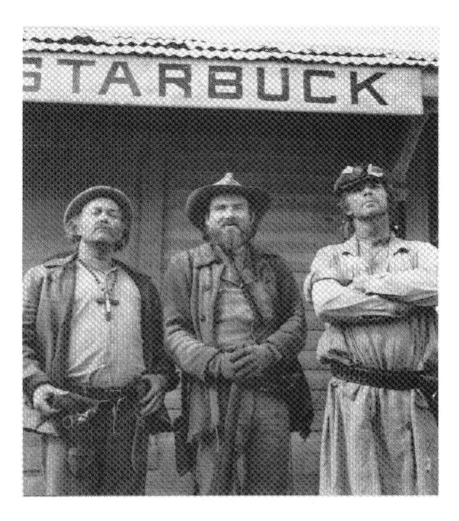

Bounty hunters Strother Martin, Paul Harper, and L. Q. Jones pose beneath the name of the town, "Starbuck," on location in Mexico near the start of production on *The Wild Bunch. (Photo courtesy of Paul Harper)*

The Bunch: Tector Gorch (Ben Johnson), Lyle Gorch (Warren Oates), Pike Bishop (William Holden), and Dutch Engstrom (Ernest Borgnine) make the last walk to free Angel from Mapache in "one final grand offensive" near the end of *The Wild Bunch. (Photo courtesy of Warner Brothers/ Seven Arts)*

Peckinpah fires a compressed air special effects gun during the filming of the bridge sequence in *The Wild Bunch. (Photo by Paul Harper)*

"Lady, nobody's ever seen you before." Stella Stevens as Hildy plays a love scene with Jason Robards in *The Ballad of Cable Hogue.* *(Photo courtesy of Warner Brothers/Seven Arts)*

"It ain't so much the dyin' you hate ... It's not hearin' what they're going to say about you ... " Cable (Jason Robards) prepares to die as Hildy (Stella Stevens), Bowen (Strother Martin, seated), and the preacher Joshua (David Warner) look on in *The Ballad of Cable Hogue. (Photo courtesy of Warner Brothers/Seven Arts)*

Dustin Hoffman as David Sumner confers with his wife, Amy, played by Susan George in *Straw Dogs. (Photo courtesy of ABC Pictures)*

Jerry Fielding conducts the score to *Straw* Dogs. "The problem with scoring the picture was that it was a terrifying film and the terror grows." *(Photo courtesy of Camille Fielding)*

David (Dustin Hoffman) is flanked by, *left,* Scutt (Ken Hutchison) and Venner (Del Henney), as his wife (Susan George) looks on during the climactic battle at the end of *Straw Dogs. (Photo courtesy of ABC Pictures)*

Robert Preston as Ace Bonner asks his son, Junior (Steve McQueen), for a grubstake in the scene set at the railroad station in *Junior Bonner.* *(Photo courtesy of ABC Pictures)*

Robert Preston and Ida Lupino as Junior's parents, estranged but still in love, grasp the moment despite their irreconcilable differences in *Junior Bonner. (Photo courtesy of ABC Pictures)*

Sam Peckinpah lines up a shot at Huntsville Penitentiary while filming *The Getaway. (Photo courtesy of First Artists)*

Steve McQueen, Ali MacGraw, and Sam Peckinpah watch the stunt work on location during the filming of *The Getaway. (Photo courtesy of First Artists)*

R. G. Armstrong as Bob Ollinger threatens Kris Kristofferson as Billy the Kid in *Pat Garrett and Billy the Kid* "l was throwin' my anger at Sam, but it all came out at Kris ... " *(Photo courtesy of Metro-Goldwyn-Mayer)*

Pete Maxwell (Paul Fix) watches as Pat Garrett (James Coburn) unleashes his rage at company man John Poe (John Beck) before he can desecrate the body of Billy the Kid in *Pat Garrett and Billy the Kid. (Photo courtesy of Metro-Goldwyn-Mayer)*

Sam Peckinpah holds the trophy for the soccer game won from John
Wayne's BATJAC company during the filming of *Pat Garrett and
Billy the Kid* on location in Durango, Mexico; Peckinpah is flanked
by, *left,* property master Robert Visciglia and editor Garth Craven.
(Photo courtesy of Garth Craven)

Isela Vega and Warren Oates as the tragic lovers in search of "the golden fleece" in *Bring Me the Head of Alfredo Garcia. (Photo courtesy of United Artists)*

A stickler for details, Peckinpah demonstrates exactly how he wants Challo Gonzales to strike Warren Oates with a shovel during the graveyard sequence from *Bring Me the Head of Alfredo Garcia. (Photo courtesy of United Artists)*

Stunt coordinator Whitey Hughes, *left,* discusses the next sequence with stuntmen Duffy Hamilton and Gary Combs during the location filming of *Bring Me the Head of Alfredo Garcia. (Photo by Garner Simmons)*

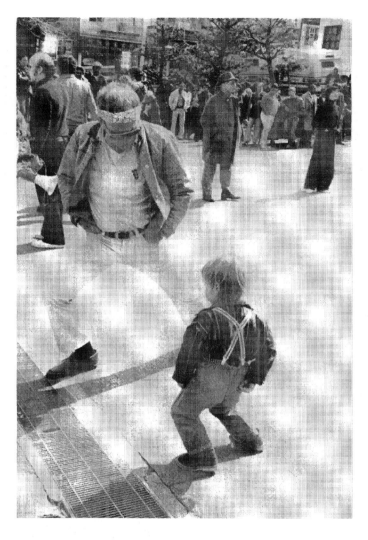

"We all dream of being a child again."   Sam Peckinpah takes
instruction from a young friend during a break in the filming of *The
Killer Elite. (Photo courtesy of United Artists)*

On location at San Francisco International Airport during the filming of *The Killer Elite,* Peckinpah, *seated center,* watches a rehearsal. With him are, *left to right,* producer Martin Baum, Tiana, unknown extra, personal assistant Katy Haber, unknown extra, Frank Kowalski, unknown extra, property master Robert Visciglia, director of photography Philip Lathrop, and Hank Hamilton. *(Photo by Garner Simmons)*

Bo Hopkins as Miller, "the patron poet of the manic depressives," practices his craft in *The Killer Elite;* note the sign on top of the taxi, part of Peckinpah's attempt at "satire." *(Photo courtesy of United Artists)*

Peckinpah, "an occasional drinker," holds an impromptu production
meeting aboard his yacht, used during the filming of *The Killer Elite;*
others are, *left to right,* assistant director Newt Arnold, second unit
director Frank Kowalski, and director of photography Philip Lathrop.
(Photo courtesy of United Artists)

Peckinpah clowns with actor/producer Helmut Dantine as second unit director Frank Kowalski, *far left,* and assistant Katy Haber look on during the filming of *The Killer Elite. (Photo courtesy of United Artists)*

James Caan as Mike Locken battles the anonymous "Ninja" during the climactic battle aboard the mothball fleet in *The Killer Elite*. *(Photo courtesy of United Artists)*

Peckinpah, *standing to the right of camera,* is flanked by cast and crew as he directs James Caan, *at left facing camera,* during the filming aboard the mothball fleet in Suisun Bay of *The Killer Elite*. *(Photo courtesy of United Artists)*

James Coburn in *Cross of Iron* as Sergeant Steiner, "the quintessential survivor ... [in] an infantile but deadly game." *(Photo courtesy of Avco-Embassy Pictures)*

Ali MacGraw and Kris Kristofferson in an intimate moment from
Convoy. (Photo courtesy of United Artists)

Two eighteen-wheelers put the squeeze on the law in a spectacular
stunt sequence from *Convoy,* "a movie in which the trucks were
the stars." *(Photo courtesy of United Artists)*

(Photo courtesy of United Artists)

(Photos by Garner Simmons)

108

Sam Peckinpah greets well-wishers at his fiftieth birthday party, "...
an impulsive little boy"; *left to right,* producer Martin Baum, Kip
Dellinger, Camille Fielding, and Peckinpah. *{Photo courtesy of
Camille Fielding)*

6 Major Dundee

"If I signal you to charge, you charge."

Because MGM was slow to realize the box office potential of *Ride the High Country,* Sam Peckinpah found it necessary to return to television for work. It was the spring of 1962 and with the preference given by the viewing audience to hourlong shows the previous year, Four Star Productions had altered its format for new shows to reflect that trend. One of these was a program called *The Dick Powell Theater,* a television anthology that presented an entirely new and different hourlong drama each week. Peckinpah was contracted to produce and direct two of these shows for the coming season.

Peckinpah's first project was a story by Harry Mark Petrakis called "Pericles on 31st Street." He and Petrakis worked on the teleplay together. It was a contemporary piece with Pericles portrayed as an elderly New York peanut vendor who sets about helping residents of a slum neighborhood free themselves from the tyranny of a local boss. Theodore Bikel was cast as the vendor and Carroll O'Connor as the heavy; Arthur O'Connell and Strother Martin were cast in supporting roles. The show was shot mid-August 1962 and telecast December 4 of that year.

For his next effort, "The Losers," Peckinpah would draw on the talents of his friend and former associate on *The Westerner,* Bruce Geller. One of Geller's greatest contributions to *The Westerner* was the creation of a character called Burgundy Smith, an eloquent hustler out to take the West for what he could get in a charming, roguish sort of way. As portrayed by John Dehner, Burgundy had become something of a semiregular second lead on the show with Peckinpah directing him in three of the thirteen episodes opposite Brian Keith's Dave Blassingame.

"The Losers" was conceived by Geller and co-scripted with Peckinpah as a 1963 update of the same two characters even to the point of employing Blassingame's dog, Brown. Like the episodes that involved Smith in *The Westerner,* "The Losers" was a comedy. This time Peckinpah cast Lee Marvin in the "Blassingame" role with Keenan Wynn as Burgundy. The sixties found these characters basically unchanged: two hard-drinking, girl-chasing, card-cheating drifters.

The show was shot during the fall of 1962. In it Peckinpah used slow motion, fast motion, and stills in addition to the footage shot at regular speed. The slow motion footage recorded a horse trader and his men tripping over a table placed in their way by Dave and Burgundy who are trying to escape. Their pursuers go down in a graceful heap. It is worth noting that Peckinpah's first use of slow motion as a device to capture "violence" occurs in a comedy.

Unfortunately, in January of 1963, Dick Powell fell seriously and unexpectedly ill. He never recovered, dying of cancer at 59. Powell never saw "The Losers" completed. The show was first televised on *The Dick Powell Theater* January 15, 1963, during the regular season. It then was repeated twice in reruns the following spring. In the course of that year, it would play a total of six hours of prime time including its summer replays. Because of this popularity, Four Star began to explore the possibility of turning it into a series with Peckinpah as producer.

This might have actually taken place except that Powell's successor, Tom MacDermott, seems to have been unable to duplicate Powell's success. When Powell died, Four Star had thirteen shows in primetime slots on major networks. Within two years, it had only a single program in prime time.

Peckinpah still remembers how close "The Losers" came to becoming a series: "'The Losers' was a funny show. We had Keenan Wynn and Lee Marvin locked up for a series with it until Tom MacDermott wouldn't pay Lee's price."

From Four Star, Peckinpah went to Walt Disney Productions as a writer-director. There he began working on an adaptation of a novel called *Little Britches* by Ralph Moody. This was the story of a family who has moved out West near the turn of the century and must fight for their land against a cattle baron who wants the range left open. Peckinpah's script, called *The Boy and the Gunfighter,* substantially altered the original. A difference of opinion with the producer assigned to the project resulted in Peckinpah's decision to look elsewhere.

As summer became fall in 1963, Peckinpah's care in making *Ride the High Country* into a motion picture that reflected his potential as a director began to pay off. Jerry Bresler, a producer whose career stretched back to the 1930s and included two Academy Awards for short subjects, had seen the film and liked it. An independent producer with a releasing agreement with Columbia Pictures, Bresler had purchased a treatment by a writer named Harry Julian Fink called "Major Dundee" that dealt with the pursuit of Apaches into Mexico by a cavalry troop composed of Union and Confederate soldiers as well as civilians. He approached Peckinpah to direct it and Peckinpah accepted.

The next step was casting the picture. Jerry Bresler recalled: "In fairness, I must explain how casting is done on a major picture. During the period of *Major Dundee,* Columbia, like all other major studios, had casting directors. They would read the script and suggest names for each part. The producer and director would do the same. Then a meeting was held and the names were discussed.

"In the case of *Dundee* it was different. I had worked with [Charlton] Heston *[Diamond Head,* 1962] and we enjoyed a warm relationship. We felt he was right for the role, so I gave him the treatment written by Harry Julian Fink. He liked it and agreed to the role subject to director approval. I suggested Richard Harris because of *[This] Sporting Life* [directed by Lindsay Anderson, 1963] and James Hutton and Michael Anderson, Jr. Sam was in complete accord. He suggested Lee Marvin for the role of Potts [the one-armed scout in the film] but could not persuade Marvin to play the role. James Coburn was suggested by Marvin's agent, and we both liked him for the part. Senta Berger was suggested by the studio for foreign box office value. In my judgment we had a great cast, including every bit part. I was in complete accord with every suggestion Sam made [with respect to casting].

"We [Bresler and Peckinpah] flew to Ravenna, Italy, together to meet Richard Harris. He was anxious to meet both of us before accepting the role. When the studio wanted to recast this role to reduce the cost, I fought against it, and Sam was proud of me ... at least at that time."

Ben Johnson, the fine character actor whose long career in motion pictures goes back to John Ford's cavalry Westerns and includes winning an Academy Award for his role as Sam the Lion in *The Last Picture Show* remembered his first meeting with Peckinpah: "First time I met Sam was when he cast me in *Major Dundee.* Before we talked, he fired a fella or two right in front of me. When he finished, why I told him, 'I can't work for you, Mr. Peckinpah.' And he says, 'Well, why not?' And I said: 'Well, if you done t' me what you just done t' that feller, I'd hit you right square in the nose, and then you'd run me out of the business. And I ain't ready to leave.' And he just smiled and said, 'That's just why I want you to work for me.' So from that day on, we got along real good." In addition to Johnson, Peckinpah cast Slim Pickens, Dub Taylor, R. G. Armstrong, Warren Oates, and L. Q. Jones.

Meanwhile Fink had expanded his treatment into an over- length first draft. Feeling that this was unworkable, Bresler hired screenwriter Oscar Saul who along with Peckinpah began to rewrite *Dundee*. Jim Silke, who eventually worked on the picture, recalled: "Harry Julian Fink's treatment was terrific. Very exciting. But it had five or six stories going through it, and the major problem with the script was that it never seemed to focus on any one of these."

Realizing this, Saul and Peckinpah redrew the screenplay so that it centered less on the pursuit of the Apache and more on the conflict between Dundee and Tyreen. These two characters were to be mirror images of one another—tied to a common heritage but with diametrically opposed responses to that heritage. Both men are contradictions: Tyreen is a rebel yet firmly bound to a traditional code of honor. Dundee refuses to dishonor his oath to the Union despite his Southern birth yet proceeds to break every rule in the book in his pursuit of the Apache.

The resolution of this conflict would take place at the very end of the film. After the destruction of leader Sierra Charriba and his band of Apaches, Dundee and Tyreen face each other in a duel of honor—the very thing for which Dundee had earlier condemned Tyreen. Before they can draw, however, their attention is called to approaching French troops. Vowing to finish the duel in Texas, they lead their men to the Rio Grande to confront the French Cavalry on the opposite side. In this final battle at the river, it is Tyreen whose gallantry saves the colors—the very flag he damned—and whose ride headlong to his death allows Dundee and the others to escape. Thus both Dundee and Tyreen have come to a tacit acceptance of each other's position: Dundee as the good Southerner, a man of personal honor, and Tyreen as the good American, a man of patriotic honor.

Despite their best intentions and a great deal of work, the Saul-Peckinpah script remained unfinished at the start of the picture. Charlton Heston, in the *AFI Dialogue on Film,* relates: "A lesson I certainly learned on *[Major Dundee]* and I suspect Sam did, too, although maybe he's not too uncomfortable working this way, is not to begin a picture without a completed script. Sam is, of course, an extremely talented writer and had the responsibility of finishing the script while directing the picture. On the basis of the experience in Mexico, I would say this is impossible."

The rewrite did delay the start of shooting on *Dundee,* which had originally been scheduled to begin October 28, 1963. As a result, a second Bresler production called *Love Has Many Faces* entered into preproduction preparations as well. It would be shot in Acapulco starring Lana Turner, Cliff Robertson, and Hugh O'Brian. Because of the postponement, Bresler would produce both pictures simultaneously at the beginning of the new year.

Meanwhile, however, Bresler and Peckinpah entered into the first of many disagreements. Bresler remembered: "Prior to seeking locations [for *Dundee]* I had to undergo surgery. To save time, I sent Sam out with an art director to pick the locations. This was unfortunate, in my opinion, as Sam never took into account the cost or logistics. He selected one location some 100 miles from the next location but could only shoot one run-through [the cavalry troop riding past the camera] at that location. It meant moving men and 100 horses with equipment a great distance for one shot, and I refused to approve. This was our first major disagreement."

Considering their success together on *Ride the High Country,* Peckinpah had requested cinematographer Lucien Ballard for the picture. Ballard recalled: "Sam had been staying at my house for several months prior to going off on *Major Dundee,* and before he left he told me that he would get me on the picture with him. Now I've always liked working with Sam because he is an incredibly talented man, so I waited to hear from him. Well, finally Columbia called me and said they had this picture for me, and I figured it was *Dundee.* Only when I got over there it turned out to be something else and I refused. Well, finally, a couple of weeks later I hear from Sam, and he's been in Mexico scouting locations. And I asked him what happened, and he says that he had this other cameraman on picture, and he couldn't jeopardize his career for me! I really got angry at that considering how long I had waited to hear from him, not to mention the fact that he'd been a guest in my house. But, of course, we've made pictures since, and I've learned to expect the unexpected from Sam. He's very strong and overpowers people. He does not overpower me, however, because I've always told him exactly what I think." The director of photography on *Major Dundee* was Sam Leavitt whom Bresler had used on *Diamond Head.*

Every motion picture requires a production team capable of functioning well together both in preparing for and completing the actual shooting of the film. The camera and lighting crews and special effects, wardrobe, and makeup departments all enter into the effort. *Major Dundee* was to be shot almost entirely on location.

Therefore, any material that was required from the studio once shooting began would mean costly delay. However, because Columbia was a major American studio and had produced many such pictures, each department prepared as it always had: what was basically needed it would bring along; unexpected needs would be improvised as best they could be. Because this attitude was almost never challenged, even by "name" directors, the department heads at Columbia had little reason to suspect that Peckinpah on his third picture would be any sort of special problem. Further compounding this error in judgment was the agreement the production would be shot in conjunction with Mexico's Churubusco Studios, the state-owned cinema complex based in Mexico City. This agreement allowed at least some of the preparation to be farmed out to Columbia's Mexican counterpart.

A good example of what was happening is the crisis faced by the wardrobe department. This department was headed by Tom Dawson, a twenty-five-year veteran at Columbia whose department had costumed such past productions as *From Here to Eternity, The Guns of Navarone, West Side Story,* and *Dr. Strangelove.*

However, the costumes being designed for *Major Dundee* were not what Peckinpah had in mind. He insisted that Dawson bring in Jim Silke who was then in the process of leaving his position as an art director at Capitol Records. Silke recalled: "I came in and talked to Dawson and told him I would do some wardrobe sketches if I had a chance to read the script a couple times and if he made sure I got two hours with the director. Now Sam was my friend not his, but I wanted to let him know I intended on doing a good job.

"So Sam and I talked for a couple of hours about the characters and how the wardrobe should reflect certain changes in them as the picture progressed. Then I did one—the Richard Harris character, Tyreen—showed him as a prisoner; then as he puts together a uniform, half Union, half Confederate; then as he deteriorates into an animal. They loved it. So I did every central character. Illustrations for each of them. The same kinds of progressions. Then we built the costumes for each of the principals."

This assignment was handed over to the studio tailors. After the costumes for the principals were tailored along the lines of Silke's illustrations, they were aged to give them the look and texture of having been worn. This work was done by Tom Dawson's

26-year-old son, Gordon, a Class 4 wardrobe man at the time (Class 1 being the equivalent of master craftsman). Each principal had costumes six deep, which meant whatever was done to one had to be done to the rest. It was an expensive and time-consuming task.

In late January, 1964, Gordon Dawson completed his work, packed the costumes into their hampers, and sent them on their way to Mexico City where the balance of the costumes for the picture was being mass produced at Churubusco as economically as possible. No one remotely suspected that the wardrobe department on this picture would ever be in trouble.

The principal photography for *Major Dundee* began on February 6, 1964, in Durango, Mexico. Only three days before, Bresler's other production, *Love Has Many Faces,* had begun shooting in Acapulco. Bresler divided his time between the two. The most pressing problem on *Major Dundee* was the wardrobe.

Silke, who had been brought down to Mexico once already to do scene sketches for the picture was recalled once more to help both in wardrobe and building props. "My problem was to rebuild the wardrobe for the Mexican extras," Silke stated. "The guy in charge was good—or at least I thought he was—but he wasn't a worker. You have to understand that in Hollywood there were guys who were very talented at one time and who had risen to positions of power that meant they didn't have to work anymore. So I literally found myself running around Durango buying clothes off people's backs, [clothes] that were worn and looked authentic as opposed to the ones that had been built at Churubusco. The problem was getting doubles and triples!"

Gordon Dawson, who today is a writer-producer (among his credits is Peckinpah's *Bring Me the Head of Alfredo Garcia),* remembered the chaos: "I was working on another picture when suddenly I got this call: 'You've got to go to Mexico tomorrow morning. You will pick up your passport in four hours, and you will stop by the office to pick up some material we need to send down to the production of *Major Dundee.* I barely had time to pack, say goodbye to my wife, and get the things I was to take to Mexico. The next morning I was on the earliest flight they could manage into Mexico City and then a connection to Durango. As I arrived at the airport in Durango, I met my father who was flying out and then went directly to meet Peckinpah, scared to death because the wardrobe department was in deep trouble, and nobody seemed to be able to get it happening.

"My assignment originally was to assist another wardrobe man named Eric Seeley who had taken over after Peckinpah had shaken up the department. Everyone was afraid of Sam because Sam would really tell you what he liked and didn't like. Well, Eric and I dug in and started to teach the Mexican wardrobe people how to build and age costumes. Christ, the production was out of sight. We had French lancers, Zouaves, American cavalry uniforms, not to mention Indians and civilians. With the exception of the uniforms for the principals, [costumes] which we had made in the States, everything else had been made out of nylon in Mexico and then lined up against a wall at Churubusco and hit with a spray gun to add brown and black specks of paint for texture. Now you place them alongside the uniforms built out of cloth and textured by taking the nap down with a blowtorch then worked over with sandpaper, and there was just no comparison. They looked like two different armies. Worse than that, of course, was the fact that we couldn't even save these Mexican-built uniforms because when you take a blowtorch to a synthetic material it melts! So we had to start from scratch.

"On top of that it was a road show where this group of soldiers starts out looking reasonably clean, and then by the end they're really ragged. So you really begin to get into fine detail work. You need the same uniform at various stages of aging, and you need duplicates, sometimes as many as six deep, in order to cover a scene where somebody gets shot up and you're liable to have re-takes. So you wind up needing twenty feet of rack space for each of your principals because you won't necessarily be shooting in sequence and therefore you can't just transform one set of costumes as you go along. Then along the way a character will add a Mexican touch. Still later he will lose his hat and add another. All of that had to be kept straight. It was very complicated but a very big point in my life because I was my own man. By making *Dundee* work as far as the wardrobe went, I was virtually able to save my father's job. After I had been on the picture for about three weeks, we were getting things together, and at least we weren't in any more trouble than any other department."

Throughout this period, Jerry Bresler's relationship with Peckinpah continued to deteriorate. "The incident that brought about a rupture in our relationship," Bresler recalled, " ... came after two weeks of photography. I became concerned on several levels: cost via length, the character relationship between Dundee and Tyreen, and tempo. I met and talked with Sam at the end of a day's shooting. I told him of my concern: his scenes were elongated; we were going over cost and way over length. It seemed obvious that

118

the way he was shooting we would have a picture over four hours, and this would be disastrous. The quality would suffer in cutting, and the loss of money, ludicrous. The meeting ended with my ultimatum: unless he agreed to change his methods, I would have to recommend a change in directors. From this point on we were completely at opposite ends."

It was at this time that Silke found himself placed in a strange position: "The second week they started shooting the fiesta sequence, which Columbia or Bresler claimed broke the back of the picture financially, and that's when I learned about the movies. Jerry Bresler came up to me and begged me to get Sam to move faster, and I was really dumbfounded. I'm a young guy who doesn't know really anything about movie making. The only thing I did know was the West, which was why I was able to do wardrobe and props. And here is the man who is producing the movie begging me, a mere *tourist,* to help him. I think I laughed out loud. Jerry Bresler never forgave me."

Because *Major Dundee* was an American production being filmed in Mexico, it was necessary for Columbia to employ a substantial number of people from the Mexican film industry. Among them was the premiere Mexican director, Don Emilio Fernandez, who was to act as codirector to Peckinpah. He had established his international reputation with *Maria Candelaria* in 1945 and had won the Grand Prix at Cannes the following year with *La Perla* scripted from the novel by John Steinbeck. When John Ford had come to Mexico in 1947 to make *The Fugitive* with Henry Fonda and Dolores Del Rio, Fernandez was his associate producer. To this day he still remembers Ford as *"mi compadre."* On *Major Dundee,* Fernandez and Peckinpah began a friendship that has grown stronger in the years since. Fernandez's support became an important factor in Peckinpah's ability to complete *Dundee.*

Likewise, casting also had to involve a number of Mexican actors and actresses. Senta Berger had been given the female lead. The two female supporting roles, however, went to Mexican actresses. The role of the prostitute with whom Dundee lives while recuperating in Durango went to the Mexican actress Aurora Clavel. For the role of Linda, the Mexican girl with whom the bugler Ryan falls in love, Peckinpah had in mind a Mexican actress who was seeing American director Budd Boetticher, then in Mexico shooting on his longterm project *Arruza.*

Peckinpah remembered: "So Budd came by and said, 'She's not going to work for you!' And I had to find another actress to play the part. So I was shown a picture of a young Mexican actress and flamenco dancer named Begonia Palacios. She was beautiful, and I ran a picture she had made in Mexico, and I thought she was very good. So I cast her in the picture and later married her—not once, but three times [twice in civil court, once in a church]. So I always tell Budd when I see him, 'Man, you really know how to fuck a guy up!'" Begonia Palacios became Peckinpah's second, third, and fourth wife.

After a month of shooting in Durango, the company moved into Churubusco Studios to film three days of interiors. Meanwhile, the picture's twenty-five stuntmen went on to Cuautla where they set up a camp to work on the stunts required in the days ahead. These stuntmen—all horse specialists—had been hired to perform the nearly 300 stunts called for in the picture and to act as the core of the troopers under Dundee.

When the *Major Dundee* cast and crew stepped off the plane at the Mexico City airport, the first thing they saw was a huge banner that read: "Jerry Bresler's *Love Has Many Faces* Welcomes Jerry Bresler's *Major Dundee.*" After the pain of Durango, while *Love Has Many Faces* had been shooting in Acapulco, this sign did little to repair the deepening split between Peckinpah and Bresler. It did even less for Bresler in the eyes of the cast and crew.

As the differences between Peckinpah and Bresler became more pronounced, Bresler informed Columbia Pictures. Bresler recalled: "Columbia had a strange attitude [toward Peckinpah] for various reasons. Under my independent banner, once we agreed on a director we both had to disagree to remove him from the picture. Columbia was excited by the selected master takes they had seen of the film shot. However, this is a trap—they fell into it. It is essential to view individual scenes as part of the whole and not just a scene. They became so intrigued, one of the executives began talking about releasing the picture in 70mm. But as the cost continued to rise and the footage estimates began to increase they became worried. I had already reported to them my conversations with Sam Peckinpah and the obligation I felt to Chuck Heston, with whom I discussed the problem. To sum it up: Sam called his agent for support; the agent called Columbia; and the agent [along] with Arthur Kramer, an executive of Columbia, visited the location. They hoped to amicably solve the problem. Sam's agent told everyone how excited the studio was with the film so that all the visit did was to bolster Sam's defiance."

Leaving Mexico City, the *Major Dundee* production company rolled south to Tequesquitengo, Tehuixtla, and Cuautla—a long caravan of cars, campers, and trucks hauling cast, crew, animals, and equipment. From this point on, until they returned to Mexico City, they would be tested. Some called it "Peckinpah's purgatory." Others were less civilized. Not all survived.

Again, in *Dialogue on Film,* Charlton Heston recounts: "[Sam Peckinpah] fired, in the course of production, some 15 people on the crew, some of them more than once, and became, in the clinically paranoid sense, convinced that he was surrounded by conspiracy and plotting. To a certain extent this is a self-generative condition because he promptly did become surrounded by conspiracy and plotting; most of it from Gower Street where Columbia Studios is headquartered. Finally we began to get those delegations of men in Italian silk suits and black attaché cases picking their way across the Mexican landscape out to where our sweaty troop of horse soldiers milled in the sun. That became a particularly difficult way of life, because the fellows in the shiny suits come down and say, 'Hi,' and have lunch with you and talk about whatever the problem is they've come down about. Then they go back into the motel and have a nice nap in an air-conditioned bedroom waiting for you to come drooping [in] at 7:30, having driven 40 miles across the desert from location. You go into the bar and there they are waiting and they say, 'Now, what about this scene?' You go to see the dailies and there they still are; you come back at one o'clock in the morning [and] you've had a drink, indeed several drinks and if lucky a sandwich. You still are in wardrobe, of course, in Sam's case, the same pair of blue jeans through the entire production. The talk goes on and on and finally you say: 'Look, fellas, we've got to get up at six.' This can go on for days at a time."

From the other side of the conflict, Bresler remembered: "Sam began to pick on the crew. He wanted me to fire some of them. I flatly refused. He got into bitter arguments with the script supervisor, who was one of the best, because the script supervisor questioned his judgement on an angle. He wanted me to fire him, but again I refused. Eventually, he [the script supervisor] went to the second unit and we got another script supervisor for Sam (one of his own choosing), but he [Sam] was not happy with him [either]."

Peckinpah disputes this: "The script supervisor was not 'one of the best'! He was incompetent from the beginning and refused to get into the river with the rest of the cast and crew because he didn't want to soil his pants. I was very happy with his replacement and have used him extensively since. His name is Frank Kowalski."

"Cost continued to rise, and my predictions were so obvious I had a phone call from the president of Columbia Pictures," Bresler recounted. "He was deeply concerned and worried. They sent their executive production manager to the location, a man of great integrity, outstanding ability and vast knowledge in his field. After a few days he was so frustrated, he was ready to leave."

"It was at my request that Ben Hirsch [the executive production manager] stayed," Peckinpah counters. "And thank God for him, because it wasn't easy dealing with the stupidity and blind ego [on this picture]."

Thriving on this kind of conflict, Peckinpah forced the production ahead. Heston continues his account in *Dialogue on Film:* "I had as close a relationship with Sam on that picture as I've ever had with any director. We were really married to each other for the whole three months we were down there.... We'd go out and drink bad Mexican brandy at night and sit up talking, telling each other how terrible They were: that's They with a capital 'T.'

"I learned a lot about the character in those talks. I guess Sam directed me as much in those times as he did on the set, maybe unconsciously, I don't know ... To a certain extent, Sam made me into Major Dundee drinking beer and brandy in those bars at night. That is the kind of mystical statement I shy away from, and I by no means mean it literally. While Sam is a highly intelligent man, a communicative man, he didn't communicate these things specifically, certainly not consciously ... There was something about the Mexican experience of living all day in a Union cavalryman's pants, sitting on a horse most of the day and spending all night in filthy Mexican cantinas."

Actor James Coburn, who had been in a number of Westerns including *The Magnificent Seven* and whose credits include such variety as *The President's Analyst* and Pat Garrett in Peckinpah's *Pat Garrett and Billy the Kid,* recounted: "I was constantly trying to get Sam to intellectualize what he wanted from me for the character of Sam Potts. Now *Major Dundee* has to be one of the most traumatic pictures ever made in terms of its production problems. I mean when we finished that picture, those of us who did finish came off saying, 'Whew, I made it!' because it was really a bitch.

"Anyway, Sam always used to come into my camper once a day because I had a good shitter in there (at that point, Columbia wouldn't have given Sam the paper much less the shitter), and I'd get a chance to talk to him alone for five or ten minutes everyday shouting through the john door. And I kept saying: 'Sam, what am I doing? What do I do in this fucking thing?' And he'd say: 'I don't know, you shithead! I don't know!' And I'd say: 'Well, what does he

122

do? What am I doing? Tell me what I'm doing. . .' And he says: 'Drier. Drier. He doesn't give a shit!' So here was a character who was dry and didn't give a shit. And that, as simple as it may sound, fed me more than three days of intellectualizing about emotional attitudes. It was simple and direct, and I didn't understand it but it worked inside me. It was an impression. He gave me an impression instead of a string of words, and that was a thousand times more powerful.

"So then I asked him, 'Sam, what is it about the character of Dundee that makes you want to make this film?' I knew I'd get an answer to that one. And Sam said: 'Because he continues. I mean through all the shit, through all the lies, through all the drunkenness and the bullshit that Major Dundee goes through, he survives and continues!' It was brilliant because suddenly I understood the script in the way Sam saw it. Despite everything, Dundee must go on. And from that point on, while the picture was still a hell, I at least understood why I was willing to go through it."

While the war on *Major Dundee* raged, another previous war that Peckinpah had fought and won made its presence felt. *Ride the High Country* had been nominated as Best Foreign Film in the Mexican Film Festival to be held in Mexico City. R. G. Armstrong who plays the preacher Dahlstrom in *Dundee,* carrying a Bible and a wired-up shotgun in one hand as he rides, still remembers what happened: "When the time came for the film festival we were still out on location, and Sam hired a limousine for himself, L. Q. Jones, Warren Oates, John Davis Chandler, and myself to ride back into Mexico City for the award ceremony. When we arrived we were taken to the Hotel Barner where Sam had arranged for rooms and a tuxedo for each of us. Then we went to the ceremony and damned if *Ride the High Country* didn't win. And Sam wouldn't accept the award until all of us came up and stood beside him for the presentation. But that's the kind of guy Sam is. He was willing to share his moment of glory with us because we had all contributed."

Peckinpah could hardly forget the aftermath of this excursion: "After winning the Mexican Oscar for *Ride the High Country,* we all proceeded to get drunker than a fiddler's bitch and jump in the car with a couple of bottles demanding to be taken back to the set. The ride back was something else. The windows were kicked out of the goddamn car. And when we arrived I was asleep, still in my half tux. I had had this son of a bitch tailored for the occasion, and when we got to Mexico City and I tried it on it was about four sizes too small sleeves up to here, couldn't get the pants on! So I ripped the fucking thing to pieces and told the tailor to shove it up his ass. Then I rented a jacket and went to the thing in cowboy boots and a pair of jeans. It was a hell of a time."

This experience for Peckinpah provided an emotional release from the pressure that had been building throughout the past months and at the same time reassured him that all his trouble was not in vain. He redoubled his efforts on *Major Dundee.*

Throughout the production, Peckinpah had added extra touches of realism wherever possible. For example, the prostitutes Dundee encounters during his drunken wanderings were real. Similarly, when they came to the point in the script where Dundee and his men are ambushed by the Apache at the river, Peckinpah brought in a small band of real Yaqui Indians to work as extras.

The setup for the river ambush called for a ten-foot platform to be built mid river so that cameras could be placed there as well as on either bank. The river was red and tepid, running only eighteen inches at its deepest. Sand fleas attacked in squadrons from either shore. Only Peckinpah and the Yaquis did not seem to mind.

As with all high-action sequences, this battle at the river involved a certain amount of risk. Whitey Hughes, a veteran stunt-man who has been on a majority of Peckinpah's pictures, recalled: "There was a group of us American stunt men riding down in there leading these Indians—real Yaquis—so that they'd go the right way and move on their cue and so forth. For them this was a lot of fun and games, and they didn't know shit from wild honey about them rifles they were totin'. So we were supposed to go down the river to a certain spot past the camera, then pull up and return to camera. Well, when we reined up, this one son of a bitch had been ridin' with his rifle cocked, and it jammed old Bobby Harron, the stunt-man nearest me, in the back and the reaction caused the Indian to pull the hammer down. Put a hole in Bobby's back about the size of a quarter, even though it was a blank load. Hell, that wadding has to go somewhere.

"Anyway, they dressed the wound down there and sent Bobby back to the States to recuperate. But the stupid son of a bitchin' doctor had only treated it as a superficial flesh wound and had sewn him up so that in three months all that crap inside him festered internally, and they had to reopen the damn thing. It was a terrible mess. I don't think Sam ever trusted the doctors down in Mexico since. He was really upset over what happened to Bobby. Sam'll ask you to do a lot of tough things, but he watches out for his people more than any other director I know."

By this time Jerry Bresler had decided to attempt another tactic to hasten completing the picture. "I suggested we talk about a second unit to shoot all the chases and battle sequences," he recalled, "with Sam Peckinpah to shoot the tie-ins with principals. We discussed it with Sam, he was against it. We had no choice. Cliff Lyons, an experienced, knowledgeable, great ex-stuntman, was engaged to shoot the second unit. Sam was antagonistic to Lyons from the beginning which didn't help. The picture at this point was estimated well over budget by one million dollars. The second unit was our only salvation to avoid a financial debacle."

Heston also vividly remembers these closing days of the production: "Finally, they pulled the plug on Sam, or were about to. When I heard this I exercised a degree of actor's muscle which I deplore, and said that I didn't think it was a very good idea. He was the director. You must recall that Sam did not have the formidable reputation he's acquired since *The Wild Bunch. Dundee* was his second film and he was very vulnerable. I think we were, by that time, $600,000 over and about two weeks. I didn't like what I did but I think I had to do it. I told the studio that and said: 'I think I should offer you my salary.' It was my old contract salary but it was what I was getting.

"They said: 'Oh no, Chuck, gee that's ridiculous, don't do that. It's very nice of you, but it wouldn't pay for it anyway.' I said: 'Well okay, I just thought I'd make the point.' Feeling rather pleased with myself, I called my agent and told him about this. He said: 'You stupid son of a bitch. They'll take it.' I said: 'No, no, they are delighted, but they said no; they recognized that I was unhappy about the situation.' He said: 'No, it was a terrible idea, Chuck.' I said: 'No, Herman, you're wrong. No, they won't take it. They said so.' And two days later he called me back and said: 'Chuck, they changed their minds.' Thus, among my other interesting experiences on *Major Dundee* was doing the picture for nothing."

This account appeared in *Dialogue on Film.* Some years later Heston, in a letter, attempted to explain the reasoning behind his actions: "I supported Sam in his controversy with Jerry Bresler for two reasons. First, he was the director and I feel the director's authority should be supported, if for no other reason than his is the prime (though not only) creative concept that shapes the film. Second, though Mr. Bresler is in my opinion an efficient producer, his creative judgment is inferior to Peckinpah's....

"I don't recall what precipitated the conflict between Bresler and Peckinpah, and doubt that it's significant. They are radically different personalities, very unlikely to work with any harmony. Sam is an extremely difficult, thorny man, and it takes a very secure man to get on with him. Someone once said, 'Even paranoiacs have enemies.' Knowing Sam, I would amend that to *'Especially* paranoiacs.[1]

"Of course, Sam is not clinically paranoid, but he has a highly suspicious nature and looks for enemies everywhere. Naturally, he finds a good many. At the same time, he is an extremely talented and highly creative man. It remains an open question as to whether he can make commercially successful films faster than he can alienate the men who must supply his financing. He does both with equal facility." The salary Heston returned to Columbia was $200,000.

By mid-April, having gone from Cuautla to Vistahermosa, *Major Dundee* would complete its location shooting with the filming of the final charge against the French lancers on the Rio Balsas near Chilpancingo. Bresler by now was so infuriated that he threatened to have Peckinpah blacklisted at every major studio in town. L. Q. Jones recalled: "You don't irritate a man like that if you can help it because when you get through that thick hide, they're very tender. Sam finally penetrated Bresler's hide, and it damn near cost him his career."

Nevertheless, the final battle sequence was committed to film. "By the time we shot that final river fight," R. G. Armstrong recounted, "Sam had pushed us damn near three months. We'd all lost weight, became tougher, and looked like the wrath of God. I think Sam planned it that way!" Indeed he had.

When the company returned to Mexico City, all that remained were the final interior scenes at Churubusco and the massacre at the Rostes ranch, which had been built at LaMarquesa, roughly twenty-five miles southwest of Mexico City. Rather than turn this opening sequence over to the second unit, Peckinpah insisted on doubling up his schedule. "I would shoot all day at Churubusco," he recalled, "and then I'd jump in a car and be driven out to LaMarquesa and shoot all night long. Then I'd get back in the car and be driven back to Churubusco for the next day's shooting. The only sleep I was getting was while we were driving. I went for five days and four nights that way with two separate crews, and it just about killed me."

The final days were spent filming the aftermath of the massacre as Dundee and "C" Troop ride up to the still smoldering Rostes ranch. Then, after seventy-four days in production, a figure that includes days lost to inclement weather and travel time between locations, *Major Dundee's* principal shooting was finally completed. Three weeks later, rested, following a brief vacation, and newly married to Begonia Palacios, Peckinpah arrived on the Columbia lot to supervise the editing of the film.

As might be expected, the editing of *Major Dundee* has given rise to a great deal of confusion and conjecture. Peckinpah speaks of the film he cut as being two hours and thirty-four minutes long when he left the project. The original running time of the release print was two hours and fourteen minutes. In varying accounts since its release, the film's length has been expanded to as much as three hours. Unfortunately, Peckinpah did not retain a print of the film as he left it (something he has learned to do since).

Jerry Bresler made the following statement on the editing of *Major Dundee:* "The picture ended up one million (1,000,000) dollars over budget and ran four hours and thirty-six and one-half minutes in first cut. [By way of clarification, the "first cut" or "rough cut" of a motion picture is *always* substantially longer than the final or "fine cut." It is not unusual for the first cut to be twice the length of the final cut. Thus Bresler would appear to be exaggerating for effect here.] I would estimate the cut footage on the cutting room floor to meet a reasonable total must have amounted to over five hundred thousand (500,000) dollars. I cannot recall how many [cuts there were], but I do know that Sam was present to all except the last one which was merely to check the cuts we had made previously.

"To cut a picture from over four hours means losing large segments. I believe we were very judicious in our judgement. The film editor, Bill Lyon now deceased [Actually three editors are credited on the picture: Lyon, Don Starling, and Howard Kunin], had won many Academy Awards for his achievements and worked tirelessly to get the best out of the film. When I left Columbia for England we had a damn good film considering all the problems. In Bangkok I received a phone call from Arthur Kramer that Columbia wanted to cut the film. They felt it was too long. I told him I would fly back immediately to argue the point, but he insisted it would not serve any useful purpose. I gathered from that that the cuts had already been made. What they were I did not know. When he told me the cuts he had in mind, I was furious. I thought them harmful and immediately put myself on record with a cable and letter to that effect.

"I believe this will be the first time Sam Peckinpah has learned the truth about what really happened to the final editing of *Major Dundee.* It is impossible for me at this writing, some 12 years later, to reconstruct the full editing process on *Major Dundee,* but I do remember we never left any stone unturned in an effort to retain the values set forth in the script. When a picture is four hours and thirty-six and one-half minutes long, it must give and we did our best. Columbia, unfortunately, did not realize they were cutting the guts out of the piece when they eliminated film after I turned it over to them. THE EDITING WASN'T BAD ... THE LENGTH WAS IMPOSSIBLE!" (Bresler's caps).

On a number of occasions Peckinpah has taken Bresler to task for recutting *Major Dundee* after he left the project. Considering their relationship during the course of the project as well as Bresler's threat to run him out of the business, one sees that Peckinpah's reaction does not seem without cause. A less impassioned point of view is presented by Charlton Heston: "I knew very little about the cutting problems on *Dundee* except that Sam was taken off the film before it was finished, and that he was convinced his editing concept would have saved it. I doubt that this is true. I did not see a rough cut, but attended an early screening. As I recall, the opinion of those involved was that it was a patchily brilliant film that finally failed to come together."

When the film was released, it met with understandably poor reviews, most critics claiming that while it had moments of excellence, it lacked continuity. Ironically, the question remains open.

"I have been asked [following the success of *The Wild Bunch*]," Peckinpah acknowledged, "'How would you like to come back to Columbia and reassemble *Major Dundee* into your version? Rescore, redub—the whole shot.' And I have said, 'No, I just don't have the time.' They were responsible for the hatchet job on the picture. If they can't live with it now, they shouldn't have fucked with it then. Mainly, however, it was Bresler. It would take me a year to get that picture back into the shape I had it when I left the first time. I don't have that year."

Unfortunately, though he could not have foreseen it when he left Columbia for his next assignment on MGM's *The Cincinnati Kid,* for a while Peckinpah would have nothing but years.

128

7 Years without Work

"Follow me and run like hell!"

In early October 1964, Sam Peckinpah reported to MGM in Culver City to begin work on *The Cincinnati Kid*. The film was being produced by Martin Ransohoff's Filmways Company in collaboration with MGM.

Adapted from the Richard Jessup novel of the same name, *The Cincinnati Kid* would run through the typewriters of a number of top screenwriters as Ransohoff searched for a script that pleased him. Paddy Chayefsky; Ring Lardner, Jr.; Charles Eastman; Terry Southern; and Sam Peckinpah all had a hand in what was to become the shooting script as the original St. Louis setting for the novel was uprooted in favor of New Orleans to take advantage of that city's colorful French Quarter. The final credit would be shared equally by Lardner and Southern.

In this story of hardnosed, high stakes poker, Spencer Tracy was cast as the old master pitted against Steve McQueen as the young lion. Karl Malden, Ann-Margret, Rip Torn, and Tuesday Weld were added in support, with Peckinpah bringing in L.Q. Jones, Jack Elam, and Dub Taylor as well. By mid-November, however, Tracy had become disenchanted with the project and withdrew from the film. The incident set the stage for a serious rift between Peckinpah and Ransohoff. "Marty Ransohoff and I never really got along," Peckinpah recalled. "He's the only guy I know who goes home at noon everyday to change his sweat. But I really fell in love with two people—Spencer Tracy and Katharine Hepburn. Tracy was originally cast but decided not to do it, so we cast Edward G. Robinson instead."

Philip Lathrop was selected to do the cinematography. His previous credits included *Days of Wine and Roses* and Blake Edwards's *The Pink Panther*. He recalled: "Sam's concept was to shoot the film in black and white. Very unusual for that time. In fact, we started the film in black and white and shot four days. But when Sam left—he was fired —the whole concept changed, and we went to color. I think we did some fabulous stuff that first week with Sam. Unfortunately, it wound up in the archives of MGM, or worse."

Jim Silke, brought in by Peckinpah as dialogue director on the film, remembered: "Sam's firing was planned. There was never any question about it. There was no production schedule in the beginning. When it did come out, we were two weeks behind.

"It came out on the fourth day of shooting, a Thursday. We had shot downtown at the railroad station during the day and had come back to the studio that night to shoot a scene which I had suggested involving Rip Torn and his whores. John Calley gave me the scene that night at six on yellow pages that hadn't even gone through mimeo yet.

"The scene called for Torn laying on his bed with these two girls sitting there suggesting what had gone on. It was the other end of the phone conversation with Eddie Robinson taking pills just to stay alive. And here's Rip Torn sated. Terry Southern had written it with the girls as cheerleaders.

"Sam eliminated one of the girls immediately. The other had pom-poms, her sweater, a vibrator, and baton. What they were doing was not clear because it was still the early sixties. But as the scene progressed Sam worked with this girl. First the vibrator disappeared, then the pom-poms, the baton, finally the fact that she was a cheerleader. At last all she had on was a fur coat, and Sam started to get something out of her that was very sad. She didn't do anything. She didn't say anything. She was just there. I think she dropped her coat from her shoulder at one point but the shot was from behind her so that there was no problem with censorship. But Sam knew what he wanted. The story was not her nudity but in Rip Tom's face. He just couldn't care. He was used.

"They fired Sam the next day for shooting unauthorized nudes at night. I called a friend of mine who suggested Sam sue Ransohoff for $3 million like Cukor did on *Gone with the Wind* and let the whole town know about it. But Sam didn't. Then I found all these press releases from Ransohoff, this outraged human being when it came to nudes, in the *New York Times* advocating nudity. Sam confronted him and Ransohoff just laughed and said, 'Okay, let's forget it. Ransohoff's motive for dropping Sam was that he didn't want to make the movie that Sam was making. He wanted to make a pretty picture. I think he got what he wanted."

On Friday, December 5th, Ransohoff shut the production down. On the following Monday, he replaced Peckinpah with Norman Jewison. After three feature films and what seemed to be a promising future, Peckinpah suddenly was on the street. Characterized as a belligerent, uncooperative director, he found himself effectively blacklisted. No one would hire him to direct a film.

It is difficult to adequately convey the enormity of what befell Peckinpah at this point in his career. He had risen through a decidedly biased system from virtual obscurity to become a critically acclaimed writer-director before the age of forty. And then, in a

130

moment, everything collapsed. Few called and fewer still returned his calls. It was worse than starting over, for now there were those who actively opposed him.

"When I was out of work and no one would hire me," Peckinpah recalled, "I had to take anything to stay alive. I wrote longhand, which can be a problem because there are times I can't read my own writing. I was about to go into bankruptcy because I was blackballed from the industry because I'm a rebel and an asshole. It was one tough mother for more than two years."

Despite his troubles, Peckinpah continued to write on speculation with Jim Silke in a house on the beach in Malibu at Trancas. And while it was difficult, it served in many ways to sharpen Peckinpah's perceptions. He no longer could just be good. He had to be better.

"I'll tell you this," stated Jim Silke, remembering those years, "Sam was at his best when he was down. This town really dropped on him. I was with Sam for two years after *Cincinnati Kid,* and they were terrific years for me. We wrote all kinds of things. Sam would write one-to five page outlines, and I would write the script from them. Now maybe it's just because we're so closely tuned, but I could sit down and write a 120-page screenplay from a one-page Peckinpah outline. Everything is there. It is so concise. Those two years were like the army—I was on twenty-four-hour call. But I would never do his laundry. And I had to make a point of it!"

Throughout 1965 and into 1966, Peckinpah's fortunes continued to decline. One of his marriages to Begonia Palacios began to fall apart. Eventually he had to sell his house at Trancas. And when Four Star Enterprises (the releasing agent for the many series made under Dick Powell) offered him $10,000 for his rights to *The Westerner,* Peckinpah reluctantly accepted. Between his dwindling resources and accelerating divorces, he had little choice.

The only project to be actually produced during this period with Peckinpah's name on it was a cavalry Western he had written called *The Glory Guys.* Adapted from Hoffman Birney's *The Dice of God* and sold to Peckinpah's former associates from *The Rifleman,* Levy-Gardner-Laven, it was filmed shortly after *Major Dundee.* Despite the fact that it was made from his script, Peckinpah dislikes the film as directed by Arnold Laven mainly because it shifts the focus away from the Indian-white conflict promulgated by a Custer-like general and concentrates on a love triangle involving a captain, a scout, and a fallen woman. It remains at best another example of the lack of communication between Peckinpah and Levy-Gardner-Laven.

By mid-1966, however, Peckinpah's luck had begun to change.

L. Q. Jones had formed his own production company, LQ/JAF (initials for L. Q. Jones and Friends), and asked Peckinpah if he would be interested in directing the company's first effort. Peckinpah agreed, offering his own property, *The Castaway,* which he had purchased from the trustees of the estate of the late James Gould Cozzens on a long-term arrangement. While Jones attended to the details, Peckinpah flew home to attend the swearing-in of his brother, Denver, as a judge in the Superior Court at Fresno; Denver was following in the tradition set by their father and grandfather.

It was shortly after this that Sam Peckinpah was approached by Talent Associates' producer Daniel Melnick. Melnick recalled: "I had always loved the Katherine Anne Porter novella *Noon Wine.* I had gotten the rights from Miss Porter and sold it, actually to ABC, as a special. Then I went to Sam to ask him to write and direct it. He was a very controversial figure at that point. . . I suppose it was a combination of an appreciation of his talent, and naivete and egotism on my part for me to feel that he wouldn't be difficult to work with and that I could handle him.

"After it was announced that I had hired him, there were a number of calls—sometimes from people whom I didn't know at all—that ranged from urging me not to hire him to pleading with me not to hire him. Obviously, there were an awful lot of people who disliked him either personally or professionally. But I was sufficiently stubborn that every time I got a call I became more convinced I wouldn't let him go. It turned out to be one of the most satisfying and stimulating creative experiences I've ever had."

Noon Wine is a tragic story set around the turn of the century in West Texas. A farmer, Royal Earle Thompson, hires a strange, laconic farmhand, Olaf Helton, who turns his poor farm into a prosperous one before being discovered by a bounty hunter who wants to return Helton to North Dakota for a crime committed years before. Attempting to protect his hired hand, Thompson kills the stranger with an ax. This act is futile, however, for Helton is tracked and killed by a posse from town, and Thompson must stand trial for murder. Although he is acquitted by the jury; neither his family nor his fellow townsmen accept that verdict. Alone, Thompson attempts to write a justification of his actions before committing suicide with a shotgun.

Peckinpah completed his script from the novella and forwarded it to Miss Porter who enthusiastically endorsed his work. On the basis of this, the project went forward as an hourlong presentation for *ABC Stage* 67. The production was shot in late October 1966, almost entirely on color videotape with Jason Robards, Olivia de Havilland, and Per Oscarsson in the principal roles.

To score the teleplay; Daniel Melnick brought in Jerry Fielding, a composer whose background had been in classical music and American jazz before coming to Hollywood as an arranger for band leader Kay Kyser at the age of only eighteen. Blacklisted for refusing to testify before the House Un-American Activities Committee in the early fifties, Fielding was someone who understood what Peckinpah was trying to do. Equally outspoken, they would work together as friends and combatants on a number of films over the next decade and a half before Jerry Fielding's unexpected death in 1980 from a heart attack at age 57.

Because a tune played on a harmonica is an essential element in the narrative, the scoring of *Noon Wine* had added significance. In the interest of authenticity; Melnick had Fielding call Katherine Anne Porter in Washington so that she could hum the tune that she had described in her short novel, a tune she had apparently remembered from her youth.

Fielding recalled their conversation: "So I called her and we talked for a while, and finally she said, 'Are you ready?' and I told her that I had a tape recorder ready and she went ahead. Well, the song she sang to me was 'Look for the Silver Lining'—just as she'd remembered it. Of course, it couldn't have been that song because that hadn't even been written when she was a child, but she didn't realize that. So when I hung up the phone, I knew that I had virtually nothing to go on and had to deal with the story Sam had created, which was probably the best starting point anyway."

Fielding, therefore, wrote music for what he saw on the screen, maintaining the haunting and ominous atmosphere that Peckinpah had created. His concern was only that the visual and music tracks work as one piece. This scoring was effective enough that in reviewing the November 23, 1966, telecast in *The Hollywood Reporter,* John Mahoney saw fit to mention: "Jerry Fielding's score was an excellent supplement in the Aaron Copland idiom, utilizing a lonely one-finger piano note to good effect at the fade out." The balance of that review, quoted in part below, offers some insight into the strength of the production:

It too often [has] seemed that ABC simply sought "names" to deliver works which were either derivative, dull or suspiciously dust-covered for this expensive but low-rated hour. And then came "Noon Wine."

Sam Peckinpah adapted the Katherine Anne Porter novella with eye and ear acutely tuned to the people and milieu of rural Western America. [They] could have found no director so committed to an understanding of the period than [Peckinpah]. In league with Talent

Associates' Daniel Melnick, fulfilling the role of creative producer, Peckinpah's realization emerged as one of the finest hours in many a season, something of a milestone in location color videotape production, and one of the few TV moments which might be termed poetic.

While Peckinpah was faithful to the original text, he amplified it in this dramatic translation and devised connective tissue and additional scenes which might well have been dictated by Miss Porter herself. His new scenes illuminate the tragedy in the story. . ..

Peckinpah created the scenes in which the farmer [Jason Robards] asks his wife [Olivia de Havilland] to claim she viewed the murder, the trial sequence, the violent montage in which the tracked hired-hand [Per Oscarsson] is killed. When the farmer pleads for understanding from his neighbors, Peckinpah created an ironic touch by making the vigilante who slays the hired-hand the one who claims not to hold with the killin', while his wife quotes from the Bible. . ...

Developing his story in visual terms he made unprecedented TV use of montage, which has never been fully exploited in TV storytelling. Other technical virtuosity which illuminated the story included circular pans, imperceptible integration of tape and film and an astounding buggy trucking shot in extreme closeup. When the farmer shoots himself at the close of the hour, an abrupt and fragmentary closeup of Miss de Havilland intensifies the personal tragedy. (© The Hollywood Reporter)

On November 25, 1966, Katherine Anne Porter wrote Peckinpah regarding *Noon Wine*. The letter began:

Dear Mr. Peckinpah:
If you couldn't manage it, no one else should try. So far as I could trace your hand in the play, and remember the script sent me, all went well. ... [However,] the music was disappointing ... because it was not the right tune and it was not heard enough to give it its meaning. . ... But the sad thing about American theater, moving pictures, TV, Radio is the awful presence and unlimited power of that nameless enemy, the Monster who limits time, gouges the heart out of every scene just enough to ruin the point, makes changes that dull action- (Why couldn't They—whoever They are—let [sic] the tragic scene of Mr. Helton running like a hunted beast with the crowd closing in on him? Why the perfectly flat and false scene of Mrs. Thompson hearing the shot sitting alone? The point was, Mr.

Thompson took himself away, as far as he could on his own land, from his family that had turned on him. She was not alone, her sons were with her trying to soothe her terror and grief. Her only real scene was her grieving scene when she shed her only tears for Mr. Helton.

She concluded with her displeasure over commercial television's shortcomings in bringing the work of artists to the public. The letter was typewritten but signed in longhand: "Sincerely yours, Katherine Anne Porter."

Katherine Anne Porter was seventy-two, and thirty years had passed since she had written *Noon Wine,* yet her concerns with Peckinpah's adaptation reflect the differences between the two mediums of expression. Because she is attempting to measure the public experience of viewing the adaptation against the more personal one of reading her novel, it is not surprising that she should find Peckinpah's work not wholly fulfilling. She probably would have been just as disappointed had she discussed the novel with a cross section of her readers, for each of them would have interpreted her writing through an individual frame of reference. In writing *Noon Wine,* Miss Porter fixed forever her own conception of the story, thus making her the least objective judge for any visualization of it.

Noon Wine, nevertheless, brought Sam Peckinpah two award nominations, the Writers Guild nomination for Best Television Adaptation and the Director's Guild nomination for Best Television Direction. Although it would still be another year before he would again be given an opportunity to direct a feature film for a major Hollywood studio, Peckinpah had at last begun the long climb back.

Following the success of *Noon Wine,* Peckinpah was given another television assignment, this time for *Bob Hope's Chrysler Theater.* The show was called "That Lady Is My Wife," a Western period drama involving a woman who becomes the "prize" in a contest between her husband and her lover. Peckinpah cast Jean Simmons, Bradford Dillman, and Alex Cord using his sometime wife Begonia as the second female lead. Filmed in late autumn of 1 966, it was televised in the spring of 1967.

It was then that L.Q. Jones and Peckinpah attempted to film James Gould Cozzens' *Castaway.* The story itself deals with a man named Lecky who is caught in the surreal world of a department store, an extraordinary metaphoric landscape against which Cozzens lays bare modern man's still primitive soul. Peckinpah and Silke had collaborated on the screenplay, and Per Oscarsson had been cast in the role of Lecky. Jones would play the stranger whom Lecky encounters.

They planned to shoot the film in 16mm on a $126,000 budget speculating on either a television release or a blowup of the negative to 35mm for commercial distribution. Everything moved smoothly until Jones's lawyer unexpectedly absconded with the money leaving Jones to face the investors. Although the lawyer was eventually caught and most of the money recovered, Jones still had to pay off Per Oscarsson as well as the investors. By the time status quo had been achieved, Jones, Peckinpah, and Oscarsson were all off in different directions. The project has never been realized.

Peckinpah still refers to *Castaway* as his "ace in the hole." Of the project, he states: "Jim Silke and I wrote the screenplay—I mean we spent years getting it just right. It reads today like it's tomorrow. It's an incredible story—Cozzens doing *Robinson Crusoe,* and we've taken it one step further. I'm very pleased with it." It still remains a future project, however.

In April 1967, Peckinpah finally managed to sell his screenplay on Pancho Villa to producer Ted Richmond. It was called *Villa Rides!* and dealt with Villa's part in the Revolution prior to his successful campaign against Huerta in 1913. This script, though substantially altered by screenwriter Robert Towne (whose credits include *The Last Detail, Shampoo,* and *Chinatown,* as well as an Academy Award in 1971 for the last of these) was filmed by Paramount with Buzz Kulik directing. Yul Brynner played Villa, a characterization that caused Peckinpah to disavow any connection with the film.

The fall of 1967 found Peckinpah at the University of California at Los Angeles as visiting lecturer on writing and directing in both motion pictures and television. It would be a limited engagement, however. More than two years had passed, but at last a major studio was again considering Peckinpah to direct a feature film.

8 The Wild Bunch

"If they move—kill 'em!"

While visiting Europe in the fall of 1965 after his troubles trying to find work had begun, Sam Peckinpah met a producer named Kenneth Hyman. Hyman, then head of Seven Arts Ltd. in England, had produced Sidney Lumet's *The Hill,* which was shown at the Cannes Film Festival that year. Peckinpah was impressed with the film and later spoke with Hyman.

The following year, Seven Arts Ltd. merged with Warner Brothers while Hyman left to produce Robert Aldrich's *The Dirty Dozen.* Returning to Warner Brothers-Seven Arts in 1967, Hyman was made vice-president in charge of worldwide production.

It was then that Hyman hired Peckinpah to rewrite a screenplay called *The Diamond Story,* a large-scale adventure centering around a multimillion dollar heist in modern Africa. It was agreed that if Peckinpah's screenplay was accepted, he would be allowed to direct the film as well.

In addition, Peckinpah also submitted another script to Hyman for consideration called *The Wild Bunch.* From a story by Roy Sickner, a stuntman and Peckinpah's longtime friend, *The Wild Bunch* had been written as a treatment and later as a screenplay by Walon Green, a writer-director whose credits include *The Hellstrom Chronicle.* It was this screenplay that Peckinpah had rewritten for submission to Warner Brothers-Seven Arts.

After some deliberation, the studio decided in favor of *The Wild Bunch* rather than *The Diamond Story* and agreed to allow Peckinpah to direct. Set along the Texas-Mexico border just prior to the First World War, *The Wild Bunch* details the last days of a small band of outlaws whose anachronistic code has no place in modern society.

Walon Green recalled: "Roy [Sickner] and I couldn't get *[The Wild Bunch]* ...made. It kicked around for a couple of years, and I was off in Southeast Asia working for National Geographic when Sickner got in touch with me to tell me he'd given it to Peckinpah, who'd really liked it. Finally, I got this call from Sickner to tell me Peckinpah had made a deal with Warners and Phil Feldman was going to produce it. He also said that Sam had done some rewriting on my script, but that he really hadn't changed it much. So I asked him to send me a copy so that I could see what he'd done.

"Actually, there were some things I liked that Sam had done, and some things I didn't. He did a dialogue polish on [it] that I thought was very good in which he made the dialogue saltier without substantially changing the flavor of the original. I had been trying a lot of oblique lines like 'If you side with a man you stick with him,' and Sam had left those alone but given the overall script a more authentic Western ring.

"He changed the opening sequence of the film slightly. In the original, I had the Bunch ride in to rob the bank and ride out through a W.C.T.U. parade. Sam added the preacher's speech and the young kid [Crazy Lee] who stays behind after the Bunch has pulled out.

"Now the scene he changed that I really disagreed with and still do is the scene in the Mexican village. In my original, the scene played entirely in Spanish, because I had only Angel return to his village promising to meet the Bunch later. I felt that he would hold the Bunch in disdain. That was the key to his character. What was to happen in the village—his girl gone, the village robbed by Mapache's men, and so forth—that was all the same. But I had wanted it to play like the scene in *Treasure of the Sierra Madre* where the bandits bring the mules to town, and the kid recognizes the brand. It's all in Spanish, but you still understand what is happening. Anyway, Sam turned it into his "Las Mañanitas" thing, which I really objected to." (In actuality, the farewell song sung by the villagers as the Bunch ride out is not "Las Mañanitas" but "Las Golondrinas."

Peckinpah also added two flashbacks: first, the capture of Deke Thornton in a whorehouse after he is deserted by Pike Bishop who escapes; second, Pike's youthful love affair with a married woman that ends in tragedy because she is killed and he is wounded by her husband. Both of these, like the village sequence, help to deepen the characterization of the Bunch, making them something more than just violent killers. Ironically, only the village sequence remained in the final American version of the film due to Warner Brothers' decision to shorten the film after its initial release. (However, in 1980 Paul Seydor, working closely with Twyman Films, Inc., a 16mm non-theatrical distributor, managed to convince Warner Brothers to reinsert almost all of the deleted footage. Presently only Pike's love affair is still missing.)

In casting *The Wild Bunch,* Lee Marvin's name came up most

often for Pike Bishop. Hyman, having produced *The Dirty Dozen,* opted for Marvin and Peckinpah agreed. Marvin, however, regarded the project as too similar to *The Professionals,* a film he had starred in two years before.

Peckinpah remembers it differently: "Lee liked the property and wanted the role of Pike. Now Lee and I have known each other for some time back. We'd both lived in Malibu, and we'd spilled more whiskey together than most people drink. It looked at first as if that would be the way things would work out. Then Lee was offered a fucking million-dollar contract to do *Paint Your Wagon,* and he took that instead. We had a bit of a to-do over that, and you might say our relationship cooled some.

"I hadn't known Bill Holden before we made *Wild Bunch,* but his performance in *Stalag 17* stuck in my mind, and I knew he could be tough enough. So we agreed to do it, and then we got Bob Ryan to play Deke Thornton. With people like that, I knew we had to have a winner."

In addition to Holden and Ryan, Peckinpah added actors he had worked with before: L. Q. Jones, Strother Martin, Ben Johnson, and Warren Oates. The character of Dutch, Pike's lieutenant in the Bunch, caused some difficulty, however. The script description reads in part: "Dutch is big, young, good-natured with a fast gun hand, strong loyalty and, like Pike, a bone-deep distaste for rules and regulations. He can sing [and] has more than his share of charm." Ernest Borgnine, who also appeared in *The Dirty Dozen,* was Hyman's choice. Peckinpah initially disagreed: "In casting *Wild Bunch,* Ken Hyman was for Ernie Borgnine in the role of Dutch, and I was against it. At that time I had never worked with Ernie and with this picture I wanted to be sure of everybody. Anyway, Ken talked me out of my reluctance, and Ernie turned out to be just one of the greatest guys I've ever worked with."

In addition to the casting, Peckinpah concerned himself with selecting the key members of his crew. For director of photography, he requested and obtained the services of Lucien Ballard, and together they screened as much footage of the Mexican Revolution circa 1913 as they could find. In scouting locations in Mexico, they then attempted to duplicate what they had seen to give the film the arid, dusty feel of a scorched land.

As his editor, Peckinpah brought in Lou Lombardo whom he had met on *Noon Wine.* Among the samples of his editing that Lombardo gave to Peckinpah to show to Feldman was an episode from the television show *Felony Squad.* "I had the show before *Bonnie and Clyde,"* Lombardo remembered, "and it had this slow-motion death sequence where Joe Don Baker falls as he is shot by the police. It had been photographed at twenty-four frames per second, but I had optically printed each frame three times to give it this slow-motion effect. Sam and Feldman really dug it, and I was hired for *The Wild Bunch.* Now I'm certain that Sam had used slow motion before, but because *Wild Bunch* was going to have a lot of death in it, we began to talk about shooting the gunfights at various speeds and intercut the slow motion with normal."

This concept of cutting together film shot at a variety of speeds ranging from normal to extreme slow motion is a key element in the power of the violence in *The Wild Bunch* as well as in subsequent Peckinpah films. Slow motion alone merely elongates time. However, by placing shots of different speeds in juxtaposition as the moment of violence is revealed, an internal tension is created within that sequence of shots. This tension has become the distinctive trademark of Peckinpah's screen violence.

Among the people Peckinpah wanted for his production team was wardrobe man Gordon Dawson with whom he had worked on *Major Dundee.* By 1967, however, Dawson had left the wardrobe end of the business behind. "I'd taught myself how to write," he recalled. "I had made a complete break with Columbia and the wardrobe department and was working as a freelance writer, mostly in television. Then I got this call from Phil Feldman saying that Sam wanted me to do wardrobe on *Wild Bunch,* and I told him it was out of the question. I just wasn't doing that anymore. So that was that.

"Then a week later Feldman calls me back and becomes more insistent. He asks me to come in and talk because Sam really wants me to do the show. So I told him that I'd come in and talk, but I really didn't do wardrobe anymore, and they wouldn't be able to meet my price to get me to even consider it. At that time a high-priced wardrobe man was $400, maybe $500, a week. So I went in and he offered me $600 a week, and I said absolutely not. I tried to explain to him: 'Look, man, I've got eight *Gentle Bens* to write. I don't do that anymore.'

"So I left, and Sam called me at home and said they'd already hired one wardrobe man and he wasn't working out at all—and the guy they'd hired had an excellent reputation in the business. So I agreed to come in and talk to Sam. I went and looked at the research stills and remembered how many times he'd crucified me on *Major Dundee*—man, he'd just eat me up and spit me out—but the project really looked good. So I said to Sam that the money had to be right, and he said that anything goes because he wanted me on that picture. They paid me $750 a week for that film.

"But the money wasn't the important thing on *Wild Bunch*. When I accepted that job from Sam, I promised myself that I would never allow Sam to catch me on one button undone! There was going to be nothing wrong with my department, because if I could do that, I knew that I would get a great deal of satisfaction. I also decided from the very beginning that whatever Sam wanted from wardrobe, I would put it together no matter what. They tried to keep me down to twenty-five costume hampers. I brought fifty and could have used a hundred!"

At the end of February 1968, Peckinpah left for Mexico in order to complete the casting for the picture and see to last minute production details. He also took along the script. "Any script that's written," Peckinpah maintains, "changes at least thirty percent from the time you begin preproduction: ten percent while you fit your script to what you discover about your locations, ten percent while your ideas are growing as you rehearse your actors who must grow into their parts because the words mean nothing alone, and ten percent while the film is finally being edited. It may change more than this but rarely less."

One of the most striking script modifications that Peckinpah was to make on *The Wild Bunch* occurred shortly after his arrival in Mexico City. He had gone to Coyoacan and the home of his friend Don Emilio Fernandez, "El Indio," with whom he had become friends on *Major Dundee*. Peckinpah had already cast Fernandez as General Mapache in the film and wished to discuss both the script and the further casting of Mexican actors for the picture with him.

"I was sitting there with Don Emilio and six girls, all of them his," Peckinpah recalled, "and I was supposed to meet this other girl I was seeing for dinner that night. So Don Emilio and I are talking about the script when suddenly he says to me, 'You know, the Wild Bunch, when they go into that town like that, are like when I was a child and we would take a scorpion and drop it on an anthill. ... ' And I said, 'What!' And he said, 'Yes, you see, the ants would attack the scorpion. . . ' And I said, 'Get me the phone!' And I dialed the producer in California and I said to him, 'I want ants and I want scorpions, and I don't care how you get them down here!' And from that point on, that was the way I saw the whole picture. I began rewriting immediately in order to get this sensational opening down on paper and when the girl I was supposed to be seeing for dinner called to find out where I was, I simply told her that I was sorry but I couldn't be bothered because I was writ- ing. I think she hung up."

Among the Mexican actors cast by Peckinpah at the suggestion of Fernandez were Jorge Russek and Alfonso Arau who play the lieutenants of Mapache, Zamorra and Herrera. Chano Urueta, an- other distinguished Mexican film director then in his eighties and virtually retired from filmmaking, was cast as the elder of Angel's village.

With the principal casting behind him and a starting date of March 25th just two weeks off, Peckinpah left for the first location, the small town of Parras, which lies along the railroad that joins Saltillo and Torreon, some 600 miles north of Mexico City. There he was joined by Lucien Ballard and his camera crew as well as the personnel of the wardrobe, properties, art, sound, and special effects departments. Parras was renamed "Starbuck" for the pur- pose of the picture. Although several of the signs on storefronts indicated the town to be named "San Raphael," it is referred to in dialogue as "Starbuck," suggesting the dilemma faced by many border towns settled by the Spanish but taken over and renamed by Americans following the Treaty of 1848.

Among the earliest discoveries for Peckinpah and Ballard in Parras was that the burnt and dusty look of the countryside for which they had selected the location in early winter was already giving way to green. This was unacceptable. The film needed a parched look everywhere but Angel's village, which was to look lush and green by comparison. To counteract the greens in the landscape, Ballard and his crew set to work making tests in order to establish which filters would yield the kinds of images they were after. Within a week this was successfully accomplished.

Peckinpah and Ballard also decided that they would travel to the set together by car each morning so that they might begin each day discussing what was to be shot. This method would prove to be so successful that Peckinpah would make it a standard operating procedure on all future productions.

Other departments were equally busy. Before the production company ever arrived on location, a complete day-by-day breakdown was prepared for the picture that included individual locations, principals, extras, essential props, livestock, and vehicles.

In shooting a scene like Angel's capture by Mapache after Angel and Dutch deliver the rifles, one case short, for example, the following elements were required:

CAST: Dutch, Angel, Mapache, Zamorra, Herrera, Mohr, Ernst, Major Perez, Juan Jose.
EXTRAS: 200 soldiers, 10 riding soldiers, Angel's double for the horse fall, soldier (roper), 60 women, 50 men, 40 children.
PROPS: Bags of coins.
LIVESTOCK/VEHICLES: Dutch's horse, Angel's horse (falling horse), Herrera's horse, 200 soldiers' horses, miscellaneous domestic and pack animals, a touring car (circa 1913).

All of this was required for the filming of approximately two and one-quarter pages of a 130-page script. This was only one of eighty-one scheduled days of shooting.

Meanwhile, Dawson had unpacked his costume hampers, blowtorch, sandpaper, and aging bench in preparation for final costuming. Each character posed an individual problem. This meant costuming not only the principal actors but those in the secondary roles as well. Add to this the need to supervise the wardrobe preparations for the hundreds of extras, duty that also fell to Dawson, and it becomes easy to understand why he had little time for anything else.

Strother Martin, who portrayed the bounty hunter, Coffer, in the picture, recalled Dawson's skill: "On *The Wild Bunch,* Sam was getting acquainted with the lowbrow side of my acting abilities. It was the kind of role he had never cast me in before. He saw Coffer as somewhere close to psychotic. Gordy Dawson, Sam's wardrobe man on the film, had made up this really seedy looking outfit with a sanded-down, greenish-colored hat that really looked weather-beaten. And Sam had looked at me and said: 'I want to see him with a piece of jewelry. What would his vanity be?' And I said: 'You know how priests have a black wooden cross? I think my character might collect those.' So Gordy got me this cross and we went back up before his eminence, his holiness, the horseshit-marvelous Mr. Peckinpah, and Sam, who has an eye like Picasso for the West, looked at the cross and said, 'Too clean!' So Gordy said: 'Strother, come here. We'll fix that son of a bitch!' And Gordy went and wired a bullet onto the cross, and we went back to Sam who gave a crooked little grin and said, 'Terrific!'"

Dawson remembered the same incident as having one drawback: "Sam wanted a 1913 Hell's Angel in two minutes! I was so damn busy right then that I really didn't think of what I was doing. I just did it. I had this crucifix, and I tore it apart, threw the Jesus away, wired a bullet in its place, and hit the whole thing with a blowtorch and handed it to Strother. And man, there were 87,000 Mexicans ready to take my head off. It hadn't even occurred to me that anybody but Sam might get upset!"

To get precisely the performance he wants from an actor, Peckinpah will involve himself down to the smallest detail. Strother Martin remembered: "In the beginning of the film, we were picking out the horses, and Sam saw to it that Eddie O'Brien had his horse and William Holden had his horse, L. Q.—everybody had a horse except me! And Sam came up to me and said: 'Strother, there's a very good horse for you, but we've got to give it to Eddie O'Brien 'cause he's got a bad back. And besides, I want you on a shitty horse!' So that's what I got. He was awful!"

Not all problems can be anticipated in preproduction, however. Ernest Borgnine, whose long career includes receiving an Academy Award for *Marty,* recalled: "I had been working on a picture called *The Split* with Gene Hackman and Warren Oates just prior to doing *Wild Bunch.* I had signed to do *Wild Bunch* because I had never had the opportunity to work with Bill Holden before. So one day Warren, who had worked with Peckinpah, said to me only half-joking, 'Wait till you meet that guy Peckinpah. He'll eat you alive!' And I told Warren, also only half-joking, 'There isn't a guy in the world I can't get along with except my former wives!' Well, by total chance as we were finishing *The Split* on this ship at night, there was a lot of action on the deck and I broke a bone in my foot. So in order to fulfill my commitment to *Wild Bunch,* I had them fit me with a walking cast on my left foot.

"Anyway, as luck would have it, the way the picture was to open we were supposed to look like soldiers while in reality we were going to rob this railway office. And fortunately, the military leggings we had to wear fit right over the cast and special boot I had to have on. So except for a slight limp, you'd never know it was there.

"Then we started shooting, and although we didn't shoot the picture in sequence, this particular thing with us dressed up as soldiers that opens the picture was scheduled first. Well, getting me inside the railway office was no trouble, but getting me out and across the street while there's this war going on with the bounty hunters who had ambushed us—that presented more of a problem.

So Sam came up to me and said, 'Borgnine, how in the Christ are we going to get you across that street?' And I said, 'Will you leave it to me?' And he said, 'What do you have in mind?' I said: 'Just leave it to me. Crank your cameras and I'll be okay.' So he said, 'Okay, go ahead,' and walked away.

"Well, they started to roll the cameras, and I came out of that office and jumped behind that bloody watering trough. Then when I got the signal to move, I rolled across the street to where the horses were, firing at the same time. So when it was over, Sam came up to me with this big grin on his face and he says, 'Ya lovable son of a bitch, that was great! Thank you!' That was all. But I had passed the test, and we never had a harsh word between us."

Not all actors have had the same peaceful experience with Peckinpah, however. "I had my ass chewed on every shot in *Wild Bunch!*" Strother Martin remembered with a smile. "But don't get the wrong idea, I have more respect for Sam than almost anybody else in the world. He was keeping me in this frenetic state for a purpose: he wanted me to portray this psychotic character as if I were on the edge of a nervous breakdown, not that that's any great struggle. But Sam is like a dirty psychiatrist—he gets inside your head and probes around with a scalpel. I worked fifteen weeks on *Wild Bunch* with Sam. I don't think I could take six pictures a year with Sam Peckinpah! There were times when I wasn't sure I could even take one! But when I saw the final product, somehow it was all worthwhile.

"In that opening sequence where we were up on the roof waiting in ambush, I said to Sam, 'Could I wink at L. Q.?' And Sam growled back at me, 'Why don't you kiss him?!' And I said, 'Well, he's too far away.' Then a little later he demanded that I kiss my rifle, which I didn't want to do because I thought it had been done many times before. I remember saying, 'I don't want to!' and Sam shouting, 'Kiss it!' And I remember how hard my pulse was racing as I kissed that rifle. So a trembling guy kisses a gun. Well, I have to admit that when I finally saw that on the screen, which must have been something like a year later, Sam had managed to get a different kind of a kiss of a rifle than anybody else has ever gotten. He got it, of course, because I was scared shitless and mad at the same time, but then that was exactly right for Coffer at that moment.

"I must say that I'm amused at my own terror. When Sam yells at me, I 'sir' him—'Yes, sir! No, sir!' That's odd because I think he's younger than I am. But Sam is hell to live with on a picture because he burns with a white-hot fire when he works, and there is no lethargy on a Sam Peckinpah set. In that way, he's like a Ford or a Hathaway.

"The character of Coffer was this strange, violent little man who probably had one friend in the world that he cared about and that was T. C. [played by L.Q. Jones]. And Christ knows what their relationship was. They'd probably go off and bugger a mule together! Now Sam will help you develop a character, but he expects you to bring something of your own. He insists on it. And that, of course, is the way I've always worked with Sam and everybody else. What happens when that camera rolls is spontaneous between me and the other actors in that scene.

"What's more, Sam will allow you—even expect you—to improvise certain scenes as you go along to give them spontaneity. For example, after the shooting stops and the bounty hunters come down into the street to check the bodies, Sam had L.Q. and I 'winging' the dialogue because it wasn't very full at that point.
That whole thing where I called L.Q. a 'liar!' and then a 'black liar!' was all improvised. I remember I was very pleased with 'black liar!' And I remember Sam saying to me, 'That's your worst line in the picture' which, of course, means he loved it!"

The associate producer on the film was Roy Sickner whose chief responsibility was coordinating stunts and action sequences in the picture. Among the many stuntmen brought down for the picture was the ever-ready Whitey Hughes. "Being a little man in the business, you're limited in what you can do by your size," noted Hughes, who is five feet six inches. "If a man is five-ten to six-two, he has a range there where he can get away with doubling just about any average-sized actor. But then [being small] works in your favor sometimes as well, because you can double women and kids, which has been a great deal of my work in this business.

"In that first sequence in *The Wild Bunch* when Bill Holden jumped out of the express office there and trampled that gal under his horse where a piece of her shawl catches in his stirrup. I was dressed as the gal and did the run under the horse. We did that so damn many times that I got so sore I could hardly move. I mean this horse with Holden's stunt double aboard would be coming down the street, and I'd run under him and try to catch his back legs with my off-shoulder so that he would just roll me in the air. I didn't want him to get a direct shot at me with those hoofs, but it had to look good for camera because it was positioned low for the shot."

To complete that particular action, Peckinpah wanted a shot

146

taken from directly overhead showing the horse and rider with the woman beneath the horse's hooves to accentuate the idea that it was not men alone who were being hurt in the violence. "I used a Mexican stunt-girl named Yolanda Ponce for the shot," Peckinpah recalled, "and everything would have been all right except the stuntman riding the horse didn't realize that he had passed over her already and backed up, catching her off guard and relaxed. Well, the horse didn't know any better and put a hoof in the middle of the girl's back, cracking her tailbone. I remember running over to her, and she was really in pain, and we sent her immediately to the hospital. Fortunately, she recovered completely from that little disaster, and I have used her in all of my pictures in Mexico since that time." The stuntman who rode the horse, however, has turned out to be one of the most unlucky and accident-prone stuntmen in all Hollywood. His work has proved him to be so dangerous to everyone including himself that if someone even mentions his name on a Peckinpah set, it costs a dollar.

Dangerous work on *The Wild Bunch* was not limited to stuntmen alone. Bo Hopkins is a young actor who made his screen debut in the picture as Crazy Lee, the kid left behind in Starbuck by the Bunch. Subsequently, he has appeared in a number of films including *American Graffiti,* in which he portrayed the leader of the Pharaohs. He recalled: "Because it was my first picture and because I guess I seemed interested, Sam took me aside on Sunday, his day off, and worked with me in his office. He told me not to be nervous, to just let everything go. It seemed like everybody was willing to help me. Lucien Ballard was really good to me because I didn't know what a key light was or about hitting a mark or any of that stuff. I learned a lot on that picture.

"I also had no idea what squibs were for when I started the picture—you know those little blood packets that have a charge wired to them that makes the blood spurt so you look like you've been shot. So they explained to me how the things worked and what would happen, and I told the special effects guy to put it where I could feel it so I'd know when I got hit. He grinned and said he'd do just that. Well, Robert Ryan and Albert Dekker were supposed to wound me the first time, and as I laid there I was supposed to say, 'Well, how'd you like t'kiss my sister's black cat's ass!' Then I'd shoot three more guys, and Ryan and Dekker would pump me full of holes to finish me off. So when I was shot the first time, the squib I was worried about feelin' went off and the blood spurted in my face and Sam shouted, 'Freeze!' Freeze, hell. I thought I'd really been shot! So we did that about fifteen more times, and then I delivered my line, which worked fine.

"Finally, we got to the place where Ryan and Dekker kill me. So Sam says that I'm supposed to be shot five times and react to each one and die after the fifth. It's that way in the European version of the picture, but they cut the shot of me dying from the American print. So I counted them—one, two, three, four, five—reacting to each one. Well, as the fifth went off, the blood spurted, and I gave a little quiver and laid still. Then the sixth went off, and I said, 'Oh, shit!' and that ruined the whole thing and we had to do it again.

"We worked until about eight o'clock that night shootin' the scene, and they had these charges planted in the walls and furniture that would go off as if they were getting hit by bullets. Well, a charge that was embedded in a bench went off about then and I caught a sliver in the eye. Sam was the first guy to me, and I'm thinkin', 'Here it is my first picture, and I'm gonna be a one-eyed actor.' They brought in this doctor, and Sam said, 'Let's break for tonight.' And I said, 'No, sir. Let's finish it.' So the doctor slit the eyelid and cleaned it out. Then Sam asked me what I wanted to drink: vodka, bourbon, or beer. I said vodka and tossed down a couple of quick shots. We finished the scene, and Sam took me out to dinner."

Filming this opening sequence of the fight in Starbuck was extremely complicated, and at times there would be as many as six of the Panavision, Mitchell, and Arriflex cameras grinding away at the same time, some twenty-four frames per second and some faster to create the slow-motion effects.

Because Parras is located in the heart of the great central plain of Mexico, a windblown, dusty desert, Peckinpah had insisted upon and received a camera mechanic permanently assigned to the production for the duration of the shooting. It was this mechanic's sole job to take the cameras every night and completely disassemble and clean them so there would be a minimum of mechanical failure on the set.

As the footage of each day's shooting was processed, the work print (a copy of the original that is made to be cut up during the editing of the film thus preserving the original from damage) was delivered to Lou Lombardo who had set up his editing room in a nearby motel. "On the street fight at the beginning of the picture," Lombardo remembered, "Sam had said to me before we had even begun shooting, 'I'm going to have the temperance union and band coming down the street, and then the Bunch is going to break out of there, and I want all hell to break loose.' So I suggested to him that he might want to shoot a lot of waiting stuff on the roof with the bounty hunters and in the street with the bank, and we could cut it together in such a way that we could build tension in sort of a pyramid between the Bunch, the bounty hunters, and the marchers. So that's what Sam did, and I cut it for tension.

"Well, when they finally did break out of that railway station or whatever it was, I cut a sequence that was twenty-one minutes long, and when you sat through that, I swear to God you thought you were caught in hell. Then Sam came in and recut it, and when he was through, it was down to five minutes. But it was a terrific five minutes because he virtually retained the essence of every action we had but fragmented and intercut it all. It was a real showpiece. Sam has a fantastic editorial mind when it comes to film, and we really work well together."

On completion of their work in Parras, the production unit moved on to other locations in the vicinity before making a major move to Torreon: the Duranzo Arroyo where Pike must put the wounded Buck out of his misery; the canyon behind the Perote Winery where the bounty hunters bed down for the night; El Rincon del Montero, the beautiful *aldehuela,* which serves as Angel's village in the film; and El Romeral where old man Sykes waits with the horses for the Bunch to return from Starbuck.

Actor William Holden, who played Pike Bishop, remembered El Romeral: "That was where Sam really set the tone of what he expected from us on the picture. Now it's difficult to do a scene involving six characters all of whom have lines, because what you are trying to do in a master take is get everyone at their peak performance so that you can build the rest of the shooting—the closeups and what have you around the master, knowing you will always be able to cut back to it. Well, of course, in any given take somebody will have a high while somebody else will have a low. So the trick is always to get everyone motivated to the same degree of excellence at once.

"Well, as I recall, all six of us this day had a low. We had supposedly just ridden into the corral where we were meeting to divide up the silver that turned out to be washers, and the first rehearsal was just absolute chaos. It was an eight-minute scene on film, which made it long and involved. Well, Sam sat there and looked at us, and nobody knew his lines because we all had somehow felt that there would be plenty of time on the set to get sharp on the thing.

"Anyway, Sam said in this very calm but menacing voice:

'Gentlemen, you were hired to work on this film as actors, and I expect actors to know their lines when they come to the set. Now I'm willing to give you twenty minutes, and anyone can go wherever he wants to learn his lines. But when you come back, if you can't be an actor, you will be replaced.' Well, you've never seen so many frantic people wandering off behind sagebrush and everything else, leaning against adobe walls, you name it, but getting those lines down. But Sam is a perfectionist and all perfectionists are taskmasters. Above everything else, Sam is a professional."

If Peckinpah is a professional, he is also impressed by others who share in that professionalism. Ernest Borgnine remembered another occurrence from El Romeral: "Now there is only one thing that really bothered me about Sam Peckinpah, and that was the fact that whenever he worked he'd always have those bloody [dark] glasses on so you could never see his eyes. I always like to look in a man's eyes when he's talking because it really lets me sense his meaning. With Peckinpah I always wondered why he wore those damn things.

"So, anyway, one day we are at this place called El Romeral, and we have this scene where Eddie O'Brien brings us coffee as Pike and I are talking. And Pike is saying that he wanted to make 'one last big score and then pull back,' and I say, 'Pull back to what?' Well, the way the scene plays, I ask Pike if he's got anything else lined up, and he says the thing about the Army payroll and the railroad. And I say, 'They'll be waiting for us,' and Pike answers, 'I wouldn't have it any other way.' So the scene goes a little further, and then, just before I go to sleep, I say, 'Pike, I wouldn't have it any other way, either.' Then after I had delivered that line, instead of rolling toward Bill and putting my face in the camera, I rolled the other way so that my back was toward the camera. And then there was this prolonged silence, and the camera kept rolling and rolling and I thought: What the hell happened? Did Sam fall asleep? And then finally from Sam I hear, 'Cut!' but there is a distinct quaver in his voice. So I waited a moment to be certain the camera wasn't still rolling, and then I turned over and looked at Sam, and there were tears rolling down from behind those dark glasses. And Sam said, 'God damn it. Now that's professionalism!'"

By the middle of the shooting schedule, the company began to film the violent, climactic battle between the Bunch and Mapache's troops. For this, the Hacienda Cienga del Carmen was transformed into the town of Agua Verde. The script called for this brutal fight to begin with Mapache's killing of Angel followed by Pike's killing of Mapache in retribution. Without interruption, the battle would then rage until all of the Bunch and most of the soldiers had been killed.

150

Peckinpah, however, decided to make a key change in this scene. Instead of an uninterrupted bloodbath, Peckinpah injected a stalemate following the deaths of Angel and Mapache. The remaining four members of the Bunch stand in the open courtyard, their guns drawn, awaiting a violent attack from the troops who, now leaderless, are unable to do more than gape at what has happened. Peckinpah prolongs the moment to show Pike, Dutch, Tector, and Lyle first wary, then gleeful at the fact that they have buffaloed an entire army. They smile knowingly at one another and Dutch laughs. Then Pike turns, and spotting the German advisor to Mapache, drops him with a single shot, and the battle begins, but it begins at the *choice* of the Bunch. They are not on the defensive but on one final grand offensive.

By making the walk to get Angel back, they had already committed themselves to a futile but necessary act to fulfill their commitment as comrades. With Mapache's murder of Angel, they have no other choice but to kill Mapache regardless of consequences. Having done this, they suddenly realize—Pike most of all—that this *is* their "last big score" and that pulling back has nothing to do with it. They have won everything that has ever really meant anything to them, for as partners in a dying profession, they stand together against an army and decimate it. That they are right or wrong, that they are good or bad, that they live or die is of no consequence. That they die the way they lived *of their own choice,* however, is essential, for it gives them the personal integrity that is denied to the hundreds they kill as well as to the bounty hunters who grotesquely parody them in the battle's aftermath. Only Deke Thornton understands what has happened, and he pays tribute to the Bunch by taking the only thing that has meaning for him: Pike Bishop's handgun (this touch was also added by Peckinpah during the filming).

As one might suspect, this battle was an extremely complex scene to shoot owing to its violent action and demand for a large number of extras. To bring it off, Peckinpah relied heavily upon his crew, including assistant director Cliff Coleman and wardrobe head Gordon Dawson.

Dawson remembered: "We called it 'The Battle of Bloody Porch,' and there were five cameras on it. We worked our way across it at a foot an' a half per day. It was difficult because we had to keep interlacing the action: first foreground action plus every thing all over again; boom! next foreground action plus everything all over again. Each time we'd set up for a new foreground action, we'd have to repeat exactly what had taken place in the previous shots in the background so that everything would cut together. Man, people were going crazy.

"I only had 300 Mexican army uniforms, and we killed over *5,000* people in that scene—blew them up, shot them—when you take into account the total number of takes. To compensate, we had to virtually set up a goddamn factory. A guy'd get blown up, shot. In the beginning we'd take his clothes off him and give him new ones, but they began dying too fast. So we set up these giant heaters—big lights—and mixed this fantastic khaki-colored paint. Now when a guy'd be shot and come to us, we had a regular assembly line going. He'd come around to where it began and get hit with a bucket of water. Then we'd put this green tape in underneath to close the holes up and at the same time rip out all the wires from special effects, then run him around so he'd hit those dryers—the hot lights. Finally, we'd hit the guy with the khaki paint while he was under those lights, and then while it was drying and still kind of looking like paint, there'd be a guy with the aging materials and the dirty gloves going over it to make it look like worn cloth. At the same time, there'd be a special effects guy standing there wiring him up for the next take. Towards the end, we were reloading guys in five minutes, which was a hell of a lot faster than the way we started. I had started *Wild Bunch* thinking I was pretty well prepared to do it, but Sam really threw one at us with that scene." The Battle of Bloody Porch took eleven days to shoot. In addition to Dawson and Coleman, Lou Lombardo was brought from the editing room to direct the second unit. This meant the cutting of this critical sequence was given to Bob Wolfe, who had joined the production as an editor. Given the enormous impact this scene has upon the audience, it is virtually impossible to overvalue Wolfe's contribution here.

By this point in the shooting both the cast and the crew had grown hard and self-assured. "Bill Holden had written a prologue for *Wild Bunch,*" Peckinpah remembered, "which he brought down to Mexico with him when he came. He wanted us to shoot it because he thought the audience might not understand what was happening. I said to him: 'I tell you what, Bill. Let's wait till the end of the picture, and if you still think we need it, we'll shoot it.' And he agreed. Then one day after we'd finished the sequences at Agua Verde, we were riding back from a day's shooting and I said to him, 'Bill, you got that prologue?' And he turned to me, and smiled and said between his teeth, 'Why don't you go fuck yourself!' By that time he *was* Pike Bishop. He had that part nailed."

The next major sequence to be filmed called for the Bunch to rob a munitions train. For this, a working locomotive of the period was employed. It ran on several miles of track located on a rail spur south of La Gama. It took six days to capture the sequence on film.

"When we got to the train sequence," recalled Borgnine, "we were rougher than hell. You know those shots of Dutch falling between the cars while the soldiers fire at him? The reason that looks so real—the reason it's so exciting on the screen—is because that's not a stuntman, and it's not rear projection. Sam doesn't go for things like that because they look phony. It was just a matter of getting the old adrenaline flowing and doing what had to be done."

Warren Oates also remembered his adrenaline flowing: "Holden floor-boarded that train about the fifth take because Sam said it wasn't going fast enough. Holden got mad and pushed the engineer out of the way and took that lever and went all the way to the hilt, and away we went! It was about a mile and three-quarters run, and we got down there pretty damn quick, and I could see guys diving off the tracks because I'm up there on that flatcar out in front of the damn engine. And suddenly I'm saying to myself, 'Oh-oh, something's wrong!' because the brakes are on and we're sliding and the sparks are flying. And up ahead is this flatcar parked on the tracks, which acted as a stopping point so that we wouldn't overshoot our mark. I don't think you can actually see it in the shot. Anyway, I saw it approaching, and it was like slow motion. These two flatcars hit like dominoes. Somebody said I looked like I was doing a ballet. I grabbed the railing on the front of the locomotive and stepped up alongside the boiler and watched it happen 'cause it was something to behold!

"Later when it came time for my part of the action, Sam really let me do what I wanted because by then I really knew my character. After I killed off the two soldiers who were sitting on the front of the flatcar, Sam wanted this one shot where I'm supposed to be really enjoying the ride. Well, Sam said to do 'something' so I pretended I was the engineer like a kid might do and, of course, the Mexican engineer always gives a little 'toot' when he's going to move the train—that's the custom—so that's what I did. I just pretended it was my train."

The two soldiers who get shot off the front of the train by Oates, of course, were American stuntmen. One of them, Gary Combs, had been brought down specifically for that shot. Combs, who has worked on a number of Peckinpah films since, including *The Getaway* and *Pat Garrett and Billy the Kid,* lost an eye working on *Little Big Man* when an Indian who had had too much to drink took the rubber tip off one of his arrows. Of *The Wild Bunch* Combs remembered: "They had built this special platform low in front of the flatcar out of view of the camera for the other guy to fall onto, so that wasn't too bad. And the side of the roadway where I went off was pretty soft, too. So it wasn't a really difficult stunt.

"The train was going, at that point, just as fast as it would go, which is about thirty miles an hour. That isn't all that fast. But you take an old train like that, steamin' and spittin' fire on the screen it looks like it's going six hundred miles per hour."

The final action sequence to be filmed involved the river crossing that takes place following the train robbery. Screenwriter Walon Green recalled: "Originally, it was a cable across the river instead of a bridge. The only reason for the change was that the river wasn't right to do a cable crossing. Now blowing up that bridge is really terrific on the screen, but it's funny to me now because I argued with Sam about it. I said, 'Christ, you're going to blow up another bridge?' But Sam had a good retort: 'It's not just blowing up a bridge; it's the way you blow up a bridge.' And he was right. It was terrific." The job of rigging the bridge was given to special effects man Bud Hulburd.

The bridge was constructed across the Rio Nazas, south of Torréon. A center section was hinged on the side away from the camera thus allowing it to swing away like a trapdoor when the charges went off. The total effect would be to look as if the bounty hunters and their horses were sent crashing into the river with the bridge, but without any of the debris being really dangerous to the stuntmen. It too called for a multiple camera setup. Some of the cameras would be positioned on rafts to catch the feeling of the swiftly flowing river.

Strother Martin recalled: "Sam really worried about that bridge with all of its balsa struts and dynamite. He was afraid for the guys who went into the river with that shot. It was a dangerous river, fast and deep and black. I saw people being swept away to be caught downstream. It was knocking cameras off, and there were black whirlpools. Sam and Lucien both went in after a camera because they needed the footage. Everyone was close to danger."

Not everyone who was involved with the stunt felt the risks were worthwhile, however. Joe Canutt, the youngest son of legendary stuntman Yakima Canutt, stands six feet four inches and doubled Robert Ryan in the picture. He recalled: "That was the last time I ever worked for Peckinpah. He had a dynamite man named Bud Hulburd who rigged the bridge. Working with explosives is a tricky business. And when I'm gonna be standing on a bridge that blows up under me, I want to have a good look at how much of a charge they're using. Well, Sam had fired all the special effects people over Hulburd for not giving him [Peckinpah] what he wanted.

"So this was the first time Hulburd had really been in charge, and he was scared to death of Sam. I looked at the rigging, and he had enough explosives to blow us clean onto dry land. My mother didn't have any stupid children. I told him if he didn't cut those charges, they'd have to find somebody else to do the stunt. Well, he eventually did, and I rode the stunt. But I told that son of a bitch Peckinpah that I'd never work for him again."

Nevertheless, the bridge sequence provided one of the most exciting moments in the film. When he returned to Hollywood after completing his work on *The Wild Bunch,* Bud Hulburd told friends: "I've just had the opportunity to hang a Rembrandt! It will probably never happen to me again."

With the major portion of the shooting completed, Peckinpah and editor Lombardo received word from Warner Brothers that a group of studio top executives was flying into Mexico City for a meeting and wanted to screen whatever footage had been assembled over the course of the shooting. Lombardo remembered: "Sam was really smart. He was making a comeback and had insisted that I be down there on location with him during the shooting instead of back on the studio lot. Now, I'm an editor and normally my job is to rough cut the films so that everything usable would be together in one long, unpolished length of film. Then, after the shooting is completed, I get together with the director, in this case Peckinpah, and we'd work and cut and polish it down to a fine cut, or final version.

"Well, Sam had this theory of how he wanted me to work, and he kept stopping me from splicing together each day's rushes as they would come in and forcing me to work on what was in reality closer to a fine cut. Finally, I said to Sam, 'Look, you've got to let me get to what's coming in because I've got a mountain of film piling up!' And Sam said to me, 'I don't care if you only cut ten reels together by the time we're done shooting. I want it cut this way.'

"So three months later, I had about seventeen reels of film cut, and I got this call from Kenny Hyman saying that they were going to have a screening ... in Mexico City for the brass from Warners. Well, I wound up taking only fifteen reels, and they just loved it.

That gave Sam the green light for anything else he wanted. That's why he didn't want to just show them shot assemblies but kept on me

155

to polish the sequences as much as I could so that they would really see how powerful the film was going to be."

Finally, in early July 1968, after eighty-one days, *The Wild Bunch* company completed its principal photography. It had been a long and grueling experience for everyone concerned, but somehow nobody seemed to mind. "What happened on *Wild Bunch*," noted Dawson, "almost never happens: everyone was there, on his toes, job and homework done, eight possibilities in each hand and his mind searching for eight more, on the dead run for [eighty-one] days. Everybody gave total, full-bore commitment or they just weren't there!"

"On *Wild Bunch*," recalled Borgnine, "it was all hard work, but we all pulled together. It was rough, but we loved it because we all felt we were creating something important."

Lombardo remained in Mexico with Peckinpah for three additional months following the close of shooting in order to make the initial cut on the picture. When they returned to Hollywood, they brought with them a cut of the film that was three hours and forty-five minutes. The next six months were spent reducing the picture's length by one-third.

To editor Lombardo the 81 minutes in cuts seemed greater: "People have asked me how I could just take a movie and cut it in half like that. Believe me, it was really tough. But Sam did it very judiciously: he would take out only parts of sequences so that their essence would be left. We brought it down to two hours and twenty-four minutes, but it was painful. If you were to get ahold of the outtakes from *Wild Bunch* and run them, you would not allow them to be out of the picture. It was just all good stuff. The problem, of course, is that the audience would not sit still for four hours, so we had no choice.

"When we finished, the picture was under two and a half- hours with an intermission. There were 3,642 individual cuts in the film— more than any other color film ever made. I had remembered I think it was Hitchcock saying one time that if you wanted to make a picture really exciting, you needed a lot of cuts. An average picture will have no more than, say, 600 cuts. So on that basis, *Wild Bunch* was the most exciting picture ever made."

Speaking before Paul Seydor successfully arranged the reinsertion of the flashbacks, Lombardo praised their use and lamented their absence in the American print: "What really made *Wild Bunch* an incredible picture though was the subliminals—the flashbacks that gave these really tough mothers a human dimension. They're virtually all cut out of the American print, but they were beautiful. The one I was proudest of was the one which occurred in the film when the Bunch are bedded down in one camp and the bounty hunters are bedded down in another the first night. I started with Strother Martin asking Ryan what kind of a man the Holden character was and Ryan saying, 'The best ... ' From there I cut to Holden in this brothel in flashback—a much younger man with no moustache— standing there holding a bottle of whiskey shouting, 'Oh, shit!' Then I cut to Holden at the camp in the present talking to Borgnine, and you suddenly realized that both he and Ryan were thinking about the same incident. Then we cut back to the brothel and completed the flashback with the posse arriving and Holden going out the window leaving Ryan wounded behind. Finally, we came out of the flashback with Ryan in the present finishing the thought he began before the flashback started, '... He didn't get caught.' Then I cut to Holden in the present and continued the scene with Borgnine and the business about 'I wouldn't have it any other way.'

"The entire subliminal was handled with straight cuts, which really made it unique for the time. Then Warners got cold feet because it had never been done that way before and they insisted on using oil dissolves to let everybody and his grandmother know we were going into the past. It was really a shame because it was really effective the first way. I wish I had a nickel for every time I've seen that straight-cut technique used since then to deal with both flashback and flashforward. But then it was something new and daring, and they wouldn't take a chance."

Because some of the visuals have problems in their accompanying sound tracks, a process known as "looping" or "dubbing" is employed to rerecord the sound. On a sound studio dubbing stage, the actor will watch himself on the screen and repeat the needed lines into an open microphone with the exact cadence and emotional intensity required. Because this process is both time-consuming and expensive, many film studios limit looping to only the least acceptable lines.

"A lot of money was spent on looping," recalled Lombardo. "We redid something like thirty percent of the sound track because Sam refused to allow a sloppy job. Holden came in and did around 150 lines; Borgnine did around 90. Over a period of weeks I think we had every major and minor character in the picture in there on the dubbing stage, and Sam worked and worked with every one of them until they got up to the right emotional pitch to deliver the line to his satisfaction. When an actor was off on some other project, Sam would send someone to where the actor was and have the dubbing done at the nearest available studio. Sam's a fanatic on lines being clearly distinguishable.

"But the most unconventional thing Sam did in terms of the sound track for *Wild Bunch* was to totally redub the sound effects track after the Kansas City preview of the film. Sam felt that the guys who had done the effects track were sloughing it, and he was right. All the gun shots—everything—he made them start from scratch. He went in there shouting: 'I want each of these guns to have a different attitude. I want Pike's gun to have a special attitude, and I want Ryan's rifle to crack with a different character than all of [those of] the other bounty hunters' on the roof. And I want Strother Martin's gun to be a fuckin' boomer—a buffalo gun! Each weapon has to have a sound that suits the man. And that train—I want that fucker to thunder to a stop!' Well, Sam raised holy hell over that effects track, but he got them to bring it up to a level of quality that won them the S.M.P.T.E. sound effects award."

For the musical scoring of the picture, Peckinpah had brought Jerry Fielding down to Mexico while the picture was shooting so that he would be able to get the feeling of the production. "Sam has made four films of value to me." Fielding stated. "I think *Cable Hogue,* which I did not score, is one of his finest films, and *Junior Bonner* is one of his minor jewels. And *Noon Wine,* the film made for television on which Sam and I met, was an extraordinary piece of work. But *The Wild Bunch* is far and away not only his best film, but, in my opinion, may be the best picture ever made of that particular kind.

"I say this for a number of reasons. More than any other single reason is the untold number of manhours that went into the production by so many talented people, all of whom cared terribly about the way the film would finally look. Phil Feldman, despite some of the mistakes I think he made later in the distribution and reediting of the picture, at least had the sense to allow Sam and I and all of us to stay on the film for months longer than I'm sure the studio really wanted. This gave us the chance to work on the film to the point at which it completely fell apart and then continue past that point to where it all fell back into place again and really worked as a whole. It was that destruction and rebirth that made *Wild Bunch* such an incredible experience in the theater.

"It was a film which very well may not have been noticed if it had not been for the excessive and explosive depiction of violence. Now there are people who rebuke Sam for *The Wild Bunch*, saying that he only did it to draw attention to himself. But even if he did do that, which I am personally sure he did not, but even if he did, it is still an incredible piece of work. I must have had to see the film 400 times in scoring it, and I must say in all that time, I never can recall a single scene which caused me to wince—something I can say for no other film I have ever been associated with.

"Now Sam's ideas on how to score *The Wild Bunch* were all wrong. Sam had wanted to do it with two Mexican guitar players-very authentic. Well, you really can't do that. You see, realism on film is not quite realism. You can't spread the theater full of horse-shit so that everybody can smell the horses. In order for the picture to look 'real' it has to be made into a movie. Sam was very stringent about one thing: the music had to be authentically Mexican, and that it was. It also was extremely 'schmaltzy,' but the picture was so violent that I went very heavily the other way. I played it like a love story between two men. The only chase we do in the film is the train robbery, really. All the rest is full of darkness and sadness. It's full of melancholy. The only bit of real fun is in the wine cellar with Ben Johnson and Warren Oates.

"Sam and I had the biggest fight of our entire relationship over the scoring for the end of the picture where all those people are carrying away their wounded and the vultures are silhouetted against that ominous gray sky. He wanted his two guitar players again. I threw a chair at him when he told me that. I think that was the closest I ever came to killing anybody. The music I had composed for that moment in the film was a dirge, and I've never felt more strongly about a piece of music in my life that I did about that."

Camille Fielding, Jerry's wife, recalled the long months during which her husband worked on the scoring for the picture somewhat differently: "Jerry was on *The Wild Bunch* working in Mexico for six and a half months, which is unheard of to score a picture, especially a Western. And I went to Sam because we had torrential rains that year and our house was on the verge of sliding down the mountain into Grauman's Chinese—as some homes actually did that year—and I said, 'I am going to sue Jerry for divorce, and goddamn it Sam, I'm naming you as a correspondent!' And I was only half kidding at that time. But with Sam Peckinpah what you have to get used to is that working for Sam is being married to the picture. Nothing else matters."

It is not surprising that Jerry Fielding was nominated for an

Academy Award for *The Wild Bunch*. What is surprising is that the film received only one other nomination, that for best original Screenplay—story by Roy Sickner and Walon Green and screenplay by Walon Green and Sam Peckinpah. Walon Green stated: "The Writers Guild had had a vote by its members, most of whom have not and never will direct a film, which resulted in the policy that a director had to have done sixty percent of a screenplay in order to have a writing credit. I voted against that proposal because I thought it was really bullshit and represented the sort of frustrated, non-directing writer.

"So when the arbitration came on *Wild Bunch* the arbitrating committee read the script and said, 'Peckinpah doesn't have enough in it to get a credit on it.' So I wrote them a memo back and said that the changes in a script cannot be measured in lines or pages. Very small changes can be a major improvement. And although he obviously had not rewritten sixty percent of the script, the point is that the changes he made were significant enough that I felt he should share screenplay credit. One of the things that is wrong with the attitude taken by the writers is that the director says to himself, 'I'd better rewrite sixty percent of the screenplay or I'm not going to get credit.' Sam didn't do that and I appreciated it. If he had changed sixty percent of *The Wild Bunch* he would have fucked it up. Instead, he did just the right things and enhanced it."

Prior to its release, every motion picture now made in America by a major studio must go before the Motion Picture Association of America to be rated. "We had a lot of arguments with the censor[s] because they wanted to give *Wild Bunch* an X rating at first," noted Lombardo. "At that time they allowed you to be there at the running of your film—something they don't do anymore. We explained to them that if you take this particular segment out, it throws off something else. They somehow understood most of that and allowed much of what we argued for to remain. But there again, much of the time Sam was way ahead of them. He made me put in certain things that he knew they would make us take out. He saw everything as relative. But we did lose some things which should have never been cut like this Mexican butcher's stall with its meat hanging in the open air. It was bloody; sure, but have you ever been to Mexico today? The butchers haven't changed down there in a hundred years. Maybe the censors were vegetarians. At any rate, they eventually gave us an R.

"Then we took the film to Kansas to preview it. Christ, what an experience! The crowd turned out to be either completely for or completely against the film. And the ones who were against it were more violent than the film itself! I remember this one lady. I was standing in the lobby next to the phone and she was screaming into the phone that she wanted the Ladies League of Decency or some damn thing [to come] down there to the theater to shut the picture down. I couldn't believe it. I thought she was going to kill us. So I grabbed Sam and said: 'Sam, we've got to get out of here. They're getting ready to kick the shit out of us.' But Sam just laughed and shouted back: 'Leave now? Hell, partner, I think we've got 'em on the run!'"

After the Kansas City preview, the picture was pulled back for final editing and revision prior to general release. Meanwhile, Peckinpah had another project under way at Warner Brothers with Phil Feldman as executive producer called *The Ballad of Cable Hogue*. While Peckinpah was on location with that film, Warners decided to release *The Wild Bunch* only in Europe, holding it back in America for a "festival" of new film releases Warner Brothers-Seven Arts was planning to hold in the Bahamas the last week in June 1969.

The "film festival" held at the King's Inn on Grand Bahama Island was, in reality, not a festival but a press junket to showcase the studio's upcoming important releases. Wherever possible the studio had flown in key people from each of the films to be showcased. For *The Wild Bunch* Sam Peckinpah, Phil Feldman, and the Bunch— Holden, Borgnine, Oates, and Johnson—attended.

As reported in *Variety* on July 2nd, *The Wild Bunch* became the center of controversy. Some members of the audience walked out in protest during the screening of the film. At a press conference held the following day, Peckinpah and his cohorts were both attacked and praised with comments ranging from the very negative (Virginia Kelly of *Reader's Digest:* "I have only one question to ask: why was this film ever made?") to the very positive (Roger Ebert of *The Chicago SunTimes:* "This movie is a masterpiece").

Released in the United States the following week, the film continued to provoke debate. Almost universally, reviewers called the film the bloodiest ever made; they were split, however, over whether this was good or bad:

Several hundred senseless frontier killings don't add up to enlightenment. They only add up to several hundred frontier killings.
~Joseph Morgenstern, *Newsweek*

[There is) little justification for discussing this ugly, pointless, disgustingly bloody film.
~William Wolf, *Cue*

161

The Wild Bunch contains faults and mistakes, but its accomplishments are more than sufficient to confirm that Peckinpah, along with Stanley Kubrick and Arthur Penn, belong to the best of the newer generation of American filmmakers.

~*Time*

[Peckinpah] is such a gifted director that I don't see how one can keep from using the word "beautiful" about his work. [There is] a kinetic beauty in the very violence that his film lives and revels in. . . the violence *is* the film.

~Stanley Kaufman, *The New Republic*

In the wake of *The Wild Bunch's* release, Peckinpah left for Hawaii both to vacation with his children and to edit *The Ballad of Cable Hogue*. Then came the call from Phil Feldman informing him that Warner Brothers was planning to cut twenty minutes out of the American release prints of *The Wild Bunch*.

"I was in Hawaii when I got the call," Peckinpah remembered. "Mr. Feldman said, 'We'd like to cut the picture because it is not opening as big as we expected.' I then asked him to hold off and give it a chance because it was going really well in Europe. The next thing I knew, they'd cut every print. But that was Ted Ashley and Phil Feldman. So they cut out all the flashbacks—the things which humanized the characters. I couldn't believe it. Here people are screaming for my head on a platter because I have too much violence in the film, and Feldman makes certain that's all anybody sees."

Many saw more than that, however. If *The Wild Bunch* was controversial, it also generated a growing admiration among film scholars as well as average moviegoers. More than a decade after the film's original release, *The Wild Bunch* remains among the most frequently rented motion pictures in the 16mm film market (primarily universities and film societies), while regularly playing to packed houses in rerun theaters throughout the United States and abroad. And despite Warner Brothers' continued claim that *The Wild Bunch* never turned a profit, the studio selected this film as one of the first twenty films it would offer for direct sale to the home video market as a "film classic." By all accounts, *The Wild Bunch* would seem to have become one of the most successful "failures" in film history.

The Ballad of Cable Hogue

"Found it where it wasn't."

After the harsh reality portrayed in *The Wild Bunch,* Sam Peckinpah needed a respite. He therefore selected for his next film an allegory, *The Ballad of Cable Hogue,* the story of a man betrayed and left to die in the desert, who finds water "where it wasn't." It is a tale of love, retribution, and the American Dream set against the passing of the Old West. Shot in the Valley of Fire, a sandstone wasteland in southern Nevada, this would be a story of survival—both in front of and behind the cameras.

Max Evans, the Western writer (*The Rounders, The Hi-Lo Country, One-Eyed Sky)* who played the shotgun guard on the stagecoach in *Cable Hogue* and later wrote about his experiences in a book (misleadingly titled *Sam Peckinpah: Master of Violence)* recalled: *"Cable Hogue* started out to be this low budget, simple sort of love story that Sam wanted to do because he wanted something which would show his gentler side. But then the storms just ripped the guts outta everybody, and the studio started saying, 'There goes Peckinpah havin' his sick fits again.' Well, that was a damn lie. Sam was one of the only people holding things together. Everybody around him was fallin' apart on him, and he fired their ass when they broke up. And those who could take the gaff, well, by God, they hung in and made the picture."

The script for *Cable Hogue* had actually been around Holly-wood for some time before Peckinpah decided to make it. L. Q. Jones recalled: "I actually bought *Cable Hogue.* The script was offered to us [LQ/JAF] for like $5,000. And I wanted to make it—it was a hellaciously good piece—because I thought it would have been better with a small company making it since you'd have fewer problems. But it didn't work out.

"Then Sam and I were going to make *Castaway,* but my attorney decided he was going to decant [abscond] with the money and the whole thing fell through. It must have been a year later

163

[that] I was out talkin' to Sam, and he said, 'I found the picture we're going to do.' And this was still when Sam didn't have enough money to eat, and everyone had to lend him money to keep alive. And he started to tell me the story, and I said: 'Stop. Let me tell you the rest.' And that was *The Ballad of Cable Hogue.* So I put up the initial money to buy it under Sam's name. But then *Wild Bunch* came along first, and finally *Cable Hogue* was made at Warners."

"Edmund Penny and Johnny Crawford had written the screenplay for *Cable Hogue,*" Peckinpah remembered, "and when I read it I knew it would be a sensational film. Warren Oates brought it to me to read. He wanted the part of Cable and L.Q. Jones wanted Joshua, but I couldn't cast them in it. I had to go with who I thought was right. When I saw *Morgan* [directed by Karel Reisz, 1966], I called Ken Hyman who came through by getting David Warner for the part, and he was superb."

In addition to Warner, Peckinpah cast Jason Robards in the title role, with Stella Stevens as Hildy, the prostitute who becomes Hogue's lady love. L. Q. Jones and Strother Martin played the evil Taggert and Bowen, respectively, with Slim Pickens as the stage driver and R. G. Armstrong as the owner of the stage line in support. *The Ballad of Cable Hogue* was originally seen by both Peckinpah and Warners as a moderately budgeted production to be shot during the first two months of 1969 with Phil Feldman as executive producer.

Gordon Dawson was secured by Peckinpah to collaborate with him on the new picture. Dawson recalled: "On *Wild Bunch* I had never been invited into the inner circle too often. I mean every time I'd really begin to get uptight, Sam'd be there with some encouragement to keep it together and I'd be off again, but beyond that, I hadn't been all that close to Sam.

"Well, at the end of the picture, Sam and Ben Johnson and I were sitting out by the river where the bridge was blown up, and Sam says to me: 'I'll tell you what. I've got another picture to do. I bought a script that needs a lot of work, and I'd like you to do some writing on it for me and be my associate producer on the picture.' Well, I really didn't know what an associate producer did at that time, but I thought it sounded sensational. So while Sam was cutting on *Wild Bunch* in Torreon, I'd rewrite *Cable Hogue* during the day. Then at night, Sam would go over what I'd written and change it wherever he thought it needed it."

The crew included Lucien Ballard as director of photography and Robert Visciglia as property master. They were two of the few who started the picture who would remain through to the end. Visciglia stated: "Sam was credited with thirty-six firings on *Cable Hogue,* but he only did seven himself. Bill Farella did most of them in Sam's name. As far as I'm concerned, Sam was one of the most reasonable men I've ever worked for. I found out what he wanted and didn't shortchange him on anything. We got along fine. I was just a mediocre prop man until I worked for Sam Peckinpah. Sam challenges you and forces you to rise to the occasion. I like working with Sam because with Sam you work twenty-four hours a day. You have to be committed. You have to live the picture."

"When you send thirty-six people home on a picture and *you've* chosen them," stated Dawson who had selected the original crew and had much of the responsibility for firing those who went, "you lose a lot of friends. The co-producer, Bill Farella, was even eventually fired. He'd been production manager on *Wild Bunch.* The production manager on *Hogue* was fired. They were never replaced, however. We replaced everyone fired in the crafts, but those of us who were left on the production team absorbed the extra responsibilities of Farella and the manager.

"You'll hear a lot of horror stories about the people we fired on *Cable Hogue.* Of course, everything depends on whose point of view you're getting. Sam requires a lot of the people who work with him—the same amount he requires from himself. That means you're generally working long hours, although on *Hogue* the weather was a pretty depressing thing for everybody. Nevertheless, Sam never fired anybody without cause. You take a guy who's been doing the same job in the industry for a long time, and he can start to slack off a bit. He's the guy Sam will fire.

"But Sam expects you to make it your picture. He expects everybody—right down to the electricians to read the script. If they do something that to him isn't consistent with the scene and wouldn't have been done by anyone who had read the script, they won't get the chance to read it. They'll be gone.

"We had 119 Labor Relations Board violations claimed against us for those thirty-six firings. I negotiated away all but three. If you did your job and kept on top of it, you didn't have any trouble."

In addition to the regular film company, two young filmmakers named Gary Weis and Gil Dennis, backed by Peckinpah's Latigo Productions and Phil Feldman Productions in cooperation with Warner Brothers, had also come to the Valley of Fire to make a movie. Theirs was to be a short 16mm film on the making of *The Ballad of Cable Hogue* to be released as part of the promotional campaign for the picture. Gary Weis at that time was also courting Sam Peckinpah's oldest daughter, Sharon, then nineteen.

The weather in the Valley of Fire was overcast the first several days, according to Max Evans's account of the events surrounding *Cable Hogue,* but then brightened for roughly one week. During this week as many scenes as possible were completed. Among these was the opening sequence that called for the blowing apart of a Gila monster, shot by Taggert and Bowen just as Hogue gets ready to kill it for supper.

R.G. Armstrong recalled: "They were rigging this Gila monster to blow it up, and Sam's—at that time, prospective son-in-law was there. He'd been given a budget of $25,000 or something [Peckinpah estimates $10,000] to make a movie of Sam Peckinpah making a movie. I don't recall his name, but he wore these Gandhi-like clothes and long hair. He wore his hair in sort of a ponytail, and he had this beard.

"So, anyway, he came up to Sam, and said, 'You're not going to kill that Gila monster just for a movie, are you?' And Sam looked at him and finally said, 'Yeah, I'm going to kill that Gila monster.' And this guy said, 'But you can't do that—kill a creature of nature just for a movie.' And Sam says: 'What's the matter? Don't you want that Gila monster to die?' And the kid said, 'No, I don't think you should do that.'

"So Sam thought a minute and then said: 'I'll tell you what I'll do. That Gila monster will live if you'll shave off that beard and cut your goddamn hair.' And the guy said, 'Well, I don't know. I don't think that's the point.' And Sam said: 'It is the point. If you want that Gila monster to live, you cut that goddamn beard and hair.' And the guy said: 'I don't know. I've gotta think about that.' And Sam said, 'Well, make it snappy.' So the kid went over to the side and then came back and said, 'I think that's irrelevant.' And Sam blew the Gila monster up.

"Now what the kid missed was the point of the whole thing. Sam was testin' him. He wanted to see just how committed the kid was to his stated beliefs. It had nothing to do with hair 'cause Sam himself had a beard at the time. But when the kid backed off, he lost respect in Sam's eyes."

In actuality, the lizard blown up on *Cable Hogue* was not a real Gila monster, a species protected under law in the United States. Jason Robards, who was close enough to check the lizard's breath, recalled: "That lizard on *Cable Hogue* was worse than a Gila monster. It was a Mexican beaded lizard. If he gets ahold of you, he'll

166

never let go. And Sam, he's standing about eighty feet away, and he says, 'Now, will you look at our crazy New York actor.' Sam's not stupid. But me—what the hell do I know?

"But Sam, he's a stickler on detail. He had 'em paint the goddamn lizard to look like a Gila monster. Then when they blew it up, they did such a good job that the camera never even saw it! And that was in slow motion, so you can figure out what kind of charge they must've had on it. So Sam made 'em put it back together again. Bobby Visciglia, the prop man, had to sew it back together just so they could blow it up again to get it on film. Hell, the first time they blew up the rock and everything." In honor of this twice-killed monster, Robards officially dubbed the cocktail bar in the motel that housed the cast and crew at Echo Bay the "Lizard Lounge."

When the weather went bad again, Peckinpah was forced to shoot interiors while waiting for the skies to clear. The scenes involved Jason Robards, David Warner, and Stella Stevens inside of the cabin Hogue builds in the desert. (The town interiors were placed at the end of the shooting schedule to be shot in a Western movie town called "Apache Junction" and located east of Phoenix, Arizona.) Visciglia recalled: "When Stella Stevens arrived on the set of *Cable Hogue* the first scene we shot was one which occurred later in the picture where Hildy is living with Cable. At any rate, she came on the set, and she proceeded to find fault with virtually everything. For example, I had made a period biscuit cutter out of a can, and she claimed she couldn't use it because it hurt her hand. Things like that. Finally, Sam turned to me and said: 'Find Stella something that works. Why are we having so many problems with this?' And I told him, 'Sam, I just don't happen to have a period Farmer's Market!' Well, that cracked everybody up including Stella, and she relaxed and was a pleasure to work with from that point on."

Stella Stevens, whose career prior to *Cable Hogue* had included *The Courtship of Eddie's Father, The Silencers,* and *Luv,* wrote of her experiences with Peckinpah in an article that appeared in the *Los Angeles Times* (March 29, 1970) at the time of the film's release. Along with a description of her career and how Peckinpah cast her in the role of Hildy, she also described the many difficulties encountered on location. And finally, she attempted to recount her relationship with Peckinpah: "[A]s I walked into the first rehearsal on the first day of work, all nervous and wary, he kissed me lightly and said, 'Welcome to the place of love.' Nobody ever welcomed me onto a picture that way before. When I was fighting down the panic before my first shot

in the film, he walked over to me and held my hand. He always listened to my questions, and he gave me honest answers.
He made a lady out of Hildy and a star out of me. He may have driven me quite mad, but maybe he saved my soul."

While Stella Stevens's account of Peckinpah's direction is, for the most part, accurate, it lacks perspective. All of the director's relationships with actors and actresses are complex and founded on a kind of "love affair." This may or may not be sexual; it will almost always be intense. For example, Peckinpah will often control an actress's performance by manipulating her emotions. One moment he may all but overwhelm her with affectionate support to obtain one kind of response. The next, he may dramatically withhold that affection to get another.

Writer-actor Evans recalled a case in point involving Peckinpah and Stevens: "Sam did a magical thing on Stella Stevens. She was uptight and he wanted to get a cryin' scene but really the right kind of cryin' scene. You see, Sam's very kind with his actors mostly and really loves 'em. But if he has to, he'll wack 'em. So all of a sudden he just blew up and told her that she couldn't act and threw this screamin' tirade. Well, Stella, she just broke down completely and started cryin'. He then brought her a bottle of ale himself and gave her a couple of drinks from it and gently calmed her. Then he set her in front of the camera and she really was able to cry with emotional conviction. It was the place where she says, 'You've been good to me Cable ... ' an' big old tears well up in her eyes. Man, it choked up pretty near everybody on the set including Sam himself."

If being an actress on a Peckinpah picture bears certain similarities to having a love affair with him, so does the aftermath resemble the end of a love affair. In a telephone interview four years after completing *Cable Hogue,* Stella Stevens hardly sounded like the same woman who wrote such high praise of Peckinpah: "An actor needs encouragement, not that reverse psychology that Sam throws at his actors. I like my performance in *Cable Hogue,* but it was mine not Sam's. Sam threw away thirty percent of my best moments—hacked them away. I saw *Cable Hogue* as a love story, something magic created by special moments between two people. That's all there is, fleeting moments. Well, thirty percent of those beautiful and fleeting moments of love are gone from *Cable Hogue,* and Sam is responsible.

"I have never been so frustrated. It was the blackest moment of my life when I saw what they had done. I was told that I would be nominated for an Academy Award with that performance. I think I would have, if Sam hadn't left some of the best parts on the cutting room floor. . . .

"Now I don't consider Sam my enemy. I just never want to be around him or his group ever again. The only thing that kept me going on *Cable* was the fact that I had a sense of humor. Well, that's just not possible anymore. I'd never work with Sam Peckinpah again. I'm a writer, an actress, a painter. I'm learning to be a potter, and I'm going to be a director. But to be a director, you don't have to emotionally destroy the people you work with."

There is clearly justification for Stevens's dislike of Peckinpah's manipulative technique. No one likes to feel that he has been used. But on the other hand, the argument must be raised that her performance in *Cable Hogue* has been enhanced by that manipulation. As for her more serious charge that the best part of her performance was lost in the editing, Lou Lombardo disagrees: "I cut the picture, and everything she did is in it. She liked the film when she saw it in preview, and there were no moments in that preview print that weren't in the release print. I don't understand what she means."

To bring the relationship full circle, two years after the telephone interview cited above, Stevens was the first person to kiss Sam Peckinpah as he walked through the door at his fiftieth birthday party. And for his part, Peckinpah still displays a photo of her that bears the inscription: "Sam of Sams—Thank you for giving me Hildy. Happy every new day. Love, Stella." In retrospect, perhaps the most important feature of this strange relationship is that some of its most emotionally moving moments were captured on film in Stevens's performance in *Cable Hogue*.

As the problems on *Cable Hogue* mounted, Peckinpah became more and more challenged to find ways of diverting his cast and crew's attention from their troubles so that they could concentrate on making a movie. Evans remembered one such event: "We had a lot of livestock on the show—I mean aside from the horses, there were rattlesnakes, a Gila monster, assorted horny toads, and such. And a bunch of Kansas jack rabbits.

"Well, one night Sam and Frank Kowalski stayed out on location in Sam's camper supposedly to get a jump on the next day's shooting. While they were out there, Sam and Frank let loose all of the jack rabbits, because Sam wanted something to raise hell about the next day. . . . 'Who the hell was the stupid son of a bitch that turned the rabbits loose? ... ' And it was calculated madness that worked. It got everybody's mind off the weather and the rest of their troubles so they'd be loose enough to give their best for the film. It may sound strange, but that's truly a bit of genius to my way of thinkin'."

Another kind of diversion took the form of several prostitutes Peckinpah had invited out to the location (a practice he had followed on other location projects as well). This time, however, it backfired because one of the girls brought with her a social disease that became euphemistically rechristened "apple valley fever." This episode was tactfully omitted from Evans's book on the production, a decision he readily explained in private: "Sure there were whores on *Cable Hogue*. But the reason I didn't write that in my book is that I've got a wife that'll kill ya, and that ain't no joke. When you're writin' with a .45 cocked in your ear, well, you write somethin' else!

"There was this one Mexican actress who'd been imported that caused such a battle that they damn near tore the hotel apart breakin' windows and doors. There was a better movie gain' on inside the hotel than Sam was makin' outside it, and that one was pretty good. So she was immediately on a plane—part of the shuttle service for hiring and firing.

"There was also some 'apple valley fever' that ran absolutely rampant on the picture. I think myself and two others missed it out of the whole crew, and that includes the waitresses, the cooks, the goddamn bartenders, and the gardener. And the few that didn't have it were so weak with worry, they could barely operate anyway."

Still another problem on *Cable Hogue* was influenza that ran roughshod over both cast and crew. For some it was a dangerous matter. "I was sick all the way through the filming of *Cable Hogue,*" recalled Slim Pickens. "And after it was over I had to have a lung operation where they took out the lower lobe of my lung. I had had the Hong Kong flu, and it had gone into pneumonia, and I had just gotten over it when the doggone picture started. So I got down there [in the Valley of Fire] and the second week of shooting, by golly, I had pneumonia again. They gave me some pills to keep the fever down, and I kept going. When I finally did get to a hospital after the picture finished, I found out that I still had pneumonia and had had it for three and a half months. The lower part of my right lung had collapsed under the strain. So when I was in the hospital, there came this box of flowers from Sam with a bottle of whiskey in it. It was a rough damn picture, but when I seen it I knew it was all worthwhile."

Among the others who suffered through this picture with Peckinpah was Lucien Ballard who also lost a lung. Ballard contracted desert fever, a malady that results from parasitic spores that grow in the lungs. In light of this kind of commitment to Peckinpah and his picture, it is perhaps easier to understand Peckinpah's shortness of temper with those who complained about routine problems.

In the midst of this came a strange ghost out of Peckinpah's past. When he had worked on *Major Dundee,* both he and the producer, Jerry Bresler, had flown to Ravenna, Italy, to obtain Richard Harris for the film. When they arrived, they discovered that the film Harris was involved with, *The Red Desert,* was shooting on a closed set. Both Peckinpah and Bresler were denied entrance to that set to meet with Harris by the film's director, Michelangelo Antonioni. Now, five years and a continent later, Antonioni was making his first American film, *Zabriskie Point,* and in the course of events found himself on a road blocked by an American motion picture company filming a picture called *The Ballad of Cable Hogue.*

Antonioni sent one of his associates forward through the mile of sand that lay between the roadblock and the American company to prevent any disruption during a sound take. Peckinpah refused to speak to the assistant and asked that Antonioni himself walk through the mile of sand to see him about whatever it was he wanted.

When Antonioni arrived, he requested that his equipment and personnel be allowed to use the road because a detour would mean valuable days lost. Peckinpah listened courteously to the request and then replied, "Maybe tomorrow, but right now I've got a shot to lay out." Peckinpah then went back to his work. Antonioni took the detour.

By now the trade papers and gossip columns began to run regular items on what was being called by everyone, Peckinpah included, "The Battle of Cable Hogue." Such adverse publicity has advantages, however, which Peckinpah was quick to recognize. "Sam doesn't mind his own legend," stated collaborator Dawson. "On *Cable Hogue,* I brought him a press release from Vegas where it said he stood up on a table in the Mint Hotel and pissed all over the crap table. I told him I could get a hold of the reporter and sue for a retraction in print. But Sam stopped me, saying: 'Now wait, wait, wait. We're not going to sue. Look at that, man. So I did that, huh?' So he gets blamed for things he doesn't always do and loves it. But that's where his legend comes from. He's done so much, people expect and believe anything."

171

On the other hand, one should never underestimate Peckinpah. Among the true stories to come off the set of *Cable Hogue,* verified by several separate eyewitness accounts, are those that place Peckinpah in numerous tackle football games held at night in the Lizard Lounge in which players used ashtrays for footballs. Another story recounts Peckinpah's leading a select group from the cast and crew out of the lounge one night with the sole purpose of washing the hotel into Lake Mead by urinating in unison against the hotel's foundation.

As the production neared the end of shooting in the Valley of Fire, a scene was scheduled that called for Hogue to drive his enemies, Taggert and Bowen, out of a hole by throwing rattlesnakes in on them. For this scene, animal handler John Walrath had brought with him a variety of rattlesnakes. The snakes' mouths were sewn shut for the purpose of shooting the scene.

"I had read the script. Knew it cold," L. Q. Jones, who plays Taggert in the film, remembered. "But somehow I had read right past that part and never even thought about it. And what's more, I got out there on the mornin' we were gonna shoot the snake scene, and there were all these people hangin' around the set. Now Sam doesn't like a lot of people on the set. If you belong in the office, you should be in the office. So I thought, 'What the hell is this?' but I didn't bother too much about it.

"And to let you know how really dumb I was, before we shot the son of a bitch, Sam wanted to shoot some stuff of me by the snake cage, which was over by the hut Cable built. So I spent a couple of hours there pokin' at this big rattler—I think he weighed around twenty pounds—makin' him strike for the camera. So he didn't like me to begin with. And it still hadn't clicked by the time we went to lunch.

"It was during lunch that the realization hit me: Sam was gonna use *real snakes.* But I couldn't very well say anything 'cause Strother [Martin] would have gone off like a three-dollar skyrocket. So as we headed out to the pit, Strother caught on to what was about to happen, and I think he grew six inches with worry alone.

"As we get down in the pit and Sam first slides that big one down the back side and the snake kind of coiled himself up and sorta fell forward. Well, Sam shouts: 'Cut. We can't have that.' So they took the snake back up and tried to figure out how to make him angry.

"Now snakes are coldblooded and detest heat, so they turned a couple of brutes [hot lights] on this big one and cooked him for a couple of minutes which really made him mad and improved his attitude tremendously as far as Sam was concerned. So they slid him down the back side again. Only this time he coiled himself up and lunged knockin' me right over on my face. He hit me 'cause Strother had already split!

"Well, now that the big one had gotten the idea, they decided to shoot the thing throwin' in a lot of smaller rattlers in such a way that you figured Hogue was walkin' around the pit. I mean it started raining snakes....

"One of 'em went down my shirt front and you want to see someone undress? I was naked in about three seconds! I completely came out of everything I had on. I mean, he was only about two or three pounds, but a two or three-pound rattler gets your attention!"

Following the completion of filming in the Valley of Fire, the production company for *Cable Hogue* moved down to Apache Junction, Arizona, for the final week of shooting. Rain delays had put them several weeks behind schedule. When the town sequences were completed, the production company wrapped up and headed home.

It had been an ordeal for everyone concerned. Considering the number of people who were either fired or who quit, property master Visciglia suggested that it resembled a war and that anyone who survived deserved a medal. Struck by the idea, Peckinpah decided to do just that. Through a local jeweler he obtained a gold medallion for each member of the cast and crew who had remained loyal. Each carried the person's name followed by the inscription: *"The Battle of Cable Hogue* for services beyond the call of duty." Beneath this was Peckinpah's brand (registered with the state of Nevada when he owned a small ranch there), the lazy SP". This kind of personal memento was to become a tradition with all future Peckinpah productions.

In reciprocation, those who had remained loyal felt it necessary to refute the charges that Peckinpah's firings had been without justification. On March 31, 1969, they bought an entire page in the *Daily Variety* to run the following statement: "It's been a hell of a ball working with Sam Peckinpah. We found it where it was." This was followed by the list of more than forty cast and crew members who finished the picture.

To edit the film, Peckinpah first engaged Frank Santillo with whom he had worked on *Ride the High Country*. Santillo had left MGM to work as a freelance editor in the mid-sixties. *The Wild Bunch* at this time was in the final stages of completion and Peckinpah divided his time between the two projects.

By the time *The Wild Bunch* was finally completed, Santillo was half finished with *Cable Hogue*. Because Santillo had a commitment to edit Burt Kennedy's *The Deserter,* Peckinpah allowed him to go and brought in Lou Lombardo to finish what Santillo had started. Among the sequences completed by Santillo were the montage sequences including the opening credits and the duet, "Butterfly Morning," which is sung in the film by Stevens and Robards.

"We took a lot of chances in the editing of that picture," Lombardo recalled. "For example, that Indian on the five-dollar bill suddenly grinning as Cable looks after Hildy and the subliminals of her cleavage that keep coming back to him as he tries to make up his mind. It was a little hokey, but we felt it was in keeping with the other experimental stuff, like the fast-motion sequences. I think it works for the most part.

"As on *Wild Bunch,* we did a lot of looping on *Cable Hogue.* Sam feels, and so do I, that some of the performances actually improved in the dubbing. Jason's performance, I know, was embellished by the chance to work still further with the character during the looping. We had to go to Rome to get it because Jason was on another picture at the time. But Sam is always concerned with the audience's being able to hear every word. If you lose a word, you lose meaning."

The scoring for *Cable Hogue* was done by composer Jerry Goldsmith and incorporated the songs of guitarist-composer Richard Gillis. One of these songs, "Butterfly Morning," is sung by Cable and Hildy as we see their relationship develop into love. Peckinpah recalled: "I found Dick Gillis working in a bar singing his own songs, and I hired him for the picture right there. He is a complete original. 'Butterfly Morning' is one of the most beautiful things I know."

Before Peckinpah and Lombardo could put the picture in final cut, however, problems developed. "Warners showed a two-and-a-half-hour version of the picture to the distributors without my knowledge," Peckinpah stated. "This was not a fine cut; it was a rough cut without the final sound track or music track. There were thirty minutes to come out of that version, and the distributors didn't know what to do with what they saw. They decided on the basis of that showing that the film was a dog and should be buried. So the picture got a very poor release in this country—no first run bookings at all.

"It was really a shame. *Cable Hogue* is possibly my best film. A real love story. I am always criticized for putting violence in my films, but it seems that when I leave it out nobody bothers to see the picture. Jason Robards and Stella Stevens gave two of their finest performances in that film. I still cry when he says to her, 'Now, there

174

is a picture.' And she says, 'You've seen it before, Hogue.' And Jason replies, 'Lady, nobody's ever seen you before.' Talk about a love scene. They were sensational."

With the release of *The Wild Bunch,* the late Joel Reisner, Peckinpah's publicity agent through good times and lean, had put together a retrospective of the director's work at the California Institute of the Arts. It had shown Peckinpah to be a talented young American director. But with Warner Brothers' mishandling of the release of *The Ballad of Cable Hogue,* Peckinpah decided to take his talents elsewhere.

10 Straw Dogs

"I got 'em all."

During the editing of *The Ballad of Cable Hogue,* Sam Peckinpah was approached by Daniel Melnick to read a book entitled *The Siege of Trencher's Farm* by British author Gordon M. Williams (a pseudonym for novelist J. Anderson Black) and consider directing a motion picture based upon it. Although Peckinpah was not overwhelmed by the book, he had confidence in Melnick's judgment and agreed to do it if Melnick could get the project off the ground. Melnick then hired screenwriter David Z. Goodman to do the first draft of the screenplay for what would eventually become *Straw Dogs.* An ironic tale of man's violence to man, it details the attempt of an American professor and his British wife to return to the tranquility of her girlhood home only to be confronted by mayhem and destruction.

At the same time Peckinpah was considering a number of other projects. The first was a screenplay called *The Summer Soldiers* cowritten by Peckinpah, writer Lee Pogostin, and actor Robert Culp, who starred in *Bob and Carol and Ted and Alice* and the television series *I Spy* and was a longtime friend of Peckinpah's. In February 1970, this project, with Peckinpah directing, had been scheduled for production later that year by Warner Brothers.

The second project Peckinpah was interested in directing was James Dickey's *Deliverance.* Peckinpah recalled: "I used to correspond with James Dickey a lot. Dickey had done *Deliverance* [the book], and John Calley gave me the galleys on it. But I already had a deal to do this thing with Culp *[Summer Soldiers],* and the script needed an enormous amount of work. I also had an invitation to go to the Scandinavian countries to lecture, which would allow me to spend some time with my son, Matthew, so Dickey eventually went to John Boorman, I think."

As a third project, Peckinpah was attempting to rough out a screenplay with his cohort Frank Kowalski based on an original story idea by Kowalski. This project would eventually be made several years later as *Bring Me the Head of Alfredo Garcia.*

Of these, *The Summer Soldiers* seemed, in all probability, to be Peckinpah's next motion picture. Then a series of events radically altered the situation. First, Warner Brothers sloughed *The Ballad of Cable Hogue* as a bill filler, which infuriated Peckinpah. At roughly the same time, he had a falling out with Pogostin and Culp, selling out his rights to *The Summer Soldiers* to them for twenty-five cents (some say a dime). Meanwhile, Daniel Melnick had convinced ABC Pictures to finance *The Siege of Trencher's Farm* on the condition that Peckinpah would be willing to direct it. Because he was no longer committed to making *The Summer Soldiers,* Peckinpah agreed to ABC's offer. He then left for Europe in early June to lecture, planning to meet Melnick a month later in England. Set in Cornwall, this feature film would be Peckinpah's first outside of the Western genre.

The man who authorized the project for ABC Pictures was Martin Baum, who had been an agent for twenty-five years representing such stars as Sidney Poitier and Gig Young before becoming a producer himself. He stated: "Sam and I got together when I was president of ABC Pictures and as such I had commissioned a film called *The Siege of Trencher's Farm.* It was a time in Sam's life when he was still regarded as a problem child by the studios. He was accused of going over budget and seen as having no respect for studio controls. But I had great confidence that what Sam could do with a picture would be worth doing. . . .

"We had a very interesting experience immediately. It was my understanding that Sam was going to write the screenplay. And I read what he had supposedly written, and I said that I didn't think it was right but I thought that there was a way to fix it. So I took the producer, Dan Melnick, to Acapulco, and I spent a week going over the script with him. And I said if these changes were implemented I thought we could make a movie. And he said: 'Don't worry. I'll get to Sam immediately and we'll work with him, and then when we're finished, I'm sure it will be what you want.' I said fine.

"Well, about a month later a script was submitted to me at a time when I was in London to meet with Sam and Melnick. So I read the script and said: 'Sam, I'm surprised at you. It's terrible. You didn't do what I asked you to do, and if this is your stamp of approval, then it's beneath what you are capable of.' And Sam looked at me and said: 'I don't know what you're talking about. I didn't write any script.' It turned out that Dan Melnick had gone to a writer named David Z. Goodman and got him to do these changes and then told me that Sam had done them. Well, Sam and I looked at Melnick, and he was abashed by this. But Sam and I said: 'Well, all right. What's done is done. Now let's talk about what's wrong with the script. 'And in one hour we had gone over the salient points of the problems, and Sam said, 'I read you and I think I can deliver.' I said, 'Good enough.' And a short time later we had the script that we all thought and hoped."

It should be pointed out that Melnick's motivation for requesting a second draft from Goodman rather than Peckinpah was simply out of loyalty to the man he had hired to write the screenplay in the first place. Goodman, whose credits include *Lovers and Other Strangers, Monty Walsh,* and *Logan's Run,* remained on the picture even following Peckinpah's rewrite and would eventually do a week's polish on another film for Peckinpah several years later called *The Getaway.* Goodman stated: "The only thing left from the book as far as the screenplay goes was the 'siege' itself. I did the first and second drafts, and Sam did a rewrite on that. It was something that Sam liked and wanted to shoot, but the producing company [ABC] was not willing to shoot immediately. As frequently happens in motion pictures, they just really weren't sure there was a picture there. And Sam wrote and changed a great deal in order to keep the project alive. . . .

"Then at the point we were actually going to make the picture there was a certain amount of editing on the script that Marty Baum wanted done in England. Sam did this, and I was never present for any of those changes. I must say though, of all the drafts of that scrip—even the ones Sam did himself—he always put my name first. He never said to Dan Melnick at any time prior to, during, or after shooting that he thought his name should be above mine or alone. And that is more charitable than many other writers would have been in this business. And I should also say that Sam doesn't fight something that is good. If he likes it, he leaves it alone. He's a good writer and respects good writing. I have always had an excellent working relationship with him."

While the central action sequence of both the novel and the film remains the same—that of an isolated farmhouse besieged by a group of locals intent on destruction and murder—the novel differs substantially from the film. Most notably, the hero, George

Magruder, is a professor of English not astromathematics; his wife, Louise, is not raped; Henry Niles is not the village idiot but a convicted child murderer who has escaped from an asylum after ten years of confinement; and Janice Hedden (a girl of eight in the book but thirteen in the film) has not been with Niles but only lost her way turning up alive the next day. The author of the book totally disclaimed the film, not because of its violence (for the book was just as violent) but because of its sex.

As Peckinpah attempted to rewrite Goodman's second draft, he found himself with a familiar difficulty. Katy Haber, a tall dark-haired English secretary, who more recently has become a production executive with producer Michael Deeley, remembered: "I was working for an English producer who was due to make a picture in the States, and it fell through so I was out of a job. But Wimbledon came along and I've always been a tennis nut, so I decided rather than worry about a job I'd just take a vacation and see the matches. Then a friend of mine—another producer named Jimmy Swann--called me and said that Sam Peckinpah was in town and he needed a script typed because he was going to start shooting soon. So I called Peckinpah and Sam said, 'Can you make it here in half an hour?' And I said, 'No, it would take more like an hour.' And Sam said, 'Too late,' and hung up. So I went to the matches.

"The very next day I got a call at Wimbledon asking me to please call Mr. Peckinpah again. So I called and Sam said, 'I need you here in ten minutes.' I said: 'I'm sorry. It will take me more like half an hour.' He said, 'Forget it,' and hung up again.

"Two weeks later, Wimbledon was over. I'd seen all the tennis I wanted and was ready to start looking for a job. So I was having coffee with Jimmy Swann, and he asked me if I was still looking for work. And I said, 'I suppose so,' and he told me to come with him. So he took me into the offices of Universal Studios [in London] and introduced me to Sam Peckinpah. He said, 'Katy, this is Sam Peckinpah.' I said, 'How do you do?' Sam said: 'Over there is the script. I want you to type it.' So I said, 'So you want to give me another chance, do you?' And Sam just gave me one of those looks like 'Where the hell did you find her?'

"He had gone through five secretaries in two weeks. They were all nine-to-fivers, and Sam is not. I started typing the rewrite on Wednesday afternoon, and on Sunday night at two-thirty in the morning we finished it—from Wednesday to Sunday around the clock. And the opening scene that I had to type was the rape scene, and I thought, 'Jesus Christ, who am I working for, Jack the Ripper?' But we went on from there, and I've been working for Sam between firings ever since."

Among the changes that Peckinpah would make on the Goodman script was to alter the title from *The Siege of Trencher's Farm* to *Straw Dogs* based on a quotation remembered by Peckinpah's close friend and associate Walter Kelley and attributed to the Chinese philosopher Lao-tse: "Heaven and earth are ruthless and treat the myriad creatures as straw dogs; the sage is ruthless and treats the people like straw dogs."

Peckinpah also reworked the basic concept of the film in terms of age. *"Straw Dogs* started out to be a much different film," recalled Haber. "The man was going to be much older. The choice was Jack Nicholson [of *Five Easy Pieces* and *Chinatown]* and Carol White [*Poor* Cow] for the girl. And people like Richard Harris and Robert Shaw and other older, established English actors for the gang. Sam brought it down, made it younger."

Screenwriter Goodman stated: "Until Dustin Hoffman said he would do it, nothing was happening. That occurred in October of 1970. Then I came back on the picture. I worked with Dustin in New York doing research on his character. We went to a couple of universities together because he was supposed to be a professor. Then I went to England where I worked with Dustin and Sam. So basically, that's what the script represents: Sam's work, my work, and in all honesty, a substantial contribution by Dustin. This continued during production in terms of his prodding Sam and myself in certain areas that he felt were murky and should be cleared up. The basic characterization of David Sumner represented an enormous amount of research and work on Dustin's part, and I think it showed on the screen."

Dustin Hoffman, an actor of considerable range whose films include *The Graduate, Midnight Cowboy,* and *Kramer vs. Kramer,* for which he received an Academy Award, remembered: "I had read the script for *Straw Dogs* and shown an interest in it. I agreed to do it after looking at the films Sam had done that I had not already seen. Then I met with David Goodman, and he and I worked for several months together on the script because Sam was not available. I think he was in London doing preproduction at the time. Then David and I went to London and showed Sam what we had done. And Sam agreed with some of it and disagreed with some of it.

"The reason I agreed to do the film was because of the script and the potential that I thought was there. What appealed to me was the notion, on paper at least, of dealing with a so-called pacifist who was unaware of the feelings and potential for violence inside himself that were the very same feelings he abhorred in society. The best example of that type of person is the liberal who professes to be antiwar and antiviolence and then goes to the boxing matches or watches the football game and screams his head off. He is totally unaware of that contradiction within himself.

"The way I envisioned the character of David Sumner in the scripting stage of the production differed somewhat from what happened on the screen. I saw him as fleeing the violent campus situation in America for the peaceful English countryside on a conscious level, while on an unconscious level he would begin to set up the situation of conflict in the small town he went to. In other words, I saw the town as being completely indifferent towards him at the outset of the film, and then in snide little ways he would turn them against him because he carried his violence with him. That was the thing that I found exciting about the script. The fact that Sam and I differed over this concept doesn't mean we didn't work well together. I must say I admire his creativity and craftsmanship as a filmmaker....

"The other area we disagreed on was the casting of Susan George as Amy. Sam sent me screen tests of her and some other girls, and I went to London to meet her. She seemed very nice and I thought she could act and we had a nice rapport, but I said to Sam, 'I just feel she's the wrong type for a guy who's a teacher in college. You're opening up a whole big can of beans as to why he married this young kind of Lolita-ish girl.' I could see a woman in her late twenties. Also the whole rape thing. I thought a woman who was a little older and starting to feel a little out of it in terms of being attractive—had a sensuality but was losing it—might be more ambivalent about being raped. Sam said he agreed and that I shouldn't worry because he could get that out of her. He even went so far as to say that he wouldn't do the picture without her. He asked me, 'Please go with my hunch.' I said, 'All right.' I still think I was right. Not that it didn't work the way we did it, but it worked in a different way." Among the girls tested but not selected for the part of Amy by Peckinpah were actress Judy Geeson (*To Sir, With Love* and *Three Into Two Won't* Go) and an English secretary named Joie Gould who was Peckinpah's girlfriend at the time.

For the supporting cast, Peckinpah selected British character actor

Peter Vaughan (*Village of the Damned, Alfred the Great)* to play the older Tom Hedden. As the four rowdies who attack the house with Hedden, Peckinpah chose younger relatively unknown London actors: Del Henney (Charlie Venner), Ken Hutchison (Norman Scutt), Jim Norton (Chris Cawsey), and Donald Webster (Phil Riddaway). Actor-writer Colin Welland, whose screenplay for *Chariots of Fire* would receive considerable acclaim a decade later, was cast as the Reverend Hood. Peckinpah also persuaded ABC Pictures to use David Warner as Niles despite the fact that he had two broken feet and was uninsurable at the time. Warner agreed to appear uncredited.

In terms of assembling a crew, Peckinpah would be restricted by the English guilds to a single American. He had planned to bring in editor Lou Lombardo to cut the picture, but Lombardo had unfortunately begun work on Robert Altman's *McCabe and Mrs. Miller* by the time *Straw Dogs* was ready to roll and had to decline Peckinpah's offer. Paul Davies, Roger Spottiswoode, and Tony Law-son, three British editors, were hired to cut the picture.

Among the other British crew members on *Straw Dogs* was Alf Fegley, a property master with a strong cockney accent. Fegley stated: "Sam Peckinpah is more demanding than any other director I've ever worked with. What I do in propping a show for Sam is to first read the script and try and figure out how many props I think will be called for. Then I go out searchin' for 'em. I always try to get a variety of each item 'cause you want to give Sam the max-imum amount of selection. Then I lay everything out on a big table and Sam'll go over it with me sayin': 'This is good. This is a maybe. Definitely not this' and so forth. When he finishes, I scrap the ones he definitely don't want and go out and start searching all over again. And we repeat the process till I've got a variety of possi-bles on every item so that the moment on the picture he calls for a certain prop, I not only can give him the one he thought was best when he first looked at 'em but I've got backups in case things have changed.

"The prop man's job is a lot of work 'cause you've got to be-come an expert on everything that's needed for the show you're on—from weaponry to ladies' shawls and toiletry. If somethin' don't work, it's my job to fix it so it does. And on Sam's show you never can coast. He's always got you thinkin' ahead, tryin' to an-ticipate. No matter how hard I try I never feel like I'm completely covered. But that makes me try even harder, which is good for the show. And if things start going too well, Sam'll sometimes give you a good shakeup just to keep you on your toes."

While the preproduction work on *Straw Dogs* continued throughout the fall and into the new year, Peckinpah brought Frank Kowalski and Walter Kelley over to England. Kelley helped Peckinpah with *Straw Dogs* while Kowalski worked on *Bring Me the Head of Alfredo Garcia.* They took up quarters with Peckinpah, writing during the day so that Peckinpah could rewrite at night. To Kowalski also fell the household chores.

"I'll never forget coming home one evening," recalled Peckinpah with a smile, "and finding Frank standing there, pissed to the gills, in an apron and holding a broom. I walked through the door, and he looked at me deadpan and said, 'Jesus Christ, you don't ever take me anywhere!'"

Strother Martin, who with his wife, Helen, also visited Peckinpah in England, confirmed the Kowalski-Peckinpah "odd couple" arrangement: "Frank Kowalski was staying with Sam at the time, and I think he coined the all-time understatement about Sam when I asked him how it'd been going. Frank just looked at me with this really hopeless expression on his face and said very seriously, 'You know, Sam isn't the easiest person in the world to live with!'"

It had been Strother Martin who, following the completion of *The Wild Bunch,* had given Peckinpah a copy of Robert Ardrey's controversial *African Genesis* because he had felt Ardrey and Peckinpah shared a common attitude toward violence in man. Peckinpah had read the book and had been impressed enough to also read Ardrey's other works, *The Territorial Imperative* and *The Social Contract.* Based on the findings of a number of anthropologists, Ardrey's writings attempt to explain the violent side of man's nature through his evolutionary descent from killer apes. As a consequence of this ancestry, man also shares a number of characteristics with the rest of the animal kingdom, especially a strong instinct for the protection of his territory or home from invasion. Peckinpah stated: "Robert Ardrey is a writer I admire tremendously. I read him after *Wild Bunch* and have reread his books since because Ardrey really knows where it's at, Baby. Man is violent by nature, and we have to learn to live with it and control it if we expect to survive." *Straw Dogs* would reflect much of Ardrey's thesis.

In January of 1971, the production company of *Straw Dogs* moved out to the county of Cornwall, a peninsula in the southwesternmost corner of England where all location shooting would take place. The cast and crew would be housed in the resort town of St. Ives located on the Atlantic side of the peninsula, fifteen miles from the rocky cliffs at Land's End. Peckinpah, however,

184

chose to forego the comforts of town and rented a small cottage for himself on the moor. He also took another cottage nearby so that his children could visit him during the production. The town of St. Buryan, some twelve miles from St. Ives, had been selected as the town described in the script. All other locations were close by.

On January 28 filming began in the middle of the raw, damp cold of the Cornwall winter. The first major problem occurred when the director of photography, Brian Probyn, left the production just shortly after the picture began shooting following a difference of opinion with the producers over the lighting of a major sequence. He was followed by Arthur Ibbetson (*Tunes of Glory, The Chalk Garden)* who walked the sets with Peckinpah one afternoon, read the script, and that evening left for what he described as "religious reasons." Finally British cinematographer John Coquillon *(The Oblong Box, Triple Echo)* was brought in. When he and Peckinpah found they basically agreed on the look of the picture, Coquillon was hired, and he remained throughout the rest of the production.

Owing to bad weather and long hours, Peckinpah contracted a case of London flu complicated by walking pneumonia. With a temperature of 102 degrees, he managed to see a doctor who gave him a shot of penicillin that kept him going another week. However, his condition continued to deteriorate.

"After we'd started the picture, I had a call from Dan Melnick to get to England immediately," recalled Martin Baum. "I was in Los Angeles at the time. Dan said, 'Dustin Hoffman is looking at the rushes every night, and I'm looking at the rushes every night, and they're terrible.' I said, 'All right, I'll come to England immediately.' I went to England and I looked at the week's rushes, and I said I thought they were really terrible and that Sam must be sick. I simply didn't think Sam in good health could do work so badly. And I rushed an insurance doctor up to see him, and sure enough he had walking pneumonia and was totally dehydrated. So we put him in the hospital and closed the picture down.

"Considering this, Dan Melnick and Dustin Hoffman discussed with me the possibility of replacing Sam and I said: 'No, I have great faith in this man. I am only doing this picture because of his concept of it, and I'll gamble that he'll be fine when he comes back to work.' And Sam continued on the picture and brought in a big winner in *Straw Dogs.*

"But I want to make it clear that Dan Melnick as producer on *Straw Dogs* did an excellent job. He had every right to question Peckinpah's ability to continue the picture in the face of walking pneumonia. With a two million-dollar picture, he was the man responsible for seeing to it that it got made."

"The goddamn doctor said they'd take me to the train in an ambulance that night and get me to the London Clinic," recalled Peckinpah. "But the weather report said we were supposed to have a little decent weather the next day for a change—everything had been so fucking awful, and we needed some long shots of the town—so I said I'd shoot the next day and then take the train.

"So we shot what we needed and about four in the afternoon I knocked off, and we went to the pub where I had a couple of scotches. The entire crew and the cast came to see me off. Then I realized that they all looked like they thought they were saying goodbye to a walking corpse. Talk about a strange sensation! That really shook me."

With one arm around his girlfriend Joie and the other around a bottle of scotch, Peckinpah boarded the train and highballed for London where he was hospitalized four days for pneumonia and overexertion. At the end of that time, he was well enough to return to the location and resume the filming of the picture sustained by alcohol and vitamin B12 shots.

With regard to the possibility of replacing Peckinpah, Daniel Melnick stated: "There was no attempt to replace Sam as director on *Straw Dogs*. If I had wanted to replace him as director, I would have replaced him as director. However, at the time Sam got so sick he had to be hospitalized, I had to make contingency plans in the event he couldn't come back to work. When Sam did come back these plans were dropped. And although there were a couple of times in the normal course of stormy events that I might have been tempted to replace Sam, not to mention a couple of others who suggested it, I never really seriously entertained such a notion.

"Obviously, my feelings about Sam are very ambivalent, and I think he generates those feelings. There are personal qualities he has that make those of us who have spent a great deal of time with him think of him as a very good friend and care for him a great deal. I have those feelings. He also has the ability to make you want to kill him a good deal of the time. He's an enormously exploitive, manipulative person. And he has the ability to convince almost anybody of anything. He's very charming while seeming to disdain charm as a bourgeois artifice. He has the ability to make almost everybody who works with him believe that he's the last person in the movie business left with integrity and guts. And then he says things like 'Hell, I'm just a good whore—I go where I'm kicked.' And to some degree, he is saying that to convince people that it is not the

186

case. The strange thing is, Sam doesn't really believe that he's as talented as he is, which is one of the problems he has in life. I think he's an enormously talented person who has dissipated himself and [who] lacks selectivity very often. But his instincts are so creative that with all of the pain he still manages to get something special on film."

As any executive with far-reaching responsibility, a director must rely on many people to keep track of the details. With Sam Peckinpah much of this burden falls on his secretary. Katy Haber stated: "Sam has so much going through his mind that sometimes he will think that he has said something when in fact he hasn't. That's why I take an abundance of notes, so that if he says something, it's down on paper. Then every night I type up my notes and have them mimeographed and distributed to the department heads. That way if Sam says, 'I asked for that,' I can either say, 'Sam, you didn't' or try to anticipate the fact that he's going to ask for it and make sure someone knows. Because if Sam has asked for something, and let's say you've forgotten it, and you come up to Sam and say, 'Sam, before you go any further, I'm sorry to say I haven't got the arc' or 'I didn't get that gun,' he's going to be cross but not half as cross as when he says, 'Now give me that gun' and you say you haven't got it.

"Sam is also a stickler for details. He will reshoot a scene if someone is shooting off a gun and they don't recoil because a blank has no kick to it. If the wardrobe guy brings Sam a hat, Sam will say: 'Take it away, and jump on it, puke on it, and piss on it, and then bring it back and show it to me again.' Sam is always testing you. And he hopes you come through, but he'll not be surprised if you don't.

"The difficult thing on *Straw Dogs* was that the exteriors were all shot in Cornwall, while the interiors were all to be shot in the studio back in London. I had to write out exactly what we'd shot and then weeks later tell Sam exactly what was needed to match continuity. This was all complicated by the fact that the last few days we were shooting in Cornwall, we had to work sixteen to eighteen hours a day to be able to get out of there with that awful weather."

All of the location shooting for *Straw Dogs* was completed by late March and the company returned to London where the remainder of the picture would be shot at the Twickenham Studios. This improvement in physical conditions resulted in an improvement in everyone's attitude. No longer having to fight the inclement weather, Peckinpah was able to devote more energy to what was going on film and to work more closely with his actors.

"Dustin Hoffman was sensational," Peckinpah stated. "An incredible actor. He was so far ahead of me through the first half of the picture, it wasn't even funny. Then somewhere about halfway, we were doing a scene and after we finished he turned to me and smiled and said, 'Got me.' That was it. He realized I had finally caught him. But an actor must bring me something. I do my work, and I expect him to do his. When you work with someone like Dustin Hoffman, you really are up against the best. He forces you to work at controlling the character because he brings so much to the part. I loved working with Dustin."

Strother Martin, who also was a great admirer of Dustin Hoffman's work as an actor, recalled: "I got to see Sam work with Dustin, and they liked each other very much. There was this one scene where Dustin first did it by coming on very strong as the scene opened and then gradually bringing things down until everything was just suggested by innuendo and gestures. 'Beautiful. Print it!' says Sam. 'Now let's do one the other way, Dustin. Where you start down at the bottom and build it right up to the goddamn, fuckin' sky!' And Dustin says: 'Okay. I'll try it. I'll whip it.' And so he did it that way and that's beautiful. 'Print 'em both!' says Sam. And then Dustin says to Sam, 'Which one did you like the best?' And Sam says, 'Well, in the first one I liked this moment, and then in the second I liked this.' And Dustin says: 'Give me one more! Give me one more!' And he tries to catch what Sam likes in both takes. He's a marvelously talented actor."

Speaking of his work in motion pictures, Hoffman explained: "You tend to find yourself in a vacuum in making a film or at least it starts to feel that way, so I always try to find different ways of keeping my performance fresh. And a lot of it has to do with humor and with shocking people and with the real life relationships that exist between the crew and the cast. An actor on stage can make use of his audience. In film you don't have an audience, but you do have the people you're working with, and I have always found that relationship very helpful. It's all intended to bring more vitality to my performance. Occasionally a producer will come on a set and say, 'What's he fuckin' around for?' But most of the time it works out pretty well.

"And Sam is a great help to an actor because the filmmaking process is something he does very well. He is one of the few natural directors I've ever worked with. I don't always agree with him in terms of his vision, and he and I have had some nice big arguments but always with an underlying affection for each other. But in terms of his being a filmmaker, he doesn't have to work at it: he's brilliant, and it seems to come naturally."

"Sam was always trying to break Dustin up," recalled Katy Haber. "There was only once on camera that he ever succeeded. I don't know whether or not you've seen *Straw Dogs* enough to be familiar with it, but you know that scene in his study where David and Amy are chewing gum and she's looking at him and he's looking at her and he starts to break into this grin and just starts to giggle? Well, Sam went down on Susan at that point off screen. Not literally, of course. He just put his head in her lap, and Dustin cracked up.

"But Dustin is worse. When Ken Hutchison [the actor who plays Scutt] had his closeup in the duck shoot sequence where he's supposed to be looking down on Dustin who was sitting on a rock, Dustin was sitting very close to camera. So while Ken was being shot closeup, Dustin began sucking on one of the gear cranks on the tripod, and poor Ken just couldn't take it and broke up completely. But it doesn't always work. Dustin tried to break up Del Henney [the actor who plays Charlie Venner] once, and Del didn't like it at all and called him a Jewish asshole or something right on camera and got really pissed off. But Dustin was always at it. He used to walk into the bar sequence where Tom Hedden and the group were with his trousers down around his knees—things like that. He's just crazy, but it really adds something to everybody's performance."

By the last week of April 1971, *Straw Dogs* moved into the final stages of production. Throughout the project, there had been much discussion over exactly how the picture would end, considering the amount of violence that takes place in the final twenty minutes. The scripted ending called for David and Amy, their attackers dead or dying, to suddenly be confronted by the children of the town led by Tom Hedden's son, Bobby. The children, all carrying sticks and clubs, survey the bodies and then close in on the Sumners who stand on the stairs. The last line of the screenplay reads:

[DAVID] SLIPS CATLIKE down the stairs toward them and AMY is suddenly at his side, their weapons ready.

Just like the rest of us. Sooner or later.

FREEZE FRAME.

Peckinpah recalled: "Marty Baum kept insisting that *Straw Dogs* have a happy ending, and I kept saying that I would try but it had to be in keeping with the story. So we got down to the end of

189

shooting and David Warner, Dustin, and I were sitting discussing the possibilities and David said, 'I don't know my way home.' And I immediately turned to Dustin, and I said, 'And you don't either!' And Dustin said: 'Right. That's the only way it could end.' So that's the way we shot it, and it worked."

This new ending is both less pessimistic than the original and more ambiguous. The exact meaning of David's reply to Henry Niles's claim of not knowing his way home ("That's all right. I don't either") is left up to the individual viewing the film. On one hand, it can be read as David's acknowledgment that he is capable of violence and can no longer deny that part of his human psyche. On the other, it may be seen as his realization that his relationship with his wife (i.e., their home) has been lost forever by virtue of her actions during the course of the fight: she betrayed him by attempting to open the door following the murder of Major Scott and failed to respond to his urgent need for her to shoot Riddaway until it was almost too late.

"When Sam directs," stated Haber, "he lives his films. He's into every part, and the actors start to take on the characteristics of the parts they are playing for him. He hated Susan George by the end of *Straw Dogs*. No, that's not entirely correct. He hated Amy and Susan *was* Amy. I suppose, from an actress's point of view, that's quite a compliment in a weird sort of way." As a gift for working on the picture, Sam Peckinpah gave Susan George a gift suited to the character she had created: a bouquet of lollipops and leeks.

The principal photography of *Straw Dogs* was completed the last week in April 1971. Within a month, Peckinpah returned to the United States to work on his next picture, *Junior Bonner,* bringing with him the uncut footage and his English editors. The picture would be cut and scored in America.

Once again, the task of writing an original score for the film fell to composer Jerry Fielding. "The only advantage I have over the rest of the people on any film," recounted Fielding, "is that I come on late, after they have all worn themselves down and talked themselves into the forest so hard that they don't know what's growing there any more.

"Straw Dogs is a very well-constructed film. It goes straight on and horrifyingly beyond where you think it is going to go. And it's the hardest picture to score that I've ever encountered in thirty-three years. Writing the music isn't all that tough. It's how to

deal with *that subject* and make it work because that picture *defies* scoring.

"As on all pictures with Sam, we had terrible fights. But long ago I gave up trying to please directors. Actually, from my point of view, I kind of gave up trying to be liked period. It's kind of hopeless in a business like this. I'd like to be liked, of course, but if I know that I'm right and the director doesn't understand why, it is usually because of a great well of ignorance about scoring a film on his part. Now, nobody expects a director to know everything about everything in this business. And like all people who visualize a finished product he has certain preconceptions about what he wants. But he depends heavily upon the people around him to tell him whether these preconceptions will work or are just infantile dreaming.

"Sam, like all directors, will express what he wants to come out in a score in terms of something specific, which is asinine, and then you have to figure out what he means by what he's saying.

"It is very difficult for Sam to surround himself with a bunch of guys who work well with him because Sam doesn't relate [verbally] very well. He's hard to talk to. You have to second-guess him, and he's a very instinctive man—I'm talking about craft-wise. You have to guess what he means, and you damn well better be right. So you can't go in on the basis that you're going to please him because that never works. If he thinks you're trying to please him, he'll kill you. If he thinks you know what you're doing, he'll fight with you, and you'd better fight back. He doesn't murder people for being wrong, but what he can't stand—and he's right there—is a weak attitude about it. I have finally gotten to the point where I can say to him either 'You're an asshole!' or 'You really don't want that' or 'You don't believe it' or 'You won't like it' or simply 'I refuse to do it.'

"And I must say that for all the battling Sam and I have done, Sam is unique from all the other directors I've worked with in that when you catch them being wrong they come to you and thank you and throw a party for you and then never want to work with you again because they realize that you know their weakness and they don't like that. Sam hasn't got that Hollywood ego problem at all. He doesn't make a practice of developing a sham personality out of horseshit and hot air. After all the fights I've had with him, he's the only director in my experience who's come back after the dust has cleared and said, 'You were right and I was wrong, and let's go at it again.'

"I sat with Sam on the spottings [a viewing of the film after it has been edited to decide at which points music is needed] on *Straw Dogs*. And you must pay no attention to Sam's idea of where to spot a movie because he wants music everywhere. Any scene he's uncomfortable with, he wants music under it and all over it, so you don't listen to that.

"Also, he will say very precisely at times, 'I want music right here,' but he'll never tell you where he wants it to stop. 'Where would you have me go out, Sam?' You'll never get an answer to that one. So you have to decide for yourself. I've largely taken to writing Sam memos about what I intend to do—half of which I'm sure he doesn't even read—but at least everything is up front when the screaming starts.

"Anyway, on *Straw Dogs* Sam came in here and we had an agonizing discussion on what the picture needed, and he used the word 'irony.' Now it's hard to say to someone, 'Now go downstairs and write me something ironic.' Irony is hard to capture in the abstract. It only exists in relation to something. However, on this picture I knew what he meant. The mocking, diabolical twists of fate in this picture which finally place the hero in an inescapable position—the word is 'ironic.'

"Now with Sam you are dealing with an illiterate musical mind. So I had to find what 'irony' meant to him in musical terms. So I played several pieces of music I thought were particularly acid and ironic, and one of them he fell in love with. So based on that indication, I wrote the entire score.

"The main title music for the picture was written the day before I left for England after being on the phone with that 'Have-you- got-us-a-singable-song-so-that-we-can-have-the-album-cover- printed?' routine and all that bullshit. The problem with scoring the picture was that it was a terrifying film and the terror grows. What do you do? You can't tip the mint and say where this picture is going as it opens, so what do you do? There is nothing lovable or lyrical about that movie—ever! So what I did was an ironclad, brass-choired thing which was very theatrical and very dramatic and which said to me: *Pay attention because something very important is going to happen in this theater.* But I didn't say what. It therefore was a unique main title.

"Dan Melnick, when he heard it, his face hit the floor. I thought he was going to have me arrested. They didn't like the score. Yet I was the only one who got a[n Academy Award] nomination on that picture, which wasn't fair in light of Dustin Hoffman's incredible performance in the film but nevertheless true. Sam loved the score, however, because I knew what he was after.

"So what I suppose I'm really saying is that with an old fashioned guy such as I see myself to be, there is a certain dedication to the end result which is all-prevailing to the point where it makes you not even a human being—your personal life is a mess, you have no friends, and there is nothing with any real meaning except

your work. You can't take the garbage handed out by these late arrivals, these certified public accountants who suddenly become great artist-producers. And if you manage to get rid of all that excess weight and get down to the actual doing and you work on a picture like *Wild Bunch* or *Straw Dogs,* it's all worthwhile."

The film was first released in London late in 1971 and met with almost universal disapproval from British reviewers. Within a month, these same writers would sing the praises of Stanley Kubrick's *A Clockwork Orange,* claiming that it should not become the "victim" of the backlash caused by Peckinpah's "irresponsible and gratuitous" use of violence in *Straw Dogs.*

Writing six months later in the British film journal *Screen* (Summer 1972), critic Charles Barr took these writers to task for their irrational and simpleminded point of view in the long article *"Straw Dogs, A Clockwork Orange* and the Critics." In it, Barr notes the antagonistic position taken by the majority of the reviewers: "Thirteen of them wrote to *The Times* [of London] in December [1971] condemning *Straw Dogs* as 'dubious in its intention, excessive in its effect.'" Then critic by critic he points out how each has rejected the film on the basis of his own emotional response. Ironically, the critics are condemning the film for allowing "passion to swamp reason," while refusing to see that very failing in themselves.

Late in December of 1971, *Straw Dogs* was released in America (although slightly cut to make the second rape less specific in order to get an R rather than an X rating from the Motion Picture Association of America) and proceeded to polarize the critics for the most part into two camps—those for ("It is hard to imagine that Sam Peckinpah will ever make a better movie than *Straw Dogs,"* wrote Paul Zimmerman in the December 20, 1971, issue of *Newsweek)* and those opposed ("I would have walked out of *Straw Dogs* if I'd been anything but a professional critic," reported Gary Arnold in the *Washington Post,* January 10, 1972). As might be expected, those who opposed the film tended to duplicate the hysteria of the English reviewers.

In an interesting follow-up, two American psychiatrists, Dr. Fedor Hagenauer and Dr. James W. Hamilton, were so struck by the intense character relationships in *Straw Dogs* that they felt compelled to psychoanalyze in effect the major characters in the film as if they were real people in order to explain in a clinical sense why they exhibited the sometimes violent and aggressive behavior that they did. In an article published in *American Imago* (Fall 1973) they conclude that David Sumner's actions are indeed credible. They also speculate on Peckinpah's motivations: "It would seem plausible that Peckinpah is struggling to master some of his own conflicts through his filmmaking, and that the quality of his work bespeaks an unusual talent and creative capacity."

As a final note, several months after the release of *Straw Dogs, Playboy* magazine made Peckinpah the subject of an in-depth interview, which was carried in the August 1972 edition. They also sent a prepublication copy of this interview to author Robert Ardrey in the hope of soliciting a printable comment. A copy of Ardrey's reply, dated July 29, 1972, was given to Peckinpah who framed it and hung it on his wall. It reads:

> *"I am sorry I can make no significant comment on the Peckinpah interview since I have never seen any of his films. I have been curious about them but living abroad, one has few opportunities to see other than dubbed versions which I abhor.*
>
> *"There is one large point on which I can firmly support him: until we have the courage to grasp the whole of human reality, we possess a small hope for improvement of the human condition. This has been my thesis that has been the total inspiration for my own work, a thesis which, as far as I know, has firmly eluded the editors of Playboy. A portion of that human reality is our propensity for violence finding testament in the whole of human history from the walls of 9,000 years ago to this morning's paper. I have every hope for a human future that accepts the challenge existing within every heart; I have none for the future dominated by those so sentimental or so cowardly, so brainwashed or so ridden with ideological dogma that they can resort to nothing but the meaningless cry of 'fascist' when confronted by inconvenient truths. Peckipah may exaggerate but so did Eugene O'Neill. So do I sometimes when what I regard as truth must be driven home. For such exaggeration might be condemned as fault were not we confronted by the dense armor of contemporary sophistry."*

Junior Bonner

"...still workin' on eight seconds."

Because the United States imposes a tax on income earned by its citizens outside the country unless they remain abroad for a certain number of months, Sam Peckinpah's intention was to stay in England following *Straw Dogs* until that time had elapsed. However, in early May 1971, two months before his time was up, Peckinpah was approached again by Martin Baum of ABC Pictures with another project: *Junior Bonner.*

Scripted by screenwriter Jeb Rosebrook, *Junior Bonner* was the story of an aging rodeo rider who returns to his hometown rodeo. It appealed to Peckinpah because it demonstrated his own values while providing a basically nonviolent story in which he could explore them. With the success of *The Wild Bunch,* the lack of distribution of *The Ballad of Cable Hogue,* and the highly volatile material he had dealt with in *Straw Dogs,* Peckinpah was concerned about being typed as a director of violent action. Although it meant a substantial financial loss in taxes, Peckinpah decided to return to California to begin preparation for *Junior Bonner,* bringing with him the uncompleted *Straw Dogs.*

The producer of the picture was Joe Wizan, a young man who had spent eleven years as an agent before becoming a producer in 1969. Since that time he produced a number of pictures, including *Jeremiah Johnson, Prime Cut,* and *The Last American Hero.* On his desk stands a wooden plaque that asks simply, "Trust me."

"Junior Bonner was my second picture as a producer," stated Wizan. "My first had been *Jeremiah Johnson.* As with most of the projects I've done, *Junior Bonner* was a coming together of the right elements at the right time. Steve McQueen wanted to do a 'soft' picture and really fell in love with Jeb Rosebrook's script. Sam wanted to do something in a more nonviolent vein. So I felt myself to be something of a catalyst in helping it all to happen.

"From the time Sam stepped off the plane from London until

we started shooting, we had only five weeks. We had to cast it, find our locations, build whatever sets we needed, everything in five weeks because the story centered around the Prescott Frontier Days Rodeo which occurs only once a year. And on top of all this and through much of the shooting, Sam was editing *Straw Dogs* at night. And despite all of this, we came in on schedule.

"Sam is not an easy man to work with. You have to anticipate him a great deal of the time. Yet the qualities he brings out in a picture are so good that it makes all the difficulty worthwhile. Sam draws on everyone around him, and he is incredibly loyal. A good example is Jeb Rosebrook who didn't know Sam before *Junior Bonner* but worked hard on the script to give Sam what he wanted. Sam kept Jeb on the picture from beginning to end even when we didn't have to. But that is because Sam is secure in his own talent."

Rosebrook had come to Hollywood in 1967 from New York where he had written his first novel, *Saturday,* which was published in 1965. He has since written extensively for both television and motion pictures, including *The Waltons, I Will Fight No More Forever,* and *The Black Hole.* Because he had suffered from asthma as a boy, he had spent his teenage years living with relatives in Prescott, Arizona. It was this experience that formed the basis for the screenplay *Junior Bonner.*

"My first meeting with Sam was in late May," Rosebrook remembered. "We were scheduled to start shooting on June thirtieth, and I hadn't even begun to rewrite yet. Sam had talked to Max Evans about doing the rewrite if I couldn't. Sam and I flew to Phoenix on about the fifth of June and went from there to Prescott. It was on that trip that Sam and I really first got to know each other. He insisted that I start immediately on the rewrite and that if I couldn't produce, he and Max Evans were standing right behind me and they would.

"I had been away from the rodeo and its jargon for so long at that point that I didn't really have a lot of its terminology and color in my original script. But Sam helped me a great deal in this area because Sam knows rewrite. He is a master rewrite man. By the time we were into production, I had Ben Johnson living on one side of me and Casey Tibbs on the other and between Ben, Casey, and Sam, I really got into the material."

Both Casey Tibbs and Ben Johnson are former rodeo hands. Tibbs, who was hired as technical advisor and rodeo stunt coordinator on the picture, won his first world championship in bronco riding at nineteen in 1949. The premiere rodeo rider of the 1950s, he won nine world championships, including being named all-around champion twice.

Johnson, who plays rodeo stockman Buck Roan in the film, recalled his days on the rodeo circuit: "I won the championship in 1953 team ropin' championship. That was the year everybody else had hard luck. I sorta just took off. I never had money enough to buy all the equipment you need to go rodeoin' before then—the horses, trailers, cars, and what have you. Then, finally, when I got in a position where I could buy all this stuff, I decided, by George, I'd just buy whatever I needed and try it. So I quit everything—the picture business and everything else—and went rodeoin'.

"And fortunately I won the world's championship. Of course, at the end of the year I didn't have any money, so fortunately they took me back in the picture business. I made quite a lot of money that year, but I had to help my friends along the way get on to the next show, y'know. And those kinda deals, they never repay you, and you don't expect 'em to. I couldn't drive off from one of those shows and leave my friends sittin' there with no money to get on to the next one. So, consequently, at the end of that year, why I didn't have a cent to my name.

"So my feelin' was that if you was the best at somethin' and couldn't make a livin' at it, you'd better do somethin' else. But the fact that I had accomplished what I'd set out to do made it a pretty big day in my life all the same. My Dad, he was a world's champion five or six times, and I'd always wanted to be a world's champion doin' somethin'. It was a good feelin' just knowin' I could do it."

These attitudes toward friends, family, and the attraction of the transitory life of the rodeo had been at the core of the Rosebrook script. Recognizing this, Peckinpah sought to bring them into sharp focus and point out their inherent conflict with the development of the American Dream in the twentieth century.

After Steve McQueen agreed to play the title role, it remained for Peckinpah to cast the balance of the picture's roles. Along with Johnson as Buck, he cast Robert Preston as Junior's father, Ace, and Ida Lupino as his mother, Ellie. Peckinpah selected Joe Don Baker to portray Curly Bonner, and Mary Murphy played his wife. The role of Charmagne, the young woman with whom Junior has a brief affair, finally went to Barbara Leigh, McQueen's girlfriend at the time.

The crew included a number of Peckinpah associates from previous films. Lucien Ballard, whose work with Peckinpah included

Peckinpah's best known features *Ride the High Country* and *The Wild Bunch,* was hired as director of photography. Frank Kowalski, the second unit director, had known Peckinpah since his pretelevision days at Allied Artists as had the picture's art director, Ted Haworth, whose friendship with Peckinpah dated from their working together on *Invasion of the Body Snatchers* (1956). And although prop man Bob Visciglia had only met Peckinpah working on *The Ballad of Cable Hogue,* he had made enough of an impression that Peckinpah requested him for *Junior Bonner* as well.

Several weeks into the preproduction planning of the film, Peckinpah found himself once again unable to keep a secretary. Katy Haber remembered: "After we finished *Straw Dogs* and Sam was leaving for the States, he said that of course he couldn't take an English secretary with him, but he was certain he'd return to England and we'd work together again. Three weeks later I get a phone call: 'Get your ass over here!' He'd tried a couple of secretaries, and it just didn't work. So I packed a couple of things and went off to *Junior Bonner,* working for expenses."

In the meanwhile, *Junior Bonner* was already in rehearsal owing to the impending start of principal photography. Ida Lupino, whose distinguished career as an actress includes such pictures as *They Drive by Night* and *High Sierra* and who remains one of Hollywood's few female directors (*Outrage* [1950], *The Hitch-Hiker,* and *The Trouble with Angels),* recalled her first rehearsal with Peckinpah: "When I was first being considered for the role of the mother in *Junior Bonner,* I had heard that Sam was 'charmingly eccentric.' Actually, I don't think that people used exactly those words, but I had liked *Ride the High Country* very much and decided to take a chance. In our first meeting on the picture, Sam briefed me on what he wanted the mother to look like, mature but still attractive and so forth.

"Then after we finished he walked up to me and hugged me and said: 'Hmmmmm. Still smells as beautiful as ever.' And I just looked at him and said, 'What on earth are you talking about?' And Sam just looked at me. He had a mustache, and a bandana around his head. And he said, 'Don't you remember *Private Hell 36* when I came up to you and asked, "What is that wonderful smell?"' And suddenly it all came back to me. Sam had been dialogue director on that picture for Don Siegel, but with the mustache and bandana I just hadn't recognized him. But in all that time, he'd remembered my perfume!"

While rehearsals and script revision continued, July and the rodeo drew closer. The use of the Prescott Rodeo as a backdrop would add a dimension of immediacy to the film not otherwise obtainable. It also would place more pressure on all concerned, for certain events would only happen once. One of these was the Frontier Days Parade that preceded the rodeo.

"The parade sequence in *Junior Bonner* was like a military arrangement," recalled Haber. "It could only be shot once, so Sam and the producer decided to go with a multiple camera setup. We sat in a room about twenty feet square with every single member of the crew and a big board with a diagram of the operation. When that session was finished I had to give notes to every camera crew. One would be on top of the cinema; one on top of the Palace Bar; one on a float—on Curly's float. Another would be a roving camera like a television news camera, and Sam was to be on that. Another was in one of the hot dog stands next to where Ida comes up to watch the parade. One was located where Ace and Junior leave the parade and cut through the crowd and another on the other side where they actually break through. Even with all this planning, we still had a couple of problems like Steve getting off Curly's float at the wrong point. But the footage was really super, and [it] cut together very well."

Then there was the rodeo itself to be photographed with the help of technical advisor Casey Tibbs. Johnson, Tibbs's longtime friend, recalled their first meeting before either was involved in films: "The first time I seen Casey was in Cheyenne, Wyoming, when he was fourteen years old. He come in there to the rodeo and tried to enter the bronc ridin'. They told him he was too young so he went home and got his mother. She came back with him and entered him in the bronc ridin', and Casey proceeded to win it. Then the next year he come back and did it again. He is some kind a rider."

Tibbs broke into motion pictures in 1951 in Budd Boetticher's film *Bronco Buster,* in which he not only played a part but doubled as stunt rider for everybody else in the picture. Since then, aside from his rodeo work, he has appeared in a great many motion pictures as a rider and stuntman. He currently runs a rodeo school near San Diego, California.

Speaking of his work on *Junior Bonner,* Tibbs stated: "Rodeo stunt work is like everything else: you've got to get the right kind of personnel geared for it. Like the bull-riding sequence. Sam had scheduled, I think, a day and a half for it, and we got it in the camera in forty-four minutes the first day. And this'll showya somethin' about Sam 'cause everybody's always on him about how he's out for blood and tryin' to kill people: the minute we had what he wanted, he made me cut it off, and I hadn't even started on the stunts yet. My stuntmen had all their gimmicks and their rigs ready to go, but we got it without having to use any of them because things just worked out in a natural way. I think we got some terrific stuff, but I think we could have improved on it without getting anybody hurt. But Sam said no. That was it."

Because the picture starred Steve McQueen, whose popular image, prior to his unfortunate death from a rare form of cancer in 1980, suggested he did his own stunt work, a word should be said about the realities of major stars doing their own stunts. For the most part, stars are not allowed to do their own stunts because of the risk involved and the resulting insurance problems. Should the star be hurt, awaiting his recovery could tie up the production for weeks; and if he were killed, everything shot up to that point involving him would have to be scrapped. Steve McQueen was something of an exception.

Casey Tibbs stated: "Steve damn sure did do some of his own stunts. He wanted to do a bunch of 'em. He's pretty game. He told me right off, he says: 'I'll tell you somethin'. I don't particularly like horses.' But he did like the one he was riding, and he got to likin' horses better than he ever did before. He even got on this one bull and insisted on coming out of the chute on him. You know, many things can happen right in the chute, and even just jumpin' off a bull can get you hurt. McQueen's all right."

However, the bulk of the extremely dangerous stunts were given to the stuntmen brought in by Tibbs. For closeups, McQueen was photographed on a mechanical bucking machine. "When Steve had to ride the mechanical bull for the closeups," recalled Katy Haber, "he was so mad that he wouldn't allow anyone to watch him. He wasn't able to do the calf roping either, although he did do his own stunts in the wild cow milking. But then there is a big insurance problem in things like that." Because of his highly competitive attitude, McQueen quickly gained Peckinpah's respect and friendship.

When the rodeo sequences were finally completed, a small problem developed. Casey Tibbs remembered: "I had completed my work there with the end of the rodeo and Ben [Johnson] had gotten a release to go home and do some dubbing on *The Last Picture Show*. Ben don't like to fly, so we drove back in his pickup. We both had releases from the company, but nobody'd told Sam about it. We were both comin' back whenever they needed us. It was just that they shouldn'ta needed us for some time.

"We had to drive all night to get back home. Then at one the next afternoon the phone started ringin'. Well, Sam and I had the same business manager, and they [Sam's assistants] called him and he called me and wanted to know why I'd left without getting Sam's permission? Well, to make a long story short, in an hour and fifteen minutes from that phone call Ben and I met at Burbank Airfield and were flown back to Prescott in a Lear Jet actually for no particular reason but that Sam wanted us there."

Johnson substantiated the story and added: "Sam really didn't care about us. The shot he wanted us for had me ridin' by in a car and Casey walkin' down the sidewalk, both of us from here to the barn from the camera. Neither of us was clearly identifiable. What Sam was after was to prove to the studio who was boss on his picture."

Tibbs summed up his work with Peckinpah in the following anecdote: "I like Sam very much. I enjoyed workin' with him probably as much as any director I've ever worked with 'cause he don't want any lightweights around, and he won't take any kiss assin'. If you think you're right and you prove your point with him, he'll say, 'Okay, let's have it that way.' But he'll damn sure put the hot iron to your feet and the pliers to your tongue till you prove it to him.

"I think I put it to him one night when we weren't too far from throwin' fists. I liked the picture and I liked the job, but I wasn't gonna get completely stomped down and I told Sam, 'One thing about it, we've got a hell of a break.' And Sam says, 'What's that?' And I said: "Cause you weigh about 140 pounds, and if you weighed 200, you'd charge everybody in the world five dollars an hour to live!'"

In the real Prescott Rodeo, there are two sessions: one during the day and one at night. In his original script, Rosebrook had used this format as well. In revising it for shooting, however, it was decided that both sessions should be held during the day with a break in between during which everyone adjourns to the Palace Bar.

What resulted was an inspired bit of character development by Mc-Queen. Rosebrook recalled: "The concept of Joe Don Baker as Steve's brother laying one on him in the bar was Steve's idea. I had originally set their confrontation at night as Steve was heading over to ride the bull and Curly would simply say to Junior the business about 'I'm working on my first million, and you're still working on eight seconds.' It was strictly verbal, nothing physical at all. I must say that Steve's idea was a damn good bit of business. And Sam picked right up on it and staged it in the Palace Bar followed by a brawl which would be stopped when the band started playing 'The Star-Spangled Banner.' Sam's instincts here were much better than mine because at this point I think I was much more into character rather than story."

201

"The barroom brawl was fun to do," Haber recalled. "All of the extras in the scene were from right there in Prescott, and they really loved it. Those people were really fighting. Those girls were just incredible. They punched each other and pulled each other's hair. And there was that little Indian guy you see in the film, Curtis, who follows the girls into the toilet. And at the end when the big guy asks him, 'Why are you always chasing girls, Curtis?' He says, "cause I lub 'em!' Well, we had to bail him out of jail every morning just to get him on the set. He would have done that role for just beer."

Not all of the fights in this sequence occurred on film, however. The script called for Junior and Ace to arrive at the Palace Bar and order a drink. Then Curly and his family would arrive followed by Arliss, the nurse interested in Ace, and finally Ellie, Ace's wife. Because Ace and Ellie are estranged and meeting here for the first time in quite a while, Peckinpah envisioned it as a highly emotional confrontation putting Ellie on the verge of tears. In attempting to get the effect he wanted, he struck out verbally at Ida Lupino in much the same fashion that he had dealt with Stella Stevens on *Cable Hogue.*

"It took seven days to shoot the barroom sequence," remembered Lupino, "and the place was filled with people. Because Sam had told me to make the character of Junior's mother mature but still attractive, I was wearing a tan base makeup to look as if I had been in the sun and just a touch of lipstick.

"Well, after the first day's rushes were screened, Sam said: 'Ida, you're looking too good. Take off that lipstick.' So I did, but my lips have always had a natural redness to them, and Sam was still unsatisfied. No matter what I did, it seemed that I just couldn't please him. He had not been in a very good mood that day to begin with, and finally he really blew up over this.

"And that, of course, made me angry, and I went over and stood by the bar very silently. And when my time came to speak, I said: 'You know who you should get for this part? I know the perfect actress. You should get Shelley Winters. I'll stay here until she arrives so that you will have someone for all the long shots where my features won't be distinguishable and you can shoot all the close shots when she arrives.' Well, at that Sam and everybody else began asking me to reconsider, but I was mad and I wouldn't. So finally that's the way we shot it for the remainder of the afternoon.
"When we wrapped for the day, I went back to my motel room and tried to unwind and began to make arrangements to leave. Well,

202

about eight o'clock that night there's a knock at my door. So I open it, and here is this boy standing there with two dozen roses and a note which reads: 'Dear Shelley: Terribly sorry. We know how much you would like this role but we have already fallen in love with Ida Lupino. Signed, Darryl Zanuck.' Well, what can you say to that? So I stayed on the picture and loved it."

In commenting upon Peckinpah's method of directing a picture, producer Joe Wizan stated: "Sam works from an emotional level rather than from an intellectual one. One of the things I like about working with him is that there is no theorizing. Everything comes out of Sam's gut reaction, which is what I personally think movies are all about. He can talk intellectually with you on almost any subject, but he doesn't direct that way."

One of the most highly personal scenes in *Junior Bonner* occurs between Ace and Junior at the railroad station. The scene called for Ace to begin talking about the old times and work the conversation around to asking his son for a grubstake that would allow him to go off to Australia to prospect for gold. The older man is so wrapped up in his scheme that he does not catch at first Junior's confession that despite his standing as a rodeo star, he is flat broke. When this finally sinks in, the old man looks stunned. At a loss for words he takes a half malicious swipe at Junior, knocking his hat across the first pair of railroad tracks. When the old man goes to retrieve the hat, a locomotive pulling several cars passes between them. Then he slowly walks back to his son, who explains that despite his lack of ready cash, he has entered them as a team in the wild cow milking.

Rosebrook recalled: "We were going to do the scene at the railroad station, and Sam told me that the way he wanted to end the scene was with Bob Preston knocking Steve's hat off. He said that when he was younger and had somehow either let his father down or gotten his father angry, Sam's dad had a way of leaning over and cuffing Sam in a way that knocked his hat off. It was then that I realized how much these two characters meant to Sam in a personal way."

However, when Peckinpah went to block the scene out for the camera, a conflict arose between him and McQueen. Lucien Ballard, the director of photography, remembered: "Sam wanted Preston to knock McQueen's hat off in the scene down by the railroad station, but Steve wouldn't go for it. He thought that it would make him look like less of a man—that it demeaned him in some way. Finally, he threw his cup of coffee at Sam and stormed off the set. And all Sam kept saying was 'I want you to try it and see if it works.' Well,

Steve would have no part of it. So I went up to him and explained that in reality, just sitting there and taking your punishment, if you want to call it that, from your father made you more of a man. McQueen seemed to come around at that, and that's the way we shot it. And I think it worked beautifully on the screen."

A habit that McQueen acquired through his years in motion pictures was that of rewriting his scenes to suit himself. Lucien Ballard continued: "Now I know Steve McQueen very well. We've even rented our home to him when we've been out on location. And I've always said exactly what I thought no matter who it was so I'm not saying this behind his back. But Steve is a difficult actor to work with in some ways. For one thing he equates money with success, which makes him very difficult to reason with unless you've made more money than he has. And for another, Steve is constantly rewriting his scenes. Not once but several times. Sam almost quit *Junior Bonner* because Steve was always rewriting. Now you must understand that Sam himself does a lot of rewriting on his pictures, and he's always ready to change a scene. But when he has something that he thinks is working, he has the good sense to leave it alone."

As cameraman on the picture, Ballard was only an observer of this situation. Lupino remembered being a victim: "The moment when Junior and his mother meet in the picture when they're outside, Sam had us adlib that, and it went very well. But when it came time to do the inside portion of that same scene, Steve had rewritten it. I had already learned what I was supposed to say, and I said that I needed more time to learn these new lines. I had loved the original but wasn't as fond of what Steve had changed it to. But I went ahead and tried to be cooperative as possible because I felt that it was necessary for a mother and a son to be motivated by a common background for the scene to work.

"Then when the scene was finally shot, Steve was even ad-libbing the new stuff he'd written. And I was blowing my cues because they just weren't there the way they were supposed to be. Well, then I blew up. Sam shut down for ten minutes to let things subside, and I went over to sit down alone.

"After a little while, Sam sent over one of the crew to ask if I would like a little wine. I couldn't accept, of course, or we'd probably still be shooting that scene. But that kind of kindness was just the right touch to bring me back into the proper frame of mind to complete the scene. The next scene, Steve made another attempt to alter my character, and I was on the verge of blowing up again. But Sam just stopped all discussion by saying: 'Okay, everybody on the set. Let's make a picture.' And I played it the way it was written, and it worked."

While dealing with the problems before the camera, Peckinpah also tested his crew, new and old members alike. Among the newer members was Chuck Wilborn, a sound man who had not previously worked with Peckinpah. He recalled: "We had a scene where Bob Preston comes along looking for Steve and can't find him so he takes off on Steve's horse. Now I work with Sam the same way I do with every director. When I have a problem, I ask him. So I asked Sam where he wanted the mikes placed in the scene and he said: 'No mikes on this. There won't be any sound.'

"So I went away. But I thought that sounded strange, so I put radio [cordless] mikes on all the principals and scattered some others around. Then they started to roll. When they went through the first take, Sam said: 'Cut, print. How was that for sound?' And I said that was just fine for sound. Now at the time I thought that was a really shitty thing to do to someone. But in retrospect, I've come to realize that is simply the way Sam finds out what you're made of. Whether I'd been prepared for that shot or not, there was never a question in my mind after that about how I should mike a scene. It forced me to think everything through. And of course, I have worked with Sam whenever the opportunity has arisen since."

Not all who were tested came through, however. While the number of crew problems did not even approach those on *The Ballad of Cable Hogue,* there were some casualties. One of these, ironically, had even survived *Cable Hogue.* The producer, Joe Wizan, recalled: "I know Sam has this reputation for firing everybody, but most of the people he fires deserve being fired. He is a very loyal and passionate person, and I think that a lot of his problems come about because someone on a picture will not give the 100 percent or 110 percent Sam gives himself. He fired his best friend, Frank Kowalski, off of *Junior Bonner.* And later, although it wasn't my picture, he fired his own daughter Sharon off of *Getaway.* So I guess you can say Sam fires people, but he's not playing any favorites."

"Frank Kowalski is a guy I've known for years," recounted Peckinpah remembering *Junior Bonner.* "And Frank has always said to me, 'We play hard, and we work hard.' He's an enormously talented guy, but on *Junior Bonner* Frank was shooting second unit and doing a half bad job of it—thousands of feet of film. And this particular time we had had a rather large night, so I had Katy

[Haber] call him to be certain he was at this production meeting the next day at noon. Everybody was going to be there—the producers, everybody. The reason Kowalski gave for missing that meeting was 'I.F.D.'—ill from drink. This was about 11:40 in the morning, and the meeting was at noon.

"So noon comes and still no Frank; one o'clock, one-thirty, still no Frank. And he's forty feet away in his room in the hotel! So I said: 'Excuse me. Let's take a break.' And I went to Frank's room and said, 'Frank, you're not at the meeting.' And Frank said: 'I know. I know what I have to do.' And I said, 'Everything has been changed, and I had Katy call you to get your ass over here.' And he said, 'Well, I'm not there, am I?' And I said: 'No, you're not. You're on the bus!' I fired him. I love him as a friend, but on a picture that's bullshit. You play hard, you work hard—his own words. And we've never been quite as close since. He sent me a note: 'Count your pallbearers. You are minus one!' He's a funny guy. I love him. I really do. But work is work." Kowalski would not work with Peckinpah again until *The Killer Elite* four years later.

Among the last things to be shot on *Junior Bonner* was the scene between Ace and Ellie in which they recognize that despite the irreconcilable problems of their marriage, they still love each other. Accepting each other for what they are, they decide to grasp the moment and go off to spend the afternoon together. Peckinpah staged this scene on the back stairs of the Palace Hotel. Lupino recalled: "For the big scene between Bob Preston and me, Sam had just told us basically what he wanted and said to go to work on it. Then, when it came time to do the scene, it rained. Every day it rained, until finally it looked as if we weren't going to get a chance to do the scene at all.

"On the last possible day it was still raining, and we waited two or three hours. Then the rain stopped but the sky was still black. So Lucien Ballard had to light the stairs with arcs.

"We played the scene a couple of times in front of the camera and Sam would say 'Save this' or 'Save that' as little bits would please him. Things like the kids on the stairs would push against us. Finally we came to the most important moment which comes at the very end where [they] stop hurting each other and go upstairs together. Sam had us do it a couple of times and didn't say any- thing. He was sitting on the camera boom with his bandana around his head, and he asked us to try it one more time.

"The sky was getting darker and darker now. But Bob and I did it one more time, and by now I didn't know what was working and what wasn't. So when that take was completed and Sam still hadn't said anything, I asked, 'Sam, was that all right?' And Sam said, with a terrible look on his face, 'That was lousy!' And he started to climb over the railing on the stairs, and I started to say, 'Well, then we'd better do it again.' And he came up to me and hugged me and said, 'It was terrific.' And I said, 'Oh, you son of a gun, you. What a way to try and scare a person!'"

With the completion of its shooting schedule, *Junior Bonner* was turned over to editors Frank Santillo and Bob Wolfe, who at Peckinpah's direction cut the picture into its final form. The picture was released in June 1972 to negative reviews by both *Time* and *Newsweek* as well as from most dailies that bothered to review it. While such reviews do not necessarily keep audiences away, they very often play an important role in influencing those who are responsible for booking a film into theaters. Rated PG (Parental Guidance Suggested) by the Motion Picture Association, the blame for the film's failure at the box office was laid to the film's inability to fulfill the expectations of those who came to see a tough action picture directed by Sam Peckinpah and starring Steve McQueen.

Marty Baum recalled: "As president of ABC Pictures, I commissioned *Junior Bonner,* and I think it is one of the best pictures Sam has ever made. But it has not been very successful at the box office. After *Straw Dogs* and being called 'the master of violence,' Sam suddenly decided he wanted to do a lyrical, thoughtful story of a family who [was] drifting apart, going in different directions, who touch each other for a brief weekend and then go their separate ways again.

"Sam cast it magnificently with Robert Preston and Ida Lupino. And Steve McQueen has never been better. It was a film that touched its audiences at every level, except nobody went to see it because somehow the people in this country don't seem to be interested in lyrical, charming stories. They want high adventure and action." *Junior Bonner* was the last film to be produced under the banner of ABC Pictures until 1979 when ABC Pictures resumed feature film production under new leadership.

Steve McQueen, whose own company, Solar Productions, had also been involved in producing *Junior Bonner,* felt, however, that the picture had been poorly distributed: "I liked *Junior Bonner* very much. It was the first time I'd worked with Sam, and we got it together. I thought the script was tremendous—one of the best properties I've come across. But I think the film is a failure, at least financially, and in this business, that's what counts.

"In distributing the picture, I was dealing with a man named

Joe Sugar who wanted to release it big—Grauman's Chinese and the whole bit. I told him that it should be released as an art picture starting in more select, smaller theaters and letting the picture catch on. He continued to disagree, and, of course, the picture was released his way and it fell flat. But I think that it's a picture that'll do very well over the long haul. Not today; not tomorrow. But give it time, and people will recognize it for what it's worth. The fact that it bombed the first time out gave me a lot more confidence in my own judgment in marketing a picture. I wouldn't let what happened there, happen again."

When *Junior Bonner* was released, by strange coincidence, several other rodeo pictures also found their way into distribution (most notably *J. W. Coop* starring Cliff Robertson and *The Honkers* starring James Coburn). These did not do well financially either.

Casey Tibbs stated: "Frankly; I don't like very many Westerns. In my opinion, *Junior Bonner* comes closest to being a good rodeo picture, but it still wasn't outstanding. With all due respect to my good friend Jeb [Rosebrook], I think he was under an awful lot of pressure to finish too much of the script on the set—to rewrite it when Sam didn't like this or that. I'm sure Jeb would have liked another two weeks on the story.

"The thing I liked about *Junior Bonner* was the fact that it was a story that could happen in any walk of life. It didn't have to be a rodeo family. It could have been a truck drivin' family or whatever. It was a good wholesome story. But it really wasn't tough enough in some respects.

"It wasn't deeply enough involved in rodeo. It's the same problem with making a film about any sporting event: the people making it—and this includes Sam—knew really nothing about the sport. And you can quote me to Sam. It really hurt the picture 'cause Jeb was the only one who really knew the rodeo, and he didn't carry enough weight. It was exactly like what Hemingway said about *Death in the* Afternoon, 'I wished I'd waited ten years to have done it.' It was the same with *Junior Bonner*. Sam knew a lot of cowboys, but him knowin' Ben Johnson and Casey Tibbs and a bunch more don't make you well versed on rodeo. You have to be there and let the manure get on your feet."

In truth, *Junior Bonner* is not so much a film about the rodeo as it is about personal values that play against the rodeo as a way of life. Thus, whatever its shortcomings with respect to the rodeo, the film remains a sensitive, often moving, portrait of a family in flux.

In it, Peckinpah examines the conflict between individual needs and familial obligations. A story of survival told in intimate terms, it is filled with human ambivalence and the bittersweet irony that success may frequently be laced with failure.

By focusing on the relationships that exist within the family—mother and father, mother and son, father and son, brother and brother—Peckinpah is able to demonstrate how people can care for one another despite deep-seated differences and the inability to live up to each other's expectations. He carefully exposes the human dimensions of each character, revealing that right and wrong are not a matter of clearly definable absolutes, but of perspective. In all of this, *Junior Bonner* must be seen as an important film in Peckinpah's career, for it is the one his detractors claim he is incapable of making—a nonviolent statement on the human condition.

12 The Getaway

"Are you kids married?"

As *Junior Bonner* moved into the final stages of editing, Sam Peckinpah attempted to maneuver himself into a position to make a film he had been preparing for three years—*Emperor of the North Pole*. This was a story set during the Depression involving a railroad train and its obsessed brakeman, Shack, who is prepared to kill to keep hobos from riding *his* train. The story revolves around a challenge to Shack's domain by an old pro—a hobo named "A-No. 1"—and a novice, "Cigarette," who becomes initiated not only into riding the rails but life and survival.

Remembering this project, Katy Haber recalled: *"Emperor of the North Pole* was Sam's picture. That was his baby. He had a big fall out with Ken Hyman over it. Sam wrote the script for it. Actually, Christopher Knopf wrote the script, and Sam did a rewrite. Sam really wanted to make that picture, but he and Ken split up and Sam made *Getaway* and Ken took *Emperor*. But if you think about it, *Emperor* is really Sam's picture. I mean it deals with the territorial imperative 'This is my train.'"

Kenneth Hyman, who had been one of Sam's supporters at Warner Brothers during the making of *The Wild Bunch* and *The Ballad of Cable Hogue,* was at this time working as an independent producer buying potential film properties on speculation. When Peckinpah approached him with *Emperor of the North Pole,* Hyman was impressed and agreed to attempt to obtain backing for the project with Peckinpah as director. Peckinpah recalled: "I wanted to direct *Emperor* so badly that I even agreed to do it for an enormous cut in salary. Ken liked it and took it around to UA [United Artists] and Metro before he finally set up a meeting with Bob Evans at Paramount. I went to that meeting with my agent.

211

"Evans said, 'I can guarantee you on my personal word that if you do *Getaway* as your next picture, we will follow it with *Emperor of the North Pole.'* I said, 'You better go talk to Ken about this.' So he went and talked to Ken and said that he would take care of everything. So I agreed to do *Getaway.* The next thing I knew, I received this fucking letter from Hyman dismissing me as director of *Emperor.* Then on top of that the Paramount brass decided not to make *Getaway,* so I'm out on both pictures. It was unbelievable.

"Fortunately, Steve [McQueen] got pissed off at this shit and said, 'All right, we'll make it at First Artists.' Now First Artists is Steve's company—his and a couple of other actors—and its president is a guy named Pat Kelly. And Kelly looked over *Getaway* and said, 'We'll do the picture.'

"But all I got out of *Emperor* was a $10,000 settlement from Ken Hyman, which I really hated because it was my property to begin with. I had put in three years on that picture trying to get it made. Then Hyman comes along and takes it over to Bob Aldrich, and they really fucked it up. Badly cast. Badly directed. Wretchedly produced. The one thing I can say about Bob Aldrich, [whom] I admire as a director—although I didn't admire what he did with this picture because it was too close to me, so I can be wrong—is that he didn't allow Ken Hyman on the set.

"Cigarette was the key, and Cigarette was totally miscast. I wanted someone like Dustin Hoffman—an actor. [Lee] Marvin [as A-No. 1] and [Ernest] Borgnine [as Shack] were tremendous. But Hyman did a rewrite on my rewrite which made no sense whatsoever, and I told him so. So I was out, and there was nothing I could do about it. I learned later that Paramount never intended to make *Emperor* and had absolutely refused to work with Ken Hyman. So to put it mildly, we're not corresponding."

The Getaway was initiated as a film project by a producer named David Foster, who had once done some public relations work for Peckinpah on *Ride the High Country.* He had since left public relations to produce Robert Altman's *McCabe and Mrs. Miller. The Getaway,* coproduced with Mitchell Brower, was to be his second motion picture as producer.

"I optioned a book called *The Getaway,"* recalled Foster, "written by an old-timer named Jim Thompson about 1957. Jim Thompson is a guy who worked with Stanley Kubrick as a screenwriter on *The Killing* and *Paths of Glory.* Anyway, I gave the book to Steve McQueen and said, 'Hey, this is something we've got to do together.' So Steve read it and liked it. So we agreed to do it. "When Steve and I talked about directors for the film, he had

212

just finished the film *Junior Bonner* with Peckinpah, and so naturally Sam's name came up. Steve said he'd get in touch with Sam and tell him I would be calling.

"So when I went over to talk to Sam, I walked into his office—and we hadn't seen each other in a while—and he threw this big bear hug on me and said, 'I'll do it!' Well, I had this paperback still in my hand, so I said, 'You don't even know what I'm talking about yet.' He said, 'I'll do it!' And it turned out that Sam had wanted to do that picture some eight years before. He had met Jim Thompson, told him what he wanted to do with it, the whole bit. But it was a rather bleak period in Sam's life, right after his debacle with Columbia, I think, so it never got off the ground. Then, here I come some eight or nine years later with that same book. I didn't believe he was serious at first. But he simply laid out the whole story for me, and I knew the book had been out of print for years, so he wasn't putting me on."

While Peckinpah had read the book and attempted to do something with it earlier, he had been attracted to the basic story of a couple on the run. In the original Thompson novel, the hero and heroine escape to an almost science fiction-like gangster retreat in Mexico where, as their money dwindles away, they eventually turn on each other. Commenting on this, Peckinpah stated: "I worked with Jim Thompson on a previous script that never got off the table. So I'd read *The Getaway* before they ever brought it to me. But I had always thought the original ending was wrong. Walter Hill wrote the screenplay and did a tremendous job."

Set in Texas circa 1949, Walter Hill's screenplay adaptation of Thompson's novel was dedicated to American film director Raoul Walsh. In particular, the script reflected something of Walsh's *High Sierra* (1941) and *White Heat* (1949) and the kind of films that have come to be known as the bandit-gangster subgenre. This subgenre involves a bandit couple (a man and a woman) who clearly adhere to a traditional Western set of values. They are associated with the rural while they carry out raids against urban society (usually banks). Because society no longer understands the meaning of the traditional code, it hunts the couple down, considering them to be gangsters. (Nicholas Ray's *They Live by Night,* Arthur Penn's *Bonnie and Clyde,* and John Milius's *Dillinger* are other films of this subgenre.) Because they have no place in modern society, the bandit-gangster couple generally are killed at the end of the film.

The Getaway is a notable exception to this because Doc and Carol escape to Mexico, a place more suited to traditional Western values.

All of this may or may not have been consciously written into the script of *The Getaway*. In retaining these themes, Peckinpah nevertheless elected to contemporize the story.

"*The Getaway* was my first attempt at satire, badly done," he stated, recalling the film. "Too many people took it too seriously. Five times in that picture I have people saying, 'It's just a game.' I was dealing with a little bit of *High Sierra* there and a couple of other things. It was a good story, and I thought I had a good ending. It made my comment."

McQueen, of course, would portray the bandit Doc McCoy. Due to the original plans to make the film at Paramount, Ali Mac-Graw, at that time married to Paramount head Bob Evans, had been signed to play Doc's wife, Carol. The balance of the casting included Ben Johnson as Benyon, Al Lettieri as Rudy, Sally Struthers as the veterinarian's unfaithful wife, and Slim Pickens as the old-timer who drives the McCoys into Mexico. In addition, Peckinpah also added several old friends—nonactors whose interesting faces intrigued him. Among these was John Bryson, the former *Life* magazine photographer, who played Benyon's brother, and Tom Runyon, a restaurateur from the Santa Monica Mountains, who played one of the gunmen. For a crew David Foster took a straightforward approach: "I simply went to Sam and said: 'I want this to be a picture that gets made with the fewest possible hassles. You tell me who you think is the best man for each position, and I'll get him for you.' It turned out being one of the smoothest running things Sam's ever done." Included in this crew were Lucien Ballard, director of photography; Gordon Dawson, associate producer; Ted Haworth, art director; Bob Visciglia, property master; Newt Arnold, assistant director; and Chuck Wilborn, sound man.

Like Joe Wizan, the producer of *Junior Bonner,* David Foster enjoyed working with Peckinpah: "I'm not saying that Sam and I didn't get into some shouting matches. We had some real ones. But basically Sam is a pussycat! Let me give you an example that really helped me to understand the guy before the picture ever started shooting.

"Sam and I both happen to have gone to the University of Southern California, and we both are football nuts. So this was the football season of '71 while we were still preparing to shoot *Getaway*. I called and asked Sam if he would like to go with me and my wife to the USC-Illinois football game. And he loved the idea.

"So we went, and it was just like Sam was back in school again. Here's this tough guy, right? Well, before the kickoff, the USC band plays their fight song which is a version of 'Conquest.' And what usually happens is that all the Joe Colleges stand up and give this crazy 'V' for victory and sing the song. Now, I'm corny up to a

214

point, but I just can't stand up at age 45 and start singing. But as the band starts to play, I turn to Sam, and he's all choked up. Then he suddenly stands up, sticks his fingers in the air, and starts singing along with the kids. It was terrific. I've never seen such spontaneous emotion.

"From then on, I realized that Sam relies almost entirely on his emotional responses. If you take him deadly serious every single moment, he'll drive you crazy. But if you keep it in perspective, and allow him to apply those instincts to the picture, there's no problem. And he gets some terrific things on film."

The Getaway began shooting in late February 1972 in San Marcos, Texas, and the surrounding countryside and included the state penitentiary at Huntsville. San Marcos, located in the southern portion of the state, is halfway between San Antonio and Austin. Huntsville, where the opening scenes were shot, lies about 150 miles to the northeast.

Peckinpah recalled: "We shot the whole opening to *The Getaway* in less than three days. We were driving up to Huntsville, and the minute I saw those deer inside the prison compound I knew that that was the opening shot of the picture. It was so peaceful you'd think it was a zoo. Then panning up to the guard tower from the animals—the incongruity of it just shattered me."

Because this opening sequence involved a prison, it recalled for Peckinpah his own beginning in the film industry and Don Siegel's *Riot in Cell Block 11*. At that time Peckinpah had been impressed by the realistic atmosphere created by filming inside a prison and using its inmates as extras. Consequently, Peckinpah placed McQueen among the real inmates at Huntsville to achieve the same effect.

More difficult and time-consuming, however, was the bank robbery with its violent aftermath that sets the stage for the chase that occupies the balance of the film. As part of their plan, the robbers, led by Doc McCoy, place a number of preset timed explosives along the escape route to cause confusion and prevent pursuit. Due to complications that occur during the robbery itself, however, Doc and Carol are delayed. As a result, they are almost caught in one of these explosions. As they attempt to drive through the fire anyway, their car goes out of control and crashes into the front of a nearby house before they escape.

For this spectacular stunt sequence, Peckinpah brought in

stuntman Gary Combs to do the driving. This tended to cause some friction because McQueen not only enjoys a reputation for doing many of his own stunts but has raced both motorcycles and cars professionally. In fact, McQueen had won the Sebring Grand Prix two years before despite having to wear a cast on one foot, which had been broken in six places in a motorcycle mishap.

Peckinpah stated: "Steve is very heavily into cars and cycles and has raced them professionally and won. He's a pro. So after I laid out the stunt, he wanted his own stunt gaffer to come in and lay it out for us. I said fine because I knew what I was going to do anyway. So they talked and worked and finally came up with exactly what I'd laid out in the first place. We shot the car going through the fire five times and the porch once. Gary Combs did a tremendous job of stunt driving."

Because of the difficulty in doing the shot of the car going through the porch more than once, multiple cameras were used. Katy Haber recalls: "On *The Getaway,* when we did that car flying through the explosion, it was really something. The special effects guys buried this large mortar in the ground, and that's what causes the explosion. Sam had five cameras and a helicopter to get it on film. Everything was coordinated by walkie-talkies. It was 'Camera 5 ready? Camera number 4 ready?' and so forth. And then 'Special effects ready? Okay, blow the son of a bitch!' Then on the first take the car caught on fire, and Steve went running through the end of the shot to see if Gary Combs was all right."

Combs, who, like all stuntmen, has a certain nonchalance about doing dangerous things, recalled that particular stunt in detail: "We did the shot in two sections: first goin' through the fire and then later goin' through the house. For the first part, the special effects people came over and said they wanted to put a bigger charge in the mortar, and I said go ahead. So they put in some five-gallon cans, and when I was comin' through the shot, I picked up one of those cans on the A-frame in the front of the car and took it with me. Well, it had some gas in it, and the gas started floatin' up over the car and burnin'.

"Well, Steve thought I was on fire, which I was but nothing serious. So he come runnin' over to help me, but there wasn't any real danger. I walked around to the front and took a look at it, and McQueen is shoutin': 'Get away! It's goin' blow!' And it wasn't gonna blow. It was in front, and the gas tank is in back. It was my number one car. We had two doubles for it, but it was the best car I had, and I had some more stuff to do. Anyway, I took a look at it,

216

and it was just some oil that had gotten on the fire wall and was burnin'. So I backed it up to where the fire hose was and let the firemen put it out. That's nothing against McQueen. He's raced some cars, and race drivers are usually spooked about fires. It's a terrible thing to be on fire, but that just wasn't gonna happen this time. I appreciated his concern."

As with his experience on *Junior Bonner*, Peckinpah found working with McQueen a stimulating, frustrating, and sometimes dangerous experience. Peckinpah recalls: "I like Steve. He's really a tough mother. On my birthday [February 21] falling shortly after filming of *The Getaway* began, we had had champagne on the set, and Steve and I had been discussing some point on which we disagreed. So he picked up this bottle of champagne and threw it at me. But I saw it coming and ducked. And Steve just laughed.

"Then when we were doing the shootout between him and Rudy at that old farm, Steve walked to where I was sitting carrying a .45 loaded with blanks and shot it off right next to my boot. He really pissed me off.

"So he laughed because he had me. He's always in terrific shape, and he outweighs me in muscle by a long shot. Well, that pissed me off even more. So there was this hole that Al [Lettieri] falls into after Steve shoots him. I was really mad, so I shoved Steve. Then I shoved him again, and he stepped backwards into that hole, still laughing.

"I figured that was all the shoving I was going to do for awhile because he was going to come out of that hole and shove both my arms down my throat, so I'd have to scratch my asshole from the inside. But instead, he came up laughing again only harder because now he really had me. He had nothing to prove. He could have taken me apart and put me back together again. He knew it, and I knew it. I had taken my best shot, and it hadn't even fazed him. So we went ahead and made the picture together. I like him. He wants to make a good picture, and he always has a lot to offer. Not many people like him, but I do."

One of the major conflicts between Peckinpah and McQueen occurred over the scene in which Doc and Carol are alone together in their bedroom for the first time in five years following his release from prison. Peckinpah recognized the moment as a clash between fantasy and reality. Confronting the woman he has desired for so long, Doc momentarily doubts his ability to perform. Perceiving this, his wife gently coaxes him past his doubt, making him realize she is willing to wait until he is ready.

Lucien Ballard recalled: "Sam and Steve got into a big argument over that first love scene in *The Getaway*. Steve wanted to rape Ali. That's the way he saw it. This guy's been in prison for five years, and he just comes home and really takes what he feels is rightfully his. He couldn't understand what Sam wanted him to do. He thought it was phony. But Sam insisted and again it played perfectly. Really one of the most sensitive love scenes on film, I think.

"Then for the scene which follows—I think it's supposed to be the next morning—Steve had written seven pages of dialogue, you know, explaining the whole thing. Well, Sam got him into that cooking thing where he's got eggs and catsup and all this stuff in a frying pan on the stove. And Steve was just really in his element. He loved it. He's very good with props. Then when Ali comes down they embrace, and I think they maybe have a couple of dozen words between them total, and that was it.

"So after they saw the dailies, Sam said to Steve, 'And that was what you wrote seven pages of dialogue to explain?' And Steve laughed and said, 'Well, you know better than to listen to me, Sam.'"

McQueen's abrasive personality often accomplished a great deal in terms of getting his own way on a set, but it also tended to make him one of the least popular actors from the point of view of those who wanted the production to run smoothly and business-like. As one of the people involved in the making of *The Getaway* stated: "To work with Steve McQueen [was] to work with a complete and thorough child. And on a Peckinpah picture there is really no time for anyone's temperament but Sam's, period. A certain amount of temperament from an actor is fine, and Sam usually deals with it in front of the camera. So you help where you can and make the guy as happy as you can. But McQueen [was] just in everybody's case, giving contrary orders and changing lines. It's all insecurity. And on top of all that he [had] this habit of taking off his shirt between takes [to get] all those rays of sunshine! Well, shit, man, it then [took] extra effort on everybody's part to get him dressed and ready when you finally do shoot the son of a bitch! Who needs it?"

Despite all of this, Steve McQueen had an electrifying screen presence that placed him among the top-grossing box office personalities in motion pictures for over a decade. He was also an extremely inventive actor, winning Peckinpah's respect by suggesting scenes like the one in which Doc holds two policemen at bay while literally destroying their squad car with a pump-action shotgun loaded with twenty-aught buckshot. "That shot was entirely Steve's idea," stated Peckinpah. "He told me what he wanted to do, and I thought it was a sensational idea. Steve [was] extraordinary with props. He [made] them his—like he[had] known them all his life.

218

On the screen he really [made] you believe in his character."

The casting of Ali MacGraw opposite McQueen was something else, however. Relatively inexperienced as an actress (her two previous films were both contemporary romances), she was hardly prepared for an action film directed by Peckinpah.

Producer Foster recalled the casting of MacGraw in the picture: "On *The Getaway*, Sam really worked with a lady. Ali MacGraw is really a cultured lady—well educated, well traveled, a former model. She'd been in two other films, *Goodbye, Columbus* and *Love Story*. And suddenly she has to deal with this two-fisted, knife-throwing, hard-drinking director. I'm sure she entered the arrangement with a great deal of trepidation.

"But Sam and Ali got along great. Sam was wonderful with her. He loves to holler and scream. It's his way of letting go of the things that have been building up inside of him. But Sam also has this tremendously gentle side, and that's the side he showed to Ali. And she really performed magnificently."

Ali MacGraw is very defensive about her performance in *The Getaway*. In a brief telephone interview in 1973, she stated: "After we had completed *The Getaway* and I looked at what I'd done in it, I hated my own performance. I like the picture, but I despised my own work. I really couldn't look at it.

"I adore Sam as a director. He is really a marvelous man, a sexy man. He really knows how to get through to a woman when he wants [her] to do something in front of the cameras. It is very difficult for me to be objective about my own work in the picture, but I would love to work again for Sam Peckinpah." Five years later, she would have her chance.

It was during the filming of *The Getaway* that Sam Peckinpah married for the fifth time, this time to Joie Gould, the English secretary he had been living with off and on since making *Straw Dogs*. It was done, Peckinpah recalled, as an act of contrition: "We had gotten into an argument, and I slapped her with my open hand. I really felt bad about it. So in a moment of remorse I agreed to marry her—in Mexico where I knew that I could get a one-day divorce. That's what I thought. Well, I was wrong. When things fell apart it took me a year to get the divorce and it cost me my shirt, my pants, and my embroidered jock strap! But some you win and some you lose. So she took all the money I got on *Getaway* and took a trip around the world at my expense. We were not exactly what you might call star-crossed lovers."

Gould commented on her marriage to Peckinpah: "All of my friends told me not to marry Sam. If you wanted to get involved, that was one thing. But nothing permanent. I said I thought I could handle it. It turned out they were right, and I was wrong."

Following their disastrous entanglement, Peckinpah would swear off the state of matrimony as being both costly and dangerous. To prevent his romantic nature from taking advantage of his better judgment, the director decided to place a clause in each of his film contracts that would stipulate that should he marry during the course of making a given picture, he would forfeit all of the money due him from the project.

As *The Getaway* moved towards conclusion, its production company crossed the state of Texas from San Antonio to El Paso. Among those responsible for making things run smoothly was the assistant director, Newt Arnold, who had first met Peckinpah on *Junior Bonner* when Arnold was called in as a replacement two-thirds of the way through the picture.

Arnold, who lists among his credentials such films as *The Godfather, Part II* and *Towering Inferno,* is immediately recognizable on the set by the distinctive black eye patch covering his left eye. In speaking of the role of the assistant director in general and *The Getaway* in particular, Arnold stated: "In production the assistant is something of a second cook who does the broad preparation so that the director, who is the master chef, can move quickly and efficiently from one scene to the next adding the proper spices and garnishes, so to speak, that make it sort of a visual meal to remember. The keys to the job are understanding what the director is ultimately after in a picture and coordinating the efforts which go into achieving those desires. At the same time, you have to be concentrating not just on what is before the camera right now but what is coming up.

"The Getaway went very smoothly. We had major moves between San Marcos, San Antonio, and El Paso. But within each of those major location settings were multiple locations so that virtually every day we were on another location. This requires a tremendous amount of planning and anticipation of what will be needed. And when you get a picture as logistically complex as this, it can often misplace the concentration from those elements which are going in front of the camera—which ultimately are the most important—to the moves themselves. When that happens, it becomes apparent in the quality of the picture. *Getaway,* however, because everybody was working together, did not lose anything to the physical effort of moving men and equipment literally hundreds of miles."

For the final sequence in the picture, Peckinpah chose El Paso as the place from which the McCoys escape into Mexico by commandeering a broken down pickup truck following a shootout in the Laughlin Hotel. The truck is driven by an old-timer, played by Slim Pickens, who takes them across the border and then sells them the truck and his silence for $30,000. It was a part that Pickens almost did not take.

"The damnedest thing when Sam offers me a part," Pickens stated, "is more times than not the danged thing is nothin' more than a bit. For instance in *The Getaway,* I said to my agent, 'Isn't there anything I could do in Sam's new picture?' And my agent said: 'I looked over everything, and there isn't anything you could do. The only thing you could do is a bit, and I wouldn't want you doin' it.'

"Then I talked to Sam, and Sam says: 'What the hell's wrong with your agent? I want you to do something for me.' So he sent the god-danged script over, and hell, the part was a nothin' part, but I was scared not to take the goddamn thing 'cause I know the way Sam shoots. What's in the dang script and what winds up on the dang screen are two different things, y'know.

"Sam told me, 'I want you to be a character just like ol' Bill Baker but dirtier.' I know'd ol' Bill. Ol' Bill just died here not too long ago. In fact, Sam went to his funeral. Baker was probably the dirtiest guy I ever knew—snaggle-toothed ol' feller—but god damn, he was a piece of the wind. You don't get but one of them very often."

In the film, the McCoys run into this Baker-like character as he stands near his pickup behind the hotel talking with a wino, portrayed by Tom Bush, who was at the time on parole from Huntsville (Bush did so well in this that Peckinpah has used him in several subsequent films including *The Killer Elite)*. When Doc commands the old-timer to drive them to Mexico, he promptly agrees.

After they cross the border, the old-timer asks them: "Are you kids married?" Although they have spent much of the picture bickering, they have resolved their differences just prior to their arrival in El Paso and now seem surprised at their ability to answer yes. The old-timer then extols the virtues of wedded bliss, speaking of his own wife as "a good ol' hide" before the McCoys tell him to pull over.

Considering they have a gun, the viewer realizes they could easily just take his truck. Instead, they decide to purchase it from him. Doc gets out of the truck and hunkers down with the old man and offers him $10,000 for his truck and his silence. Considering the condition of the truck, Doc is shocked when the old man asks for $20,000. Amused by this, Carol, who is counting out the payment, does not wait for Doc to continue the bargaining and says, "Why don't we make it thirty [thousand]." Overwhelmed with gratitude, the old-timer takes his money in disbelief and saunters back up the road as the McCoys drive on together.

Peckinpah recalled: "I said to Slim, 'You read the lines in the script?' And Slim says, 'Yeah, I read 'em.' And I said, 'Well, I want you to talk about marriage and love and morality.' And I gave him about three lines that weren't in the script and let him play it the way he felt it. I said: 'Turn these kids on. See what they can do.' And when Slim asked them if they were married, it really threw them badly. But they stayed with it, and it worked.

"That's the way I like to work. That's 'indirection.' I can work that way with Slim, Ben [Johnson], Warren [Oates], Strother [Martin]. You've got to know who you're working with and set them up for a certain situation, turn on the camera, and let it happen."

Pickens remembered the scene with McQueen and MacGraw: "Sam said to me, 'Throw some dialogue at McQueen, and find out if he can act.' So none a that stuff was in the script. Sam, by golly, he just told met' talk t' 'em about morals and such. So I just ad-libbed the goddamn thing as we went down the road.

"Then for the part where McQueen's supposed to buy my truck, Sam said to me: 'I think you'd be horse tradin'. You just kind a hunker down while you're talkin'.' So, by golly, that's the way we did it. Then when they gave me the money an' I go off there, I don't know why, but I just felt so good I reached down an' picked up that goddamn rock 'an threw it. None of that was in the script. It just felt right, so that's the way we did 'er."

With the completion of shooting, *The Getaway* became the problem of editors Bob Wolfe and Roger Spottiswoode who cut the picture to Peckinpah's specifications prior to turning it over to Mc-Queen and First Artists for preview and release. The scoring for the picture would be done once again by Jerry Fielding. Problems developed, however, when following the picture's second preview, McQueen exercised his prerogative as a member of First Artists. Composer Jerry Fielding remembered: "Sam was delighted with the scoring on *The Getaway*. Everybody was until Sam and Steve started having a war of some sort. And McQueen simply came in after I had finished the picture and rescored it. Sam did the best he could and took out an ad in the paper. But nothing changed. I got paid. But that wasn't why I wrote the music."

The ad Fielding refers to was a full-page ad in the *Daily Variety,* November 17, 1972, which carried a reprint of an earlier letter Peckinpah had written to Fielding concerning the scoring of *The Getaway.* The letter read:

222

Dear Jerry,

I know you will be pleased that the second preview of "Getaway" was as great as the first. In fact, it was even more enthusiastically received. Which is surprising since it was attended mostly by industry people.

I want to thank you for the beautiful job you did with the music. I have heard many marvelous comments, particularly on the second showing. Possibly because no one there had impaired hearing and we had no problem with malfunctioning equipment.

Once again, congratulations. I am looking forward to the next one.

Best regards, Sam Peckinpah

Commenting on the two scores, associate producer Gordon Dawson stated: "Jerry Fielding's score for *Getaway* was a beautiful score. It was like a man in a green suit walking in a forest. That was important because there were a lot of source sounds—radio station stuff and creaking shoes, things like that. It gave the film a real presence, like you were really there. The Fielding score never went over the top of a thing. He and his sound editor really worked on it. Then all of a sudden, it gets yanked out, and the more obvious score goes in, and there goes your presence.

"In fairness to McQueen, though, I guess he redid the effects track as well. And cars are really his thing. So he really did a job on that and I guess it won the golden microphone or whatever it is for best sound effects. But it wasn't worth the loss of the Fielding score, to my mind."

Al Lettieri also found reason to be upset with the film as it was finally previewed and released. David Foster recalls: "Both Al Lettieri and Sally Struthers were incredible on *Getaway*. Al used to be a writer and is a very funny guy. He has a very quick mind. And Sally is also pretty inventive. Well, they'd come up with some really great bits. Then when Steve recut the picture, some of those things were cut out, and Al really got upset at Sam because he thought Sam had done it. At the preview for Steve's cut, I thought he was going to kill Sam, and I mean literally. I've never seen anyone so angry, except maybe Sam. But it was Steve's picture, and he was right."

McQueen made apologies to no one: *"The Getaway* meant more to me in a financial and professional way than *Junior Bonner.* I take full responsibility for it. Not full credit but full responsibility. It's made money for everyone connected with it. That says all there is to say. I know Sam wasn't happy with some of the changes, but I had my reasons. Sam and I are still friends. And of course, personally, *Getaway* was a film that I met my lady on. Ali and I had a chance to meet and got to know each other, so it has a sentimental value for me as well. [McQueen and MacGraw were eventually married following the completion of *The Getaway.*]

"I feel that Sam Peckinpah is an exceptional filmmaker. He is a little bit hard on himself sometimes, and I worry about him for that. But I have a great respect for anyone as committed as Sam is to his work. He surrounds himself with people who are honest and who are personally committed to what he does. Sam has made a personal commitment to his work, and I feel that a man isn't worth a shit unless he has."

Despite mixed reviews, *The Getaway* exceeded everyone's expectations at the box office. It became the first picture to ever pay Peckinpah beyond his initial salary. As with most motion picture contracts for name directors, Peckinpah's deal to direct *The Getaway* included a number of percentage points of the adjusted gross. This meant that Peckinpah would receive a portion of whatever revenue was produced by the picture after all the bills have been paid including advertising. However, it has been Peckinpah's policy to give away some of these points to those who have worked closely with him on his pictures. Among others, Lucien Ballard and Gordon Dawson received part of Peckinpah's percentage of *The Getaway.* Lucien Ballard states: "After we'd completed *Wild Bunch,* Sam said to me: 'Well, pard, we made it. I want you to get a piece of the profit.' I tried to turn it down but Sam insisted, and his lawyer drew up a paper to that effect. Well, because we must go by Warner Brothers' bookkeeping, I'm still waiting for my dividend on that one.

"On *Getaway,* however, Sam did the same thing, and it has amounted to a sizable sum. That's why I don't listen to Sam when he tells me about how little money he has."

The Getaway grossed more than $18 million in the United States and Canada (and double that worldwide). In terms of market value for a director attempting to assure himself of future financial backing, this has been Peckinpah's most important commercial success. Indeed, this film was instrumental in promoting Peckinpah as a "bankable" director, one whose name alone when connected to a project would help attract investors. He had risen to the top of his profession.

224

13 Pat Garrett and Billy the Kid

"Who do you screw to get out of this game?"

For his next project, Sam Peckinpah agreed to direct a version of the legendary confrontation during the Lincoln County cattle wars between Pat Garrett and Billy the Kid. Made for Metro-Goldwyn-Mayer, this film would test all who were involved, especially Peckinpah. In fact, it became such an acrimonious experience for the director that he eventually forbade anyone from even mentioning the names of those at the studio who thwarted him or forfeit a dollar for each verbal offense. To avoid paying the fine himself, Peckinpah invented penalty-free pseudonyms that inevitably included a change in gender.

"It was my worst experience since *Major Dundee,*" Peckinpah recounted in anger and recrimination. "Who was responsible? Those fucking assholes at MGM, who else? I'm suing every god-damn one of them—Jennifer Mulberry, Dorothy Carrot—every fucking one of them."

It is not surprising that there should have been conflicts on *Pat Garrett and Billy the Kid.* There are conflicts on every Peckinpah film. When there are none, Peckinpah will manufacture them himself on the theory that conflict keeps his creative juices flowing. He also believes conflicts keep everyone connected with a production more alert and sensitive to detail. However, even for Peckinpah, conflict is not always a successful creative tool. *Pat Garrett* was to become a case in point.

James T. Aubrey, president of MGM at this time, had come to the motion picture industry in 1969 after heading CBS television. He brought with him a reputation for being coldly pragmatic concerning marketing, with no regard for creative sensibilities. He thought nothing of reediting a work if he thought the result would be more commercially successful and was frequently accused of betraying trusts. This had earned him the epithet "the smiling cobra." Apparently, Aubrey viewed the conflict between Peckinpah and MGM as one that could be ultimately resolved in the cutting room after the picture passed out of Peckinpah's control. Caught in the middle of this conflict was the film's producer, Gordon Carroll.

The project was originally proposed by Carroll, whose credits as a producer include *How to Murder Your Wife, The April Fools* (both vehicles for Jack Lemmon), and *Cool Hand Luke* (starring Paul Newman). He believed the story of Billy the Kid to be the quintessential American myth—the young individualist pitted against a society that eventually pays to have him killed to make way for the masses. That this myth had been the basis of thirty or more motion pictures in years past did not dissuade Carroll. In 1970 he hired scriptwriter Rudolph Wurlitzer to write the screenplay.

What followed over the next several years is condensed by Wurlitzer in the introduction to his published screenplay *Pat Garrett and Billy the Kid* (Signet, 1973). There he attempts to explain what he tried to accomplish in writing the screenplay.

Basically, Wurlitzer concerned himself with the last three months of Billy's life, the months following his escape from the Lincoln County courthouse. This allowed Wurlitzer to create Garrett and the Kid as two separate and distinct forces locked into a collision course, forces that would not meet until the final shoot-out at the end of the picture. It was, by his own admission, an "existential" approach to the legend. If the Kid chose to die as he had lived rather than change, Garrett had consciously elected life at any cost.

Wurlitzer's first draft of this screenplay was sold to MGM and director Monte Hellman (*The Shooting, Ride in the Whirlwind)* was contracted to direct it on the strength of his most recent film at that time, *Two-Lane Blacktop,* which had also been scripted by Wurlitzer. *Two-Lane Blacktop* starred country-rock singer James Taylor (whose portrait had recently adorned the cover of *Time* magazine) and Warren Oates in a story vaguely reminiscent of *Easy Rider.* When *Two-Lane Blacktop* failed to do well at the box office, Metro decided to pay off Hellman rather than allow him to direct *Pat Garrett.* Gordon Carroll took the script to other studios in the hope of making the film with Hellman but nothing materialized.

After what was apparently a more commercial rewrite of the screenplay by Wurlitzer, the project, still at MGM, was shown to Peckinpah who tentatively agreed to direct it. Writing in his introduction, Wurlitzer describes Peckinpah without naming him as "a director famous for his tantrums, rages, macho passions and banal, highly embarrassing pronouncements." He then goes on to explain how Peckinpah altered his original concept of the script by incorporating the relationship between Garrett and the Kid at the outset of the film.

James Coburn, who plays Pat Garrett in the film, remembered Wurlitzer's anxiety over what Peckinpah did to his script: "Rudy wrote a beautiful script. I thought it was one of the best scripts I've ever read. And Sam destroyed it. But the script has to crumble and die in order to be reborn in the form of a film. Now I've worked on films where the scripts were not destroyed. But then those films were never really anything special. Creation involves destruction. Sam understands that process so well. But it hurt Rudy because he didn't understand that process. He thought Sam was simply destroying his creation, which was true but necessary."

On the same subject, Peckinpah himself stated: "I liked Rudy. He's got different ideas than I do, but he's a poet—a really fine writer. If I'd shot his screenplay, I would have had five hours of screen time. It was an epic confrontation with a great lyric quality to it. I brought it down some, but I attempted to retain its lyricism, and I was really pleased with it—proud of it. It wasn't all shoot-outs. Then those emotional eunuchs back at MGM—the ones who have become bellhops—cut all of the character and humor and drama out leaving, or at least trying to leave, only the shootouts. And it didn't work."

The approach employed in the rewriting of the screenplay for *Pat Garrett* was patterned after Peckinpah's first draft of *The Authentic Death of Hendry Jones,* which had become Marlon Brando's *One-Eyed Jacks.* In that screenplay, Peckinpah told the story of a young outlaw called "The Kid" in flashback, using the outlaw's funeral as a framing device. He decided to enclose similarly the story of *Pat Garrett and Billy the Kid* using Garrett's death in 1908 as both prologue and epilogue so that the story of Billy's last days becomes Garrett's memory at the moment of his own demise. He also insisted on beginning Billy's story with a meeting between him and Garrett thereby voiding Wurlitzer's existential approach.

There was a purpose to Peckinpah's additions, however. By having Garrett first come to old Fort Sumner to give the Kid warning followed by Billy's capture and escape from the courthouse, Peckinpah sets in motion the circular construction of the film. Like two halves of a great circle, Garrett and the Kid ride their separate trails until they meet once more at Fort Sumner for their final showdown. Thus Peckinpah's construction of the narrative reflects his vision of Garrett and the Kid as two halves of the same man. Pat Garrett is not only riding against his friend, he is riding against his surrogate self.

It was agreed by both MGM and Peckinpah that the project could be filmed most economically in Durango, Mexico. Casting was another matter. They had little trouble agreeing on Coburn as Garrett. For Billy the Kid, however, Peckinpah wanted someone fresh while MGM wanted someone with established box office value. Peckinpah suggested Bo Hopkins on the basis of his work in *The Wild Bunch* and the more recently released *Culpepper Cattle Company.* MGM suggested Jon Voight. Peckinpah recalled: "I was looking at a lot of film over at MGM trying to cast Billy. And they were turning down my people, and I was turning down theirs. Then I saw Kris [Kristofferson] in a picture called *Cisco Pike,* and I said: 'I know I can work with that guy. I know I can work with him.' So I went to see him at the Troubadour."

The Troubadour was a Los Angeles night spot that at the time specialized in folk-rock singers. Kris Kristofferson's success helped to establish its name. Kristofferson remembered meeting Peckinpah for the first time: "Sam and Peter Falk had come by to see the show, and those assholes at the Troubadour couldn't find them a seat. The only thing I ever asked them to do was get Sam and Peter seats. Well, they're both hammered, and I walk in late and look up and in the very last seat in the balcony there's Sam and Peter. Later when I went up to talk to 'em, Sam says, 'You really have got the pull in this place.' It was really embarrassing. But Sam and I hit it off because I had worked construction up in North Fork, which is right below Peckinpah Mountain. So we got along right from the start."

In casting the balance of the picture, Peckinpah relied heavily upon long-established Western character actors whom he had known and worked with throughout his career—actors like Slim Pickens, L. Q. Jones, Dub Taylor, R. G. Armstrong, and Jack Elam. In addition to these he invited a number of name stars to take cameo roles. Jason Robards agreed to do a brief portrayal of Governor Lew Wallace; Barry Sullivan was brought in to play John Chisum; Katy Jurado would play the wife of Slim Pickens's Sheriff Baker, and Emilio Fernandez would play the Mexican sheep herder, Paco.

Peckinpah further decided to cast Kris Kristofferson's entire band in parts. Keyboard man Donny Fritts stands out as a character called Beaver who spends the entire film repeating verbatim whatever is said by whomever he is with. Rita Coolidge, Kristofferson's

Folk-singing girlfriend and later wife, was cast as Maria, Billy's mistress. Also, through Kristofferson, Peckinpah brought in singer-composer Bob Dylan to play an unscripted character named Alias.

Kristofferson stated: "I think Bob Dylan wanted to be in *Pat Garrett*. I called him up, and I may have talked him into it. Unfortunately, Sam was going through so much shit with MGM that he was never able to sit down and figure out what Dylan was in the movie. I had an idea that he was gonna be sort of like the Fool in *Lear*—an observer through it all. But Bob, he wanted to know what Sam thought he was doing in the picture and of course, Sam wasn't thinking about it. Bob kept sayin' to me, 'Well, at least you're in the script.'"

James Coburn remembered Peckinpah's reaction to Dylan on *Pat Garrett*: "When Dylan came down to Mexico, Sam didn't know who the fuck Dylan was. But when he heard Dylan sing, Sam was the first to admit that he was taken with Dylan's singing. He heard Dylan's 'Ballad of Billy the Kid' and immediately had it put on tape so that he could have it with him to play."

With the film to be made in Mexico, many of the other parts as well as a substantial portion of the crew would again have to be filled by Mexican personnel. Gordon Dawson, then acting as associate producer, was sent ahead with the unit production manager to hire the Mexican crew. It had already been decided that John Coquillon's British camera crew would form the first unit and that Ted Haworth and Newt Arnold would function as art director and first assistant director, respectively. Bob Visciglia once again would act as property master, and Chuck Wilborn would handle sound.

Dawson recalled: "I was spoiled. We ran *Getaway* so good—no problems. We had 114 moves along with three major city moves—trains, staging gunfights in towns, going through houses, finding a hotel we could literally shoot up. And we came in right on schedule and on budget. It was a good feeling.

"By comparison, *Pat Garrett* should have been a walk in the park: stationed in Durango, shooting in a hub around it, never making a major move, all Western, totally controlled sets because you're not shooting in practical locations where you have to worry about crowd control. Instead, it turned into a disaster."

The disaster began with the hiring of the technicians needed to make the picture. It has always been Peckinpah's policy to go after and get the best possible personnel regardless of cost. However, at the time MGM wanted to make *Pat Garrett and Billy the Kid* another company was also filming in Durango: John Wayne's BATJAC production of *Wednesday Morning* (finally released as *Cahill, U.S. Marshal*). Many of the people Peckinpah wanted had already been hired for the Wayne picture by its unit manager, Bill Davidson. When Davidson learned that the Peckinpah production was about to overpay technicians in order to get them to jump their agreements with BATJAC, he asked Dawson to consider the long-range effects of filming in Mexico. When this caution was ignored, Davidson did the only thing he could: he hired replacements at the going rate.

Ironically, in spite of this confrontation, Davidson still managed to bring in his picture fourteen days ahead of schedule while *Pat Garrett* would wind up running twenty-two days over. But Davidson held no grudges. He even allowed Peckinpah to rent the only available Chapman crane, while BATJAC took a Christmas break, despite the fact that Peckinpah's crew had soundly defeated BATJAC's in a soccer game held for charity the week before. On his next film, Peckinpah would hire Davidson to work for him.

Following the start of production in mid-November 1972, the *Pat Garrett and Billy the Kid* company found itself confronted with an epidemic of influenza. Peckinpah caught the virus early and had to fight its effects virtually throughout the production as did many of the cast and crew. Thousands of people would die of the disease in Durango that winter. Among them would be Bud Hulburd, Peckinpah's special effects man on *The Wild Bunch,* who visited Peckinpah on location and died shortly following his return to the States.

To all of this was added conspiracy. For whatever his reasons, the unit production manager became concerned that Peckinpah was neither physically nor mentally fit to direct the picture. He began openly to question Peckinpah's production decisions, thereby alienating himself from the director.

After shooting began all of the exposed film was shipped to MGM's laboratory in California for processing and printing. This in itself was not unusual inasmuch as the color process used was the studio's own Metrocolor. MGM, however, continually assured Peckinpah that the footage was being screened in California and was usable. What they did not say was that MGM's screening procedure for daily rushes called for projecting them at 96 frames per second (four times normal speed). This meant that problems with zooms, lens flares, strobing pans, or any other mechanical difficulties went virtually unnoticed until the rushes were screened in Mexico at normal speed, six to twelve days later. This oversight was then complicated by the MGM policy of dismissing actors im-

230

mediately following the completion of their scenes. These practices made reshooting both difficult and costly.

As if this were not enough, a new Panavision lens developed focus problems. Owing to a slightly bent mounting flange, this lens could only bring into sharp focus the right half of the image. Because MGM had rejected Peckinpah's request for a camera mechanic on location, the problem went unnoticed for several weeks. As a consequence, a great deal of film had been shot with this lens before the failure was discovered and the lens replaced.

In the midst of these problems, the unit manager's questioning of Peckinpah's ability finally irked Peckinpah to the point that he requested that MGM remove the man from the picture. The unit manager, who had apparently put himself on record with the studio, refused to go, suggesting that it would be Peckinpah who would be replaced instead. When MGM delayed making any decision on the matter, open warfare broke out between Peckinpah and MGM.

This conflict disturbed producer Gordon Carroll greatly. He had been in strong support of Peckinpah since his name began being mentioned in connection with the picture. He had personally negotiated a contract for Peckinpah that called for two director's cuts of the film rather than the customary one. It also assured Peckinpah of a "play or pay" position on the project—MGM either had to make the film with Peckinpah or pay Peckinpah a substantial amount of money. This placed Carroll in the role of pacifier when MGM and Peckinpah squared off.

If Carroll did not agree with MGM's policies toward Peckinpah, he also did not feel that Peckinpah's weakened physical condition was conducive to making a good picture. Moreover, he disagreed with Peckinpah's easily aroused aggression toward the studio and felt too much energy was being spent attacking MGM and not enough making *Pat Garrett* into what it should be. Because he did not wholly support Peckinpah, he became Peckinpah's enemy as well.

At this point in the conflict, MGM decided to exclude Dawson, the associate producer, from all production meetings because they felt that he was Peckinpah's man. Dawson was made second unit director. He recalled the deepening split between Carroll and Peckinpah: "Although Sam and Gordon Carroll got along very well at the beginning of the picture, Carroll was a studio producer. I mean when it came down to choosing between Sam's group and MGM's, he went with MGM. There were some real confrontations between him and Peckinpah. He'd say: 'I forbid you to shoot such and such a scene. You are not authorized to shoot it.' And Sam would say: 'Oh, yeah? Watch me!' And Carroll would say, 'If you do, you will be in breach of contract, and MGM will have to take a legal position.' And Sam would say to me, 'Gordy, go out and get it prepared.' Then we'd be in a race to see if I can get there and wrap it up before they can get there and rip it out.

"With that kind of game playing, where's your energy going? Right down the tube. It's not on the screen where it belongs. With my energy, it's okay because I am a troubleshooter on a picture. I enjoy that kind of challenge if it's constructively solving problems. But when the guy you're supposed to be working with is in competition with you, what have you got if you win? And when it's Sam's energy that gets tapped in pointless battles, it's really a waste."

An attempt to see things more objectively came from Kristofferson: "Sam surely had his troubles on *Pat Garrett*. It was a regular horror show. But I have to see both sides of it. I can't even mention Gordon Carroll's name around Sam because it [already] has cost me four bucks. But I admire Gordon for sticking it out. I don't know all the sides, except that I know that Gordon put up with a lot of abuse that I know I would never have stood around for." Meanwhile, the disagreement with the unit production manager finally came to a head when he confronted Peckinpah one evening. After a long and heated exchange of words, he threatened to put a contract out on Peckinpah's life. Among those present when this threat was made was a friend of Peckinpah's whose father holds a high position in the Mexican military. Taking the statement at its face value, the friend immediately picked up the phone and called Mexico City asking that Mexican gunmen be dispatched to eliminate the unit manager. After the manager had finally departed and the dust cleared, Peckinpah tactfully took his enthusiastic friend aside and explained that the threat had been spoken in anger and that he must call Mexico City and head off the gunmen. Several days later, MGM finally recalled the unit manager to Hollywood.

One of the other casualties of this affair was Peckinpah's personal secretary, who had her loyalties undermined and was forced to depart. She had been Katy Haber's replacement after Peckinpah completed *The Getaway*. Katy Haber recalled: "I had been fired or let go following all three of my pictures for Sam at that time—*Straw Dogs, Junior Bonner,* and *The Getaway.* It was great because it meant I had a chance to return to England to see my mother. The only problem is that by the time Sam gets around to rehiring me, I have to go through all the files to find out where things are at.

"On *Getaway* Sam, of course, had married Joie so there wasn't a whole lot of room for me, was there? So I went back to England and saw my mother as usual and then got a job on a picture called *Reata* that Sam Fuller was making in Spain. Well, that was terrific, except that after five weeks Warner Brothers came in, looked at the rushes, and canceled the production. By coincidence, that was the very day Sam's secretary on *Pat Garrett* quit.

"Sam called Camille Fielding in California and told her he needed a secretary and Camille said, 'What about Katy?' And Sam said, 'That bitch is working for Sam Fuller in Spain.' And Camille said, 'No, she isn't. She just called, and the picture's been canceled.' ... So I packed my bags and flew to Mexico. But *Pat Garrett* was by far the most emotionally draining experience I have ever been involved with. I think I'm a fairly placid person, but after *Pat Garrett* I was as close to a nervous breakdown as I ever hope to come. It was awful."

Despite all of its difficulties, *Pat Garrett and Billy the Kid* is a film of striking visual beauty. Among those responsible for this was art director Ted Haworth, whose credits include the production design of such films as *The Longest Day, The Professionals, Marty, Strangers on a Train,* and an Academy Award for his work on *Sayonara.*

"It is difficult to discuss *Pat Garrett* because there were so many problems connected with it," Haworth recalled. "I remember arguing with Sam about the location. I had found a town I thought was absolutely right for Lincoln, but it needed work, and it meant traveling each day to shoot there. Sam considered my suggestion but insisted that the Western town in Chupaderos would be fine. That decision alone saved the production easily $100,000. But I kept getting these MGM people telling me how much Sam was costing them when in reality the picture probably would have come in on time and within budget had they only just let him alone.

"That doesn't mean that Sam looks for the cheapest way. Absolutely not. But he is concerned about quality. He responds only to the best, either in front of the camera or behind it. All the rest is bullshit.

"There was one scene in *Pat Garrett* that I really fought Sam over. That was the room where Billy was jailed. I had purposely left it bare—only a table and a couple of chairs. Sam doesn't like that. He likes things a little overdressed so that he can remove things to get the look he wants. But that room had to be devoid of clutter. I knew it, and I refused to change. Sam insisted on more. I had this calendar that duplicated the year 1881 exactly. I said, 'Sam, what would you think if I hung up a calendar from 1881?' And Sam just smiled and said, 'Perfect.' Not another word about change this or change that—just 'perfect.' It was the perfect detail to complement the sparseness of the room. He understood what I was after, and that was all he needed to shoot it."

The setting that Haworth describes was used for the scene in which Garrett's deputy, Bob Ollinger, threatens Billy, setting the stage for the Kid's break from jail. R. G. Armstrong, who portrays Ollinger in the film, vividly recalled the scene and his own confrontation with Peckinpah over it: "Sam allows you to improvise on the set if he trusts you. There were about three or four lines in the jail there that I put in because I needed them as transitions. The line there near the opening of the scene where I tell Billy, 'And just before that rope snaps it's gonna hit you like a bolt a lightnin' that what I been tellin' you's the truth'—Sam let me put that in so it'd be obvious that I'd been talkin' to this guy over a longer period of time.

"One of the other things we added was the place where I go up to Billy and say, 'On your knees.' And he says, 'Kiss my ass.' That wasn't in there. I said to Sam that we needed somethin' in here to motivate my knockin' him sideways. And Kris says, 'I'll say, "kiss my ass."' And I said: 'That's good. I'll knock you clear over the table if you say that to me.'

"So, finally, we were doin' one more rehearsal before shooting a master take of the scene, and suddenly Sam says, 'I don't believe a goddamn thing you're sayin' or you're doin'.' Just like that—outta nowhere. And you talk about my ego! I didn't say anything. I just closed my eyes. And it got all quiet on the set as Sam let me stand there for what must have been five or ten beats thinking and getting my head together.

"Finally, I said, 'Let's do it over,' and I walked back to the chair in the corner ragin' inside. Sam said, 'Let's shoot it.' And man, I came out of that corner, and I was on fire. I was throwin' my anger at Sam, but it all came out at Kris Kristofferson.

"I said, 'On your knees,' and he said, 'Kiss my ass,' and man, I exploded. I knocked him down and then pulled him up by the hair. He said to me, 'I want you to really pull my hair.' Well, the way I was feelin', he didn't have to worry about me pullin' as much as he did about what he was gonna have left when I finished. "Then at the end of the scene I threw in the lines: 'I'm goin' across the street. I'm thirsty as hell!' And as I walked past Sam I heard him say, 'Cut ... Whew!' And he slid down in his seat. I mean I was angry, and Sam knew it. But he got me to put that anger into the part."

As with all Peckinpah pictures, *Pat Garrett* required the services of several professional stunt men, among them Gary Combs. "The things you really bust your keester on in stunt work are the simple things," stated Combs. "Like a saddle fall. Happens in every Western. A guy is whippin' down the road, and he gets shot off his horse. I'm tellin' you that is the most underpaid, hardest thing to do in the picture in terms of wear and tear on your body.

"I had to take a horse fall for Kris in *Pat Garrett* right after where he breaks jail and the horse bucks him off in the street. I was workin' with an old Mexican buckin' horse which wasn't the best in the world. I had taken him out two or three days before and rehearsed him. And he bucked pretty good down in the soft sand. But on that hard street the old horse was hurtin' his front feet when he'd hit, so he was tryin' to quit me.

"Well, when I finally got him lined up in the right direction, I decided I'd bail off and make it look like he bucked me. Only as I started to do that he really fired one, which sent my feet straight up in the air and I landed on my head. If he'd been buckin' good, I couldn't have gotten off any better as far as the picture was concerned. It knocked me cold and broke a little bone in my ankle that never did heal right so I had to have it taken out."

Peckinpah also recalled that fall: "It was late in the day, and I was afraid it wouldn't work out—that he might get hurt. I wanted to wait. But he said—he insisted—that he was ready and the horse was ready. So I finally said go ahead because Gary is a pro. Well, he landed badly on his head and he was out. A little bit different and he could have broken his neck. I don't want that. A good friend of mine, Roy Sickner, had the top of his head taken off in a stunt involving a jeep, and another good friend of mine is dead. When you get around four o'clock in the afternoon and you start pushing, don't do it. That's when I want to get closeups and reactions. I don't want anybody hurt. Anybody."

Meanwhile, the battle between the studio and director continued undiminished as Hollywood gossip columns regularly began to run items about Peckinpah's excessive drinking on the set. Peckinpah characteristically fought back, sometimes with a sense of humor. He took out a full page ad in *Daily Variety* picturing himself on location with many of the cast and crew who remained loyal to him, all with drinks in their hands raised in a toast. The caption read: "Dear Sirs: With reference to the rumor that seems to be spreading around Hollywood that on numerous occasions Sam Peckinpah has been carried off the set taken with drink. This is to inform you that those rumors are totally unfounded. However, there have been mornings ... " (Peckinpah's ellipsis).

This conflict did not make Peckinpah any easier to work with. Wurlitzer, who had gone on location with the picture to rewrite scenes as needed, found Peckinpah close to unbearable. Kristofferson stated: "Sam drove poor Rudy crazy. Sam would call Rudy up at like four in the morning and say, 'Come on over here, and we'll rewrite the script.' By the time Rudy'd get over there, Sam'd forgotten that he called him, and he'd chew Rudy's ass out for coming over. Rudy is such a great writer, but by the end of the picture, he could barely keep it together. Damn, Sam was tough on him. But Sam's tough on everybody, especially himself."

Between the conflict and the flu, Peckinpah's health throughout the making of *Pat Garrett* remained shaky at best. In the face of this adversity, Peckinpah regarded himself as "an occasional drinker—drinking whenever the occasion arose." To steady his nerves and relieve tension, he would throw knives at a large oak door. On the set, however, he was in complete control.

Jack Elam, the wild-eyed, often bearded character actor whose many films include *Support Your Local Sheriff* and *Once upon a Time in the West* and who portrays Alamosa Bill in *Pat Garrett and Billy the Kid,* recalled: "Twenty-five years ago—fifteen—even ten years ago, when there were still stars in this business of the caliber of Gable—there still are some around today like Jimmy Stewart or Henry Fonda. Well, on the set there was traditionally a procedure you go through that was automatic when it came to setting up a scene. What happens is that the director first talks over the shot with his key people and the important actors involved, and they decide to do it a particular way. Then everybody but the crew can go do anything they want while the shot is set up.

"So the cameraman and his lighting crew and the grips all set the shot up and, say, forty-five minutes later it's ready to go. So the assistant director's first call is for all the extras and he sets them in their places. Then he calls in the one-line bit players and sets them up. Then you call over your supporting actors. And then you call the director over. And nine times out of ten, he's already sittin' there looking over the script or something. And you get virtually everything ready to shoot and then you go get your major stars that when they walk on the set, you are ready to run through it once and shoot it.

"Now on Sam's picture it's not quite like that. Everything is the same except that last part. You bring in your supporting players, and then you get your stars. And then you get Sam after everybody's in his

236

spot. So what I'm sayin' is that Sam is the star of his set. And actually in terms of money power and publicity to get a picture made, Sam is the star of his own pictures in a very real sense."

There was doubt about star Bob Dylan, however, who despite his experience as a performer had never worked as a professional actor before. Kristofferson related: "Bobby Dylan is the most unusual dude I have ever known. I think he's a genius or somethin'. You can't really ever understand him completely. He is so much like a kid in a way. But you don't think that when you're around him. You think, 'That son of a bitch is doin' numbers on everybody.' But I think really his mind just doesn't go ABCDE; it goes AFWQ...But he stuck it out the whole movie without knowin' what he was really supposed to be doin'. . . .

"This one scene, Sam wanted him to come riding up to me, and as usual, it wasn't in the script. So they put Bobby on a horse and told him what they wanted. Now it's hard for Bobby to hit his marks in a scene with his own feet 'cause he doesn't think like that. But he's supposed to come through these sheep to where I'm standin', and old Sam says, 'Okay, Bobby, you just come straight by the camera here.' Well, Bobby went into a gallop, man, scaring sheep, horses, cameramen, and everybody. And I was laughin' so hard I was in tears. So was Sam. And old Sam says, 'No, Bobby, I really didn't mean that.' The strange thing is, I don't know yet whether Bobby did that on purpose or not.

"The really big scene that Bobby kind a screwed up was the one where Garrett is supposed to be ridin' off into the sunrise at the end of the movie after killin' Billy. Only they were shootin' a sunset for sunrise and they had like five minutes of what they call 'golden time' when the sun is just right.

"Well, the night before it had been the extras screwin' the shot up—lookin' at Sam or somethin'. So we were doin' it the second time. Well, Bobby wasn't in the shot, and he and Harry Dean Stanton [the actor who plays the outlaw Luke in the picture] decided they were goin' on a health campaign and run five miles. Only the first part of the five miles was right through the shot.

"I came out on the set, and it was like a tomb. I asked what happened, and I hear, 'The Dylan boys just ran through the shot.' And everybody is sitting around not sayin' a word as Harry Dean comes walkin' in. It was about as quiet as a church, and old Harry Dean is sayin' 'Hi Sam!' And everybody is sayin' to themselves, 'Oh, shit,' and Sam growls, 'You just cost me $25,000!' And Harry Dean says, 'Sam, I knew it was wrong, and I was runnin' after him to tell him to stop.'

"Now Sam throws a pretty mean knife. He can pretty near always make it stick. Well, he's got this knife in his hand, and he lets 'er fly, and it sticks in the wood next to old Harry Dean, who flies through the door like nothin' flat shoutin' behind him: 'I promise Sam. It'll never happen again.' And when Dylan heard about it, he just said, 'Well, let's have a concert and pay him back.'
It's like I said. I never know when he's doin' a number on Sam or not."

Kristofferson, because of his lack of experience as an actor, came in for a good deal of criticism. One complaint was that he refused to take much instruction about firing a handgun. Peckinpah supported him throughout the production, however.

James Coburn recalled: "The interesting thing about Kris was the boyish quality he brought to the part of Billy, which I thought was brilliant. And Sam saw that in Kris when the producer and everyone else was down on Kris—thought he was too inexperienced. Sam saw the kind of brash naivete in Kris that really made Billy come alive on the screen. For me, Kris was a pleasure to work with. He didn't have much experience in this sort of work, but he was always there, always prepared, always ready to do what was required of him. I helped him as much as I could, but Sam was the one who really helped Kris the most."

With the size of the production and the fact that it was being shot in Mexico, a number of small speaking parts went to members of the crew as much for the ability to speak English without an accent as anything else. Property master Bob Visciglia plays the barber who shaves Garrett, Dawson plays an outraged citizen of the town of Lincoln, and Wurlitzer portrays the tall, bearded O'Folliard who is shot to death when Billy is captured early in the picture. Even Sam Peckinpah got into the act, playing a coffin maker at work on a child's coffin who speaks with Garrett just before Garrett closes in on the Kid. James Coburn continued: "I think they cut most of what Sam said in the way it's released but his line to me was: 'I'm going to take everything I've got and stick it in this box [casket] and bury it in the ground. Then I'm getting out of this goddamn territory.' Then I offer him a drink from this flask I'm carrying, and he refuses it, which was hilarious because that's the only drink Sam's ever turned down and we got it on film. And he says: 'So you finally figured it out. Well, go on. Get it over with.' And as I turn to go, he shouts after me: 'Go get him, you bastard! Go get him, you son of a bitch, you asshole lawman!' I mean he was really into the part.

"But that's the way Sam directs—everything's spontaneous. If you know something about the scene and a lot about the character you're playing, the part develops a life of its own. There's a real interaction between the characters in the scene. That scene with Sam was a very heavy experience. I think I did my best work on the picture."

The scene is of interest on another level as well. Peckinpah, perhaps more than any other director currently working, seems to have set himself the task of not allowing the Western hero or the values for which that hero died slip unnoticed into an unmarked grave. What Garrett has figured out is that Billy will not run, for it is not death but the meaning of life that is at stake. That is the theme at the center of the film as Peckinpah intended it. In this respect, MGM's reediting of the film eliminated several key scenes that deserve attention.

"There were three scenes that justify [the film] that are missing from the MGM version," Coburn recounts. "It was to be told from Pat Garrett's point of view rather than from Billy's, and it was done so purposely. The studio didn't understand that at all. They apparently wanted some sort of balance going. So the studio eliminated three scenes that were keys as well as portions of others. It was those scenes that placed [Garrett] in his quandary. Garrett had made a choice, and the film portrayed him working his way through that choice. He had to deal with his own conscience, and he suffered greatly."

The three scenes that Coburn is referring to are the death of Garrett in the prologue and epilogue, the conflict with his wife that reveals him not as just some killer but as a human being with pressures and problems with which he must somehow come to terms, and a meeting between Garrett and John Chisum that points up Garrett's sellout to society as he discusses a loan Chisum made available to him to purchase some bottom land. Ironically, it is this land that Garrett dies on in the original opening and closing moments of the film that framed the story of the killing of Billy.

Coburn continued: "As the film opens, Garrett's old—an old, crotchety son of a bitch living with this thing on his back all these years. It's about thirty years later, and he's got a long, white, drooping mustache. And we're riding out [Garrett is being driven out to see his land by another man] in this buggy, and [John] Poe is riding alongside. And I look up, and I see all these sheep, and I say to Poe: 'Get all those fuckin' sheep off my property. Get 'em off! I've told you, you son of a bitch!' And I'm yelling. . . And Poe says back to me, 'It's my land.' And I say: 'Not no more it isn't. I'm breakin' that lease!' And he says, 'That's not legal.' And I say: 'What kind of legal you talkin' about? You and that Santa Fe bunch legal? Is that it? You're gettin' off my property.' And he leads me into the ambush and says, 'That's the last time you're gonna talk to me like that, Old Man.' And he starts to go for his gun, and there is another guy up behind me in ambush, and I reach for my old gun. I've got that blanket coat. . . over my legs, and I whip that off and go for my gun and—'Bang'—I'm shot in the back, and I whip around like that and then this guy shoots me—'Pow'—and then that guy shoots me—'Baf'—and I start to fall over out of the buggy in slow motion.

"Well, with each crack of the gun, Sam cut in the shots of a chicken's head being blown off. It was all cut together with flash cuts against the slow motion of my—or Garrett's—death until as I topple out of the buggy, we are into the scene where Billy and the rest of them are shooting at the chickens buried up to their heads in sand, and I ride up—some thirty years before. So the entire narrative of the film becomes Garrett's flashback at the moment of his death."

This scene was brilliantly edited by Bob Wolfe, one of six editors whose names appear on the final credits of the picture. In it, Wolfe intensified the meaning by cutting it so that not only was Garrett's death interlaced with the shooting of the chickens at old Fort Sumner some thirty years before, but the resulting montage made it appear that both the younger Garrett and Billy were shooting at the older Garrett as well. Since the men who really kill Garrett work for the same Santa Fe ring that hired Garrett to kill the Kid, Garrett's death atones for his killing of Billy thus allowing Peckinpah's main theme to come full circle.

When the cast and crew finished shooting *Pat Garrett and Billy the Kid* in March of 1973, they were nearly a month behind schedule. At that point there were only two editors working on the film, Garth Craven and Roger Spottiswoode, both English and therefore a problem as far as the American Editors Guild was concerned. Coupled with this problem was the fact that MGM had committed the film to a number of first-run theaters from Memorial Day to the Fourth of July. Assuming the picture would be successful, MGM knew controlling these theaters would mean considerable revenue. However, to edit a film of this size in roughly two months verged on the impossible.

Craven, whose first association with Peckinpah was as sound editor on *Straw Dogs,* and who since has worked as both a film editor *(Bring Me the Head of Alfredo Garcia, The Killer Elite)* and director (second unit on *Carny),* recalled the situation: "The editing credits on *Pat Garrett* are really very simple. Two things happened: First, we got back to Hollywood, and there was no time left to cut the film. MGM wanted it like a week after Tuesday, and they said to us, 'Is there any way you can do that?' And first we said no, but then we said: 'Wait a minute; yes, there is: just give us *carte blanche.'* This meant hiring vast crews but, more importantly, hiring Bob Wolfe.

"This was then complicated by the fact that the union stepped in and said to Roger Spottiswoode and I that they didn't want us working because we weren't Americans. So that was a big battle that went on for a couple of weeks, and actually they won that round so we couldn't work. What we then had to do was hire this whole list of other men, and Roger and I had to stand behind the Moviolas not actually touching film but with these guys running the stuff for us. And they all had to be credited.

"Bob Wolfe would have come on the picture anyway simply to get us out of trouble timewise. There were certain things that were given to Bob that hadn't been worked on yet, for example, the whole title sequence involving the death of Pat Garrett which MGM eventually lifted from the film anyway.

"There was a cut—I mean not a first cut, but one which had gone through several stages in Mexico and which we brought with us when we came back to Hollywood. The work done afterwards was based on that cut. But we didn't actually physically do the cutting."

At the same time Jerry Fielding was brought in to supervise Bob Dylan's scoring of the picture because this was Dylan's first attempt at such a project. Fielding stated: "It was total frustration. Wasted effort. First of all, I was called in late on the picture after Sam began to doubt that Dylan's music alone could hold together a two-hour-plus motion picture.

"The producer, Gordon Carroll, was the one who subsidized Dylan as the major creative force musically on *Pat Garrett.* But just because you play a guitar and sing doesn't qualify you for scoring a picture. Everybody knew it, and everybody kept giving Dylan advice. The problem was he didn't know enough about the situation to tell good advice from bad. And then, of course, he looked at me, and all he could see was 'establishment.' So he wouldn't listen to me at all. And I resent that kind of superficial shit. I paid my dues in this business, and I've got the scars to prove it, but that's beside the point.

"I give Bobby Dylan credit for writing seven great pieces of music and a lot of nonsense which is strictly for teenyboppers. I also give him credit for having a way with words that is often very effective but just as often meaningless. He plays a simple blues pattern and a number of repetitious chords that I honestly must say offend me as a musician. On that basis, considering the complexities of scoring a picture,. Bobby Dylan has no more business attempting it than Sam Peckinpah has selling popcorn in the lobby of the theater.

"But he was their boy, and I was supposed to make it happen. I set up two dubbing sessions. Dylan had this song he'd written for which he had a limitless number of verses that he would sing in random order. Actually, Kris Kristofferson had written a song as well which I thought had more potential in terms of scoring the picture, but I was overruled. So I had to tape Dylan's song, because he had nothing written down, and have it transcribed. It was my idea that by having Dylan sing a relevant verse as it fit the story at roughly nine separate points throughout the picture, it might be coherent. Dylan never understood what I wanted.

"At the same time I asked that he write at least one other piece of music because you cannot possibly hope to deal with an entire picture on the basis of that one ballad. So, finally, he brought to the dubbing session another piece of music—'Knock-knock-knockin' on Heaven's Door.' Everybody loved it. It was shit. That was the end for me.

"They all got into it. Bob Dylan—he talked to them all and he listened to them all and he believed them all and he tried to do what he thought they wanted in his limited way. And it was infantile. It was sophomoric. It was stuff you learn not to do the second year you score a piece of film. And for me to go back and try to do that shit and tell them why I can't be a part of that—why it's wrong that he's singing 'Knock-knock-knockin' on Heaven's Door' with a rock drummer in a scene where a guy is dying and the emotion speaks for itself. If I've got to explain that to a producer, then I've got to get out."

"They didn't use the song I wrote for *Pat Garrett,*" stated Kristofferson. "But at the time I wrote it, I didn't realize that they were asking Bob to do the whole thing, or I wouldn't have even bothered to try and put a song in it. I've rewritten what I did then, and we use it as part of our [Kristofferson and his band's] act. It's called 'One for the Money' now. What I did was keep the chorus. I was writing about Sam and all of us and MGM anyway. It was about Garrett and the whorehouse scene in the picture—'caught in a circle of strangers and who do you screw to get out of this game.' But I like

Bobby's work, and Sam sure liked it."

Following the terms of its contract with Peckinpah, MGM allowed him two cuts on the picture and a preview screening after each. By the second screening, however, it became apparent that the studio was not concerned with what Peckinpah had done because it had editing plans of its own.

"Sam wanted a showing for cast, crew, and friends," stated Katy Haber. "We sent out invitations and everything, and at the last moment MGM said no. Then they said only sixteen people selected by Peckinpah could attend each preview, and we'd already had the first one so Sam was really only allowed sixteen of his friends total to view the film. He wanted people with some influence in the industry to see the film—Henry Fonda, Marty Baum. We sent the list to MGM and they removed all names they felt were influential. So that left only Sam's family and a couple of people [that] I was able to sneak in under assumed names as boyfriends of Sam's daughters—three newspaper reviewers. After it was over, MGM began re-cutting the film.

"So basically what MGM did was to hire Sam for who he was and then use his name to publicize the picture even though it was no longer his cut. The sneaker ads in the *Los Angeles Times* were a four-by-four box with the name Sam Peckinpah in it and nothing else. I thought it was an obituary when I opened it up. I thought it was a joke."

Craven, who suddenly found himself locked out of his editing room following the second screening of the film, stated: "I must tell you that the time spent in Durango when it was just Roger, Sam, and myself—an awful lot of midnight oil and heartache went into that cut. It was a big picture. It was this sort of epic film, and that was not apparently what MGM wanted. They apparently wanted something to go on a double bill with the *Kansas City Bomber* or something.

"I have not seen the film at the cinema. But people who were in the film have come along and said, 'Whatever happened to that scene such and such?' And all I can say is that it was there when I last saw the film. Whole scenes and people were eliminated. It was more than a little bit heartbreaking."

As if to justify Peckinpah's fury and disgust at what MGM had done to the film, *Pat Garrett and Billy the Kid* in the studio version did extremely little business when it was released. Peckinpah openly denounced the film as not being his and informed his lawyers to file suit for $2 million in damages. It was not a suit he expected to win but rather a gesture he felt was necessary. Nevertheless, in a very real sense, *Pat Garrett and Billy the Kid,* along with numerous other films that failed to do well at the box office, caused a drastic reorganization at MGM culminating with the resignation of James T. Aubrey less than six months after the film was released. To whatever extent Peckinpah won this encounter, however, he also lost. Far too few people went to see what must be considered one of Peckinpah's most memorable Westerns.

Among the executives who remained at MGM following the exodus of James Aubrey was vice-president in charge of production, Daniel Melnick. During a telephone interview in November 1974, Melnick stated: "Sam has reedited *Pat Garrett.* I have spent some time with him working on it, consulting with him on it. And it is unresolved at this point as to when and if it will be released [again]. It's really subject to discussion between ourselves and UA [United Artists, then the distributor for MGM]. My own feeling is that it is really an extraordinarily good film, and that it may be flawed in various ways, but it remains an important film. I would like to see it rereleased, but it will come down to economics and people's judgment as to how much it's going to cost to do that."

Unfortunately, economics won out. MGM never rereleased the film in its original form, and Melnick has since left the studio.

14

Bring Me the Head of Alfredo Garcia

"We're going to find the Golden Fleece."

Soon after the release of *Pat Garrett and Billy the Kid,* Sam Peckinpah began working on his next feature film, *Bring Me the Head of Alfredo Garcia,* an unsettling tale of vengeance and love involving an American ex-patriot in South America. "I'd been working on the project for four years," Peckinpah recalled. "Driving up to make *Cable Hogue,* Frank Kowalski presented me with the initial idea. He said: 'I got a great title: *Bring Me the Head of.* . . —and he had some other name—and the hook is that the guy is already dead.' I thought the idea was sensational. We worked on it both here and then in England when I was making *Straw Dogs.* But it was finally Gordy Dawson who collaborated with me on the shooting script."

Meanwhile, producer Martin Baum had formed his own independent production company following the demise of ABC Pictures. This new company; Optimus Productions, had a distribution arrangement with United Artists and was looking for interesting possibilities.

"Sam came to me one day;" recalled Martin Baum, "and said: 'I've got an idea for a script. It's about twenty-five pages. How would you like to take a look at it?' It was called *Bring Me the Head of Alfredo Garcia.* I read it and I thought, yeah, this could be exciting. So I went to United Artists, and I said that I could make a deal with Sam's agent for so many dollars down and so many dollars at the time of shooting. They said fine, pay the money. So I went back to Sam and said, 'I've got the money for you to write the script.' And Sam said: 'You don't understand. I don't want any money to write the script. I'm doing this for you. I owe it to you. If they like the script, they can pay me; if they don't like it, it costs them nothing. This one is for you, and I'll do it only on that condition.' So Sam sat down and wrote the script, and obviously they liked it."

In mid-August 1973, Peckinpah arrived in Mexico City to begin preproduction work on the film. With him was his secretary, Katy Haber; writer-producer Gordon Dawson; and unit production manager Bill Davidson. With the exception of Alf Pegley, who was coming from England to act as property master, the entire balance of the crew would be Mexican. Working in conjunction with Churubusco Studios, Dawson and Davidson would select that crew.

Among the key Mexican personnel was the director of photography, Alex Phillips, Jr., a strikingly handsome blond, blue-eyed Mexican Indian-Russian, who had been trained by his father, a Russian emigre who had become one of Mexico's premiere cameramen.

When they met for the first time in Peckinpah's suite at the Aristos Hotel, Phillips and Peckinpah realized they shared a dislike for wide-angle lenses and a fondness for zooms and multiple camera setups. "I shoot a lot of film," Peckinpah said at last, "possibly between 150,000 and 200,000 feet of film on this picture. I make very few takes, but I shoot a lot of film because I like to change angles. I shoot with editing in the back of my mind." Phillips nodded his head. They had much in common indeed.

Preproduction work on *Alfredo Garcia* took its cues from Peckinpah. Out of habit, Peckinpah would wake up daily around 4:30 in the morning. During the production of a film he uses the several hours between then and the morning call to do his "homework" for the day's shooting. However, without a day of shooting before him, he would attempt to fall back asleep, often taking a sleeping pill to do so. This would result in his missing the morning call altogether, a frequent occurrence during the preproduction work on *Alfredo Garcia.*

Nevertheless, the preparation for *Alfredo Garcia* moved ahead without much difficulty. Each day Dawson, Davidson, and their Mexican counterparts would accompany Peckinpah out to one or more possible locations for the film—the town of Huixlac in fiesta, a hacienda near the pyramids of Teotihuacan, a myriad of grave-yards, a tenement off Reforma. In selecting or rejecting each location, Peckinpah would consider whatever was shown to him, relying heavily upon his intuitive response. He wanted the picture to reflect a particular kind of gritty reality he sensed was Mexico.

Because Peckinpah had to be driven out to each of these potential locations, he was often caught in traffic during the Mexico City rush hour. Because Mexico City streets were laid out long before

246

the invention of the automobile, the chaos that occurs during this period each day rivals the worst in the world. To add to the general discomfort, August and September are also the rainy season in Mexico. Each day at rush hour, the sky would become cramped with dark gray clouds wetting down the streets and making the traffic accidents more interesting for the native population. Faced with these conditions, Peckinpah insisted that his driver, Camillo, always travel with glasses, ice, and several bottles of liquor. These comforts did not make the traffic move any faster, but they improved Peckinpah's attitude toward the situation immeasurably.

One particular rush hour it took exceptionally long for Camillo to pick his way through traffic back to the Aristos. By chance, this was the day that Peckinpah was scheduled to interview several actresses for the part of Elita, the heroine of the picture. They were being brought to the hotel that evening by a casting agent named Lanca Becker with whom Peckinpah had worked on previous films.

They finally arrived at the hotel an hour and a half late. As he stepped from his car, Peckinpah drained the last of his brandy and ginger ale, handed the glass to a companion, hitched up his pants, and moved through the hotel's revolving doors. In the midst of the confusion of the lobby stood Lanca, a matronly woman in her forties, expensively dressed. With her was a beautiful Mexican actress in her early twenties, quietly aware of the overeager glances from bellboys and tourists. Peckinpah spotted them easily and moved toward them. Lanca whispered something to the young actress, and they both smiled in Peckinpah's direction. Peckinpah, however, completely ignoring the younger woman, walked directly to Lanca and dropped to his knees before her. Then, taking both of her hands in his own, he apologized in his most eloquent Spanish, telling her she was the most beautiful woman in the room. Finally, he kissed her hands and arose to escort her to the elevator, leaving the young actress to awkwardly fend for herself. Once in the elevator on the way to his suite, Peckinpah graciously allowed Lanca to introduce the actress to him before complimenting the girl on her looks and Lanca on her eye for casting.

In his suite, Peckinpah was joined for the informal casting session by Dawson and Davidson. Lanca presented several photographs of other actresses whom she thought Peckinpah might be interested in casting. She had arranged for several to come by. Introducing himself as "San Samuel," Peckinpah greeted each warmly and discussed the range that would be required from whoever landed the part. Davidson assured Peckinpah that provisions had been made for screen tests of all actresses with Warren Oates, who had already been cast as Bennie, the American ex-patriot. Oates would arrive in Mexico the following week.

The last actress to arrive was Aurora Clavel, whom Peckinpah had cast in all three of his previous films made in Mexico (as the prostitute in *Major Dundee,* the lost love of Pike Bishop in *The Wild Bunch,* and Pat Garrett's wife in *Pat Garrett and Billy the Kid).* After all of the other actresses and Lanca had left for the evening, Peckinpah asked Aurora to remove her makeup. When she had done so, he announced to Dawson and Davidson that she *was* Elita. She smiled and kissed him affectionately. Peckinpah then asked the others to leave them alone. The casting session was over.

Out in the hall, Davidson asked Dawson why they must go through the time and expense of shooting screen tests with all the actresses if Sam was convinced that Aurora was right for the part. Dawson smiled, shook his head, and replied that Sam's mind really would not be made up until he actually saw how each of the actresses worked with Oates. Davidson, whose concern was with finding the most economical way of getting the picture made, shrugged and followed Dawson off to find a restaurant and a late dinner. The next day a leading gossip column in a Mexican newspaper would prematurely run a story about Aurora Clavel's selection as the leading lady in Peckinpah's new picture.

Much time was spent in search of the right bar to serve as Bennie's work place. Peckinpah and his associates personally checked out a great variety of drinking spots in different sections of the city. None of them satisfied Peckinpah, although in one establishment he was taken with a fourteen-year-old Mexican girl and her younger brother who were cleaning it prior to its opening for business. He inquired about her family and found that the father was dead and there were seven children. Peckinpah then had Davidson get their names and addresses, promising that he would use them all as extras in the film.

At last, Peckinpah and company arrived at the Plaza Garibaldi with its mariachis and rough clientele. They tried several bars but finally wound up in one called "Tlaque-Paque." After Peckinpah's Mexican associates from Churubusco explained to the owner of this bar their interest, the owner agreed to allow "Senor Peckinpah" to look around and to use the place if he liked it. His voice had the texture of gravel-blasted *pulque.*

Peckinpah moved through the bar with his entourage. He was excited by something for the first time in several days. "This is dressed. This is for real," he murmured. He looked at his Mexican art director, Augustin Ituarte: "Augustin, I want you to overdress the set anyway. Pictures of

Pancho Villa. Guns. A piano over here." "Would you like sarapes on the walls?" Ituarte inquired. "You are the art director. The decisions are up to you. But overdress it. I like to be able to walk on a set and find what I want by eliminating things that are already there," Peckinpah replied. Ituarte nodded and continued to write and sketch in his large notebook.

Suggesting that they have a drink here, Peckinpah moved to a table and sat down. The owner shouted from his table to make themselves comfortable and ordered a bottle of Ponche de Granada sent over, compliments of the house. Ponche de Granada is a drink made from tequila and pomegranate juice, served with ice and pecans. As Peckinpah poured, Alex Phillips, Jr., promised that it would give everyone "a tenday hangover." "I'll drink to that," Peckinpah smiled. *"Salud!"*

The Mexican members of the production team then softly explained that the owner of the bar was notorious in the area. It was rumored that he once killed a woman in his bar, but he served very little time in jail because he was able to bribe the right people in high places. He sat at his table across from his seventh wife with a mistress on each knee. All were somewhat hefty. His meaty hands constantly massaged the flesh of the women on his lap. Shouting in Spanish to Peckinpah as the filmmaker arose to leave, the owner asked that when he come back he bring beautiful women, not ugly men like the ones he was with. Peckinpah smiled, thanked him in Spanish for his hospitality, and said that he was thinking of setting up his office in the bar.

The owner laughed and stood, forcing his mistresses into chairs. Dressed in an expensive silk suit, his fingers adorned with diamond rings, he escorted them to the door while telling a coarse joke. Obviously excited by the obscene words and gestures required by the story, he laughed louder than those to whom he told it. As the production team finally returned to their cars, Peckinpah muttered: "And they call me *macho?* They don't know the meaning of the word."

By the first of September, Peckinpah had become so disenchanted with his accommodations at the Aristos that he moved into the older Hotel Bristol located blocks away. Aurora Clavel had suggested the hotel, claiming the governor of Guadalajara liked to stay there. A blue, concrete and iron, six-story structure, the Hotel Bristol fronted surreally on a picturesque, eighteenth-century cobblestone street. Its main dining room was a red and yellow Denny's restaurant decorated in American plastics that, some guests suggested, doubled for the food as well. Peckinpah, calling into question the taste and good judgment of the governor of Guadalajara, redoubled his efforts to find a suitable house to rent while working on the film.

Preproduction rolled on. One bright midmorning, sunshine forced Peckinpah behind his dark glasses as he stepped from the elevator and, moved unsteadily across the lobby towards a late breakfast in the dining room. Consumed by a case of what good ol' boys in California cattle country would have called "the whips and jingles," he arrived at a table where Dawson, Davidson, and Haber sat over morning coffee. Since Haber had ordered Peckinpah's breakfast ahead of his arrival— two soft-boiled eggs, dry toast, and tea—he slid loosely into the unoccupied seat and attempted to put the demons of the night behind him. Allied with the alcohol, the high altitude, and the Aztec twostep, however, those demons rendered Peckinpah closer to his two-minute eggs than to the hard-boiled director so often portrayed to the public.

Sam's spoon spasmodically rattled against the lip of the egg cup as he attempted to master his mouth. Bedeviled, he let the spoon slide back into the cup. "Shit!" he mumbled. "These bastards really have me this morning." Davidson shot a worried glance at Dawson who responded by standing up.

"Sam, we've gotta be moving. We've got men sitting out at the locations we're supposed to see today since six this morning. Bill and I'll go ahead. Drink your eggs, Sam, and you can meet us there."

Sam lifted his head and raised his dark glasses from his eyes so he could look directly at Dawson. A slow smile curled his lip. He nodded, then, removing the spoon from his egg cup, raised it like a wine glass. *"Salud!"* he said and quaffed his eggs in a long, slow swallow. "Not a bad idea," he said setting the cup back down. "I should do that more often." A smile flashed across his face again as he wiped a drop of yoke that mingled momentarily with the gray of his beard. "You and Bill go on. We'll see you out there." Dawson and Davidson moved off to their waiting car.

News has reached them that morning from America that the renowned director of Westerns John Ford had died at the age of 78. "I only met John Ford once," Peckinpah recalled. "On the steps of MGM one evening. We were introduced by mutual friends. People spend a lot of time comparing my work to his. Most of that's bullshit. In the first place, I don't like most of his later films. I loved *The Informer* and *Grapes of Wrath* and—what was that other one?—*Tobacco Road.* His best Western was *My Darling Clementine.* Fonda was sensational in that. I hated *The Searchers.* I loved the book, but I thought the movie was shit. But I suppose he didn't like much of what I did,

250

either. I think we're very different." Peckinpah lit a cigarette, finished his tea, and moved towards his waiting car.

The day was spent scouting locations that might serve as the spot where Bennie and Elita stop for a picnic and are accosted by two motorcycle bums. As the day wore on, nothing that was shown to Peckinpah proved to be what he wanted. By late afternoon, as a fine rain began to fall, Dawson stated that he was certain that he could find what Sam wanted. He said that he would take a driver and go out the following day, Sunday—his day off—and take pictures of all the suitable locations he could find. Peckinpah could then look at the photographs and decide from them which site he might want to look at more closely. Peckinpah agreed and Dawson returned to the city with Davidson and most of the Mexican production people for a meeting at Churubusco.

Peckinpah elected to stay behind at the last location they had looked at—a mountain meadow high above Mexico City—with a few friends and enjoy the quiet of the approaching evening. They stood beneath a cluster of pine trees that sheltered them from the gentle rain, drank tequila straight, and shared stories until the rain finally sifted through the pine needles. At last, Sam Peckinpah raised his glass: "To John Ford." It was time to go.

For the screen tests, Peckinpah selected several scenes out of the script that would test the range of equipment they planned to use as well as help choose a leading lady. These scenes included the opening confrontation between Bennie and Elita when he first learns of Alfredo's death, a compilation scene made up of several sequences that occur as Bennie and Elita drive, and the scene between them at night in the room before they go to the graveyard.

In the course of these tests, Warren Oates worked with eleven different actresses: "I went down to Mexico to do the tests for the picture, and I was a little jumpy. But Sam has a way of directing you that's like shorthand. I went through this one scene with the first actress, and Sam comes up to me and says: 'Don't screw around with it. Right there is where it's at, so don't screw around with it.' Then with another girl, he comes up to me and says, 'Who do you think you are, John Dillinger?' Or with another girl: 'Who do you think you're doing, Warren Oates? Now don't screw around with it. You had it, so don't screw around with it.' He talks to you in terms of what he knows about you, so you can always tell where you're at and what you have to do to get where he wants you to be."

After looking at the screen tests, Peckinpah selected the Mexican actress Isela Vega to play the role of Elita. She had never acted in a Peckinpah picture before and, in fact, had only appeared in one other American film prior to *Alfredo Garcia, The Deadly Trackers*. Nevertheless, Peckinpah felt that on the screen she managed to capture the character of Elita better than any of the other actresses including Aurora Clavel, who completely understood Peckinpah's decision: "Sam is a very loyal man, but his first loyalty is to his picture. I can take that. If I had been right for the part, it would have been me. I was not, therefore it is someone else. I still love Sam the same."

Among the others cast by Peckinpah in *Alfredo Garcia* were Emilio Fernandez as El Jefe, Mort Sahl as Quill, Helmut Dantine (who coproduced the picture with Martin Baum) as El Jefe's right-hand man, Janine Maldonado as El Jefe's daughter, and Kris Kristofferson and Donny Fritts as two motorcycle toughs. With the approval of the script by the Mexican censor, the film went into production in late September.

On October 10, *Variety* ran a small story on the production of *Alfredo Garcia* in which it quoted Peckinpah as saying: "For me, Hollywood no longer exists. It's past history. I've decided to stay in Mexico because I believe I can make my pictures with greater freedom from here." Within the month, the National Conference of Motion Picture and Television Unions, meeting in Detroit, openly censured Peckinpah for his statement and threatened *Alfredo Garcia* with union boycotts upon its release, claiming that it was a "runaway" production (one which could have been made in the United States but was being made outside the country for reasons of economy).

"My own quote down here [in Mexico] which they misquoted in the States," recounted Peckinpah, "was 'If MGM is an example of Hollywood, Hollywood is dead.' All they printed was the last part. This picture could never have been a 'runaway.' Anyone who has read the script could see that. There are only half a dozen roles in the whole fucking movie for Americans. On top of that, shooting in Mexico is no cheaper than in the States due to the going price for talented people being the same everywhere.

"I'm in favor of internationalizing unions so that if you work in the film industry, you can work for anybody making a film anywhere. I'm in favor of breaking down borders instead of building them up. I'm a member of three of the unions who are supposedly going to boycott this picture, so I've got to speak up for the unions. They've been beaten into the ground so many times by the studios that they have to take strong measures. But now I think a summit meeting is in order so that we can get on with making pictures."

Speaking as a producer on the picture, Dantine stated: "There are certain industries that are international—and should be and must be. Motion picture making is no longer a national industry but an international one. And you must do more to satisfy the more cosmopolitan audiences. You can't do the pyramids in lot 3 any more. There are too many millions of students and secretaries and G.I.s who have traveled all over the world. They can smell and taste the real from the phony. This picture could not have been made in the United States regardless of the cost." In their own good time and before the picture was released, the unions relinquished their opposition to *Alfredo Garcia.*

Despite a week's time lost to inclement weather, the production of *Alfredo Garcia* moved along as smoothly as any normal Peckinpah production could hope to move. Kris Kristofferson noted: "I was really glad we went down to Mexico on *Alfredo* because it gave us a chance to see Sam work under good conditions. *Pat Garrett* had been such a war with MGM, it was really nice to see Sam create without hassles.

"Right after we got down there, Donny [Fritts] and I went to see the rushes with Sam and took a look at the scene that's supposed to come just before the one we're in. It was this really tender love scene between Warren and Isela. Warren is kinda this loser dude who figures on makin' a lot a bread by scarfin' up this head that somebody has a price on. Anyway, it's her ex-boyfriend and Warren's sittin' there tryin' to explain this to her while they're havin' this picnic. And the scene was supposed to end in a certain place where she says, 'How come you never asked me to marry you?' And he says: 'I don't know. I guess it never occurred to me' or somethin' like that. And that kinda awkward place was where they were supposed to stop.

"But she didn't stop. She says: 'Well, ask me. . . 'And he says, 'What?' And she says, 'To marry you.' And I swear to God, Warren just looked like every other guy who's ever been confronted like that. But he didn't break character. He says, 'Will you marry me?' And then she starts crying. And every time I saw it—from every camera angle they had—it broke me up. Warren said to me: 'I just knew there was no place to hide in that scene. She had me, and I was cryin', too.'

"So I said to Sam that this is one of the heaviest scenes I'd ever seen. Now Sam, he don't ever say 'Hey, that's a good idea' or what-ever. But he picks up on what you react to. And he ended up changin' my scene with Isela, which was supposed to be a rape scene. He took all the macho outa it."

Kristofferson's scene with Isela is perhaps the most important scene in the film in terms of understanding the love relationship between Bennie and Elita. In this scene, when they are confronted by the bikers, Bennie allows Elita to be led off by Paco (Kristofferson) while the other holds Bennie at gunpoint. Elita, who at this stage is stronger than Bennie, tries to protect them both. When Paco strips her to the waist, she makes it very clear that he will never be able to dominate her, slapping his face twice. When he slaps her back, she defiantly takes it without tears, thereby destroying the masculine fantasy that he can sexually overpower her.

Unsettled by this encounter with reality, Paco turns and walks away. Now Elita becomes the aggressor, forcing a sexual encounter on her own terms to prevent Paco from taking out his frustration on Bennie. Thus, by the time Bennie does overpower his guard and race after them with a gun, he finds them in an embrace and is forced to recognize that no rape is taking place. This would seem to make his rescue effort superfluous. Rather, it makes Peckinpah's point: in killing Paco and his partner, Bennie is not rescuing Elita but *himself.*

In the scene that follows, Bennie takes Elita to a motel for the remainder of the night. Finding her sitting in the shower crying, Bennie sits before her and says for the first time without her asking him, "I love you." He has at last totally committed himself to her and is consequently more vulnerable through her than he knows. This then sets up Bennie's obsessive need for revenge after Elita is killed.

Among the problems that arose during the course of the shooting was one involving comedian Mort Sahl who had been cast by Peckinpah in the role of the gangster named Quill. Apparently Sahl had arranged club dates for his comedy act around the original shooting schedule. When his scenes were postponed due to production difficulties, Peckinpah phoned him to ask him to rearrange his show dates. Sahl said this was impossible, and an argument ensued. After calling each other a variety of turgid descriptive phrases, they both hung up. Two weeks later Peckinpah sent Sahl a bouquet of roses with a note of apology. In return he received from Sahl a wreath accompanied by a simple instruction: "Drop dead."

After his return to America following the completion of *Alfredo Garcia,* Peckinpah resumed his friendship with Sahl. Nevertheless, Sahl's refusal to alter his schedule at the time placed the production in serious trouble. Producer Martin Baum quickly solved the problem by asking two of his former clients, Robert Webber and Gig Young, to take the roles of Sappensly and Quill, respectively. The late Gig Young may be most remembered in recent years for his Academy Award performance as the master of ceremonies in *They Shoot* Horses, *Don't They?* while Webber has had a long stage career in America and Europe as well as roles in such films as *Twelve Angry Men,* Harper, and *The Dirty Dozen.* Out of friendship for Baum, both agreed to work for screen actors' minimum wage.

Speaking of this casting change, Peckinpah stated: "It's just one more reason why Marty Baum is such a great producer to work with. [Young and Webber] were both his suggestions. Two real pros. Gig Young [was] one of the most professional, on-time, ready-to-go, imaginative, and dedicated actors I've ever had the pleasure of dealing with. And Bob Webber is another one—a sensational actor to work with. Both have the ability to work on multiple levels at once— to take a character that is one dimensional and breathe life into it."

In the original script, the characters of Quill and Sappensly were not greatly distinguished from the other thugs who work for El Jefe. Young and Webber, each standing well over six feet, brought a certain physical presence to the roles as well as the ability to play against that masculinity. Robert Webber stated: "What is interesting to me is that Sam and I come from different schools. Sam is essentially a motion picture director while I come basically from the Broadway theater. And yet we both have the same way of working.

"It really started the first day on the picture. There was no dialogue. It was just a scene where Gig and I were supposed to meet Helmut at the Camino Real. So I was just standing there while Sam was blocking out the shot, and I saw a little eight-year-old girl standing there. And I went over to Sam, and I said, 'Hey, Sam, I just got my character.' He said, 'What's that?' And I said, 'A little eight-year-old girl.' And he looked at her, and without missing a beat he picked right up on it. He said, 'Wait till you see where I'm going to put you.' And there was this horseless carriage sitting in the outside lobby of the Camino Real. So Sam took the little girl, and he put her up there. Then he said to me, 'Sit up there beside her.' So he ... opened up to me. He ... accepted my insight on my character and [took] it a step further. And that's the way it [went] the entire picture. . . "

From Webber's initial insight, he and Young developed their portrayal of the gangsters by allowing the allusion of homosexuality to accentuate their relationship on screen. Considering their physical size and profession, Quill and Sappensly quite obviously represent violence. But it is their perverse attraction for one another that gives that violence its frightening potential.

Meanwhile, Peckinpah's personal life had managed to retain its status of ubiquitous chaos. He had taken a six-month lease on a beautiful, three-story house located in the San Angel section of Mexico City. Dating from the eighteenth century, this home, with its whitewashed walls, tile floors, and beamed ceilings, was filled with many of the mementos Peckinpah had accumulated through the years: photographic portraits of his father, brother, children, and close friends; location stills from his features; several pictures of Pancho Villa; a photograph taken by his brother, Denver, of Sam kneeling beside an eight-point buck he killed; a poem entitled "Bill," which colorfully describes an old packer named Bill Hendricks and which was written by Sam's nephew David, a talented writer in his own right; a door splattered with red paint, khaki cloth, and squib ignition wire bearing the inscription "Para Sam Peckinpah-Push button and destroy painting yourself" from the crew of *The Wild Bunch;* the ancient wooden board with the conglomeration "WATLE" painted on it—Cable Hague's unwritten union of his own name with "water"; and before the living room fireplace, one of a half dozen that heated the house, the large bench swing from the porch of Pete Maxwell's ranch house in *Pat Garrett and Billy the Kid.*

At first Peckinpah had lived here with his secretary, Katy Haber, and his daughter Sharon, who had come down to work as dialogue director on the picture. Along with a housekeeper and a cook, they formed the Peckinpah household. Despite Peckinpah's propensity for knife throwing and occasional target practice on the wall in front of his bed with a handgun, both Katy and Sharon had enjoyed living there.

However, when Begonia Palacios, Peckinpah's second, third, and fourth wife, took up residence with him, both of the other women moved out. Ironically, although he had been married to Begonia three times and never fathered any children with her, he managed to accomplish this feat while they were divorced. Born prematurely in October, Peckinpah's baby daughter Lupita remained in a hospital incubator for a month while he brought his ex-wife to his home to recuperate. When Begonia began expressing a desire to make the arrangement permanent once again, however, he sent her away.

Alfredo Garcia continued shooting into the month of December as the picture's demands, both physical and mental, began to take their toll on the cast and crew. The strain on everyone seemed to reach the breaking point with the filming of the sequence at the Tlaque-Paque with its macho owner. Realizing this, Peckinpah, along with Dawson and Davidson, bought out the bar and threw an impromptu party in an effort to lift everyone's spirits.

This seemed to work with the single exception of Emilio Fernandez, whose car was followed by three toughs as he left the party in the company of two young ladies. When the toughs forced Fernandez's car off the road into a ditch, Don Emilio drew a pistol from beneath the seat and drove off his assailants with gunfire.

It should be pointed out that aside from being one of Mexico's premiere motion picture directors, Fernandez also enjoys a colorful reputation as a fighter. It is said that in duels of honor he has killed seven men, including a critic who panned one of his films. And at seventy-three, he was jailed for shooting a man over the love of a woman. A robust man with a volatile temper, he once unloaded his revolver into the radiator of a bus that was tailgating him in rush-hour traffic. From his skirmish with the toughs following the party at the Tlaque-Paque, Fernandez received two broken ribs. Despite these, he would still portray El Jefe in the film a few days later.

On the morning of December 10, Peckinpah was faced with another casualty. Katy Haber, his personal assistant on the film, fell victim to acute appendicitis and had to be rushed to the hospital. Despite complications, she would recover. But her absence intensified Peckinpah's difficulties in completing the picture.

The final sequence to be shot involved the Hacienda de San Juan "Tlacatecpan" located north of Mexico City near the pyramids of Teotihuacan. Nearly two centuries old, this fortress-like structure with its thick walls and open interior courtyard dominates the plain on which it stands. All of the land that is visible to the mountains on either side of it and the pyramids before it belongs to its owner. Among its rooms is a private chapel, dominated by a gold altarpiece twenty feet square, bounty of the Lord delivered by the years of revolution. The hacienda's current landlord is a Mexican beer baron who breeds racehorses there and whose family uses it only on weekends. Before *Alfredo Garcia* he had leased it occasionally for films.

Although Peckinpah had been impressed by the authenticity he found at the hacienda, he was most intrigued by a huge empty room with a thirty-foot ceiling. Peckinpah moved to the center of the room intently looking at its size and measuring its possibilities. After asking for the opinions of his key production people, he nodded: "This is the room for a man who likes to play God. This is where

257

El Jefe holds court. Augustin, overdress it." It would become the primary setting for the opening and closing of the picture.

The transformation of this large empty room into the chamber where El Jefe dispenses his "law" took place in less than two months. Its scope and detail provide an insight into a motion picture's ability to create the illusion of reality. Ornately carved wooden gates and arches were fashioned to divide the room into three parts. In front of a shallow alcove in the center of the room was placed El Jefe's antique desk. The alcove itself was decorated to resemble a personal altar with a crucifix, coat of arms, and swords hung like crosses. Directly across from the desk, a massive stone fireplace was constructed, embellished with a twenty-five-foot oak mantelpiece. Although it had no flue, it was rendered functional provided the fire would be extinguished after each take. A hand-crafted chandelier set with candles was suspended from a beam in the ceiling, and the walls were lined with original oil portraits and tapestries of the period. The tile floor was covered with well-worn oriental rugs. By the time this set was finally completed, the extras who were brought in to help fill it could not believe that it had not always looked that way.

At the end of the first day's shooting at the hacienda, Emilio Fernandez arrived to talk with Peckinpah about his role and drink a little brandy for his health. Peckinpah was overjoyed to see him, for he had heard about Don Emilio's "accident" following the party at the Tlaque-Paque. With a few friends, they adjourned to Peckinpah's camper.

As several bottles of Mexican brandy were placed on the table, Don Emilio attempted to explain to all who were present what was special to him about Sam Peckinpah: "Cortez [the Spanish conqueror] came here, and he seemed to have found everything in Mexico. John Ford came here and now Sam Peckinpah, and they show us Mexicans things about our land that we are unable to see ourselves.

"John Ford was my master and *mi compadre*. Sam Peckinpah is my son—no, my grandson. John Ford was a divine man. Sam Peckinpah, in an age when only the very best survive, has surpassed everybody in the field of directing. He is able to tell a story in a way that makes the world take notice when it notices very little. Sam Peckinpah is like a rough and powerful painter—the most powerful painter in motion pictures today."

On the day he was to begin shooting the complex scene in El Jefe's imposing "hall of God," Peckinpah awoke early and began setting clearly in his mind what it was he wanted to get on film. At

258

nine o'clock he met with Phillips to establish the camera position for the master take at the far end of the room. It would be shot with a 20mm wide-angle lens to establish the location of the many people who would be in the room. Then Peckinpah roughly explained to Mexican assistant director Chu Chu Marin how he wanted the extras distributed throughout the room. With this done, Peckinpah returned to his camper for a little breakfast, a large drink, and a shot of vitamin B_{12}.

When he walked on the set two hours later everything had been laid out to his specifications—an approximation of how he wanted it to look on film. Peckinpah moved directly to the camera and looked through the viewfinder to get an initial impression of what it looked like. Then he began moving both principal actors and extras. Some he simply repositioned; others he eliminated entirely as he attempted to create a meaningful relationship between El Jefe and those who surrounded him.

Returning to the camera, Peckinpah checked the shot once more by looking through the viewfinder. Walking back into the room, he placed one of the servants in the foreground of the shot. Going back to the camera again, he directed his assistants to make minor alterations within the scene while he viewed it through the camera. Then, having made a slight pan of the camera to achieve precisely the framing he wanted, Peckinpah joked with the camera crew in Spanish and complimented Phillips on the lighting.

As Peckinpah moved to El Jefe's desk, assistant wardrobe men moved silently and quickly through the room, dusting shoes and straightening the costumes of the more than seventy actors and extras involved in the scene. Deliberately Peckinpah removed the clutter from the desk until only the glass-globed candelabra remained.

Looking for something to give the scene the feeling of continuing action as El Jefe's daughter is brought in, Peckinpah discovered an old Latin Bible on the shelf behind the desk. Taking this volume, Peckinpah spread it before Emilio Fernandez and asked him to read it aloud as the scene opened. He then instructed him to snap his fingers without looking up from the page, at which point his manservant would bring a humidor of cigars and a match. With the exception of these additions, the scene would play as it had been written with El Jefe asking his dishonored daughter to name the father of her child.

Smiling, Peckinpah returned to his chair positioned directly beneath the camera. After watching carefully as the actors ran through the scene, he repositioned the girl's mother so that she was somewhat apart from her ladies-in-waiting. At last he stated, "Let's make one."

His dark glasses propped above his forehead, Peckinpah watched tensely as the scene unfolded. As each line was delivered, he silently mouthed the words, his fingers crossed, his eyes fixed on the action. As the girl's arm is broken by her father's guards, Peckinpah visibly winced, his eyes filling with tears. Almost unconsciously, he reached for his dark glasses and dropped them across the bridge of his nose. Only after the scene had been completed did he finally relax, smile, compliment the girl on her performance, and request a second master for safety.

Following the second master, the company broke for lunch. Peckinpah retired to his trailer, and a light meal was brought to him. There he met with producer Martin Baum who had driven out for the day to observe the film's progress. Peckinpah estimated that they would be able to wrap up shooting by the end of the following week. Baum agreed. They then discussed the possibility of reshooting several thousand feet of film that had been misprocessed by the laboratory at Churubusco Studios.

When Peckinpah returned to the set, he stopped at the sound table. With a smile, he greeted the Mexican sound engineer who sat there and commanded, "Roll sound." Surprised, the sound man turned on his recorder and adjusted the sound level. Peckinpah announced into the microphone: "Wild track for Churubusco Studios. Take one." Then with a grin he turned around, broke wind loudly into the open mike, and walked away.

The remainder of the afternoon and for the next several days, Peckinpah concentrated on the individual shots of the elements and people in the room that when cut together with the master would effectively develop the action: a shot of the girl being brought into the room; another from her point of view; shots of El Jefe reading, lighting his cigar, and looking up to question his daughter; shots of those in the room in reaction to what is going on; cutaway shots of the fireplace and the paintings on the wall.

Then on Saturday afternoon, ten days before Christmas, Sam Peckinpah finally returned to his house in Mexico City for the first time in a week to relax, bathe, change his clothes, and prepare for the final week's shooting.

On his orders, Katy Haber had been brought to his house to recuperate from her operation mainly because Peckinpah had two servants who could help her. On Sunday, however, she insisted on working. During the afternoon, while Peckinpah relaxed with a few friends, making ten-peso bets on the American football games broadcast over Mexican television, Haber worked on the correspondence that had accumulated in her absence. She also helped Peckinpah draw up the customary list of gifts for the members of the cast and crew. During the week to come she would see to their purchase and inscription.

Then in the evening she sat down with Peckinpah to rewrite the ending for the picture one more time. The original script had Bennie winning the shootout and getting away with the million dollar reward. Earlier that week, Peckinpah had come to the realization that Bennie had to die if he took the money. "I was playing chess with Helmut [Dantine], and I said to him, 'You know, Bennie can't get away alive.' And Helmut said, 'I know, Sam.' So that's the way we rewrote it." Then, before Peckinpah left for the drive back out to the location, Haber typed this final script change.

At last, just before midnight Sunday, Peckinpah, bathed and well oiled with Mexican brandy, headed back out to the hacienda. The shooting of the picture verged on completion. As usual, Peckinpah had become close to this cast and crew. Since no two pictures are ever alike, this particular group of people would never be assembled again. It was a long and melancholy ride back.

For the shootout at the close of the picture, stuntman Whitey Hughes, who plays one of the guards Bennie kills, was asked by Peckinpah to help supervise the execution of the various falls. In his fifties, Hughes is in better shape than many men half his age. He stated: "I'm still doin' stunt work 'cause I know *how* to do the stunts. I feel better today than when I was in my young years, as I call 'em. When I was younger, I used to do things just on guts. Now I take the time to figure it out so that I can give you the same shot except with thought. Sam has taught me that. He doesn't want anybody hurt. He says he doesn't want you to go out and show him how tough you are but how smart you are. He expects a professional job, and that's what I give him. When I get to the day that I can't give it my all, then I'll quit."

Despite the added complexities of the stunt work, however, the shooting of *Bring Me the Head of Alfredo Garcia* was completed three days before Christmas. Sam Peckinpah thanked his cast and crew, distributed the gifts Haber had secured for him, and left to spend Christmas week on Mexico's Pacific coast before settling down to oversee the editing of the picture.

During the first few months of 1974, *Alfredo Garcia* was both edited and scored. The supervising editor on the picture was Garth Craven, and Jerry Fielding composed and conducted the musical score. For the most part, all of this went smoothly with Peckinpah staying more on the wagon than off. However, there were moments when he would let things rip, such as the night in mid-March when the American Film Institute held a retrospective honoring James Cagney.

Variety (March 15, 1974) made special mention of Peckinpah's contribution to the festivities in its account of the affair: "And then there was Jack Lemmon, teamed on stage with Shirley MacLaine for some personal rambling tributes. Lemmon's ruminations occasioned an unexpected heckling by Sam Peckinpah who loudly suggested that Lemmon knock off telling the audience how great he thinks Cagney is...."

"While Peckinpah's surprise outburst was considered by many to be in dubious taste, had a secret ballot been taken on the merits of his remarks, Ensign Pulver [Lemmon's role when he acted with Cagney in *Mr. Roberts*] would have been restricted to quarters indefinitely." Peckinpah eventually had to be escorted from the premises following the ceremony after he supposedly insulted a bartender.

Kris Kristofferson, who was looping his lines in the picture at the time of the Cagney ordeal, recalled: "[Sam] had been on the wagon, but then he started drinkin'. . . [He] had to buy a tuxedo for the Cagney show. So me an' old Max [Evans] and Sam's driver, Juan, went over to this place. Well, we just musta terrorized the shit outa the poor guy who made Sam's tux. I mean he's tryin' to talk to me and watch Juan while old Max is stealin' socks and Sam's tryin' on the tux. So after that and some other stuff, we finally had to take Sam home and put him to bed.

"Well, the next day I saw Sam, and he was straight. We had lunch together, and I begged him, 'Tonight, pace yourself, Man.' He went to the Cagney thing in his new tux and a rented Rolls Royce, and you saw what happened. He got into that shouting match with Jack Lemmon and wound up with his picture in *People* magazine being bounced by the bartender.

"You see, Sam's got reasons for all the shitty things he does. I just wish he wouldn't do 'em 'cause it makes him less than what he is. And he's killin' himself with booze. He can be such a good guy. I mean he hires the walkin' wounded, Man. Every loser who would come to Sam on the picture, Sam would find a part for a way of helpin' 'em out. I don't have any way of knowin' whether me an' Donny [Fritts] will ever have a chance to work with him again, but I do know we'll always be friends. It's strange. I think in his heart of hearts, Sam'd rather be a songwriter than anything else. He's a superstar, but he really don't know it."

262

In mid-August, Sam Peckinpah's *Bring Me the Head of Alfredo Garcia* was released to the general public, first opening in New York, Los Angeles, and Chicago. Everywhere but Chicago it met with hostile reviews.

So grotesque in its basic conception, so sadistic in its imagery, so irrational in its plotting, so obscene in its effect, and so incompetent in its cinematic realization that the only kind of analysis it really invites is psychoanalysis.
                    ~Joy Gould Boyum, Wall Street Journal (August 12, 1974)

A catastrophe so huge that those who once ranked Peckinpah with Hemingway may now invoke Mickey Spillane.
                    ~ Michael Sragow, New York Magazine (August 12, 1974)

A masterpiece—a strange, weird masterpiece that will turn off a lot of people but it will be remembered for a long time. . . It's a definitive Peckinpah work.
                    ~Roger Ebert, Chicago Sun-Times (August 11, 1974)

Because of this predominantly negative response, the film was quickly sloughed by its American distributors, thereby preventing it from finding its audience. At the same time, it was censored in both Germany and Sweden. Only in England, the country that had almost universally decried Peckinpah's *Straw Dogs,* did the film find acclaim. There, when the nine critics for *Sight and Sound,* the journal of the British Film Institute, listed their selections for the ten best films of 1975, *Alfredo Garcia* was included by four of the nine.

In recent years, friends and enemies alike have found it fashionable to condemn Peckinpah's films as being fascist or reflecting an overbearing machismo attitude towards life in general and women in particular. In *Alfredo Garcia,* every major movement in the film is initiated by women who are stronger than the men who attempt to dominate them and equal to the men who love them. It is El Jefe's daughter whose pregnancy and defiance cause her father to demand Garcia's head in the first place. It is Elita's love that gives Bennie the strength to do things he never thought possible. It is Alfredo's grandmother whose relentless pursuit leads to the death of her entire family. And fittingly, as Bennie and El Jefe confront each other at the end of the film, it is El Jefe's daughter who commands Bennie: "Kill him!" In this film, Sam Peckinpah both acknowledges and refutes his critics.

At the San Francisco Film Festival held in 1974 at which Peckinpah was honored with a retrospective of his work, he answered an inquiry about whether he ever hoped to release a "pure Peckinpah" film with "I did *Alfredo Garcia,* and I did it exactly the way I wanted to. Good or bad, like it or not, that was my film."

15 The Killer Elite
" ...patron poet of the manic-depressives."

Following the completion of *Bring Me the Head of Alfredo Garcia,*
Sam Peckinpah returned to California to begin work on his next film,
The Insurance Company, to be produced at Twentieth-Century-Fox by
Joe Wizan. Wizan was a major consideration in Peckinpah's accepting
the project. However, after months of revisions and countless story
conferences, Fox got cold feet and backed out. While this did not hurt
Peckinpah financially because of a "play or pay" contractual agreement,
it was extremely frustrating and left him anxious to begin another
project immediately.

By the beginning of 1975 he had agreed to direct a film for United
Artists based on the book *The Killer Elite* by Robert Rostand, the pen
name of British writer Robert Hopkins. The rights to the novel had been
purchased by producer Arthur Lewis: "Originally; I made a development
deal with EMI and Westinghouse. And I engaged Reginald Rose to do
the script, and Reggie and I worked on the script in London for a quite a
while. . .it was that script that Peckinpah agreed to make," Lewis
recounted.

Because of Peckinpah's interest, United Artists became involved
and bought out EMI. At the same time, producer Martin Baum, who
had brought the script to Peckinpah's attention at the behest of Lewis,
agreed to act as coproducer on the film. At this point, all, including
Peckinpah, were in complete agreement that the film, like the novel,
should be set in England.

However, after seeing James Caan in Karel Reisz's *The Gambler,*
Peckinpah and his producers agreed to cast Caan as the lead, Mike
Locken. This unfortunately created a problem. Refusing to do the
picture outside the United States, Caan went to Mike Medavoy; then
head of production at United Artists, and Medavoy agreed. Peckinpah
and his producers reluctantly conceded to rewrite the script for San
Francisco.

The novel, *The Killer Elite,* had dealt with a quasi-CIA agent
shepherding an exiled African leader back to his country from England. The original adaptation of this novel by screenwriter Reginald Rose had attempted to remain true to this story line. With the

change in location, however, the original script was dropped and a new one commissioned from writer Marc Norman (author of *Oklahoma Crude)*. Peckinpah's dislike of this script resulted in a third try, this time by Stirling Silliphant, whose credits included *The New Centurions* and *Towering Inferno* in the seventies as well as an Academy Award in the late sixties for *In the Heat of the Night.*

A devotee of the martial arts (Silliphant was a student of the late Bruce Lee) and married to the Vietnamese actress Tiana, who held a brown belt in karate, Silliphant rewrote the script to accommodate his interest as well as provide a starring role for his wife. San Francisco with its thriving Chinatown provided him with an ideal locale.

Peckinpah, however, wanted to emphasize the more satiric aspects of the traditional action film, something he had attempted in *The Getaway* without success. It was over this that the director and producer Martin Baum began to clash.

In January, Baum began meeting with Silliphant privately in order to secure the kind of straightforward action script he felt *The Killer Elite* should be. Meanwhile, Peckinpah had informed Silliphant of his desire for more satiric humor. And Silliphant, caught in the middle, attempted to please both. He managed to satisfy neither.

Baum went to Mike Medavoy for support. Medavoy called Peckinpah and what resulted was the following exchange of memos:

January 27th 1975
MIKE MEDAVOY
SAM PECKINPAH
As per our conversation of January 24th it is my understanding that you have instructed me to do "no writing on the script." However, I feel that we both agreed that I should proceed along the line that a hyphenate could as defined by the Writers Guild of America and the Directors Guild.

Would you please confirm this by memo because this is the road I am taking.

S.P.

Because he felt these memos made his creative position with respect to the project clear, Peckinpah had them printed on T-shirts with his query on the front and Medavoy's response on the back. At the start of shooting, each member of the cast and crew received a T-shirt, compliments of Peckinpah.

Throughout this period, producer Arthur Lewis, who was still dividing his time between London and Los Angeles, was never informed of the controversy by either Baum or Medavoy. "As far as Sam wanting to do *[The Killer Elite]* as a spoof on American action-adventure films," he recalled later, "after we had switched the location back to the States, if Sam or anybody else had ever said to me, 'Let's go with a spoof,' I think I would have supported it enthusiastically. I felt Reggie Rose's script was superb. But changing locations from England to California radically altered the entire concept, and it no longer really worked for me. But Sam, for whatever reason, never openly said to me, 'I want to make this a satire.'"

In selecting a crew, Peckinpah again surrounded himself wherever possible with men and women he had worked with before and felt he could trust. These included Katy Haber, Newt Arnold, Ted Haworth, Bob Visciglia, Chuck Wilborn, and Ron Wright. For the first time since *Junior Bonner,* Frank Kowalski would be Peckinpah's second unit director and script supervisor. And finally, after ten years, Peckinpah would have the opportunity to work with Philip Lathrop, the cinematographer he had collaborated with briefly on *Cincinnati Kid.*

In addition to James Caan, Peckinpah would cast Robert Duvall as Caan's friend and betrayer. Arthur Hill would portray the opportunistic department head who plays both sides; Gig Young was cast as Hill's sardonic superior at COMTEG, the fictional agency Caan worked for. As Caan's accomplices, Peckinpah cast Bo Hopkins as a young killer for hire and Burt Young as the getaway driver. Mako was cast as the

Oriental politician entrusted to Caan, and Tiana would play his daughter.

Since the martial arts were not one of Peckinpah's prime interests, he brought in a number of professionals, including Hank Hamilton, who doubled as Duvall's assistant, and Tak Kubota. All would work under the supervision of stunt coordinator Whitey Hughes.

Given the costs of three screenplays by major writers, a name director, and a "bankable" star, *The Killer Elite* was virtually over-budget before a frame was exposed. With April 7, 1975, set as the start of production, the producers issued the following memo:

> *TO: ENTIRE CAST AND CREW*
> *FROM: MARTIN BAUM AND ARTHUR LEWIS*
> *Due to the high projected cost of THE KILLER ELITE, the producers and the director have given back a considerable portion of their fees in order to induce United Artists to start principal photography on this film. It is urgent that we all maintain constant vigilance in keeping all costs down. There is no money available for food and beverage at staff meetings, or at cast crew parties. Any such expenditure will have to be at the expense of the participants.*
> *Your cooperation in this matter will be greatly appreciated by both.*
> *All best,*
> *Martin Baum   Arthur Lewis*

This was followed two days later by a countermemo:

> *TO: The Production*
> *FROM: Sam Peckinpah Gentlemen and Ladies:*
> *Regardless of memos to the contrary, there will be at least two cast and crew parties on whatever date we feel like it. We are not United Artists and we are not Optimus Productions. We are just a crew who want to make a good picture in the only way we know how.*
> *SAM PECKINPAH AND FRIENDS*
> *P.S. James Caan has now volunteered to pay for the coffee at all staff meetings from now on.*
> *P.P.S. Cast and Crew parties will be by invitation only!!!*
> *P.P.P.S. Please sign and return if you wish to participate.*

These memos also became a T-shirt. The battle lines had been drawn. The war was about to begin.

268

Shooting began on April 7 in San Francisco. With its steep hills, diverse ethnic mix, and picturesque locales, this city has become one of the most frequently photographed in America. It fell to director of photography Philip Lathrop and his crew to give *The Killer Elite* a fresh look.

"Over the years since *Cincinnati Kid,*" Lathrop recalled, "Sam and I have kept in touch and talked about making a picture together. But I've always been busy. And much of the time Sam's had Lucien Ballard, whose work I've admired. But this picture happened to work out. In fact, I turned down a couple of pictures to do it—*Midway* for one—but I felt this had more stuff to it.

"Of course, this has been a very tough picture logistically. Altogether I guess we had around thirty locations, which is average. But they were really tough locations: the mothball fleet out in Suisun Bay, the Bethlehem Steel pier, Chinatown. Everyone of them I thought was going to get easier, but they all got worse.

"It's really a very intricate piece, but I enjoyed working on the picture. Sam's got a lot of balls. You always know that you've only got one man to please, and that's the director. I've worked on too many where you've got all sorts of guys, each one telling you something different. Sam never gets in my department. He tells me what he wants and lets me do it. Then he runs interference so I can.

"I always try to work with the same people. For the last five years I've had the same key grip, gaffer, and camera crew. I try to light the set with the fewest number of lights I can. Simplicity is the key. More lights mean more shadows. Then I always follow the picture right on through to completion. I have it in my contract that I must be present at the run-through with the timer from the lab. It's at my own expense, of course, but it's worth it because the picture comes out the way you intended.

"Sam understands that. He also had a very good idea which saved us a lot of time. He had us mount three cameras for all the interior car shots. The main trick is keeping the cameras and lights out of camera range so it takes about an hour to set up. But from that point on you can just drive wherever you want. One trip and everything matches. And you get some terrific stuff—especially the spontaneous dialogue that you can't go back and expect an actor to duplicate word for word."

An excellent example of this three-camera technique occurs early in the picture as Caan and Duvall take an early morning drive across the bay bridge to relieve their partners who are guarding a defector named Vrodny (Helmut Dantine). Caan has just spent the night with a girl. Duvall claims he went through her purse and discovered a letter from the girl's doctor informing her of "vaginal infection." While this scene is only briefly sketched in the script itself, Peckinpah was able to discuss the possibilities with the two actors and simply allow them to play off of each other's responses. The result is a humorous scene that at the same time serves to define the relationship between the characters played by Caan and Duvall: Caan implicitly trusts Duvall because he is his friend, but Duvall betrays that trust for his own amusement and gratification. While this case is a practical joke, in the scene that follows, Duvall, who has gone over to the other side, sadistically cripples Caan. By virtue of the triple camera technique, Peckinpah was able to capture the ribald humor that was part of their friendship and at the same time set up the audience for the harsh contrast of the violent attack that is to follow.

The production work in San Francisco moved ahead without major setbacks. As for his relationship with his producers, Peckinpah had narrowed the field. "At the beginning," Arthur Lewis recalled, "the first five or six weeks, [Sam and I] had a lot of laughs together.... This went well past the start of production. It was Baum, strangely enough, who Peckinpah asked be barred from the set. In a memo to Eric Pleskow [then president of United Artists], he literally said, 'The only one I want to deal with is Arthur Lewis.'"

As the picture wore on, however, Lewis began to discover that there was little he could do that pleased Peckinpah. Annoyed at the production company's tightfisted money policy, Peckinpah would intentionally accuse his producers of "petty thievery." Ignoring this, Lewis continued to function as best he could. But the harder he tried, the more difficult Peckinpah made it. It was a war of attrition to which Peckinpah was infinitely better suited than he. Surrounded with technicians and actors more loyal to Peckinpah than himself, Lewis's energies were siphoned in futile struggles, often of his own making.

One such struggle occurred at San Francisco's International Airport where a plane and concourse docking area had been secured through the cooperation of Western Airlines. The scene to be photographed involved the arrival of the Far Eastern politician and his daughter, who are immediately set upon by a group of Ninja assassins. At the same time the Duvall character, also at the airport, takes a shot at the politician and misses, hitting another passenger instead. Since it is Duvall's presence at the airport that convinces COMTEG to rehire Caan, the scene was essential.

270

Lewis, however, became concerned that Western Airlines might be upset by the implication that airport security had broken down. He therefore went to Peckinpah and insisted that no one appear to be shot during the deplaning. Peckinpah deadpanned that someone would fall down, but that it could always be explained as a heart attack. This seemed to mollify Lewis, and Peckinpah assigned Charles Titone, a young actor and editor who worked as production assistant on the picture, to take the fall. No squibs would be used.

After watching Titone descend the steps from the plane with the other passengers and suddenly fall lifelessly to the runway, Lewis walked up to Peckinpah and restated his concern: Titone looked like he'd been shot. The airline might sue. Peckinpah smiled stiffly, "Trust me, Arthur." This and similiar incidents served only to feed the growing conflict that would ultimately result in Peckinpah insisting that Lewis not be allowed to even talk to Garth Craven, the film's editor.

"Sam's conflict with Arthur Lewis put me in a very embarrassing position," recalled Craven, "because Arthur would try to make contact with the film through me. If I was busy, which was frequently, I would just say to him, 'Arthur, I really just don't have the time.' And he would say all right and go away. Other times I really wouldn't have minded talking about the film.

"But Sam's conflict with his producers is a constant game. This time it was pretty bad, but Sam needs that anger to work off of. If you so much as said 'good morning' to Arthur you were betraying the cause. It really came to the point where I had to say, 'Arthur, I don't want to be rude, but by talking to me, you put me in a very uncomfortable position. . . ' And actually, he was fairly understanding about that, which is to his credit, although Sam would hate me for saying so." Nevertheless, Lewis continued to be the only member of the production team, aside from Craven, who religiously attended the daily screenings of the previous day's shooting.

With the completion of location shooting in San Francisco the production returned to Los Angeles in late May. There were filmed the remaining interiors, including the offices of COMTEG, the house in Chinatown where Caan first meets Mako, and Mac's garage.

During the filming of the scene in the garage, the following interview with James Caan took place in the trailer that served as his dressing room. Burt Young, Bo Hopkins, Walter Kelley, and Sondra Blake were present as well.

CAAN: There's only one thing I want to say about Sam Peckinpah: he's a fucking maniac! [Laughter. Caan distributes sandwiches, purchased by Burt Young, part of the ongoing feud with the production company over food. Young turns down a sandwich because he is on a diet.]

CAAN: Well, what do you want to ask me? Get the fuckin' thing over with. What do I think of Peckinpah? If I get two more signatures, I'm going to have the man put away. [More laughter] I only need two more. Wanna sign? Is this his autobiography?

GS: No, biography.

CAAN: Of course. Don't try to make me feel stupid, fella.
       No, the man is definitely deranged. I mean in a marvelous way, you understand. But they are going to put him away. First, they're going to put his liver at UCLA Medical Center. It will never rot. [Laughter] His liver will never rot. It's fucking fermented. It's going to be like one of them fossils. A thousand years from now they're going to be saying, 'There's Sam Peckinpah's liver still bouncing around, having a coke, and wearing dark glasses.' [Laughter] Sam's body is rotten. It will decay in ten seconds, but his liver will live on. We could do a science fiction picture about his liver: 'The Liver that Drank New York.' [More laughter] Is this helping any? I'm sure Sam's going to love this. But seriously, there is no more style in life. You know what I mean? No more Hemingways. No Brendan Behans. Sam's one of the last guys with that kind of mad style of living. I mean the man will do anything. He's fun. He's fun-loving ... and his liver is incredible.

GS: Have there been many script changes since you began shooting?

CAAN: We have not had a script. I mean there's been one around, but I haven't looked at it. Sam hasn't looked at it. Sam will say, 'What do you think?' And I'll say: 'I don't know. What do you think?' And Sam'll say back, '$5 million in the hands of insane children.' So Burt [Young] and Sam will work it over and try to make something out of it. When we put it all together it will probably be a mess. I don't know. Sam's very creative, very funny. It's his style.

GS: How has it been working with Tiana?

CAAN: No comment.

GS: What made you decide to make the picture?

CAAN: A combination of Sam and money. It certainly wasn't the script, I'll tell you that. But Sam can make something out of this.

GS: So it's been a relatively easy picture?

272

CAAN: Well, no. It's had its rough spots. For Sam and I, it's been easy. We haven't had two cross words between us. But there's been a lot of shit on this production. There's been a lot of heat. . .

GS: Would you like to work with Sam again?

CAAN: Yes. With the proper vehicle. But not this. I would never do this again.

GS: How do you prepare for a scene?

CAAN: It's something I try not to think about. Try not to prejudice something somebody else is going to do. I have a character that I understand, and I just try to be available to what's going to happen or what might happen. Sam understands that and directs you by sort of indirection. Not giving you specifics but impressions.

GS: This film aside, what do you look for in a script?

CAAN: What I generally look for is something that's both good and different from what I've done before. On this picture I didn't even look at the script before I signed. Without Peckinpah that never would have happened. It won't happen again.

[At this point, Frank Kowalski enters the trailer.]

KOWALSKI: I've got some good news and some bad news. The good news is that I have in my hand checks for each of us covering Sam's losses in liars' poker the other night.

YOUNG: You're kiddin'.

CAAN: I don't believe it. I should be able to retire.

KOWALSKI: And the bad news is rehearsal in five minutes.

The rehearsal that followed involved a complete run-through of the garage scene in which Caan convinces Burt Young to act as his driver followed by the arrival of Hopkins and their departure in Young's modified taxi. Walter Kelley ran through their lines quickly with them before Peckinpah arrived. When Peckinpah arrived, the rehearsal began.

He sat and listened carefully as they ran through the scene once more for him. His purpose was to see how the dialogue would play. It had several rough spots. After another run-through, Peckinpah retired with Young and Haber to rewrite some of the dialogue.

On the set itself, the interior of a downtown Los Angeles garage temporarily converted to a sound stage, the scene was played and replayed before the cameras over the next two days capturing the action from various angles. Between takes Caan kept himself loose by entertaining the cast and crew with an unending barrage of bad jokes.

The final shot in the sequence called for Caan, Young, and Hopkins to get into the taxi and drive out of the garage, Young at the wheel. Because of the taxi's turning radius, it was impossible for the vehicle to negotiate the turn required for it to make it through the doorway. On the first take, however, neither Young nor Peckinpah had any way of knowing this. Consequently, Young who is a natural comic, revved the engine, slipped it into gear, and drove directly into the wall. Caan fell on the floor of the cab. Not from the impact—from hysterics. When he finally managed to get out, he placed his arm around Young and quipped, "Of all the people in the world, I picked *you* to be my getaway driver!"

Because the film's distribution would be handled through United Artists, the final editing of the picture would be done at MGM studios in Culver City where United Artists' main West Coast offices were located. This placed the production under the direct supervision of UA's head of production, Mike Medavoy, the young, former agent whose impressive string of successes for United Artists (including *One Flew Over the Cuckoo's Nest* and *Annie Hall)* would eventually result in his leaving (with four other former top executives at United Artists) to form the independent production company Orion Pictures. It had been Medavoy's memos instructing Peckinpah to stick to directing that launched the first T-shirt campaign.

A fan of Peckinpah's earlier work, Medavoy had attempted to promote an atmosphere at UA that was conducive to the best kind of creative filmmaking. With a number of other filmmakers, including Woody Allen and Blake Edwards, Medavoy was successful. With Sam Peckinpah, whose personal penchant for creating out of conflict has frequently led to infighting with studio brass, Medavoy was not.

The situation came to a head following a screening of several hours' worth of daily rushes for *The Killer Elite* at United Artists. Both Medavoy and Peckinpah were present. As the screening ended, Medavoy shook his head and remarked: "That was the worst editing I've ever seen."

Considering the shots were in random order and introduced by clapboards, one may well think Medavoy's remark was a lame joke. Peckinpah failed to see the humor. Instead, he elected to view it as a sign of Medavoy's ignorance of the filmmaking process. From that point their relationship swiftly degenerated.

The editing of the picture continued throughout the summer of 1975 with its aim an action picture emphasizing Peckinpah's brand of "satire." As it did in *The Getaway,* however, Peckinpah's instinct for action sometimes got in the way of what could properly be called satire. Nevertheless, the finished film clearly shows Peckinpah's intentions.

In *The Killer Elite,* myriad details constantly work in counterpoint to the reality of the situation being portrayed. In the midst of the confusion at the airport as the body of one of the assassins comes up the conveyor belt with the baggage, a "flasher" walks up to one of the security personnel and opens his raincoat exposing himself to the mortified guard before melting into the crowd. The sign on the top of Mac's cab reads: "Don't forget. Ripley's Believe It or Not." A high ranking pseudo-CIA official reads aloud from a listing of current stock options: "MGM is going down. Oh well, they're in the hotel business anyway" and "This I don't believe. The stock is going up, and they don't even have a company!" In a scene designed to humorously reverse the audience's expectations about the film's love interest between Caan and Tiana, she tells him she is still a virgin. He replies, "Look, kid, I don't want this to sound too harsh, but I really don't give a shit!" As Mako and Tak Kubota (both of whom are shorter than 5 feet) square off near the end of the film for what should be a ritualized fight to the death with traditional swords, Caan at first attempts to dissuade the combatants by suggesting they just shoot the Kubota character outright. When that fails and the fight begins, Caan turns to Burt Young and quips: "Lay me 7 to 5, and I'll take the little guy."

While these examples are several of the more obvious attempts to poke fun at the conventions of the Hollywood action picture, they lacked the kind of explicit punch needed to allow the audience in on the joke. Moreover, the film as a whole failed to live up to Peckinpah's own expectations. There was nothing special, nothing to make it stand out among the others of its genre. Realizing this, Peckinpah made one last attempt at a statement. He had shot two endings—one as scripted, and one he called "Brechtian."

The scripted ending called for the Caan and Young characters to sail off on a ketch following the climactic fight aboard the mothball fleet in Suisun Bay. The second ending was similar except that Bo Hopkins's character, Miller, joins them carrying a can of beer, despite the fact that we have just seen him killed in the previous fight with the Ninja. Laughing, Caan and Young grab Hopkins and start to throw him overboard as the tail credits appear.

"I loved Sam's ending for the picture," stated Garth Craven. "In fact, before there was any discussion, when I saw that shot in the dailies, I just automatically used it as the ending. I thought it was an exciting concept because it forced the audience to rethink what it had just been shown. What is all this espionage business if it isn't theater of the absurd. Sam wanted the ending to be more 'Brechtian.' That shot made it, and I could never understand why other people couldn't see it."

Among those who could not see it were Peckinpah's producers. Having believed all along that they were making "a Sam Peckinpah action-adventure," they were hardly prepared to accept anything as surreal as a character inexplicably reappearing after his death, even if that character had been canonized as "the patron poet of the manic-depressives." Worse, they feared the ticket-buying public would react the same way. As a consequence, they insisted that the picture end as written.

In an attempt to alter this thinking, Peckinpah previewed the film in MGM's main theater on the Culver City lot using both endings. In attendance were the various heads of United Artists including Medavoy, the film's producers, and a few selected friends of Peckinpah.

It was an exercise in futility. United Artists' mind had already been made up. And in fairness, Peckinpah had done his best to help them. Aside from having alienated virtually everyone in the room who might have been able to aid him in getting what he wanted, Peckinpah had also allowed the action on the screen to overpower the "satire." Thus his "Brechtian" ending served only to momentarily confuse the studio brass rather than convince them. The original ending would remain.

Because it would mean a considerable increase in potential revenue, the studio also asked that the film be conformed to meet whatever concerns were voiced by the Motion Picture Association of America Board in order to secure a PG rather than an R rating. Release had been set for mid-December to take advantage of the Christmas season. That left barely enough time to complete the final editing, scoring, and dubbing.

On Friday, November 28, 1975, Peckinpah arrived at Warner Brothers' Burbank studios where scoring stage number one had been reserved for the live recording session of the music track for *The Killer Elite*. Present was an orchestra of 100 under the personal direction of Jerry Fielding whose music they would be performing. The film's preview date was only a week away.

The process of recording music on film is a complex one involving the simultaneous screening of the sections of the film to be "scored" while the orchestra plays each note at precisely the correct moment in the film. To accomplish this, the scoring stage is equipped with a carefully monitored projection system that operates in synchronization with the banks of tape recorders that capture the sound. When the music is transferred to film, it must maintain the exact relationship with the images that it does in the recording session.

As the session began, Fielding faced the orchestra and placed a headset over his ears. Tapping the podium with his baton, he spoke into the microphone before him and asked the projectionist to roll the first piece of film. The musicians finished tuning their instruments and gave their attention to Fielding as Peckinpah and the others present took their seats and fell silent.

On the wall behind the orchestra, Fielding watched as the first "cue" to be scored appeared on the screen. Because the black and white work print was the same one Fielding had run over and over again while composing and arranging the score, it was lined with signs of wear. A pale blue "streamer"—a vertical line drawn on the film beginning at the left and moving to the right—signaled the approach of the starting point. Fielding raised his baton and as the streamer touched the righthand edge of the screen and disappeared, the music began. At the same moment, a clock at the right of the screen started to keep its count. Other streamers drawn on the film indicated particular moments within the sequence calling for musical emphasis. Fielding read and incorporated each into his conducting. At last, a red streamer brought the sequence to a close. The images and music ended as one.

As the technicians in the control booth rewound the tape for playback, Fielding shook his head, "We can do better. . ." Then he listened to what had just been recorded and shook his head again, "I can do better than that." To his right, a musician tuned his cello and deadpanned: "It's perfect. So we'll do it once more to make it better."

The same sequence was then repeated. But this time as the screen went dark, a voice from the control booth broke in: "That was excellent, Jerry." Fielding removed his headset and glanced across to where Peckinpah sat listening. Their eyes met, and Peckinpah nodded drolly, "All I ask is a little perfection." And so the session went, taking each sequence of the film and repeating it until it was precisely the way Fielding had intended it. It would be a long day.

On the evening of December 5, the Village Theater in Westwood had to open its balcony and turn away a large number of customers who had come to see what the papers had advertised as "A new Sam Peckinpah picture starring James Caan and Robert Duvall." The audience reception to the film was mixed. Medavoy, nevertheless, spoke in confident tones about having "another winner." Others were less satisfied.

Fielding stood by himself looking pained. Finally he approached two friends. "What these people do not understand," he began with a look that indicated he meant all the studio brass who now stood in the lobby of the theater smiling and waiting for the preview cards to be returned, "is that you cannot possibly build tension in a film if that sound track is a dense black line. The problem with this picture is that there is too much sound *all* the time. The audience's senses are dulled to the point where you try to subtly give them a music cue, and they miss it because they just don't care. We've got a lot of work to do on this picture yet, but I doubt that they give us the opportunity.

"It's really difficult. I'm not on speaking terms with half of the people here because I tell them what they don't want to hear while they stand around like a bunch of glad-handing, backslapping jack-asses congratulating each other on what they don't understand to begin with. All they want to hear about is what a hit they've got, not what really has to be done to make it one."

In another part of the lobby, Peckinpah kissed the girls, shook the hands of well-wishers, and sipped Campari and Calso water. "Wait till tomorrow," he smiled.

The following day, Peckinpah and a small group of friends flew up to San Francisco to attend the second preview. Everyone stayed at the Fairmont Hotel at Peckinpah's expense. That evening at the Northpoint Theater it was again standing room only with as many turned away as admitted. Because it had been filmed in San Francisco, the crowd was considerably more responsive than the previous evening.

"Sam's ending occurs in reel 14," recalled Garth Craven, who stood at the rear of the theater during the performance. "So around reel 12, when I was certain they couldn't stop it, I told one of Medavoy's assistants to watch what was coming very carefully. He asked why, and I told him that I'd been a bit naughty. He grinned and said, 'Given my position, I really have to tell Medavoy, but that's okay because there's bloody little he can do about it.' So Medavoy came storming back to me and said, 'What did you do?' I said, 'Put in that ending.' 'Why?' 'It's my last little joke.' 'Yours or Sam's?' 'Well,' I said, 'I guess it was both of ours.' And Medavoy just glared at me: 'He'll never work again! He's finished! Finished!'"

The preview cards from the San Francisco preview were considerably more positive than the Westwood screening had been. The ending, however, would remain as before. United Artists had ordered 450 prints for national distribution beginning December 16, just ten days away.

The picture had cost in excess of $6 million, far over the original projections. But within the first month of its release, *The Killer Elite* returned its investment and began to turn a profit. Unfortunately, it would do little more than that.

The reactions of the critics were mixed, ranging from "wasted effort" to "Peckinpah's best." The most positive review, however, came from Pauline Kael, in an article that appeared in *The New Yorker* January 12, 1976: "For all [Peckinpah's] ceremonial exhibitionism, his power plays, and his baloney, or maybe because of them there is a total, physical elation in his work and in his own relation to it that makes me feel closer to him than I do to any other director except Jean Renoir. . . .

"Peckinpah has become so nihilistic that filmmaking itself seems to be the only thing he believes in. He's crowing in *The Killer Elite,* saying, 'No matter what you do to me, look at the way I can make a movie.' The be-devilled bastard's got a right to crow."

Several days before he departed for Europe and his next project, a World War II epic entitled *Cross of Iron* to be scripted by Julius Epstein, Peckinpah received the following letter dated December 11, 1975, from Lewis:

> *Dear Sam:*
> *You're a talented man. Too bad you're not a gracious one.*
>
> *I have no idea why you singled me out as an adversary, but I think I helped you a lot.*
>
> *I got us our PG, and Eric Pleskow thinks that's worth a million and a half over whatever our gross would have been as an R. If that's so, next Christmas I'll buy you a drink—either here or in the South of France. Even if it isn't, I'll buy you a drink.*
>
> *I'm glad it's over. However, it was an experience I will always remember, an experience unlike any I've ever had, and believe me, I've been there, man.*
>
> *Anyway—good luck on your next one. Make [Cross of Iron] a hit, and don't be too harsh on my old and good friend, Julie Epstein.*
>
> *I wish you well.*
> *All best,*
> *Yours,*
> *A.L.*

After reading this, Peckinpah wrote the following message across the
bottom of the letter and returned it to Lewis:

Dear Arthur:

*My problem is, I do not suffer fools graciously and detest
petty thievery and incompetence. Other than that, I found
you charming, and on occasion, mildly entertaining.
Thank you for the PG. Everyone is proud of you.*

S.P.

Nothing had changed

Epilogue: Cross of Iron, Convoy, and Beyond

"I wouldn't have it any other way."

Before the completion of principal photography on *The Killer Elite,* Sam Peckinpah was approached by a German producer named Wolf C. Hartwig to direct an American-German-Yugoslavian coproduction of the German novel *Cross of Iron* by Willi Heinrich. Peckinpah read the book but remained uncertain about whether or not he should accept the project. At the same time, he was sent scripts for two other projects, Dino De Laurentiis's *King Kong* and Ilya Salkind's *Superman.* Experience had taught him that it was always wise, as a hedge against bad reviews, a poor showing at the box office, or both, to be contractually involved with another film prior to the release of the one currently in postproduction. But after weighing the gimmickry of both *King Kong* and *Superman* (respectively, a gigantic ape and a man who flies) against the hard-edged reality of the Second World War, Peckinpah opted for *Cross of Iron.*

In taking the project, Peckinpah saw an opportunity to make an atypical war film. Set against the Battle of Krymskaya, which took place in southern Russia near the Black Sea in mid-1943, the novel sought to dramatize the disastrous retreat by the Germans in the face of the Soviet offensive. By portraying the Germans as protagonists, Peckinpah felt he had a chance to make an antiwar statement unlike any other.

"I want to capture on film the thousand-mile stare you can only see in the eyes of men who have been at the front too long," he confided to friends as he began to prepare the project in late 1975. Julius Epstein, whose credits included an Academy Award for *Casablanca* in 1942, was hired to write the screenplay. Actor James Coburn would portray the leading role of the German Sergeant Steiner.

"I asked Sam why he was going to do it," Coburn recalled. "And he said, 'Well, I haven't done World War II yet.' So I said:

281

'That's a good enough reason for me. I'd like to see you do World War II.'"

In preparation for the film, Coburn joined Peckinpah in Europe to research the project in early 1976. "I saw him over in Munich," Coburn continued. "We were going through all of the various files and film of the time [German and Russian war footage circa 1943]. We went to the war museum in London, the film archives in Koblenz. And we saw a lot of really fascinating film on that time that really turned Sam around. It was really difficult to get an accurate view of that time that wasn't prejudiced one way or the other. We saw [two films] cut from the same stock ... a captured German war film that had been used for [German] propaganda and a Russian propaganda film cut from virtually the same footage. It was very interesting to see what amounted to the same shots edited differently to be used by two so totally different ideologies for their own purposes. So what we realized—and this really hit Sam—was that they were both liars. The truth, if there is a truth, has to [be] somewhere else."

When Peckinpah read Julius Epstein's first draft of the screenplay, however, he felt that it was far too conventional. "As far as the Julius Epstein script went," James Coburn commented in March of 1976, "he tried to make it into a good guy-bad guy thing. And that just isn't what Sam is after in this picture. . . We don't have any good guys or bad guys. Just a bunch of human beings working out their destinies within. . . the conflict of the war and the internal rivalries of the German command." Peckinpah brought in Walter Kelley to work on the script.

It was on this same front that a more familiar conflict began surfacing as well. The first signs of friction between Peckinpah and producer Wolf Hartwig emerged during several script conferences prior to the start of shooting in Yugoslavia. Considering Hartwig had served in the German army as a young man and actually been wounded in the battle to be portrayed in this film, he felt justified in making certain creative demands.

"Wolf and Sam have had at it a couple of times already over the script," Coburn recounted during a preproduction interview. "I remember one script conference where Wolf said, 'I think a cut here.' And Sam came back with, 'What do you want cut?' 'Well, something ... it's too long. It doesn't play.' And Sam, of course, says, 'Okay, why don't you take it, and cut it then?' And this is something Wolf doesn't know what to do with. He says: 'Well, I don't know. You're the director. You're the screenwriter. Let's see what you come up with that would be satisfactory to me.' And Sam says: 'No! *To* me! It must be satisfactory *to me.'* 'All right. All right,' Wolf says. 'To you then. But you must cut it out.'"

As it would turn out, the script would not be the only issue over which Peckinpah and Hartwig would disagree. Because he apparently had needed Peckinpah's commitment to the project in order to secure the bulk of his financing, Hartwig had readily assured the director that whatever his needs in making "a Sam Peckinpah film" they would be met without consideration of cost. Unfortunately, the producer did not have access to the funding necessary to underwrite such a potentially expensive film. (Because of the need for large quantities of explosives, special effects, and dangerous stunt work, war films tend to be among the most expensive motion pictures to make.) The resulting conflicts would eventually siphon the creative energies of virtually everyone connected with the picture.

"Hartwig doesn't really know what he is getting into," Coburn observed prophetically just before leaving to join Peckinpah in Yugoslavia for the start of the picture. "He keeps trying to hedge his bets, and Sam keeps making him come up with whatever it is he's committed to. Sam's not asking for anything out of line. He just wants the best possible production that he can get."

As the start of production drew near, Peckinpah and several key members of the crew flew to Zagreb, Yugoslavia, to scout locations and prepare for the weeks of shooting that lay ahead. In this group were Walter Kelley and assistant director Ron Wright and his wife, Bitsy. Despite some initial problems with the weather, most of the necessary locations for filming were found in northern Yugoslavia between Zagreb and Trieste, Italy. The script unfortunately still remained a problem.

Faced with the somewhat unsettling reality of having to deal with a multilingual production company drawn in large part from Germany and Yugoslavia, Peckinpah had insisted that as many key department heads as possible come from the ranks of those with whom he had previously worked. These would include (in addition to Kelley and the Wrights) assistant director Cliff Coleman, property master Bob Visciglia, production designer Ted Haworth, cinematographer John Coquillon, special effects man Sass Bedig, and makeup artist Colin Arthur. Once again, Katy Haber would act as Peckinpah's personal assistant. All things being equal, this caliber of production talent would normally have been capable of producing an extraordinary film. Unfortunately, in Yugoslavia all things would not be equal. Around American actor James Coburn, Peckinpah assembled an international cast including British actors James Mason (Colonel Brandt) and David Warner (Captain Kiesel), and Austrian actor Maximilian Schell (Captain Stransky). The supporting roles were given to German and Yugoslavian actors. Austrian actress Senta Berger, who had worked with Peckinpah on *Major Dundee* more than a decade before, was cast in the lone female role, a German nurse whom Coburn encounters while he is recuperating from a wound.

As the starting date drew near, a final script had still not been completed to Peckinpah's satisfaction despite work done on it at different times by Kelley, Ron Wright, Haber, and himself. Because Kelley would be working as second unit director and dialogue coach, writer James Hamilton was brought in by Peckinpah to work on the screenplay as well.

At the same time, owing to a limited budget, Peckinpah sought to bring the actors to Yugoslavia for a week's unpaid rehearsal prior to the start of shooting. James Mason's reply to this request was to say that he always arrived on the set fully rehearsed, but if the American director wanted a week of rehearsal, let the director rehearse. At Peckinpah's insistence, Hartwig's production company, Rapid Film, paid the additional week in order to have Mason come in early.

"It was money well spent," noted Ron Wright, recalling the incident. "The real basis for the final script evolved during that week of rehearsal between Sam and the actors. In two and a half months, that script had gone nowhere. But the minute the actors arrived and began discussing who their characters were and what their motivations were, the whole script really fell into place."

Shortly after the beginning of principal photography, Peckinpah injured his leg. The contusion was severe enough that Peckinpah found it too painful to walk. As a result, assistant director Cliff Coleman transported Peckinpah to and from the set in an ancient BMW motorcycle with a sidecar. Still later, when Peckinpah's injury worsened, Coleman, who stands six feet five, was drafted to carry Peckinpah around on a stretcher with the help of a Yugoslavian assistant. When asked why he would agree to such a chore, Coleman replied: "It's just the knowledge that anytime I want to I can drop the son of a bitch." Along with his other responsibilities, Coleman would remain as chief litter bearer.

From the first, the biggest problem to be faced by Peckinpah and his production crew was a debilitating lack of communication between the various nationalities involved. Without a common language, efforts were frequently duplicated or wasted. One of the areas in which this problem became most noticeable early in the production was the wardrobe department.

As with every Peckinpah production, the director demanded that the clothing worn by the actors look "lived in." Attempting to accomplish this, the Yugoslavian and German wardrobe people resorted to a concoction that approximated watery cement applied with large paint brushes. The results were so unsatisfactory that Peckinpah demanded that Hartwig bring in Kent and Carol James with whom he had worked on *The Killer Elite*. Reluctantly, Hartwig, whose problems in financing the picture were mounting daily, agreed. As soon as they arrived, the Jameses went to work.

"The first day we got on the set," Kent James remembered, "we aged the costumes of 300 extras in about half an hour using the supplies we had brought with us—aerosol cans of paint, grease bags, Fuller's earth, everything—while [the German and Yugoslavian] crew of twelve couldn't get it done without paintbrush lines that looked awful. They had been using this dark mud that they painted on with brushes. Only when it dried under the hot lights, it looked almost white. So there were times when Sam'd shoot different angles on a scene, but they wouldn't cut together because the early stuff had guys in dark uniforms while the later stuff looked like these same guys had joined a different army."

"James Mason literally went around through the entire picture with a large 'X' painted on the back of his uniform," Carol James confirmed. "There was nothing we could do about it. We just came in too late. The damage had already been done. If they had wanted to save money, they should have brought us in at the beginning to set things up. Then, if they wanted to cut corners, they could have let us go. At least things would have run smoothly. But they did just the reverse, and it was nothing but pain. We had to communicate with the Yugoslavian wardrobe people using sign language. But they really picked up on what we were doing. The Germans were different. I think they really resented our being there."

Even the addition of Kent and Carol James could not relieve the difficulties that developed during the photographing of the battle scenes, however. With English, German, and a variety of Slavic dialects all being spoken at once, there were frequent miscues. A great deal of time was squandered attempting to coordinate the principals, extras, and special effects so that everything would take place before the cameras.

Among the most frustrated in this regard was special effects man Sass Bedig, who would carefully prepare and ignite his charges on cue only to learn that the extras had misunderstood the signals and failed to move. A great deal of time and money would then be spent as Bedig and crew would have to go back and rig everything again. Whole days were lost this way, and the morale of the company began to wane.

Although the picture required 300 extras to stage these mock battles before the cameras, of those only five were stuntmen. This lack of expertise in itself made it difficult to create the illusion of battle. "The problem," lamented Ron Wright, "was that once you killed those five stuntmen in closeup, where do you go next? Obviously, we became heavily dependent upon makeup. Fortunately, we had a makeup man who was absolutely brilliant. Colin Arthur was a real artist, a sculptor. And he took these five guys and made them different over and over again.

"One of the most amazing things he did was with one of the Yugoslavian stuntmen who had been in an accident and had half his face blown off some years before. He had a fake eye and half his face looked like something out of the *Phantom of the Opera.* Well, Colin, for one of the disguises, literally recreated this guy's face— rebuilt his cheekbone and everything. When the poor guy looked at himself in the mirror, it was too much. He just broke down and cried."

In addition, despite Peckinpah's insistence on having an American stunt coordinator for the picture, none could be found. The difficulty was that no stuntman was willing to risk his life without at least one other American stuntman along on whom he could rely. Always in a bind for funds, Hartwig had refused to pay for two American stuntmen, plus their gear, to be brought over for the picture.

The result was Peckinpah's dependence once again upon assistant director Cliff Coleman to assume the role of stunt coordinator. Coleman, who had had some experience in stunt work previously, brought with him to Yugoslavia all of the necessary equipment he felt he would need to perform the various stunts required by the script.

"Cliff Coleman was spectacular," recalled Ron Wright, who shared assistant directorial responsibilities with Coleman. "He did some of the toughest stunts in the picture, including all of the stunts for James Coburn. At one point, dressed as one of the German soldiers, he had to run past a tree as a bomb goes off. As the explosion hit him, he had to go up in the air and land on barbed wire just as a tree falls on him—all in one take. To do it, he used the small trampoline he had brought over with him because the Yugoslavian stunt people didn't use anything like that. He had to teach them how to use all the gear he'd brought along. Well, Cliff did this stunt with the barbed wire and the tree just perfectly. It was really a dangerous stunt, but Cliff pulled it off. Then, ironically, he never got paid for it because Hartwig was starting to run low on cash."

Hartwig's financial troubles that had developed early in the days of preproduction never really were resolved. The money committed to the picture by the Yugoslavian interests had been earmarked to pay for the Yugoslavian actors, crew members, and facilities. To offset this, Hartwig had managed to get most of his German crew members to work for a small salary and a promised share of the profits. This still left the production expenses (equipment rental, special effects, etc.) as well as the American and English cast and crew. As a result, Hartwig went weekly to Munich, attempting to dredge up funding to finish the picture.

All of this came to a head late in the filming when James Coburn received word from his agent in America that he had never been paid. Coburn promptly informed Hartwig that he would not walk on the set until he heard from his agent that the necessary funds had cleared his bank. The production continued to shoot around Coburn while awaiting the resolution of this situation. Ironically, Hartwig would succeed in paying Coburn only to run out of money to complete the final portion of the picture.

With more than three-quarters of a motion picture completed, Hartwig was forced to shut down production while he searched for someone willing to finance the final shooting and editing. He met with success in England where EMI Films agreed to provide the money for a substantial profit consideration. Hartwig had no choice.

The final days of shooting were completed in Yugoslavia under the aegis of EMI with editing to be completed at EMI facilities in England. Peckinpah, however, still searching for a satisfactory ending to the film, would eventually convince EMI to allow him to shoot additional footage of Coburn and Schell. This would be done in England, however, and cut in with the location footage.

Through all of this, Peckinpah remained in a good deal of pain both from his leg and general dissipation resulting from long hours and too much alcohol. At one point in the production, Peckinpah's leg had swollen so seriously that a doctor was called in to discuss the possibility of an operation. But in examining the director, the physician found that Peckinpah's liver was enlarged and his heart was showing some strain. On this basis, the operation was postponed and eventually forgotten.

Once in London, Peckinpah was forced to give up alcohol entirely in order to allow his body to mend. As the film's editors, Murray Jordan, Tony Lawson (who had worked with Peckinpah on *Straw Dogs)* and Michael Ellis, completed the final editing on the film, Peckinpah was placed on a medication that when combined with alcohol would cause him to vomit. It was prescribed as an aid in helping him resist the temptation to take a drink. "It really works," he deadpanned to a friend at the time. "I puke about eight times a day."

It was while he was recuperating and completing the post-production work on *Cross of Iron* that Peckinpah was offered the opportunity to direct another script for EMI called *Convoy.* Based upon a popular American song of the same name by country and western singer C. W. McCall, the script had been written by B.W. L. Norton, Jr., whose other credits included *Cisco Pike* and *Outlaw Blues.* The American producer would be Robert Sherman.

Again concerned that he involve himself in another project before the release of the one on which he was working, Peckinpah agreed to direct the picture. In it, he would cast two people he had enjoyed working with previously, Kris Kristofferson, who would portray the lead trucker known in the film by his nickname "Rubber Duck," and Ali MacGraw, who would portray the photojournalist he picks up along the way. Peckinpah began thinking of the project as a modern day *The Wild Bunch,* using truckers as the Western heroes of today. This was not an original notion. In a number of contemporary films and songs, the trucker has been commemorated as the modern cowboy. And although Peckinpah would attempt to explore some familiar themes from his work through this project, it would never reach a satisfactory conclusion.

Set in the American Southwest, *Convoy* was shot entirely on location, primarily in New Mexico during the late spring and summer of 1977. The single exception was a confrontation between Rubber Duck and the forces of justice near the end of the picture that was shot at Needles, California, on the Colorado River.

In addition to Kristofferson and MacGraw, Peckinpah cast Burt Young as a trucker named Pig Pen and Ernest Borgnine as Dirty Lyle, the evil policeman who preys on truck drivers. In a departure from the original script, Peckinpah attempted to add an extra dimension to the material by casting a pair of black actors as members of the convoy: Madge Sinclair, a star from the television drama *Roots,* became Widow

Woman, a female trucker, and Franklin Ajaye was cast as Spiker Mike, the young driver busted by Dirty Lyle.

Predictably, the film's crew would again be comprised primarily of longtime Peckinpah survivors. However, despite a general feeling of optimism as the project began, few would remain by the time filming was complete. And only editor Garth Craven would manage to stay with the film from the start of shooting until Peckinpah left the picture the following spring. Looking back on the ordeal, Craven recalled: "There were enormous problems on this picture. And I think Sam knew it early on. He had cast Kristofferson, whom he had worked with and liked on both *Pat Garrett* and *Alfredo Garcia.* The difficulty was that Kristofferson had undergone a number of personal changes including quitting booze. He was a totally different figure with whom Sam had little rapport.

"As for Ali MacGraw, I think Sam always knew she was no actress. But on *Getaway* he had felt she worked very well because she had a lot of business to do. She was always on the run. But that just wasn't the case in *Convoy.*

"So fairly early on, I think Sam realized he was stuck with these two people sitting in the cab of a truck with three or four basic camera angles he couldn't deviate from. And since he couldn't give them a whole lot of business, he had to rely upon acting, dialogue, and facial expression. It really made him desperate.

"He wound up getting into shouting matches with Ali between takes. Eventually, he just started running the camera—thousands and thousands of feet of film in the hope that something would come up that he could use. And in fact, this did work. Occasionally you would get something really extraordinary—a moment like a gold nugget. But this in turn created other problems like how to connect one nugget to the next without a jump cut or the story straying all over the place. It became a very difficult picture to cut."

In addition to problems with actors, Peckinpah had to face some very real physical and mechanical problems. The script called for 100 eighteen-wheel semitrailer trucks in a convoy through a substantial portion of the picture. To get them lined up and ready to move for one take would be fine. But if he wanted a second take, it would require substantial time and effort. In order to communicate between himself, the crew, and the actors and teamsters in the trucks, Peckinpah had to rely upon citizens band radios that sometimes functioned and sometimes did not. Originally budgeted for $6 million, the film's cost would eventually double.

"I think that there came a conscious realization on Sam's part," Craven commented, following the picture's release, "that we were involved in something of very little worth. He therefore began

289

looking for ways to justify what he was doing by adding bits of pseudo-philosophizing in the hope of giving this thing a wider scope. He needed to feel that he was saying something meaningful, something important. And it just wasn't there."

Nevertheless, Peckinpah steeped himself in a love affair with trucks and truckers in an effort to make the film into a contemporary Western. He would send people out to contact and record truckers' conversations on long night hauls. He tried getting inside the trucker psyche in the hope that out of this would come some basic truth upon which he could build his film. He wanted to turn the world of the trucker into a microcosm of modern American society. But the harder he tried, the less he succeeded.

"He desperately wanted a *big* picture," Craven continued. "And in his defense, I believe his concern was an honest one. The producers never attempted to justify what they were doing in this picture aside from the hope that it would make them rich. But that wasn't enough for Sam. His pride wouldn't let him accept the fact that this was a real piece of shit from the beginning.

"When he began to realize that the pseudo-philosophizing wasn't going to hold up, he tried to bring in elements reminiscent of Kafka or Pirandello. For example, he staged the scenes involving the governor of New Mexico in the ballroom of the Hilton Hotel in Albuquerque. Sam just walked in and was completely taken by what he saw—this sort of surreal room with convention chairs piled one upon the other in sort of towers all over the room. He spent the next three hours arranging these towers. Then he shot the scene from a series of angles with the governor [Seymour Cassel] and his people in the foreground while men in white coats flitted about mysteriously in the background among the towers [of chairs].

"In another scene, the one where Pig Pen [Burt Young] gets into an accident with an ice cream truck near the end of the picture, this crowd gathers to gawk. And in the crowd, watching Pig Pen, is Pig Pen. It's a character watching himself. And they looked at each other and smile. None of this, of course, made it to the screen, although it was shot. I give Sam credit for trying. But in the end, there was no way to save it."

As the problems continued to mount, the picture ran far over schedule. Kristofferson had a previous commitment to do a concert tour with his band (who were also in the picture as a strange quasi-religious sect in a microbus) in August. Because so much money had already been committed to the project, EMI elected to do something unprecedented. It shut the film down for a month while Kristofferson went on tour, resuming when he returned. This did even less for the morale of the company, however, and few of the original crew (who had not already left or been fired) elected to come back. As the picture finally drew to completion, Peckinpah tried to find words to express his frustration. "The most significant thing Sam said to me on this picture," recalled Craven, "was on the last day of shooting when he said, 'I haven't done one good day's work on this whole picture— not one day that I really felt I'd put it all together.'"

The film's principal photography was completed in September of 1977, and Peckinpah returned with Craven to Los Angeles to edit it. Unfortunately, the problems persisted.

"When we finished shooting and actually went to cut [the film], there was a point where we had to screen the rough cut for the executives from EMI. All things considered, that screening went quite well. I think even Sam was surprised. Until that moment, I really don't think Sam actually thought he had a film, something with a beginning, a middle, and an end.

"We really had some spectacular footage. But there just wasn't much of a story. We tried everything. Sam had even shot thousands of feet of Ali running down to where Kris's truck has just gone into the river at the end of the picture. It was done at various camera speeds from slow motion to normal. And Sam had us insert these shots throughout the film as a sort of pre-echo. But even that didn't work, and we had to pull all those shots out."

Leaving Craven to wrestle with the editing, Peckinpah flew to Rome at the request of a young producer he knew named Jerry Harvey, who along with director Monte Hellman was producing a film called *China 9, Liberty 37*. An offbeat Western, the film company had completed shooting the film's exteriors in Spain and was now finishing up on an Italian sound stage. In a change of pace, Peckinpah would act in the film, portraying a character modeled on real life Western entrepreneur Ned Buntline. "I remember talking with Lee Marvin," the director recalled just prior to his departure, "and I told him I hated actors. And Lee just looked at me with a smile and said: 'Every actor does.'"

While in Italy, Peckinpah also appeared in a low-budget science fiction film entitled *The Visitor* starring another well-known American director, John Huston. However, Peckinpah's performance as a seedy gynecologist was photographed in silhouetted profile using someone else's dubbed voice and is hardly worth noting.

By early 1978, Peckinpah had returned to California to finish *Convoy*. In March of that year, he screened his version of the film for EMI and turned the project over to them. It was significant that

Peckinpah, the *enfant terrible* of American cinema, did not choose to defend his version of the film.

"Personally," Garth Craven concluded, "I think Sam was very relieved to be relieved of the film, because what we had was a movie in which the trucks were the stars. And they looked pretty good. And there were some extraordinary stunt sequences. The actors, on the other hand, didn't have much to work with. Sam made the best of what he was given. He just couldn't transcend the material."

Neither *Cross of Iron* nor *Convoy* is representative of Peckinpah at his best. Yet each found success of a sort at the box office. *Cross of Iron,* while failing to attract an American audience (due most probably to an American audience's inability to identify with the German soldier in World War II), was so successful in Europe that it eventually spawned a sequel. When Peckinpah was approached to possibly direct this film, he immediately declined. The original had given him a chance to say all he had ever wanted about war. He had no desire to repeat himself. Moreover, he felt certain such a project could only damage his career, a perception that was borne out as the sequel, eventually directed by Andrew McLaglen and starring Richard Burton, was unable to find an American distributor willing to release it.

Convoy, on the other hand, did well in the American South as well as abroad, especially in Japan where Peckinpah's work is greatly admired. But because this film was taken over by EMI and recut to the specifications of executive producer Michael Deeley, former head of British Lion Films, it is less a Sam Peckinpah film than it is an EMI Film. Deeley even brought over his own supervising film editor from England to prepare the final cut of the film, a cut for which Peckinpah had little empathy.

Of the two, *Cross of Iron* remains the most interesting with respect to Peckinpah's work as a director. At best, it is not an easy picture to like. Nevertheless, following its American release, Peckinpah did receive a letter from Orson Welles calling it the finest antiwar film he had ever seen. Bleak and loveless, it has no hero, only a protagonist, Sergeant Steiner, the quintessential survivor. Despising officers and elitists alike, Steiner reserves his loyalty for the men of his platoon and perceives war as an infantile but deadly game.

The film is strongest when portraying the chaos of battle and Steiner's madness while recuperating at a German hospital and weakest when philosophizing about man's condition. At times, it is condescending and pretentious. Yet, ironically; it leaves the viewer with what is perhaps the only correct response to war: a loathing for the ugly, stupid pandering to man's basest instincts. There is nothing romantic, beautiful, or stirring, and nothing for young minds to emulate. Only revulsion and a sense of futility persist.

Following his difficulties on *Convoy*, Peckinpah left Hollywood for Mexico where he attempted to set up a production company with Emilio Fernandez; Alex Phillips, Jr.; and Isela Vega. However, owing to circumstances beyond his control, the partnership failed to materialize and Peckinpah returned to the States where his friend actor Warren Oates had purchased a large piece of property in the Big Sky country of Montana. Peckinpah had visited Oates there on several previous occasions and talked the actor into selling him a portion of his land. The director intended to settle there. He built a cabin, did a little fishing, and tried to put the film industry behind him.

Then on May 15, 1979, Peckinpah suffered a heart attack. Rushed to the hospital in Livingston, Montana, Peckinpah underwent surgery in which doctors implanted a corrective pacemaker. He was placed in intensive care. Denver Peckinpah, his brother, who had survived a similar attack, flew in to be at his bedside. Despite some difficult moments, Peckinpah would fully recover. Given the fact that the incident would finally force him to limit his drinking, the heart attack probably saved his life. He continued to live quietly in Montana.

Several months later, however, producer Albert Ruddy; whose credits include *The Godfather* and *The Longest Yard,* called Katy Haber, who was then employed in EMl's Beverly Hills office as executive assistant to Michael Deeley. There she had worked on a number of films including the postproduction of *The Deer Hunter.*

"He asked me what I thought of Sam as a director," Haber recounted, "and I told him that Sam is an enormously powerful personality. It takes a strong producer to be able to deal with Sam. But if you can manage that, he's liable to make an extraordinary film."

On the strength of this recommendation and what he had seen of Peckinpah's work in the Western genre, Ruddy contacted the recuperating director in Montana and offered him a script entitled *The Texans*. Originally written in the early seventies by John Milius, whose credits include *The Wind and the Lion, Big Wednesday,* and *Apocalypse Now,* it was the story of the head of a modern Texas conglomerate who decides to test the mettle of his younger corporate executives as well as that of his own son by forcing them to drive a herd of Longhorns up the Chisholm Trail. Intrigued by the possibilities, Peckinpah agreed to do a major rewrite with the understanding that he would direct the picture.

Over the next six months, Peckinpah reworked the first half of *The Texans* and submitted it to Ruddy for approval. Among the actors discussed for the leading role was William Holden, whose work on *The Wild Bunch* made him Peckinpah's first choice.

Peckinpah continued to work on the script through the summer of 1980.

It was during this time that the National Cowboy Hall of Fame and Western Heritage Center in Oklahoma City awarded Peckinpah the John Ford Award for his contributions to Western film-making. Peckinpah traveled to Oklahoma City to accept the award with his brother, Denver, and Denver's son, David. The day after this was reported in the Hollywood trade papers, Peckinpah's agents received three separate inquiries about the director's availability. One of these was from Peckinpah's former nemesis, Martin Ransohoff, who had recently optioned Edward Abbey's best-selling novel *The Monkey Wrench Gang.* "We didn't see eye-to-eye on *Cincinnati Kid,"* Peckinpah recalled, "but we've had a couple of laughs since. And God, what I wouldn't give to do *The Monkey Wrench Gang."* Clearly, Peckinpah appeared to be back in business.

However, when Peckinpah's deal with Ruddy to make *The Texans* unexpectedly fell through, the director became dissatisfied with the way in which his agents were handling his career. Predictably he cast about for new representation.

It was then, with no small sense of irony, that he turned to Martin Baum, his former producer on *Alfredo Garcia* and *The Killer Elite,* who had since returned to agentry and joined the firm of Creative Artists. Once again elements in Peckinpah's life had come full circle. His rationale behind selecting Baum was not personal but pragmatic: while they had had their creative differences, Baum remained an extremely effective agent. As if to offer proof of this, Baum promptly secured a project for Peckinpah entitled *Hang Tough,* then under development by producer Herb Jaffe at United Artists.

Based on the 1980 novel *City Primeval* by Elmore Leonard, whose other books *Hombre* and *Valdez Is Coming* had also been made into films, *Hang Tough* was a contemporary police drama set in Detroit. Originally scheduled to begin shooting on location in Detroit in late autumn of 1981, the project was delayed by the three-month Writers Guild strike as well as a threatened walkout by the Directors Guild. A member of both guilds, Peckinpah actively worked as a negotiator in helping to avert the directors' strike. It was only after these labor differences had been settled that Peckinpah finally collaborated with Jim Silke on a revised script for *Hang Tough* and then traveled to Detroit to scout locations.

At the same time, he continued to do the unexpected. At the request of his longtime friend and mentor Don Siegel, Peckinpah agreed to do several weeks work as second unit director on Siegel's production of the Frank Gilroy novel *The Edge,* a love story of a blackjack dealer and a change girl out to beat the odds, starring Bette Midler. As second unit director, Peckinpah would only be permitted to handle the action sequences. Inasmuch as this was a Herb Jaffe project as well, Jaffe agreed. Ignoring the title of the project—now called *Jinxed*—Peckinpah went to work.

Although he significantly contributed to the Siegel picture, Peckinpah's own project was terminated with the sale of United Artists to MGM late in 1981. At another time in his life, this might have panicked Peckinpah into accepting the first available project, much as he had done following Fox's cancellation of *The Insurance Company* when he was offered *The Killer Elite.* But he had learned that lesson the hard way. Having given up smoking and drinking as well, he seemed to have put his demons behind him. This time he would wait for the chance to make something worthwhile.

By the spring of 1982, Peckinpah's patience finally paid off. Producers Peter S. Davis and William Panzer approached him with an offer to direct the film version of Robert Ludlum's bestselling novel *The Osterman Weekend* from a script by Alan Sharp *(Night Moves).* After reading both the book and Sharp's screenplay, Peckinpah agreed. The film was scheduled to begin principal photography in early autumn on location in the Eastern United States. The tide had turned at last.

Through all of the tribulation following the release of *Convoy,* Peckinpah had remained philosophical. He still maintained his cabin in Montana as well as a trailer on the beach at Malibu. He still saw many of his old friends. His son, Matthew, had gone off on his own, joining the Marines. His daughter Sharon was about to make him a grandfather for the first time. Yet one element alone continued to dominate his life.

During a foray into Hollywood on business in the spring of 1980, Peckinpah had learned of a screening of *The Wild Bunch* for a class on Western film at the University of Southern California and was persuaded to attend. Warren Oates, who also happened to be in town at the time, came to the screening as well. The film was well received and afterwards the director parried a number of questions with offhand humor and self-deprecating asides.

At last, a student was prompted to ask the director what was the most important thing to Sam Peckinpah. Peckinpah stared at the young man for a long moment.

"Making films," he said at last. "Working with people like Warren [Oates] and Strother [Martin]. That's everything. Nothing else matters."

Postscript:
The Osterman Weekend

"The truth is a lie that hasn't been found out.,,

By the time Sam Peckinpah had begun preproduction on his next film, *The Osterman Weekend,* this book, *PECKINPAH: A Portrait in Montage,* was at last about to make it into print in its first edition. In the late spring of 1982, at my then publisher's request, I had attended the American Book Association convention held in Anaheim, California, to promote the upcoming publication. Having read the manuscript, Peckinpah had agreed to join me there only to back out at the last minute. By way of apology, he sent me the following note laced with his own brand of wry humor and dated June 24, 1982:

> *Dear Gar:*
>
> *I would love to have a couple of copies signed by the author. I send you my love.*
>
> *I apologize for not being where I should have been, but I am trying to pay the rent. I trust you'll understand.*
>
> *My love to your wife—In name, not in fact, and your*
>
> *adopted children.*

It was signed in Peckinpah's characteristic scrawl: *"Send money to your friend, SP."*

Thus when I received the first copies of the book from the publisher in the autumn of 1982, I called Sam to see when we could get together. By then, *The Osterman Weekend* was well into production and shooting at a private home in the Pacific Palisades. Peckinpah was living in the guest quarters. Answering the phone, he sounded like a man looking for a fight. He had been waiting on a call from one of his producers and was surprised to hear my voice. Pleased to hear the book was finally out, he suggested I take a ride out to the set so we could talk. They were shooting nights. I said I'd stop out after work. "Don't forget the books," he said. I promised I wouldn't.

At the time, I was working as story editor on a television series for CBS. On the evening of November 17, armed with a half-dozen copies of the book fresh from the printer, I found myself driving into the Santa Monica Mountains. Up Mandeville Canyon after dark, the winding road led to a sprawling ranch-style house with a pool that had once belonged to the late actor, Robert Taylor. Peckinpah had told me to come as early as I could since the evening's filming consisted of a difficult stunt involving a burning swimming pool. The pre-rigging would take them until well after midnight. "We'll have some time," Sam had said. "Better bring your long-and-woollies. There's a bite in the air."

Based on the Robert Ludlum novel, *The Osterman Weekend* was a somewhat convoluted story involving corruption, compromise and betrayal within the American CIA. Published as Ludlum's fifth novel, it was more ragged than his earlier works, the kind of novel that gets written and goes unpublished until the author becomes successful. It had been optioned by the producing team of William Panzer and Peter Davis, who commissioned a screenplay from Alan Sharp before approaching Peckinpah to direct. And while Sam had expressed an interest, they had not secured Peckinpah's services with any kind of firm financial commitment. "They're shopping it all over town with my name attached, and there's nothing I can do about it," he had once lamented, knowing that he was no longer in a position to turn down any legitimate offer. When Panzer-Davis secured a distribution agreement from 20th Century-Fox and the film was greenlighted for production, Peckinpah said yes.

Sitting across the desk, Sam looked older and more fragile than I had remembered him. The time without work, the insecurities of the movie business, the grind of production and, not least of all, his years of alcohol and drug abuse had all taken their toll. A plastic mask dangled from his neck giving him the look of a surgeon. The mask was attached to a small canister of pure oxygen to help him deal with the lingering effects of a bacterial infection as well as the long hours. Still, there was a familiar fire burning deep in his eyes. Resembling a graying warrior unable to resist the smell of battle, he smiled and talked about old times. About our first meeting in Mexico and the long journey that had finally led us here. I handed him the copies of

298

the book. He shook his head. "You never could write worth a shit," he said, looking pleased. "God knows I tried to stop you." I answered that I remembered.

Having recently read *White Hunter, Black Heart,* Peter Viertel's *roman a clef* based on his experiences with director John Huston during the preproduction of *The African Queen* in 1950, I had been struck by certain undeniable similarities between Viertel's surrogate for Huston, the character John Wilson, and Peckinpah. Looking at Peckinpah, I asked if he'd read it. He stared at me for a long time without speaking. "Why?" he said at last. I told him I had a theory: Not only had he read it, he'd lived it. His entire lifestyle had been patterned after Huston's ever since. He looked very serious, then broke into smile: "So you finally found me out ... Took you long enough."

He picked up a copy and read the opening page, his dark eyes darting quickly. He smiled again. "But at least you got some of it right." Outside, the sound of laughter drifted through the fogged window panes. A moment later, Helen Shaver, the actress cast as Virginia Tremayne, the drug-addicted wife of a celebrity doctor played by Dennis Hopper, came in to join us. Discovering Sam was not alone, she apologized but explained that she needed to talk to him. "It's about the scene where we die," she said. Peckinpah nodded, then introduced us. "We'll have time to talk before the fireworks," he assured her, referring to the upcoming stunt. Watching her exit the room, Sam smiled. "You know what they say about unbelievably beautiful actresses who can't deliver lines?" I nodded, repeating the phrase I'd heard him use before: "God doesn't give with both hands." His eyes lingered on Shaver, who had stopped just outside to rezip her coat. At last, he grinned: "Yeah, well when God made that one, He really had His hands full. 'Cause she's got it all."

Helen Shaver, who more recently has become a director herself, remembers going to meet Peckinpah for the first time and thinking she was in for a rough time:

"I thought I was going to meet a misogynist—a man who hated women. The only reason I went was because of who he was—this incredibly gifted director. But I was expecting the worst. So I walked in and here's this small man behind a very large desk who is so charming that I couldn't help myself—he completely turned me

around. Within ten minutes, I was blushing and giggling and feeling like this schoolgirl. Sam just adored women. He made you feel so beautiful. . . so important. By the time the meeting was over, I real- ized that everything I had expected had been wrong.

"Acting for Sam as a director, it was the same thing. He made you feel honored and protected—safe to create a character on the edge, which was what my character was. The role was very dangerous. As a former addict, two-and-a-half years into recovery, I wanted to play the character exactly as she would have been. It was very risky. But Sam completely understood. The first scene I played was my side of the conversation with Dennis Hopper trying to get him to come home. It was written as very sexual, almost like phone sex. But the whole subtext had to convey her desperate need for drugs. Sam understood that. During rehearsal, he came over and asked me how I wanted my bed- room to look. And we decided on peach colored sheets. And what color the walls should be. He didn't want it to be just any room. He wanted it to be my room. Then before we shot the scene, he got on the bed with me and together we made this kind of nest of the sheets. What Sam understood better than any director I'd ever worked with was how vulnerable you are as an actress. He was my protector. He made me feel incredibly safe.

"But the other thing that made Sam such a great director was his understanding of who each character was and how to get that on the screen. At the end of Osterman Weekend my character is killed along with her husband and another couple in a camper trying to escape. And Sam and I discussed it. He felt that before she dies my character needs a moment of truth. So I suggested that maybe she sees herself in the mirror with her face smeared with cocaine. Only I also wanted the child in this character to emerge and find a kind of salvation just before she dies. So I asked Sam: 'How can I show this?' And Sam said: 'What if you sing?' And I just immediately picked up on it. I said: 'How about a prayer?' Sam thought that was fantastic. So I sang 'Jesus loves me, this I know. . . ' And after the first take, he said: 'Cut, print. That was sensational.' But I couldn't help it. I said: 'Let me do one more.' And Sam looked at me with this twinkle in his eye and said: 'You're just like me. We live our lives between action and cut. It's like the only time we're really alive.'"

300

When he would cast a picture, Sam had always trusted his instincts and never went with an actor he didn't believe in. Craig T. Nelson, who plays the character of a successful television writer, Bernie Osterman, in the film complete with a moustache reminiscent of the late Dalton Trumbo (the blacklisted writer who served a year in jail as a member of the "Hollywood Ten"), remembers:

"I was pretty much an unknown at the time. But I had an office over at Sunset Gower Studios where Sam was casting the film. And I'd been so blown away by *The Wild Bunch* that I would have given any-thing to be in a Peckinpah film. So I'd watch him. I mean just stare at him day after day, every time I'd see him. Finally he came up to me and said: 'What do you want?' And I said: 'I want to read for a part. I want to be in your picture.' And he said: 'Sorry. We're only looking at name actors.' But he gave me a chance. And the minute I read for him, there was just this connection between us. I know it's a cliché, but Sam was like a father to me. He was my mentor, my friend. Through the pic-ture, after the picture, right to the end. He was the guy I'd call when I needed to talk. Sam had such a big heart.

"We spent a lot of time together on *Osterman*. Sam was staying at the guesthouse out at the Robert Taylor estate because he was ill. He had a deep cut on the index finger of his right hand that wouldn't heal. They even had a grip stand with a sling on it for Sam on the set while he'd be directing. So after we'd wrap, I'd stick around just to talk with him. And I learned so much. He went out of his way to make sure I understood everything he wanted my character to do. He knew what he wanted. It was all in his head. But he was at the end of his life, and nothing was easy.

"After the movie, we kept in touch. He used to call me 'Fish' because my character in *Osterman* was underwater so much. I remember being on this other film and calling him in Malibu at his trailer [in] Paradise Cove. And he was shooting cockroaches off the wall with a .45. I hear this 'Blam...blam...blam.' I said: 'Did you get 'em?' 'Yeah, I got 'em. Go ahead.' And I was having such a miserable time on this picture, I just opened up. Very emotional.

"Then there's this long pause—maybe he was reloading, I'm not sure. Finally he says: 'Fish, just remember one thing—acting is looping.' And we laughed. He knew just the right thing to bring me out of it. He was great. Sometime after that, I got another call from him while he was trying to finish *Osterman*. It was brutal. He said: 'Fish, I need $5,000 bucks to finish the film.' So I sent him the check. And then went to this screening he had of his cut of the film somewhere down in Orange County. It was worth it just to see it Sam's

301

way once. Because it was never going to be that way again."

The Osterman Weekend is a parable. Anticipating the information overload the world is now mired in, it asks the question: Who will watch the watchers? As Peckinpah once remarked to the critic now a film editor, Paul Seydor: "Burt Lancaster's performance is as close to Alexander Haig [Richard Nixon's chief of staff in the waning days of Watergate] as I ever hope to get." The demise of the Western with its clear-cut values had left Peckinpah less able to define what America had become. *The Osterman Weekend* in some ways reflects Peckinpah's disillusionment at America's loss of direction. It's like *Straw Dogs* turned inside out. A man on his own turf confronted by his friends. No longer the America that he had known as a boy and attempted to fix on film in such classics as *Ride the High Country, The Wild Bunch* or *Cable Hogue,* he seems to bear a grudge against the America he now finds. At the far end of a difficult and stormy career, he is like a Jeremiah revealing uncomfortable ancient truths. Having seen the film again recently, albeit not in Peckinpah's cut (which to my knowledge, no longer exists) but the producer's, I was struck by how much of the film, indeed, seems prophetic. In retrospect, it emerges as more of a cautionary tale for our times than any of us realized.

On the wall of my office hangs a photograph I took of Sam the first time we met in Mexico a quarter century ago. We had been scouting locations for *Bring Me the Head of Alfredo Garcia* and had stopped to look at a hacienda not far from the pyramids outside Mexico City. He wears a denim jacket, arms resting on the wooden fence rail, a glass of Campari in his hand. Looking across the paddock, he seems momentarily to have put his demons to rest. Across the top of the photo he has written: "I hope the end is always the beginning—Sam Peckinpah."

* * *

On December 28, 1984, in Los Angeles, California, Sam Peckinpah died. Some said too soon, others not soon enough. The cause of death was listed as heart failure. Which has to be a lie. For of all the things in life that failed him, it could never have been his heart.

Sources

Since much of the material that forms the core of this book evolved out of extensive interviews and research, it seems appropriate to provide the reader with relevant documentation without repetitive footnoting. Consequently, the following is an attempt to briefly bring into focus the primary sources of information for each chapter.

In addition, Sam Peckinpah graciously took the time to read through an early draft of the manuscript and provide comprehensive notes and additions. These were then evaluated against the factual data available and used where appropriate.

1. A California Heritage

Most of the factual material presented in this chapter was gathered in California in a series of interviews: Fern Church Peckinpah, Fresno, September 16, 1973; Jane Visher, Bass Lake, June 8, 1974; Mortimer Peckinpah, Fresno, June 11,, 1974; and Denver C. Peckinpah, Fresno, September 16, 1973, April 4, 1974, and June 11, 1974.
The undated letter from Louise Derrek Church to her son, Earle, was kindly made available by Denver C. Peckinpah. As for the change in spelling of the family name, the following quotation is from Elezabeth Peckinpah's diary furnished through the courtesy of Mortimer Peckinpah:

A few months ago our family were talking about our name having so many letters. We all thought it would be a good idea to shorten the name if it did not change the pronunciation. Last night the subject came up again and I told the family that the only way we could change the name and shorten it without losing the pronunciation would be to leave out the "u" and the "g" from "paugh" and end the name in "pah." Mr. P. agreed with me so we all voted on the change 100 per cent. From now on our name shall be spelled "PECKINPAH."

Early morning, April 6, 1853.

303

Additional material was obtained from the following sources: Ben R. Walker, *The Fresno Blue Book* (Fresno: Cawston, 1941), pp. 42-43; John Anderson, "Moses J. Church: Father of Fresno Irrigation," *Fresno Bee,* January 4, 1942, magazine supplement; "Young Belles of Army and Congressional Sets Just Introduced Who Won Popularity," *Washington Post,* February 1, 1914, p. 5.

2. Growing Up

The account of Sam Peckinpah's youth resulted from the interpolation of information gathered in Mexico City and California in a series of interviews: Sam Peckinpah, Mexico City, August 28 and 29 and December 9, 13, and 14, 1973; Fern Church Peckinpah, Fresno, September 16, 1973; Denver Peckinpah, Fresno, September 16, 1973, and April 4 and June 11, 1974; Fern Lea Peckinpah Peter, Malibu, September 6, 1973; Slim Pickens (telephone), Westlake Village, September 12, 1973; Blaine Pettitt, Fresno, June 10, 1974; Al Pettitt, Bass Lake, June 9, 1974.

For further discussion of Peckinpah's background and influences, see Paul Seydor, *Peckinpah: The Western Films* (Chicago: University of Illinois Press, 1980), pp. 251-281.

3. Learning a Trade

The depiction of Sam Peckinpah's career prior to becoming a feature film director as presented in this chapter was derived from information gathered in a series of interviews: Sam Peckinpah, Mexico City, August 27-29 and December 16, 1973; Denver C. Peckinpah, Fresno, September 16, 1973, and April 4, and June 11, 1974; Fern Lea Peckinpah Peter, Malibu, September 6, 1973; Don Siegel, Los Angeles, June 12, 1974; Joel McCrea (telephone), Camarillo, California, June 16, 1974; Strother Martin, Chicago, August 21 1973; Frank Kowalski, Studio City, California, September 12, 1973; R. G. Armstrong, Los Angeles, September 10, 1973.

In addition, the work done by Paul Seydor for his book *Peckinpah: The Western Films,* pp. 251-281, especially his diligence in unearthing Peckinpah's master's thesis, was extremely helpful.

When I originally interviewed Peckinpah regarding his work at the University of Southern California, he staunchly maintained that his thesis was "mercifully lost." Taking this at face value, I was pleasantly surprised when Seydor, while teaching at USC, found a copy on file there. Peckinpah's reluctance in this seems attributable to the common fear among directors and writers of his generation that such information might render him unemployable by producers and studio executives with less education.

All comments pertaining to Peckinpah's master's thesis were the result of a careful reading of the document itself: David S. Peckinpah, "An Analysis of the Method Used in Producing and Directing a One Act Play for the Stage and for a Closed Circuit Television Broadcast" (Master's thesis, University of Southern California Department of Drama, June 1954).

4. The Deadly Companions

The examination of Sam Peckinpah's first experience as a feature film director and his conflicts with producer Charles B. FitzSimons are primarily the result of interviews with both Peckinpah, Mexico City, August 29 and December 13, 1973, and FitzSimons (telephone), Los Angeles, June 13, 1974.

5. Ride the High Country

This chapter is the result of integrating material obtained in Mexico City and California through a series of interviews: Sam Peckinpah, Mexico City, August 29-31, 1973; Richard Lyons, Tarzana, June 16, 1974; Joel McCrea (telephone), Camarillo, June 16, 1974; Burt Kennedy (telephone), Los Angeles, June 14, 1974; L. Q. Jones, Los Angeles, September 5, 1973; Randolph Scott (telephone), Palm Springs, September 4, 1973; Warren Oates, Los Angeles, September 13, 1973; R. G. Armstrong, Los Angeles, September 11, 1973; Frank Santillo, Malibu, September 6, 1973; James Silke, Beverly Hills, March 3, 1976; Fern Lea Peckinpah Peter, Malibu, September 6, 1973.

6. Major Dundee

The examination of creative conflicts over the making of this picture as well as the detailing of the production itself are the result of interviews in Mexico City and California with the following individuals: Sam Peckinpah, Mexico City, August 28-29 and December 13, 1973; Ben Johnson, Sylmar, October 24, 1974; James Silke, Beverly Hills, March 3, 1976; Lucien Ballard, Malibu, June 6, 1974; Gordon Dawson, Mexico City, August 25, 1973; James Coburn, Beverly Hills, September 7, 1973; R. G. Armstrong, Los Angeles, September 11, 1973; Whitey Hughes, Mexico City, December 11, 1973; L. Q. Jones, Los Angeles, September 5, 1973.

In addition to these interviews and Peckinpah's notes on this film, I received two letters of importance: one from the film's producer, Jerry Bresler, dated June 23, 1974, and another from the film's star, Charlton Heston, dated September 12, 1974.

Initially, Bresler had consented to a telephone interview, but he subsequently recanted everything he had said, preferring instead to be quoted for the record by means of the letter cited above. In terms of fact, there was no difference between the information made available during the interview and that supplied in the letter. All information attributed to Bresler in this chapter comes directly from his letter according to his instructions.

As for Heston, he was unable to break into an extremely crowded schedule on numerous occasions and, therefore, graciously elected to supply a transcript of a previous interview (American Film Institute's *Dialogue on Film* 1, no. 1 [1972]) in which he dealt with his experiences on *Major Dundee* as well as comment in the personal letter cited above.

7. Years without Work

The primary source materials for this chapter were the following interviews in Mexico City and California: Sam Peckinpah, Mexico City, August 28 and December 13, 1973; Philip Lathrop, Culver City, June 11, 1975; James Silke, Beverly Hills, March 3, 1976; Daniel Melnick (telephone), Culver City, November 21, 1974; Jerry Fielding, Hollywood, September 5, 1973.

In addition, the letter written by Katherine Anne Porter to Sam Peckinpah, dated November 25, 1966, was kindly made available by Peckinpah. It is interesting to note the phrase "Why couldn't They— whoever They are—" in light of the similar phrasing used in *The Wild Bunch* when the Bunch discover they have stolen washers instead of gold:

LYLE
Who the hell is "they"!?

SYKES
(laughing, cackling)
"They?" Why "they" are just plain
and fancy "they." Knock down and
drag-out "they!" "They."

(*The Wild Bunch,* p. 24)

Considering Peckinpah was working on the script in the months following this letter, this dialogue would appear to have been inspired by Miss Porter's remark

8. The Wild Bunch

The detailing of this production resulted from the integration of information gathered through interviews with the following individuals: Sam Peckinpah, Mexico City, August 27, 28, and 31 and December 13, 1973; Walon Green (telephone), Los Angeles, November 11, 1974; Lou Lombardo, Los Angeles, September 10, 1973; Gordon Dawson, Mexico City, August 25, 1973; Strother Martin, Chicago, August 2, 1973; Ernest Borgnine, Los Angeles, September 13, 1973; Whitey Hughes, Mexico City, December 11,1973; Bo Hopkins, Los Angeles, September 10, 1973; William Holden, Los Angeles, June 14, 1974; Warren Oates, Los Angeles, September 13, 1973; Gary Combs, Mexico City, December 10,, 1973; Joe Canutt, Buellton, California, August 15, 1975; Jerry Fielding, Hollywood, September 5, 1973; Camille Fielding, Hollywood, September 5, 1973.

9. The Ballad of Cable Hogue

The account of the extreme difficulties surrounding this production and its aftermath resulted from interviews with the following individuals: Sam Peckinpah, Mexico City, December 13 and 18, 1973; Max Evans (telephone), Los Angeles, July 2, 1974; L.Q. Jones, Los Angeles, September 5, 1973; Gordon Dawson, Mexico City, August 25, 1973; Robert Visciglia, Los Angeles, September 13, 1973; R. G. Armstrong, Los Angeles, September 9, 1973; Jason Robards, Lake Forest, Illinois, July 6, 1973; Stella Stevens (telephone), Los Angeles, September 8, 1973; Lou Lombardo, Los Angeles, September 10, 1973; Slim Pickens (telephone), Westlake Village, California, September 12, 1973.

10. Straw Dogs

The material presented in this chapter is based largely on a series of interviews with the following individuals: Sam Peckinpah, Mexico City, August 30 and December 13, 1973, and Los Angeles, June 3, 1974; Martin Baum, Mexico City, December 13, 1973; David Z. Goodman (telephone), Beverly Hills, California, January 13, 1975; Katy Haber, Mexico City, August 30, 1973, and June 3, 1974; Dustin Hoffman (telephone), New York, February 6, 1975; Alf Pegley, Mexico City, December 18, 1973; Strother Martin, Chicago, August 2,

1973; Daniel Melnick (telephone), Culver City, California, November 21, 1974; Jerry Fielding, Hollywood, September 5, 1973.

1. Junior Bonner

The material presented in this chapter is based largely on a series of interviews in Mexico City and California with the following individuals: Sam Peckinpah, Mexico City, December 13, 1973; Joe Wizan, Los Angeles, September 11, 1973; Jeb Rosebrook, Studio City, September 13, 1973; Ben Johnson, Sylmar, October 24, 1974; Katy Haber, Mexico City, August 30, 1973; Ida Lupino (telephone), Los Angeles, September 8, 1973; Casey Tibbs, Los Angeles, June 14, 1974; Lucien Ballard, Malibu, June 6, 1974; Chuck Wilborn, Los Angeles, June 10, 1975; Martin Baum, Mexico City, December 13, 1973; Steve McQueen (telephone), Malibu, September 6, 1973.

2. The Getaway

The material presented in this chapter is based largely on a series of interviews in Mexico City and California with the following individuals: Sam Peckinpah, Mexico City, August 28 and 29 and December 13, 1973, and San Francisco, October 26, 1974; Katy Haber, Mexico City, August 30, 1973; David Foster, Los Angeles, September 11, 1973; Gary Combs, Mexico City, December 10, 1973; Lucien Ballard, Malibu, June 6, 1974; Ali MacGraw (telephone) Malibu, September 4, 1973; Joie Gould, Malibu, June 2, 1974; Newt Arnold, Encino, September 7, 1973; Slim Pickens (telephone), Westlake Village, September 12, 1973; Jerry Fielding, Hollywood, September 5, 1973; Gordon Dawson, Mexico City, August 25, 1973; Steve McQueen (telephone), Malibu, September 6, 1973.

3. Pat Garrett and Billy the Kid

The material presented in this chapter is based largely on a series of interviews with the following individuals: Sam Peckinpah, Mexico City, August 27 and 29 and December 13, 1973; James Coburn, Beverly Hills, September 7, 1973; Kris Kristofferson, Chicago, April 19, 1974; Gordon Dawson, Mexico City, August 25, 1973; Katy Haber, Mexico City, August 30, 1973; Ted Haworth, Westwood Village, California, September 9, 1973; R. G. Armstrong, Los Angeles, September 11, 1973; Gary Combs, Mexico City, December 10, 1973; Jack Elam, Studio City, California, September 10, 1973; Garth Craven,

Hollywood, September 5, 1973; Daniel Melnick (telephone), Culver City, California, November 21, 1974.

14. Bring Me the Head of Alfredo Garcia

Much of the material presented in this and the following chapter on *The Killer Elite* is the result of Sam Peckinpah's generously allowing me to be present on the set to observe the filming of these projects firsthand. In the case of *Alfredo Garcia* this meant numerous trips to locations in and around Mexico City both prior to and during principal photography.

In addition, I drew on material gathered from interviews with the following individuals: Sam Peckinpah, Mexico City, August 26, September 1, and December 12, 13, 14, and 16, 1973, and San Francisco, October 26, 1974; Martin Baum, Mexico City, December 13, 1973; Warren Oates, Los Angeles, September 13, 1973; Alex Phillips, Jr., Mexico City, August 26, 1973; Aurora Clavel, Mexico City, December 9, 1973; Helmut Dantine, Mexico City, December 14, 1973; Kris Kristofferson, Chicago, April 19, 1974; Robert Webber, Mexico City, December 11, 1973; Emilio Fernandez, Mexico City, December 14, 1973; Whitey Hughes, Mexico City, December 14, 1973.

15. The Killer Elite

As noted with regard to the previous chapter, much of the material presented here was made possible through firsthand observation during the production. In the case of *The Killer Elite* this entailed work in both Los Angeles and San Francisco.

In addition, I was able to draw on material gathered from interviews in California with the following individuals: Sam Peckinpah, San Francisco, May 13-14, 1975, and Los Angeles, June 10-11, 1975; Arthur Lewis, Los Angeles, August 24, 1981; Philip Lathrop, Culver City, June 11, 1975; Garth Craven, Malibu, January 31, 1976; James Caan, Los Angeles, June 10, 1975; Jerry Fielding, Westwood Village, December 5, 1975.

Epilogue: Cross of Iron, Convoy, and Beyond

The material in this chapter is based largely on a series of interviews in California with the following individuals: Sam Peckinpah, Burbank, November 28, 1975, and Malibu, March 28, 1982; James Coburn, Beverly Hills, March 3, 1976; Ron Wright, Van Nuys,

November 30, 1976; Kent James, Van Nuys, November 30, 1976; Carol James, Van Nuys, November 30, 1976; Garth Craven, Malibu, October 5, 1980; Katy Haber, Beverly Hills, March 7, 1980.

In addition, I had the good fortune to be present May 1, 1980, at a screening of *The Wild Bunch* for a class on the American Western being conducted by professor Rick Jewell at the University of Southern California's Norris Theater when Sam Peckinpah arrived unannounced and agreed to answer questions.

EDITOR'S NOTE: Of necessity, in republishing *Peckinpah: A Portrait in Montage* in the current format the original "Index" was rendered meaningless. Therefore has not been included in this edition. Anyone wishing to consult the index is encouraged to consult the 1998 Limelight Edition.

Afterthoughts: 50 Years After the Release of "The Wild Bunch"

Through a Glass, Darkly:
Sam Peckinpah's The Wild Bunch

From the moment of its release, Sam Peckinpah's *The Wild Bunch* polarized audiences everywhere. At issue was the film's troubling depiction of violence employing a relatively new technology – the use of blood packs and electronically triggered simulated bullet hits (known in the movie business as squibs). Two scenes in particular – the blood-soaked opening shootout on the streets of Starbuck and the cathartic ending in which the Bunch confront and decimate a Mexican army as they meet their deaths in Agua Verde dominated the conversation. Either you accepted the film's depiction of violence as valid or reviled it. There was simply no middle ground.

As a result, Peckinpah's creation of screen mayhem has had many imitators, and the director himself has frequently been both exalted and pilloried for inspiring so much cinema bloodletting. Even today, labels like "Master of Violence" and "Bloody Sam" continue to be attached to his name. The irony, of course, is that Peckinpah himself despised such epithets recognizing full well that they undermined any true understanding of what he was attempting to create.

Nevertheless, fifty years after its release (and nearly thirty-five years after the director's death at 59 in 1984) the fact that the cinematic power of *The Wild Bunch* still resonates with audiences prompting legitimate discussions on the part violence plays in both art and life suggests that there is something much deeper at work. Indeed, *The Wild Bunch* can legitimately be seen as a watershed moment in American cinema. As a

311

consequence, to fully appreciate what Peckinpah was able to achieve requires something more than a cursory examination of his demanding directorial style.

In April 2004, a group collectively known as the "Dog Brothers" – Peckinpah historian / editor / filmmaker Paul Seydor, writer / producer David Weddle, writer Jesse Graham, documentary filmmaker and preservationist Nick Redman and myself – returned to the Mexican town of Parras in the state of Coahuila along with Sam Peckinpah's youngest daughter, Lupita and Nick's brother, cinematographer Jonathan Redman. Our purpose was twofold: to take part in a documentary Nick was making to be titled *A Simple Adventure Story: Sam Peckinpah, Mexico, and The Wild Bunch* (2005) and to experience firsthand the locations of a film that had so profoundly touched us all.

*****

David Samuel Peckinpah was 42 in 1967, a controversial writer-director whose small body of work – just four short years writing and directing television followed by three feature films in quick succession: *The Deadly Companions, Ride the High Country* and *Major Dundee* – was seen by a number of critics to announce the emergence of a major, if somewhat quixotic, talent. His open conflicts during the shooting and editing of *Major Dundee,* primarily with the film's producer, Jerry Bresler, had created such a schism that Bresler eventually had him barred from the cutting room and blacklisted in Hollywood as a director. This in turn would lead to his being fired off of his next film *The Cincinnati Kid* only a week into production followed by more than two years of virtual unemployment, the details of which can be found elsewhere. His feature directorial career seemed to be over almost before it had begun.

Finally, after several seasons in hell, Peckinpah got lucky. Hired by producer Daniel Melnick to adapt and direct a television version of Katherine Anne Porter's *Noon Wine,* he was able to once again demonstrate his unique gifts as a

312

filmmaker. This in turn brought him to the attention of two men who would change his destiny: Ken Hyman, newly appointed head of Warner Bros. / Seven Arts and producer Phil Feldman. Peckinpah had met Hyman in Europe at Cannes in 1965 following a screening of a film Hyman had produced called *The Hill* directed by Sidney Lumet and starring Sean Connery. Impressed by the young director, Hyman remembered him two years later when he assumed the reins at Warner Bros.

Having come out of the world of independent filmmaking, Hyman was looking for young producers and directors who shared his passion for off beat iconoclastic filmmaking. With only one credit as producer, (Francis Ford Coppola's *You're a Big Boy Now*), Feldman was brought in to oversee the development of a project titled *The Diamond Story,* an action adventure set in Africa. As a result, Hyman sent Feldman to approach Peckinpah about rewriting the script for *The Diamond Story* with a promise to direct if the script he delivered received a green light. Clearly looking for a way back in, Peckinpah accepted.

At the same time, Peckinpah possessed a slim, edgy screenplay titled *The Wild Bunch* by a writer named Walon Green based on a story from stuntman-aspiring producer Roy N. Sickner. Sickner had originally approached Peckinpah with a rough treatment of the project during the shooting of *Major Dundee*. Now with a finished screenplay and Lee Marvin – the same actor Hyman was courting to play the lead in *Diamond Story* – tentatively attached to play Pike Bishop, Peckinpah saw *The Wild Bunch* as a possible second project at Warners should the first one actually come to fruition. As a result he began reworking the screenplay for *The Wild Bunch* as well.

Several months later after Peckinpah had rewritten the Green-Sickner script adding depth to the characters and substance to the story, Lee Marvin jumped ship signing to star in Paramount's adaptation of the stage musical *Paint Your Wagon*. But to Hyman's credit, he felt so strongly about Peckinpah's newly revised screenplay for *The Wild Bunch* as well as his vision for the film that he decided to go with it instead of *Diamond Story*, recasting William Holden to replace Marvin as Pike Bishop. As Paul Seydor has noted, "[Holden was] an actor of considerably greater range and depth of feeling than Marvin, one who could take the character much further in the tormented, guilt-ridden direction [Peckinpah] was already developing.." In short, the replacement of Marvin with Holden would significantly contribute to making *The Wild Bunch* into the extraordinary film it was to become.

At the same time, given the debacle of *Major Dundee* and the years without work that had followed, Sam Peckinpah was acutely aware that his talent as a screenwriter had simply provided him with the opportunity to save whatever was left of his floundering directorial career. It is not surprising that Peckinpah's rewrite of *The Wild Bunch* solidified Hyman's faith in his abilities to capture his creative vision on the page. The newly revised screenplay was rife with fast paced action scenes and memorable lines of dialogue. However, it would be his ability to transmogrify those words into images on film that would make or break him.

Having heavily researched the pre-World War I world of revolutionary Mexico, Peckinpah felt it necessary to open his screenplay with a voiceover narration:

> *NARRATOR*
> *To most of America in 1913,*
> *the Age of Innocence had arrived and*
> *the stories of the Indian Wars and the*
> *Gold Rush and the Great Gunfighters*
> *had become either barroom ballyhoo or*
> *front-porch reminiscences… But on both*
> *sides of the Rio Grande men still lived*
> *as they had in the '70's and '80's –*
> *unchanged men in a changing land.*

Although this narration would ultimately not be used in the finished film, Peckinpah's phrase "unchanged men on a changing land…" would be appropriated by the Warner Bros.

publicity department and prominently included in the movie poster to be used in the film's advertising campaign.

Haunted by the photos from the period, Peckinpah insisted to Feldman that the film's location needed to reflect that same look. Feldman agreed. But while both favored shooting the picture in Mexico, Feldman preferred the town of Durango, a frequent backdrop for many Hollywood Westerns. However, having shot portions of *Major Dundee* there, Peckinpah wanted something fresh, something that would more accurately reflect the look of revolutionary Mexico. As a result, he bypassed the Warner Bros. location department insisting the studio hire someone he personally trusted to do a preliminary reconnaissance.

Chalo Gonzalez had met the director on *Major Dundee* (he was, in fact, the uncle of Peckinpah's former wife, the Mexican actress Begonia Palacios who appears in that film). After sharing the photographic research and going over the script in significant detail, Peckinpah sent Gonzalez south. Over the next two weeks he traveled across Mexico's arid northern plain. In the state of Coahuila, he found the small Mexican village of Parras. Situated halfway between Saltillo and Torreon, it had the authentic Mexican look Peckinpah had been searching for. In fact, it was so far off the beaten path that in 1967 the town still lacked electricity. Further, in 1913, it had served as the site for several battles between Pancho Villa and the forces of Mexican President Victoriano Huerta. Given that *The Wild Bunch* would be set against this same historical backdrop, the photographs Gonzalez returned with from Parras fired Peckinpah's imagination. Preproduction now began in earnest.

On February 21, 1968 (coincidentally Peckinpah's 43 birthday), Warners shipped the necessary production equipment to begin filming *The Wild Bunch* to Mexico. The Bill of Lading ran 144 pages involving 1184 shipping containers weighing 210,103 lbs. at a total cost of $304,139.46. And this was just the beginning. Aside from cameras, lights and sound equipment, the shipment listed five pages of weaponry including 35 Winchester rifles and 75 Springfields plus assorted shotguns and pistols plus 60,000 rounds of blank ammunition. By April 2, just one week into filming, Feldman was forced to requisition an additional 138 boxes of blank ammo followed by 20,000 electric squibs. By the time the company moved on to Torreon at the end of May, Warners would have to ship an additional 16,500 rounds of blank ammo as well. As the studio soon realized, Sam Peckinpah was not your average journeyman director, and *The Wild Bunch* was not going to be just another run-of-the-mill Western. While all these cost overruns raised red flags at the studio, it must be noted that to his credit Ken Hyman never wavered in his support of the director or his film.

Sam Peckinpah was an instinctive filmmaker. Instead of relying on a shot list or any kind of preset plan, he almost always trusted his own insights and intuitive responses to whatever presented itself when he stepped onto the set. But because filmmaking is a collaborative art form, he also expected everyone around him to be as prepared as he was. Thus, in order to fully understand and appreciate what Peckinpah accomplished in *The Wild Bunch,* it is necessary to look beyond the director alone.

In this regard, the contributions of three critical members of his production team deserve special recognition: Lucien Ballard, the cinematographer, who had previously worked as Director of Photography on *Ride the High Country* and most recently Peckinpah's adaption of Katherine Anne Porter's *Noon Wine;* Gordon Dawson, who had headed up wardrobe on the grueling production of *Major Dundee*; and Cliff Coleman, the assistant director who had no prior experience with Peckinpah and had been brought aboard at the last minute after Peckinpah had fired the studio's original hire for first assistant director, Phil Rawlins. In truth, Rawlins had been in trouble for some time. As Assistant Director, his extensive credits included features like *Two on a Guillotine* and *Gidget Goes Hawaiian* and, most recently, two seasons on the comedy Western TV series *F Troop* none of which would have inspired Peckinpah's confidence. In a memo dated March 14, 1968, only eleven days before the start of principal photography, Feldman sent a blistering reproach to Rawlins copying both Peckinpah and Unit Production Manager William Faralla reprimanding him for his handling of an incident involving Lucien Ballard and costing the company $300. Given that Peckinpah viewed *The Wild Bunch* as his comeback film, it is hardly surprising that he demanded that Rawlins be replaced.

With respect to Ballard, he had first worked with Peckinpah on the critically acclaimed, short-lived television series *The Westerner*. As David Weddle records, after the series was canceled, Peckinpah sent a note of appreciation to Ballard that ended: "…I would like you to know that 'The Courtship of Libby' and 'Jeff' were by far the two best things I have ever done, and I hold you directly responsible. I would like us to get together as soon as possible to discuss future projects." Given their previous collaborations, Peckinpah clearly trusted Ballard's creative instincts.

Gordon Dawson had grown up in the industry. His father, Tom Dawson, had been the head of wardrobe at Columbia Pictures. Having begun in Columbia's wardrobe department in 1960, Gordy Dawson had been assigned to *Major Dundee*. Given the difficulties of that production, Dawson had impressed Peckinpah through his meticulous attention to detail, his resilience and his ability to deliver under extreme pressure. As a result, Peckinpah insisted that Feldman pay whatever it took to entice Dawson to head up wardrobe on *The Wild Bunch*. Since Dawson had been attempting to change the trajectory of his career by teaching himself to write, Feldman was forced to make Dawson a substantial deal, which he reluctantly accepted. As it would turn out, this was money well spent as the wardrobe department under Dawson's leadership functioned extremely well despite the demanding circumstances. As a bonus, Dawson was able to draw upon his experience on *Dundee* to help other key members of the crew deal with Peckinpah's irascible, demanding style and survive.

Cliff Coleman arrived in Parras late. After Peckinpah insisted that the original A.D., Phil Rawlins, be fired for various offenses, including failing to anticipate the director's demands (no easy task under any circumstance), Feldman notified Warners to send down a replacement A.S.A.P. Given such short notice, the studio may well have seen Coleman as a temporary replacement until someone more suitable could found.

The production was only two days away from the start of principal photography when Cliff Coleman arrived in Mexico. At the time, he was relatively inexperienced with only three feature credits to his name: *Harlow* staring Carroll Baker plus two Robert Aldrich films: *The Flight of the Phoenix* and *The Legend of Lylah Clare*. Recognizing Coleman's lack of experience as something that might work in his favor, Rawlins decided to stick around Parras presumably waiting for Coleman to fail. And given the complexities of the opening sequence and Peckinpah's mercurial disposition, Rawlins's expectation was not entirely without merit. From his perspective, once Coleman screwed up, Warners would be forced to override Peckinpah and reinstate Rawlins as First Assistant Director since he was already familiar with the script and readily available.

However, like Dawson, Coleman's father, Charles C. Coleman, had had a long and stellar career as an assistant director with over 100 credits dating all the way back to 1927. And by chance, three of those credits were on important films in the career of William Holden: *Sunset Boulevard* (for which the actor was Oscar nominated), *Stalag 17* (for which he won the Oscar for Best Actor) and *Sabrina*. As a result, over the years Charles Coleman had developed and maintained a personal relationship with Holden. Knowing studio politics, the elder Coleman promptly contacted Holden asking him to put in a word on behalf of his son should things get rough. As a result, with Holden's support, plus his own unique talents for organizing and marshaling complex background action, Cliff Coleman had a fighting chance.

In an interview at age 82 in 2017, Cliff Coleman recalled: "My dad was an A.D. So I grew up playing on Hollywood backlots. Then in the late '50s there was this shortage of A.D.s and one day my dad said to me, 'Get your ass over to Paramount. Here's who you ask for. Tell him you're my son.' And literally overnight I became a third assistant director.

"By the time I got the call to go down to Mexico on *Wild Bunch,* I was a first. But given the circumstances at the time, I felt that they were setting me up to fail. Phil Rawlins had been Warners first choice. He had been fired by Sam but was still there hanging around Parras when I showed up. Given that this was only my fourth show as a First, I figured these guys expected me to fall on my ass so they could turn right around and force Sam to take Rawlins back. What they didn't expect was that I always said exactly what I thought and, for whatever reason, Sam really responded to that.

"They were two days away from rolling film when I walked into my first production meeting. Feldman was there along with Sam and Lucien [Ballard] and all the key department heads. And they were debating how they were going to shoot this huge goddamn opening. Feldman wasn't crazy about the ants and scorpions thing – he thought it might come off as too hokey. As I recall, he thought Sam should start on the meeting of the Temperance Union then pick up the Bunch riding into town dressed as soldiers. Save the ants and scorpions as a pickup to be shot separately so that it could easily be cut if it didn't work.

"Having only just read the script on the plane down from L.A., I had decided to keep my mouth shut when Sam turned and looked me straight in the eye and said: 'What do you think?' The word on Sam was he was a no bullshit guy so I gave him a no bullshit answer. I said, "Start with scene one – they ride in past the ants and scorpions – then from there on shoot the sequence in continuity." I finished and Sam just stared at me. Then he turned to Feldman and said, 'Exactly what I've been saying all along. So let's stop fucking around and just do it.' And that's what we did."

Without question, the screenplay for *The Wild Bunch* by Green as revised and polished by Peckinpah provides the basis for a solid action Western. In staging these action sequences, Peckinpah would distinguish himself, immediately placing him among the first rank of action directors who have ever worked in the medium. However, what differentiates *The Wild Bunch* from virtually every other Western made up until that time and indeed from those made since was the director's uncanny ability to significantly elevate seemingly inconsequential nonaction moments, expanding them in ways that indelibly fix them in our memories. As is evidenced throughout the film, Peckinpah's obsessive insistence on controlling every aspect of the filming of *The Wild Bunch* reveals his absolute determination to impose his vision – his stamp – on the final film.

On the evening of Saturday March 23, 1968, Peckinpah arranged for a screening of Arthur Penn's *Bonnie and Clyde* for the entire cast and crew. Released by Warners the previous year, it had garnered ten Oscar nominations and generated a great deal of debate about screen violence, especially the film's finale in which the two outlaws are ambushed, dying in a hale of bullets. According to Gordon Dawson, "Sam said, 'We're going to bury *Bonnie and Clyde*.' That was his goal, to do it a thousand times better than that picture." Though few present for that screening understood it at the time, clearly Peckinpah was absolutely serious.

As with all U.S. productions requesting permission to film in Mexico, Warner Bros. was obliged to hire an established Mexican director as "codirector" even though he would have no actual power and would not be credited as such. As a consequence, although he had been cast by Peckinpah in the role of "General Mapache," Emilio Fernandez, known as "El Indio" for his Mestizo heritage, arrived in Parras early for preproduction. Easily the premiere Mexican film director (his film *María Candelaria* had won the Grand Prix at Cannes in 1946 and his adaption of John Steinbeck's *The Pearl* won the Golden Lion at Venice in 1948), Fernandez sat down with Peckinpah to discuss the script. As recorded elsewhere, Peckinpah's decision to incorporate ants and scorpions into the opening sequence was inspired by El Indio, who said that reading about the shootout in Starbuck had reminded him of how as children they would drop a scorpion on an anthill. His imagination stoked by Fernandez's visceral description, Peckinpah immediately contacted Feldman in L.A. to demand he secure the necessary insects and have them delivered to the location in time for the first day's shooting.

Taking it a step further, in rewriting the scene, Peckinpah included children in order to make his point: that Man's ability to inflict thoughtless cruelty and violence is an innate part of the human psyche. Aware of the potential danger posed by combining young children and live scorpions, he discussed the sequence with Lucien Ballard then ordered his art director, Edward Carrere, to have his crew construct a mound of earth beside the railroad tracks leading into town. Then within that mound, they hollowed out a kind of shallow pit shoring up the sides with sticks. This would allow the children to appear to be watching something going on below the line of sight of the camera while the actual tight closeups ants and scorpions could be shot as inserts.

Thus in the finished film, a dozen children can be seen huddled together poking at something obscured by a kind of miniature stockade made of sticks as five U.S. Cavalrymen approach along the railroad tracks at the edge of town. As they ride past, Pike Bishop, the apparent officer in charge, glances down at the children as does Dutch, his second in command.

Peckinpah, however, saves the reveal of what they see until after the Bunch has ridden past: three scorpions trapped at the bottom of the pit being swarmed by hundreds of fire ants. To underscore his intention, Peckinpah then spends a full minute of screen time on this as the children, totally insensitive to the suffering they are inflicting, laugh and poke at the writhing scorpions. It is an image that would serve as a metaphor (or as Paul Seydor has noted an "epic simile") for Peckinpah throughout the picture. As realized on film, the entire opening is brilliantly handled by Peckinpah in visuals alone without a single word of dialogue.

At the same time, instructed by Peckinpah, Carrere turned the central square in Parras into the West Texas border town of Starbuck (leaving sporadic evidence of the town's original Mexican name, San Rafael, still visible in places as a touch of realism). To accomplish this, Carrere concealed the actual storefronts of Parras behind turn of the century façades. The streets surrounding the square were covered in footdeep sand that provided both the look Peckinpah was after as well as serving as a cushion for the numerous stunts – high falls and horse falls – that the opening sequence would require.

From the moment the Bunch enter Starbuck, Peckinpah begins to construct one of the most complex and compelling sequences ever committed to film. In addition to the innocent onlookers, there are three independent elements at work here: (1) The Bunch, (2) the Temperance Union and (3) the bounty hunters who lie in wait on the roof overlooking the railroad office. Critical to building maximum tension within the scene would be the director's ability to capture and integrate all three elements as they converge. Thus over the next six days of shooting, Peckinpah would expose 25,290 feet of film employing 131 camera setups using a variety of lenses and camera speeds. The resulting sequence reveals an extraordinary attention to detail. Relentless in his pursuit of perfection, Peckinpah insisted that the entire crew be over prepared and ready for whatever he might throw their way. Anyone who wasn't would be replaced.

In speaking with David Weddle, Gordon Dawson explained: "No one was prepared for the demands Sam made for that opening shootout. He started saying, 'Give me more people here, I want more people there. Now I'm going to run them here and I want to shoot down the street. Now I want to shoot up there.' The first few days of shooting were very difficult. The first day's call sheet called for sixty-three extras and twenty-three animals. By the time noon rolled around we had 230 people in costume and fifty-six horses on the set. Sam just wanted more and more and more."

The task of accommodating Peckinpah's needs regarding the marshaling of background action for these complicated, overlapping camera setups (at times there would be as many as six cameras rolling at once) fell to Cliff Coleman.

At 6'5" Coleman can be spotted towering over actors and extras alike in Paul Seydor's 1996 Academy Award nominated documentary short, *The Wild Bunch: An Album in Montage.* Wearing a U.S. Cavalry campaign hat, white T-shirt and jeans and carrying a riding crop, Coleman has the demeanor of a drill sergeant, which in many ways he was.

"That first day," Coleman remembered, "when Sam got into the main street in Starbuck taught me a lot. A normal 400 foot magazine at 24 frames per second runs just under four and half minutes. But we also had these goddamn 1,000 foot magazines which were mainly intended for slow motion where you're shooting at 90 or 120 frames per second. Except Sam would tell Lucien [Ballard] he wanted to shoot certain masters using those same 1,000 foot mags at 24 fps. That meant that once we started rolling it would be 11 minutes before the film ran out.

"Part of the chaos of that first day was realizing we were going to need background action for 11 minutes as Sam shot each separate master. First we'd shoot the Bunch riding into town past the Temperance Union tent all the way to the hitching post where they dismount, then march into the railroad office bumping into the old lady with the packages. Then we'd go back and shoot the Temperance Union from the point where they strike up the band and begin marching down the street all the way to the point where Holden shoves the clerk out and the bounty hunters on the roof open up. All that had to be choreographed and coordinated on the fly. As we kept rolling, Sam'd be shouting for more people to fill street – townspeople, kids, old ladies, businessmen, you name it. And every time the background had to be exactly the same so that it'd all cut together. Then we'd go in for coverage the shots of the Bunch, the bounty hunters, the band and the Temperance Union. By the end of that first day we'd used so many extras Gordy almost ran out of costumes. I knew he must've hated me. But there was nothing else I could do.

"Sam never had a plan. He was always winging it. The minute I caught on to that I realized that I had to put together enough background action to run the entire 11 minutes. So I invented bits of action then organized the extras so that each bit was linked to the next. Every damn time the background action had to happen exactly at the same point and in sync with the main action… Sam had this great energy but you had to anticipate what he wanted. We shot everything from every angle. Multiple cameras going at once. A shitload of film. But Peckinpah was smart. He knew what he wanted and knew the more raw footage he shot the more he'd have to create with when he got to the cutting room. So we just kept shooting.

"But it was Gordy Dawson who saved my ass. He was the one who'd worked with Peckinpah and he clued me in. We weren't friends at the start of the picture but by the end I knew I couldn't have survived without him."

"By the end of that first day on *Wild Bunch* I could've killed Cliff," Gordy Dawson recalled with a shake of his head. "I had gone down there overprepared. Warners had tried to limit me to twenty-five costume hampers. But having gotten my ass chewed by Sam so many times on *Major Dundee*, I had insisted on bringing fifty. I should've brought 100. The call sheet on day one said something like 63 extras. By noon we had over 200, then 350. Every one of them needed to be costumed and the ones being shot on camera had to be squibbed. We were going crazy. So to say I was pissed at Cliff would be an understatement. But he was good. And he really 'got' Sam. Whatever Sam needed to make the scene work, Cliff was on top of it."

While it is undeniably true that Peckinpah, as noted, was an improvisational director, it would be wrong to assume he created without any sense of how seemingly random shots would cut together. Just looking at the opening shootout one is struck by his exceptional attention to detail, his ability to create cause and effect thereby tying individual elements together. For example, as Pike Bishop reaches his horse to make his escape, Peckinpah cuts to Thornton on the roof spotting him and taking aim. At the same time, Pike spots Thornton as a tuba player from the Temperance Union parade attempts to rush past. Thus as Thornton takes aim at Pike, the tuba player steps in front of him and is shot instead with Peckinpah positioning his camera behind the musician so that we see the impact of the bullet as the squib explodes giving the appearance of the bullet passing through him. Cutting to a new angle on Pike as the tuba player falls away, Bishop takes aim at Thornton missing and dropping the bounty hunter beside him as Thornton ducks. Rising up, Thornton attempts another shot only to find that he needs to reload allowing Bishop to remount and start to ride off. For all its complexity, this entire sequence takes less than eleven seconds of screen time.

Similarly, in covering the bounty hunters as they fire down from the roof at civilians and outlaws alike, Peckinpah uses separate setups to capture both Coffer (Strother Martin) and T.C. (L.Q. Jones) firing over the parapet at the street below. Later after turning his cameras on those in the street being shot, he specifically uses two separate camera angles to photograph an innocent bystander in a business suit being struck by bullets from above. Later in the editing room, Peckinpah and his editor Lou Lombardo bring these seemingly disparate elements together then pay the moment off when, in the aftermath of the massacre, Coffer and T.C. stand arguing over the corpse about who killed him. It's worth noting that while Peckinpah wrote brilliant dialogue, he also encouraged his actors to improvise when the moment called for it as is evidenced here:

TC
(to Coffer)
Why you know I shot this man.

COFFER
Liar...! Black liar!

TC
You shouldn't talk to me like that.

COFFER
I'm sorry... Com'on, T.C. Help me
get his boots.

In speaking about the scene in 1973, Strother Martin recalled: "...[A]fter the shooting stops and the bounty hunters come down into the street to check the bodies, Sam had L.Q. and I 'winging' the dialogue because it wasn't very full at that point. The whole thing where I called L.Q. a 'liar' and then a 'black liar!' That was all improvised. I remember I was very pleased with 'black liar!' And I remember Sam saying to me, 'That's your worst line in the picture.' Which, of course, means he loved it.!'"

With the completion of the opening shootout in Starbuck and its aftermath, Peckinpah turned his attention to those scenes whose locations lay close by. Based upon Chalo Gonzalez's initial location report, Peckinpah was able to stage roughly 70% of the movie within a 20mile radius of the town of Parras (the remainder of the film including the railroad and river sequences, the caves where the Bunch hide the guns following the robbery and the turn-of-the-century bordello would be filmed in Torreon, 100 miles to the west).

What is striking about visiting these locations 35 years later is the way they reveal Peckinpah's gift for taking what he found and transforming it into what he envisioned. For example, the location for Old Man Skykes' camp where the Bunch ride in from Starbuck following the aborted robbery is a seemingly innocuous spot beside the road to Parras only 22 km (13 miles) from the center of town. Remarkably, it is less than 50 meters from roadway itself. By carefully choosing his camera angles and shooting away from the highway, the director was able to create a sense of isolation by portraying what appears to be a vast wasteland stretching to the west with the distant mountains.

Further, given the complexity of the scene involving six main characters – Pike, Dutch, the Gorchs, Angel and Sykes – plus horses, the Mexican *mamacitas* and children, Peckinpah brilliantly uses the physical geography of the camp to set up the conflicts and alliances within the Bunch through his staging. Using a stone fire pit in the center of the corral, he establishes Pike and Dutch to one side with Tector and Lyle opposite. Angel sits apart, his back against the fence while Sykes hovers off to one side. The scene begins on a note of discord as the Gorch brothers challenge the right of Angel and Sykes to an equal share of the spoils. Without hesitating, Pike angrily calls their bluff. This allows Peckinpah to have Angel then taunt the brothers establishing the mutual animosity that lies just below the surface. That along with the fact that Angel is the lone Mexican in the Bunch lets Peckinpah define Angel from the start as an outsider, a crucial fact as the story unfolds.

As the Gorchs grudgingly concede the point, the Bunch turn to dividing the "gold" only to discover the bags are filled with steel washers. This only increases the tension as Peckinpah, in a moment of seriocomic inspiration, provides partial relief by having Old Man Sykes (Edmund O'Brien, all but unrecognizable beneath heavy makeup) deliver his outrageous monologue that begins "They... who the hell are 'they...?'" But perceptively attune to the underlying insecurities and latent hostilities he had woven into the fabric of the script, Peckinpah uses this moment to simultaneously reinforce the sense of bad blood between the brothers and the old man, a situation that will also continue to fester. Thus by the end of the scene, Peckinpah has clearly established the dynamics of the Bunch, a set of complex, conflicted relationships that will play out through the remainder of the picture.

Equally inspired is the location of Angel's village. By appropriating a grove of willow trees beside a small pond and creek that meandered through the grounds of the Hotel Rincón del Montero where the production offices and key personnel from the company were housed, Peckinpah had Carrere, create a rustic Mexican village. As Peckinpah wrote on p.45 of the final draft of the script: "The natural beauty of this location should contrast with other landscapes in the picture. The village and its inhabitants represent a complete and green contrast to the arid world of the Wild Bunch." Indeed, these scenes as Peckinpah filmed them, including the Bunch's unforgettable ride out that he will reprise at the film's close, are among the most lyrical and emotionally moving in the film. That he was able to stand in the midst of the hotel grounds and completely envision it is a testament to Peckinpah's remarkable creative instincts.

By the middle of the production schedule, the company moved to the Hacienda Cienega del Carmen, a visually striking abandoned winery that would serve as General Mapache's stronghold, Agua Verde. Remote and difficult to reach, the Hacienda had no available source of water or electricity and would require moving trucks and equipment (not to mention cast and crew) some 12 kilometers down an unpaved dirt road in the middle of nowhere. As producer, Phil Feldman quite rightly objected. As he would tell David Weddle in an interview some years later: "Sam said, 'I can't get along without that winery, it's the greatest. I've got it all in my head, I know just how I'm going to shoot all the scenes. Here's the row of shacks where all the whores will be, and this is where their last march will be. I've got that all mapped out.' The truth of the matter was Sam rarely mapped anything out, as I found out later. He was a directorial genius, but mostly improvisational, which I didn't realize. So I thought: yeah, he's got it all mapped out and choreographed and I'm not going to interfere with that, so let's give him his way on this one."

By 2004, the year we travelled there, the Hacienda Cienega del Carmen was no more accessible than it had been in 1968. The 12 kilometer unpaved road that the motion picture company had cut through the barren landscape to reach it remained an unmarked rock and dirt path through the desert. The fact that we blew a tire halfway there and had to walk the rest of the way while the driver struggled to repair the flat firmly underscored the demands of the location. Yet upon reaching the Hacienda itself with *The Wild Bunch* firmly fixed in our minds, it was easy to see how Peckinpah had become obsessed with the possibilities. The Gothic arches, iron-caged windows, the abandoned bodega and crumbling out buildings all spoke to him of authenticity. Here was the look of revolutionary Mexico capable of fulfilling the promise of his screenplay. What was less readily apparent was how, 35 years before, Peckinpah had somehow looked at these ruins and imagined the remarkable sequences he would eventually film there. Given its difficulties and demands, here was a location only a visionary could love.

Location set map: "The Wild Bunch"

In the weeks leading up the company move to the Hacienda, Peckinpah ordered Carrere and his crew to construct and age a pair of wooden gates that would serve as the entrance to Agua Verde. In order to preserve the main courtyard with its elevated veranda and stone stepped approaches for two key sequences: (1) the Bunch's arrival in Mapache's lair where Angel kills Teresa followed by her funeral procession as they plan the train robbery and (2) the final confrontation and shootout that would become known among the crew as the "Battle of Bloody Porch," Peckinpah had Carrere also turn the immediate area inside the gates into an open air plaza complete with a gazebo and a drive wide enough to accommodate General Mapache's grand entrance looking every inch a tin pot dictator as he lounges in the back of his red convertible 1912 touring car.

This secondary staging area would serve as the backdrop for a number of key scenes including the exchanges of guns for gold, Mapache's infatuation with the machinegun, and Angel's capture and eventual torture.

The last of these, Angel's torture, was originally written with Mapache and his lieutenants sitting around a table celebrating the delivery of the guns as Angel is tied to the packsaddle of a donkey and dragged through the courtyard. But in a moment of inspiration, Peckinpah decided to replace the donkey with Mapache's touring car. This allowed him to place Mapache and his henchmen inside the car making them active participants as opposed to observers. It also provided a way of prolonging the inevitable fight to come. As the Bunch arrive and and Pike offers to buy Angel back, Mapache refuses ordering the car to drive on. Unable to bring themselves to act on impulse, the Bunch do nothing but watch thereby compounding their sense of guilt.

Thus Peckinpah begins the escalation of events that will lead to the final violent confrontation. He starts in the darkened rooms that serve as a brothel by beginning on Pike with a young prostitute. Their lovemaking over, the young woman's infant lies nearby as Pike drains a bottle of tequila attempting to drown the memory of Angel's disfigured face as well as those of all the women he has loved and left in similar places. At the same time, from the adjoining room separated only by a blanket hung in the doorway, come the sounds of Tector and Lyle arguing with another prostitute over the price she wants to charge for taking on the two of them. Meanwhile, just outside, Dutch sits alone, his back to the wall, mindlessly witling as he struggles to soothe his own pangs of conscience. At last, filled with self-loathing, Pike rises. As Peckinpah described it in the final draft of the script dated 2/13/68:

330

PIKE WATCHES THE WOMAN AND THE BABY FOR A MOMENT LONGER THEN SUDDENLY SWINGS OUT OF THE HAMMOCK and steps into the adjoining room.

LYLE GORCH LOOKS UP AT HIM BLEARILY FROM A HAMMOCK. Tector is on the floor embracing a disheveled woman.

Pike watches them, weaving a little:

> PIKE
> *(finally)*
> *Let's get Angel... let's get him*
> *back from that dirty greaser!*

Tector blinks his eyes and reaches for his gun. Lyle gets to his feet as if he's just been given an important order by a commanding officer.

> LYLE
> *Can't trust 'em.... Give 'em a*
> *chance and they'll shoot you in the back.*

However, when it came time to commit the scene to film, Peckinpah cuts through all the expository dialogue reducing the exchange to simply:

> PIKE
> *Let's go.*

> LYLE
> *Why not...?"*

Peckinpah's use of minimalist dialogue and restraint adds to the power of the moment. Wordlessly, Pike overpays his prostitute then moves out passing through the adjoining room and into the street as Tector and Lyle follow. One look from Pike and Dutch

331

knows it's time. Getting to his feet, he moves with them to their horses as they begin to arm themselves for the final battle. In a script change issued 2/12/68 Peckinpah describes the scene like this (p. 120):

THEY CROSS TO THEIR HORSES, THEIR DRUNKENNESS LESSENING with every step.

Pike and Dutch pull rifles or shotguns from their saddle-scabbards as do Lyle and Tector, then they move up the village street.

FOUR MEN IN A LINE AND THE AIR OF IMPENDING VIOLENCE IS SO STRONG around them that as they pass the celebrating soldiers, the song and laughter begins to die.

In 2017, Cliff Coleman recalled: "That scene where the Bunch comes out of the whorehouse, we all assumed Sam would cut from there directly to the Hacienda. But Sam had a different idea. Total improvisation. There was this brand new experimental Panavision lens – 1000mm with this incredibly deep focus – that Lucien had ordered for the film but hadn't been able to use. At the same time, given they considered it an unnecessary expense Warner Brothers was screaming at Feldman that they wanted the lens returned to Panavision for credit. But Sam and Lucien had gotten together and decided to create this walk up to the Hacienda using that lens. Feldman was on him, but Sam ignored the studio because he knew what he wanted. So he lined them up four across Holden and Borgnine, the Gorchs and started them walking forwards until they were out of frame. Meantime I began setting the background action – groups of soldiers, women, kids – all watching these guys without really knowing what the fuck they were up to."

For the next setup, Ballard had his crew lay down a hundred feet of dolly track inline with the direction the Bunch now walked. Then placing the 1000mm lens on an Arriflex with a 400' mag, he mounted it on a camera dolly as Peckinpah instructed the Bunch to walk straight ahead as he filmed them from behind. As Ballard started filming, the Bunch moved past camera with Peckinpah directing them towards a break in the brick wall beside the bodega. Owing to its extreme depth of field, the 1000mm lens compressed the distance while holding all four in focus as they walked away from camera. Then as they approached a brief incline, the camera began to dolly forward, pushing in and rising as they moved up and through the break in the wall.

Next, Peckinpah had Ballard reposition the Arri so that the Bunch now walked directly towards camera. Once again the ability of the special lens to foreshorten distances allowed Peckinpah to stay on the Bunch as they approach, shouldering their way past and through the groups of extras Coleman had carefully positioned to impede their progress. Simultaneously using a separate camera, Peckinpah had Ballard photograph telling moments – a cluster of soldiers drunkenly singing, a mother with crossed bandoliers sitting with her children seemingly oblivious to the danger around them. Meanwhile, Coleman's exceptional attention to detail allowed Peckinpah's main camera to catch glimpses of everyday camp life: a bare chested soldier lathering his face with shaving cream; another with a armload of tamales watching them come, then hurrying out of the way. As the Bunch continue to march on, Peckinpah ordered Ballard to add a moving shot from the Bunch's point of view. Then another angle as the Bunch march relentlessly toward their own destruction. Finally, Peckinpah, again instructing Ballard to shoot the Bunch from behind, had them proceed along the bodega wall and turn right disappearing out of frame, a perfect match cut as they enter beneath the arches to confront Mapache.

Until we traveled there in 2004, I had always assumed the Bunch to be marching along some street in the fictional village of Agua Verde. To discover that Peckinpah had actually created the entire sequence on the fly, cobbling it together from various unrelated parts of the location to give the impression of a street, stands a testament to his creative genius. In two and half minutes of screen time without a single word of dialogue, Peckinpah demonstrates his virtuosity as a director setting the stage for the final shootout. It is a remarkable moment that would be further enhanced in the finished film by the martial drumbeat of Jerry Fielding's magnificent score.

It is no small irony that Feldman had originally disapproved of Peckinpah's insistence that Jerry Fielding score *The Wild Bunch*. Having met on *Noon Wine*, Peckinpah and Fielding had both survived being black listed and shared a common distaste for mindless authority. In an undated memo, Feldman writes with obvious disdain: "He [Fielding] scores television pictures. Still thinking of an opening song – Glenn Campbell or Trini Lopez." Even as late as three months into postproduction, Feldman was lobbying to limit Fielding to writing the opening theme before committing to him for the entire picture. The fact that Fielding's score was one of only two Academy Award nominations the film would receive (Peckinpah, Green and Sickner for Best Screenplay being the other) clearly vindicated Peckinpah's faith. And in fairness to Feldman, once he actually heard Fielding's completed score, he would become one of the composer's greatest champions

Given the size and scope of the closing battle of *The Wild Bunch*, it is hardly surprising that Peckinpah initially felt all but overwhelmed as the moment to actually film it finally arrived. But what is truly remarkable, however, was his ability to rise above any self-doubt and come up with an extraordinary plan on the spot. Much of this has been catalogued in detail elsewhere. In speaking of it again in 2017, Cliff Coleman remembered: "Sam had this amazing ability to see what nobody else could. But that day, standing there looking at this giant goddamn empty space in the middle of the Hacienda and knowing he had to stage a fight with hundreds of extras, it fucking hit him right in the gut. At first, he didn't know what to do. Anybody else would have been devastated. But Sam sent us all away. Then he sat down and over the next three or four hours thought the entire thing out in his head. As soon as they shoot Mapache, there's this Mexican standoff. So Sam decided the way to start the battle was to have Holden shoot the German. From then to the end, he'd mapped out the whole thing in his head. Where did Holden go? Where's Borgnine? What about the Gorchs? Who shot who and how the hell did the fucking machinegun figure into it? When he had it finally straight in his head, he sat down with Lucien and figured out the camera angles. Put all the cameras on the porch with different lens and shoot the whole thing. Then move the cameras closer and do it again. Meanwhile, I'd organized the Mexican extras – every move was preset, choreographed to cue off the main action. It was all linked together. I said to Sam: 'If you change anything now, it won't work.' So we shot it one way then turned the cameras around and shot the reverse. Then we spent days doing coverage. Sam shot everything. He said to Gordy [Dawson] and me, 'You know what I want.' And the truth was by then we did. Gordy was un-fucking-believable. Every take meant a change of wardrobe only he worked out a way to use this khaki colored paint to repair the damage and get 'em back for the next take. Gordy was a genius. On *Wild Bunch*, he saved my life every day."

Dawson remains equally impressed with what Coleman accomplished. Speaking in 2017, he described it this way: "What's amazing about that final shootout is the way Cliff had drilled the extras. Every background action matched. The reason that scene all cut together was no matter which take you used the background action was the same. Cliff has a volatile personality. And we butted heads throughout the picture but became friends later. He had a little trouble communicating with the Mexican actors. But we had a Mexican first A.D., Chuchu Marin, who was able to translate what Cliff wanted and it worked beautifully."

On Friday May 31, having completed filming all the scenes in and around Parras, the company at last moved west to Torreon. Much of the work to be done there centered around the railroad and the Rio Nazas which doubled for the Rio Grande. Contrary to a persistent rumor (inadvertently started by

Phil Feldman in an interview with David Weddle), the train robbery sequence was not improvised by Peckinpah on the spot. It exists in the draft of the script as early as 9/25/67 and was crafted by the director almost shot for shot (50 separate setups described over eight pages). He even instructed Edward Carrere to design and build the water tower beside the tracks making certain that the housing for the water spout was large enough to conceal Angel as he waits with a sawed off shotgun for the fireman to lower it. In fact, of all the action sequences in the film, it is perhaps the one Peckinpah was best prepared to shoot.

Among the changes that Peckinpah did make during the filming, however, was the one having to do with the Bunch crossing into Mexico. As Walon Green had originally conceived of the border crossing, it was not the Rio Grande but simply the railroad tracks. In the 9/25/67 draft, it appears like this:

EXT. BORDER – DAY (SUNSET EFFECT)

PIKE AND THE OTHERS ARE staring at a distant range of mountains on the horizon.

ANGEL
(to himself)
Mexico lindo!

Pike looks at him a moment, then rides down the slope toward:

THE RAILROAD THAT MARKS THE BORDER. Slowly the others follow…

Then in a subsequent draft dated 2/7/68, Peckinpah penciled the following exchange of dialogue beside the scene:

ANGEL
Mexico lindo.

> LYLE
> *What's so lindo about it? Just more of*
> *Texas as far as I'm concerned.*

> ANGEL
> *You have no eyes.*

However, when the time came for Peckinpah to commit it to film, he reimagined the scene, responding to the actual location. In place of the mundane railroad tracks, he elected instead to make it a river crossing using the Rio Nazas to stand-in for the Rio Grande. At the same time, Peckinpah gave half of Lyle's original line to his brother, Tector. Thus, the scene plays as follows:

THE BUNCH PULL UP at the river that marks the border and look out into Mexico.

> ANGEL
> *(softly)*
> *Mexico lindo...*

> LYLE
> *I don't see nothin' so 'lindo' about it.*

> TECTOR
> *Just looks like more o' Texas far as I'm*
> *concerned.*

> ANGEL
> *That's because you have no eyes...*

Thus not only does Peckinpah make the Bunch's entrance in Mexico more visually arresting, the net effect of the adjusted dialogue is to reinforce the previously established tension between the Gorch brothers and Angel. Just another of the subtle ways in which Peckinpah consistently enhanced the drama.

The final piece of major action to be filmed was the bridge being blown up with the bounty hunters on it. As originally conceived by Walon Green, it was not a bridge at all but a cable crossing, something Green felt strongly about as it had never been done on film before. The Bunch would steal the guns and then, using a wagon with large empty barrels lashed to the wagon box to help float it across, would tether it to a thick rope cable. Peckinpah found this overly cumbersome and somewhat unbelievable since placing the Bunch in the river escorting the wagon across they would be sitting ducks for the bounty hunters. As a result he opted for a bridge instead.

Interviewed in 1974, Green recalled: "Originally, it was a cable across the river instead of a bridge. The only reason for the change was that the river wasn't right to do a cable crossing. Now blowing up that bridge is really terrific on the screen, but it's funny to me now because I argued with Sam about it. I said, 'Christ, you're going to blow up another bridge?' But Sam had a good retort: 'It's not just blowing up a bridge, it's the way you blow up a bridge.' And he was right. It was terrific."

On Thursday June 20, 1968, William Faralla sent the following memo to Peckinpah: "The actual date & hour of the Blowjob on the Bridge is an eyeball estimate at the moment. We all, you, me. Lucien, spfx [Special Effects head Bud Hulburd], Carrere & the actual stuntmen should discuss all the 'angles' this Sunday."

Following that meeting, Carrere and his crew began construction on the bridge complete with a hinged drop-away trapdoor and balsawood breakaway struts. To make certain there was enough water in the river to protect the stuntmen, the Rio Nazas had been dammed up downstream for several weeks before. To ensure maximum coverage, Peckinpah and Ballard used all six cameras, several placed on barges, to shoot this once in a lifetime stunt. Set for Saturday, Peckinpah hesitated checking and rechecking every detail, fully aware that there would be no chance for a second take. As the hour grew later and later, they began to lose the light forcing the shot to be postponed until the following day. Finally, on the afternoon of Sunday June 30, all was in readiness. As the stuntmen rode their horses out onto the bridge, the cameras rolled. And as everyone held their breath, Peckinpah called "action." Moments later, the charges blew sending the men and animals plunging in to the dark water below. Miraculously, the only mishap was the loss of an Arriflex camera when one of the camera barges broke free.

All that remained was a final day of pickup shots at Churubusco studios in Mexico City. Then, after 81 days of production, having shot more than 333,000 feet of film (a total due in part to the large number of high speed / slow motion takes that would forever become associated with Sam Peckinpah's unique style of filmmaking), the shooting of *The Wild Bunch* was complete.

*****

Among the criteria defining a classic is that it is able to withstand the test of time. When I first saw *The Wild Bunch* in 1969, I knew I had seen something extraordinary. It altered the course of my life causing me to pursue a career in filmmaking. Now fifty years later, having viewed this film more times than I can count, I still find myself transported from the opening frame. When I first met Peckinpah in Mexico of 1973, he asked me why I wanted to write a book about him. My answer then is my answer now: A hundred years in the future, assuming people are able to watch motion pictures, the films of Sam Peckinpah will still be in high demand. And first among them will be *The Wild Bunch*.

The Deadly Companions Revisited

A fresh look at Sam Peckinpah's first feature film.

O ver the quarter century since his death, Sam
Peckinpah's reputation has evolved out of critical
acclaim for eight of his fourteen features. By general
consensus, his best work can be seen in the exceptional *Ride the
High Country, The Wild Bunch, The Ballad of Cable Hogue,
The Straw Dogs, Junior Bonner,* and *The Getaway,* along with
his two flawed masterpieces *Major Dundee* and *Pat Garrett &
Billy the Kid* and the television adaptation of Katherine Anne
Porter's *Noon Wine.* It is no small tribute to Peckinpah's talents
that these nine films span barely a dozen years an intensely
creative period from 1961 to 1973. This fact seems even more
remarkable when one takes into account the years immediately
following the debacle of *Major Dundee,* which resulted in
Peckinpah being deemed as "difficult" and essentially
"unemployable."

While much has justifiably been written about these core
films, considerably less time has been spent examining the film
that effectively launched Peckinpah's career as a feature director
– *The Deadly Companions.* Despite the fact that Peckinpah
himself repeatedly attempted to dismiss it as flawed beyond
redemption and unrepresentative of his artistic intent, the film
still bears his undeniable stamp. Yet over the years, *Deadly
Companions* has failed to attract more than a smattering of
serious critical consideration. Clearly, the time for
reexamination is long overdue.

In 1973, the year I began to write *Peckinpah: A Portrait
in Montage*, it was impossible to view *The Deadly Companions*
due to legal wrangling over who controlled the copyright. Since
I had not seen the film in its original release in 1961, I was

anxious to locate a print. Upon my arrival in Los Angeles having spent three weeks with Peckinpah in Mexico where he was preparing to film *Bring Me the Head of Alfredo Garcia,* I managed to track down a 16mm copy of the film at a company called Bartco located in Hollywood on North Cole Avenue. Despite reluctantly admitting they had the film, they were unwilling to screen it for me. After some discussion, I finally managed to persuade a gentleman who worked there named Pat Duram to allow me to "borrow" the print for 24 hours. I then contacted the AFI, housed at the time in the Doheny mansion in Beverly Hills, who were good enough to allow me the use of a screening room. Given the difficulties I had experienced in just viewing the film, I ran it twice out of concern I might never see it again. What immediately struck me were the similarities it shared with Peckinpah's other work in terms of look, tone, and thematic concerns, despite his efforts to disclaim it.

Today, of course, it is possible to purchase a DVD of the film. Seeing it again recently reminded me of how much the film reflected Peckinpah's fledgling style. It also made me wonder anew about what really went on between Peckinpah and producer Charles B. FitzSimons during the making of the film. Having interviewed FitzSimons in 1974, I had included a portion of that interview in the chapter of the book that dealt with *Deadly Companions.* And while I had interviewed Peckinpah extensively, he had had such a negative experience during the making of the film that he refused to discuss it in any depth. However, in rereading the transcriptions that I had made of those interviews, I began to see how things that seemed irrelevant then now warranted closer examination. What had always been lacking, of course, was the original source material, mainly the script itself. In my initial research for the book, I had learned that the writer, A. S. Fleischman, had actually turned his screenplay into a novel published under the title *Yellowleg.* However, since it had been a paperback original with no hardcover printing, I had been unable to track down a copy at the time. With the advent of the Internet, however, this was no longer an obstacle.

342

After locating a copy of the novel online, I purchased a first edition for a mere ten dollars. But despite the claim by FitzSimons that Fleischman had adapted the novel directly from his screenplay, there were inconsistencies with respect to the finished film that made me wonder if this was correct. With both Peckinpah and FitzSimons no longer alive, I decided to go in search of A. S. Fleischman.

Born in 1920, Albert Sidney Fleischman was a newspaperman turned novelist who had adapted his own novel *Blood Alley* into a screenplay for John Wayne and director William Wellman. This, in turn, led him to write *Yellowleg,* which would eventually make it to the screen as *The Deadly Companions.* However, Fleischman is better known today as a writer of award-winning juvenile fiction. Taking a chance, I decided to contact him through his website and discovered that he still lives and writes in Southern California. Agreeing to meet with me, he not only was willing to talk about his experiences on *Deadly Companions*, but also provide me with a copy of his screenplay. This new infusion of previously unknown source material, coupled with the transcriptions of the interviews mentioned above, form the basis for this study.

It seems decidedly prophetic that Peckinpah's career as a feature director should begin with a film titled *The Deadly Companions,* considering the acrimonious conflicts that would develop between Peckinpah and FitzSimons. Peckinpah had just come off of *The Westerner*, the television series he had created for Dick Powell at Four Star Productions, a prolific television company in the 1950s and early sixties. As producer, writer, and director on the series, Peckinpah had effectively been given full creative control. Clearly accustomed to making all creative decisions himself, Sam Peckinpah was young, talented and ill prepared for his encounter with Fitzsimons. Ironically, this primal conflict can be seen as a paradigm for the struggles Peckinpah would have with producers throughout his career.

Charles B. FitzSimons was Irish by birth and a lawyer by training. As both a producer and actress Maureen O'Hara's brother (born Maureen FitzSimons, she had taken the stage name of O'Hara to capitalize on the popularity of Scarlet O'Hara in *Gone with the Wind*), FitzSimons had been on the lookout for a script that would take advantage of his sister's talents. At the same time, such a film would allow him to make the transition to full producer. Hence, he had taken a proprietary position with respect to the material long before Peckinpah arrived on the scene.

Speaking about the film in June 1974, FitzSimons maintained: "*The Deadly Companions* originated as a long treatment by a very fine writer named A.S. Fleishman that I fell in love with. The treatment was originally optioned by Marlon Brando. And I waited and waited to see what Brando would do with it, and when Brando decided to do *One-eyed Jacks*, he dropped his option on the treatment. So I met with Fleischman and talked to him about what I wanted to do with [the project] and he and I became firm friends and partners forming a company called Carousel Productions. He then wrote what I considered to be a fairly brilliant screenplay..."

Interestingly, Fleischman remembers it somewhat differently. Today A.S. Fleischman, who prefers being called Sid, is 89 and a Newbery Award winning children's author. When we first met in April 2009 to discuss *The Deadly Companions*, he was hard at work making a final pass on his current project, a book on the comedian and filmmaker Charlie Chaplin. According to Fleischman, *The Deadly Companions* – originally titled *Yellowleg* – began as a screenplay (he does not believe in or use treatments when he writes). He recalled: "I had gotten an option for the screenplay from Marlon Brando. So to support [Brando's attempt to set the film up] and to give it a little more dignity, I turned it into a novel. I don't recall how long Brando had it – and he helped himself to a couple of ideas which he used in *One-eyed Jacks* by the way – but when he let it go, Charles came into the picture."

Working together, FitzSimons and Fleischman struggled to get the financial backing to mount a production. According to Fleischman at least some of the difficulty came from the kind

344

of film they were attempting to make. "The picture was really Maureen's picture," he recalled. "But of course having a Western as a woman's picture gave us all sorts of problems at the time in terms of marketing. But Charles was determined, and he eventually put the deal together."

Similarly, FitzSimons remembered: "We found it very, very difficult to get financial backing for the motion picture because it was this morality play and required the carrying of a dead child in a coffin throughout the film. Many people wanted us to change the story... but we refused to do it.

"Then we got lucky. Fleischman had written it as a novel from his screenplay which was published by Gold Medal in paperback and was enormously successful – it sold around 250,000 copies. So based on the success of the novel, [James S.] Sam Burkett, who at that time was head of sales for Pathe Laboratories, persuaded Pathe to co-finance the picture along with the Theater Owners of America.

"My first choice for the role of Yellowleg was Brian Keith. Maureen was going to play the girl... At that time I had other ideas as to who I wanted to direct it. But Brian had some form of moral commitment to Sam Peckinpah with whom he had done the television series *The Westerner*. And Brian asked if we would consider Peckinpah for the picture. So I ran some of the episodes of the series and agreed to give him a chance..."

It is possible that FitzSimons' claim that Brian Keith was his first choice for the role of Yellowleg was in deference to his relationship with Keith at the time, but Sid Fleischman remembers the casting somewhat differently: "We were going to do it with Errol Flynn. But Flynn died unexpectedly. So we decided to form Carousel Productions with Maureen O'Hara, Charles' sister. Given her status as a major star at the time, Maureen agreed to do the picture for scale but take a fifty percent stake in the company; Charles and I owned a quarter each. Maureen had just done *Parent Trap* with Brian, and they had gotten along very well. So we decided to offer him the role. We then hired Peckinpah on Brian Keith's recommendation for $15,000. We only paid Brian $30,000. The entire picture was done for $300,000 to $400,000 – unheard of for a picture of that quality at the time. (The actual budget was $530,000).

"Sam, when I knew him, was a much different director than he would become. This reputation he developed for being a wild man – arrogant and difficult – was not evident on *Deadly Companions*. In fact, one of the very few times I remember Sam losing his temper was the scene where Brian Keith is supposed to shoot a rattlesnake. But the sharpshooter we had hired didn't kill the snake with the first shot and had to shoot it a second time. And Sam really blew up because it wasn't a clean kill. Of course in the final cut all you see is one shot and the snake's dead. But Sam obviously hated to see it suffer. I liked Sam but Charles did not, and I think that the picture suffered because of that.

"*Deadly Companions* had become Charles' passion. Getting it made took us years. He felt he knew what he wanted literally in every shot. And that made it very tough for Peckinpah. Now Peckinpah went to Tucson ahead of us. And when we got there, he had hired a secretary and had begun to rewrite the script. That's where the trouble started because Charles didn't even bother to read his notes. He simply said to Sam: 'We hired you to shoot the script.' Charles and I had worked hard on that script. Now I was far more flexible than Charles because I always felt that if something wasn't working, I could come up with another idea. But Charles wanted that script shot as is. And they were both fairly bullheaded when it came to artistic decisions. And that was a problem."

FitzSimons concurred: "Now I believe that everyone is entitled to his opinion, but I also believe that there has to be a boss. Unquestionably, Sam thought that everything he was suggesting was right, and I felt that, having spent two years on what we had, there was no reason to change. I couldn't believe that the author and I could be that far wrong. So we went ahead, and we made the picture according to the original screenplay without any of Peckinpah's changes. And as he would try to change it during shooting, we would lock horns."

However, irrespective of FitzSimons' stated belief that he had prevented Peckinpah from straying very far from the script, a comparison between the original screenplay and the finished film reveals a number of striking differences. In fact, after a careful examination of the film, it is possible to discern Peckinpah's unique imprint despite FitzSimons' resistance. And it begins with the very first scene.

Both Fleischman's screenplay and the novel open in daylight with three riders – a former Union Cavalry Sergeant called Yellowleg (Brian Keith), Turk (Chill Wills), and Billy (Steve Cochran) – headed for the town of Gila City, ostensibly to rob the bank there. The film, however, opens quite differently. Entering an out-of-the-way barroom at night, Yellowleg passes a man (Turk) balancing on a barrel, his hands tied behind his back, a noose around his neck, and five aces pinned to his shirt. Reaching the bar, Yellowleg catches sight of the teeth marks in Turk's left hand and instantly realizes this is the man who attempted to scalp him on a Civil War battlefield some years before – the man he's been pursuing ever since. When he asks what's going on, the bartender refers to Turk as a "five-ace card player," while the men he cheated lay bets on how long it will take him to slip off the barrel and hang himself. Unwilling to allow Turk to die before he can claim his revenge, Yellowleg intervenes. Knocking out one of the card players, he starts to cut Turk down when Billy enters, shirt undone and a pair of sixguns in hand, from a backroom in the company of two prostitutes. Seeing what's happening, Billy reacts, shooting the rope before Yellowleg can finish cutting Turk down. The three men then leave together. Once outside in the dark, Yellowleg takes charge suggesting he knows of a town with "a new bank and an old marshal" that they might rob. Mounting up, they head off together for Gila City.

While Fleischman does not remember the details of writing this opening scene, he does recall that the suggestion of a man balancing on a barrel with a noose around his neck as being Peckinpah's idea. Despite how protective FitzSimons was regarding Fleischman's screenplay being the sole source of the film, the staging of this new opening sequence would seem to be pure Peckinpah. It has an almost improvisational feel to it. The dialogue, of course, is minimal and would have been written by Fleischman, who was present on the set for much of the shooting. But none of the bit players in this scene including the bartender and one of the gamblers, both of whom have speaking parts, receive credit (a common practice at the time). Given the nature of the scene, at least two of them are stuntmen (Big John Hamilton and Chuck Hayward, both of whom worked frequently for John Wayne). However, the quirkiness of the bar's patrons, a scruffy, unkempt lot, is reminiscent of the habitués of other bars from both Peckinpah's television and later feature work (the saloon in "Jeff," the opening episode of *The Westerner* cowritten and directed by Peckinpah immediately comes to mind as do the saloons and bordellos to be found in films like *Ride the High Country* and *Pat Garrett & Billy the Kid)*.

The same is true of Peckinpah's orchestration of the action including William Clothier's camerawork, which opens with a tight shot of Brian Keith's "yellowleg" cavalry breeches as he enters the saloon. As Paul Seydor has noted: "This opening is significant because it introduces one of Peckinpah's basic storytelling techniques: he rarely opens a film or a scene with an establishing shot. Instead, his camera will light upon a naturalistic detail that leads to another detail and still another, until gradually the setting is built from and revealed through a careful process of selection and accumulation of significant details."

Concurrent with this is a heightened sense of edgy and unpredictable danger that is unlike anything else in the film. From the inspired dilemma of Turk's precarious balancing act to the staging of Yellowleg's fight with one of the card players that directly impacts the very rope used to string Turk up, Peckinpah begins his career as a feature director by creating an uncertain world where nothing is either safe or entirely what it seems.

Similarly, when Billy emerges from the back room to find Turk, his neck in a noose, he must shoot the rope in order

348

to free him. However, unlike the typical Western convention where the gunman is such a marksman that he severs the rope with a single shot, Billy's first attempt misses the rope requiring him to take careful aim in order to free Turk with his second. This serves both to underscore the reality that even a practiced gunman can miss and to reveal Billy as less accomplished than his ego might allow. It is the kind of obsession with imperfection that will continue to mark Peckinpah's world throughout his career.

And finally, as if to punctuate this auspicious directorial beginning, Peckinpah has Billy, guns in both hands, turn to leave only to suddenly come upon his own image in a mirror hanging from the barroom wall. With a wild impetuous grin, he shoots his own reflection, fracturing the glass before dashing out the door.   It is a signature moment that Peckinpah will use again, most notably following the final shootout at the end of *Pat Garrret*. In *Deadly Companions*, this simple act allows Peckinpah to define Billy's character as someone who acts before he thinks, failing to recognize his own image as he opens fire. In *Pat Garrett*, however, Peckinpah uses the device to reveal Garrett as repelled by what he sees – a man who has just shot his friend and who therefore opens fire out of a sense of self-loathing and remorse.

Having rescued Turk, Yellowleg now initiates a plan for the three of them to ride to Gila City to rob the bank. What is interesting about this arrangement is the way in which Peckinpah establishes the dynamics of the gang. Though he is essentially the outsider, Yellowleg immediately assumes command, implying that their success depends upon his leadership. While this is unquestionably a dynamic that Fleischman establishes in both his screenplay and his novel, it clearly appeals to Peckinpah and is a running theme he developed throughout *The Westerner*. In the series, Dave Blassingame, the lead character also played by Brian Keith, frequently would fill a void wherever leadership was required, thereby bringing him into conflict with men of lesser ability.

Yellowleg is a flawed hero, also a Fleischman conceit, demonstrated by the scalping scar hidden beneath his hat, as well as a minié ball he carries from an old war wound in his right shoulder that compromises his skill with a gun. There is no question that this is the kind of handicap Peckinpah responded to as well. We see Peckinpah employ it in an episode of *The Westerner* titled *Hand on the Gun* (another episode cowritten and directed by Peckinpah) where a character named Oresquote, played by Michael Ansara, attempts to deter an impetuous young would-be gunfighter named Cal, played by Ben Cooper. At Blassingame's urging, Oresquote raises his shirt to reveal a bullet scar from a gunfight that put him down for many months. Unimpressed, Cal, who, much like Billy in *Deadly Companions*, is constantly practicing his fast draw, ignores the warning only to die in the street when the gunfight he longs for becomes a reality. Similarly, wounds will impact other Peckinpah characters in future films like Samuel Potts, the one-armed scout, or Amos Dundee whose arrow wound compromises his command in *Major Dundee*. In *The Wild Bunch*, Pike Bishop carries a bullet in his leg from a gunfight that resulted in the death of the only woman he ever loved. And Mike Locken, the former quasi-CIA agent, is so severely wounded in the opening sequence of *The Killer Elite* that he literally must walk with a cane.

When I interviewed Fleischman, he was good enough to lend me a copy of his screenplay, titled *Yellowleg*. Tucked into the back cover page of this script was a Thermofax copy of a set of typed change pages. Brown and weathered, their edges curled with age, the Thermofax changes carry a title page that reads:

TREK
Screenplay by A. S. Fleischman
From the Novel
YELLOWLEG
By the same author

When I questioned Fleischman about this, he remarked that *Trek* had been one of the titles under consideration before they settled on *The Deadly Companions*. The set of changes amounts to 44 pages, less than forty percent of the original script. And in truth, most of the changes are minor, dealing primarily with dialogue adjustments made during the course of production. However, there are also several more specific changes in action that require closer examination. For purposes of clarity, from this point on let me refer to Fleischman's original complete screenplay as the "Script" while referring to the Thermofax pages as the "Change Pages."

The first of these revisions deals with Kit Tilden's son, Mead. In the Script, the boy (who is referred to as being six years old, though from his appearance – and for obvious practical reasons – Billy Vaughan, the young actor playing Mead in the film, would seem to be closer to ten) is introduced on page 8 when he and his mother first enter the saloon turned into a temporary house of worship. In the Change Pages, however, Mead first appears on page 4 coming down from the roof of the dancehall (presumably the one where his mother works) as Yellowleg, Turk, and Billy ride into Gila City:

EXT. DANCE HALL – MEAD

With an air of curiosity and excitement, he shinnies quickly down a drainpipe to the ground. He turns to silently watch the three strangers riding into town.

Since the boy does not appear at this point in the story in either the original screenplay or the novel, it would be logical to assume that this revision, though clearly written by Fleischman, reflects Peckinpah's involvement as director.

Further evidence of Peckinpah's touch here can be seen in the staging of the scene on film. As the three gunmen ride into town, Peckinpah starts with the camera on Mead standing on the roof playing a harmonica – a bit of business that also is neither present in the Script nor Change Pages. It is significant that Peckinpah visually establishes the harmonica with the boy so that he can use it to poignant effect once the boy has been killed. In the street below, a group of other boys are roughhousing with wooden swords. Spotting Mead, they stop to ad lib taunts chiding him for not having a father, thereby establishing him as an outcast. But by placing him physically above the other boys, Peckinpah visually implies Mead's moral superiority. At the same time, this allows Peckinpah to capture both the gunmen and Mead all in one shot as they ride past.

As the scene progresses, Turk heads towards the Blacksmith's to have one of his horse's shoes replaced while Yellowleg and Billy ride ahead and dismount at a hitching rail. In the Script, Fleischman uses the moment to underscore the developing conflict between the two men by having Yellowleg hand Billy the reins to his horse, telling him to take both horses around to the livery stable. When Billy chafes at this, Fleischman initially takes the edge off the moment by having Billy back down. But in the Change Pages, he introduces the boy at this point, who intercedes, offering to take the horses for them. Fleischman describes it this way:

[Yellowleg and Billy] stare at each other, tension mounting – and then Mead comes into the shot, swinging under the hitch rail.

MEAD
I'll take the horses for you.

Mead takes the reins of both horses and leads them away, leaving Billy and Yellowleg still staring at each other. Then Billy cracks a grin.

BILLY
There's some men is just plain lucky.

But Peckinpah builds on this by expanding the moment between Yellowleg and the boy. As Mead steps up to say: "I'll take the horses for you, Mister." Peckinpah gives Brian Keith as Yellowleg an improvised response: "You look like an honest man to me." He then fishes a coin out of his pocket to give to the boy, who takes the reins and leads the horses off.

This addition is significant since the incident brings the boy into direct contact with Yellowleg prior to the accidental shooting. In both the introduction of Mead on the roof and again here with his taking the horses, Peckinpah burnishes the boy's character and expands the moment. He achieves this by making a more tangible connection between him and Yellowleg, thereby deepening the eventual pangs of guilt the man will feel after he accidentally kills the boy.

Peckinpah follows this with another unscripted exchange between Yellowleg and Mead as the boy and his mother, Kit, enter the saloon as it is being readied for the church service. As Kit and her son come through the swinging doors, the impetuous Billy is immediately attracted to her commenting: "That's what I call pretty." But recognizing Yellowleg, the boy smiles and calls out "Howdy, Mister." To which Peckinpah has Brian Keith smile and ad lib: "Hello, boy." Clearly Peckinpah is attempting to reaffirm the connection beginning to form between them. Having created the television series *The Rifleman,* which centers on the relationship between a man and his young son growing up in the West, this is clearly familiar territory for Peckinpah.

Entering the saloon, Yellowleg and Billy are surprised to discover the room being rearranged to accommodate a church service that is about to begin. Fleischman's plot requires that the saloon be temporarily converted to a place of worship in order to introduce Maureen O'Hara's character Kit as a mother first and a dancehall girl second. Since we now have already met Mead, this also serves to establish him as her son. At the same time, Fleischman needs to have the bank across the street open for business in order to stage the daring daylight robbery that will occur shortly. He neatly solves the dilemma by having the bartender explain that it's been so long since the town's seen a calendar that some townsfolk think it's Sunday, while others hold that it's Monday. Hence both the makeshift church and the bank across the street are conducting business simultaneously.

The bartender in this scene is played by character actor Hank Gobble, clearly cast by Peckinpah (he appeared in five episodes of *The Westerner* as a cowboy named Digger) as were the prostitutes, who appear both in the opening scene and later here in Gila City. As Fleischman recalled: "The prostitutes in *Deadly Companions* were real prostitutes. Sam insisted on going down to the whorehouse and hire real prostitutes. They couldn't act, but then I'm sure he tried them all out." Regarding the casting, FitzSimons recalled:

"Brian Keith, I happen to believe, is one of the finest actors in the business today [1974]. I also happen to believe that he is the only actor who has the silent virility of John Wayne. I don't think that Brian, in this instance, understood the morality play [aspect]. And I think because he was Sam's booster, he obviously felt that Sam had enormous talents and he felt that he had the responsibility to take his direction from Sam, which, of course, is as a good actor should. So I can hardly fault the actor for what happened.

"I also think that both Steve Cochran and Chill Wills were brilliant in the picture... I had always admired Steve Cochran, but he had always played a heavy-heavy. I told him when I cast him in the role of Billy that I wanted him to play a likeable heavy. I wanted him dangerous but likeable so that at the end of the picture, the audience isn't sure just who they are rooting for. I told him that I wanted to lighten his hair one shade and put a wave in it. Cochran laughed and said okay because he trusted me. And he did play the picture with a light quality – a likeable villain."

However, the character of Billy as portrayed by Cochran embodies a contradiction that Peckinpah would explore in the future as well. Half courtly valor, half animal lust, Billy becomes a reflection of conflicts Peckinpah found within himself. It is possible to see in Cochran's Billy a foreshadowing of the character of Billy Hammond played by James Drury in Peckinpah's *Ride the High Country*. Both characters possess what Peckinpah himself once described as a kind of "little boy bravado" and a preening selflove that presumes every woman he desires, regardless of her protestations, really desires him as well. Just as Cochran's Billy attempts to force himself on Kit, Billy Hammond attempts to physically force himself on Elsa after her arrival in Course Gold. Assuming FitzSimons sincerely believed that this kind of prideful, self-absorbed behavior made Billy into someone the audience might be secretly "rooting for," Peckinpah clearly did not. All of Billy's actions are overstated. From his showy gun-twirling to his brocade vest to the red arm-garter he wears on his left sleeve, Billy, as Peckinpah presents him, is a source of self-parody not to be admired.

The character on which Peckinpah and FitzSimons agreed was Turk, a character whose creation should be properly attributed to Fleischman. In both the screenplay and the book, Turk is portrayed as uncouth and disheveled, an animal in a man's skin. In the novel, Fleischman introduces him as he is about to answer nature's call: "The short, big-eared man, the one who called himself Turk, pulled away and dismounted along the cutback. He began humming a little tune and unbuckled his breeches in the area of some bunchgrass. He rejoined the others about ten minutes later." This was the kind of offbeat character moment that would have caught Peckinpah's attention. Clearly, throughout the film he attempts to capture Turk with all his twitches and itches and bearlike mannerisms intact. Peckinpah's directorial flourishes, like having Turk attempting to scratch his back against a giant saguaro cactus, or having him draped over the leaning trunk of a tree, reveals an innate talent for exploring Wills' strengths as a character actor.

"Oskar Homolka had been considered for the role of Turk," FitzSimons recalled. "But I had always felt that Chill Wills was the undiscovered Wally Beery. And I felt that this was a Wally Beery role. We discussed Homolka because he was a slightly bigger name at the time, and one of the problems we faced in obtaining financing was that they did not feel that

Brian Keith had a large enough name. They hadn't wanted Brian and I had to fight to get him. And then when Brian wanted his own director, it made it tougher still. Sam had virtually nothing to do with the primary casting, because most of it was already set when we hired him. However, he did confirm my feelings about Chill Wills, although I believe he originally wanted R.G. Armstrong. Sam did suggest first Slim Pickens and then Strother Martin for the role of the preacher, and of course, I agreed with both of those choices, and Martin got the role. We had no conflict at all over casting, only in the interpretation of the script."

Once they started filming, Peckinpah's instincts as a director, while not wholly appreciated by FitzSimons, impressed Fleischman: "When I watched Sam direct on the set of *Deadly Companions*, it was as if he was inventing it all on the spot. I mean, we never had a meeting the night before on what the direction was going to be on the set the next day. So the day would start and Sam would show up and see several actors milling about and say something like 'Why don't we hang somebody today' just to get their attention. But Sam brought something to the film that was extremely spontaneous. It was like here's a camera and there are the actors, and he'd simply say to them – show me something. It was as if there was no one else around. And he'd feed off that improvisation."

An example of this can be seen in the film following the prayer service, when an unexpected band of outlaws attempts to rob the bank. Ironically, Yellowleg, Billy and Turk must take the law into their own hands, shooting it out with the fleeing robbers. In the course of the shootout, the lead ball lodged in Yellowleg's right shoulder causes such pain that he fires wildly, his stray bullet accidentally killing the boy. Improvising on the fly, Peckinpah begins on the boy playing his harmonica. As he wanders past the bank, he looks through the window. Spotting the robbers inside, he turns and runs, then stops to watch the ensuing gunfight. Then as the final outlaw spurs his horse in a futile attempt to escape, Peckinpah has the boy make a dash up a set of stairs. By placing him higher than the street action,

Peckinpah justifies the possibility of Yellowleg's errant shot striking the boy as it misses the mounted bandit.

After the smoke clears, Yellowleg spots the boy's body. Going to him, he picks him up and carries him down, laying him in the boardwalk as his mother arrives. Though other voices start to suggest that the boy was killed by the outlaws' wild gunfire, Yellowleg refuses to allow the lie to stand and admits the bullet was his. This moment is in Fleischman's original screenplay as well as the book and was no doubt part of what attracted both Peckinpah and Brian Keith to the project: a moral man who admits to his own actions, regardless of how repugnant they may be. But as Kit lifts her son and carries him off in her arms, Peckinpah, improvising once more, has Clothier's camera find the harmonica lying in the street. A significant detail as it, too, has been robbed of life without the boy's breath to play it. Later that night, in another unscripted moment, Peckinpah has Yellowleg spot the harmonica still lying there. As he picks it up, it serves as tangible evidence of his culpability, an unspoken motivation that will cause Yellowleg to accompany Kit on her sad journey.

Among the most discussed elements of the film is its central conceit – the transport of the boy's dead body across the desert in the heat, in order to bury him beside his father's grave in the far off abandoned town of Siringo. In the novel, Fleischman has the blacksmith tell Yellowleg: *"...They fixed the body to travel in the heat, and I heard them nailing the pine box just before you walked in..."*

But for some reason this explanation does not exist on film. It is not in the Script, nor the Change Pages. However, in the film in the bar where Turk and Billy play cards while waiting for Yellowleg, a character does say: *"She got Doc [Caxton] to take care of the body..."* presumably referring to some sort of preparation against the desert heat.

In reality, nothing short of mummification would have been effective against the decomposition of the boy's corpse. Indeed, in desert communities around the world, bodies are buried or burned as soon as practicable out of concern for infection and disease. But since this element was so central to Fleischman's story – what FitzSimons referred to as "a morality tale" – they would simply have to take the license and hope the audience didn't over think the point. Unquestionably, the lack of verisimilitude troubled Peckinpah and was a source of conflict with FitzSimons. But Peckinpah's objections, as usual, were quickly dismissed.

Clearly this matter was not easily dismissed by Peckinpah himself. Though it would take him a dozen years, he would eventually return to these issues in *Bring Me the Head of Alfredo Garcia*.

Like *The Deadly Companions*, *Alfredo Garcia* is a story of revenge. In talking about Peckinpah, Fleischman remembers on more than one occasion witnessing Peckinpah's ability to turn things upside down. "It was a trick Sam had of turning things around, reversing the order. In doing it, he was sometimes able to discover things you never expected. For example, on the trail they discover the corpse of a man who's been scalped. The traditional way of shooting this is to start on the actors. You see them react, then you show what it is they're reacting to. But Sam did just the opposite. He started on the body and panned up to their faces. That way it's the audience that gets hit with the full impact of the moment."

Consequently, while *Deadly Companions* is a journey to bury a boy beside his dead father, *Alfredo Garcia* is just the reverse – a journey in which the character of Bennie, played by the exceptional Warren Oates, must exhume the head of a dead man and return it to a ruthless Mexican overlord for enough money to retire in style with the woman he loves.

Where *Deadly Companions* uses the transport of the dead boy as a metaphor for the past that both Yellowleg and Kit must put to rest, *Alfredo Garcia* would probe the dark underbelly of such an experience and the toll it takes on the human soul. In the end, the burial of the boy in Siringo would be an act of liberation. But in *Alfredo Garcia*, the personal and emotional price that Bennie must pay in delivering the severed head leaves him with nowhere to go. It is no surprise that

Peckinpah would end the latter film with Bennie's death, essentially an existential choice.

In *Deadly Companions*, Yellowleg's journey of discovery causes him to recognize that vengeance is a poor substitute for love. However, in *Bring me the Head of Afredo Garcia,* Peckinpah takes us on a journey of self-discovery in which Bennie gambles everything for wealth, only to lose the one thing he truly values – the life of the woman he loves. Ironically, both men must come to recognize the redemptive nature of the love of a good woman. Yellowleg elects to take love over revenge. But Bennie, confronted by the loss of Elita, elects to die in a hail of bullets. Clearly, from Peckinpah's perspective, the darker of these tales holds closer to the truth.

Another point of friction in the film was the relationship between Peckinpah and Maureen O'Hara. In discussing *Deadly Companions* in his book *"If They Move, Kill 'Em!" – The Life and Times of Sam Peckinpah,* David Weddle states: "FitzSimons stood beside Peckinpah on the set every day, telling him how to stage and shoot the scenes, and forbidding him to give direction to his sister Maureen."

However, in discussing this with Fleischman, the situation appears to be less clear cut: "The fact that Maureen chose to underplay her role as Kit is very important because on the set, she complained to Charles that Peckinpah was not directing her. He may have done the same thing with Brian Keith, but particularly with her, he never gave her a clue as to how he wanted the scene played.

"Now she was far more experienced as an actress than Sam was a director. So it's hard to say whether that was the factor or possibly he was more comfortable directing men at the time. Now someone like Bill Wellman would have had her tearing her hair out, but Sam just let her do what she wanted to do. In fact, he paid so little attention to her that there's a scene where she's running away from Billy and she twisted her ankle. But she was such a pro that she didn't let it show. But you could tell that something was wrong. And Sam never even went up to her to ask her if she was all right. He just ignored her."

In truth, when it came to dealing with actors, Peckinpah was a master of mind games. As Strother Martin once remarked: "Sam is like a dirty psychiatrist – he gets inside your head and probes around with the scalpel." Thus, his treatment of Maureen O'Hara would seem to be a classic case of Peckinpah eliciting a performance through what he liked to refer to as "indirection." By ignoring her, Peckinpah would seem to have been attempting to manufacture the kind of frustration and anger in the actress that he wanted her character to express towards Yellowleg on screen. In recalling Peckinpah's directorial style, Fleischman was struck by his taciturn approach: "I don't remember him doing a lot of second takes. He got what he wanted and moved on. Sam had the ability to make others uncomfortable and thereby get them to do things they might not otherwise do. Which is frequently a sign of a gifted director."

This kind of direction by indirection was something Peckinpah would employ throughout his career. For example, in his very next film, *Ride the High Country*, he would instruct the actors playing the Hammond brothers to distance themselves from everyone else in the cast and crew, with the result being the kind of realistic clannish behavior that underscores the intensity of their performance. With Maureen O'Hara, however, this technique was only partially successful. This was due in a great degree to the fact that she was both the majority stake holder in the production company as well as the sister of the producer, not to mention an established motion picture star.

While Peckinpah had come out of television, a medium that, at the time, was perceived by many in Hollywood as inferior, O'Hara was part of a star system that treated leading actors as a kind of royalty. The fact that Peckinpah lacked the properly deferential attitude towards her no doubt rankled O'Hara. And while some of this infected her performance, it also so poisoned her relationship with Peckinpah that her brother actively fought with him on her behalf throughout the production.

Yet over the course of the film, despite being prevented from rewriting the material, Peckinpah managed to find ways to embellish it. For example, when Yellowleg goes to visit Dr. Caxton, the town doctor, about removing the minié ball lodged in his shoulder, Peckinpah has the doctor begin to prepare for the surgery by offering Yellowleg a couple of shots of "medicinal" whiskey, while drinking directly from the decanter himself. None of this exists in either the book or the script. As both men drink, Yellowleg asks how long he'll be out of action. When he's told a month (in the script it's a week), he declines the operation, and Peckinpah has the doctor react, brusquely adlibbing: "Then stop wasting my time."

Peckinpah's visual style could be subtle as well. Fleischman recalls: "I remember one scene that got ruined in the cutting. I think it was the first time I saw a flash of genius in Sam because I didn't understand what he was doing at first. The two bad guys – Chill Wills and Steve Cochran – are riding along on horseback. And maybe you'd shoot that head on or from an angle. But Sam has the camera on their backs as they're riding side by side. And I thought, what the hell is he doing? But when I saw the dailies, I suddenly understood, because what you first see on the screen are two horse's asses. But Charles ruined it because he cut that part out, and all you have are two men riding. But Sam had visually captured in a sly way the essence of Turkey and Billy in one fleeting image. I actually think Sam communicated best visually."

This is clearly reflected in Peckinpah's attention to the details that define each character through wardrobe. Throughout his career, Peckinpah's vision of the world would demand a lived-in look. After years of working for him, his assistant, Katy Haber once noted: "Sam is also a stickler for details... If a wardrobe guy brings Sam a hat, Sam will say: 'Take it away and jump on it, puke on it, and piss on it, and then bring it back and show it to me again." In *Deadly Companions*, Peckinpah saw to every item from Turk's ragged buffalo coat, sweat-stained shirt, and beat up derby to Yellowleg's worn buckskin jacket and frayed cavalry breeches to Billy's dandified vest and perfectly blocked Stetson. When it came to Maureen O'Hara, Peckinpah had the wardrobe department gradually age her dress from starched and prim to torn and soiled as the trek across the desert takes its toll. One only needs to compare Peckinpah's future body of work to FitzSimons' television productions (*Nanny and the Professor; Love, American Style* et al.) to realize that this touch is Peckinpah's alone.

Ever concerned with details, Peckinpah continued to improvise throughout the shooting to help clarify any point that required it. For example, as Kit and Yellowleg cross the desert, they witness a mock attack on a stagecoach by a drunken band of Apaches. Having lost a horse, Yellowleg waits until nightfall, then sneaks into the Apache camp to steal a replacement. In doing so, he stampedes the rest of their horses before riding off without incident. In the screenplay and the book, Fleischman creates a separate solitary Apache, not one of the band, who begins to stalk them. But in the film, Peckinpah has Yellowleg be discovered by one of the Indians who wakes and tries to stop him. Knocking the Apache out, Yellowleg drives off the other horses and rides away before the rest of the band realize what's happening. This act provides the motivation for this lone Apache whose loss of face now demands that he confront Yellowleg and kill him. As a consequence, the Apache separates from the band and begins dogging them.

This game of cat-and-mouse continues for several days with the Apache taunting them with arrows that narrowly miss until Yellowleg realizes he must face the Apache and finish it one way or the other. Ironically, this, of course, results in Kit, not Yellowleg, having to finally kill the Apache.

In the book, Fleischman has the Apache killed by Kit between chapters. Chapter 20 ends with Kit waiting in a cavern while Yellowleg goes in search of their tormentor. With the focus on Yellowleg, the last line of the chapter reads:

"And then, from somewhere behind the sun, the blast of a shotgun rolled out over the haze."

Chapter 21 begins on the next page with:

"Yellowleg found the Apache almost on his feet, a young giant in bronze and blood, blown back into the spiked branches of a staghorn cholla and held there like a grotesque scarecrow..."

In the screenplay, however, Fleischman gives the Apache a name, Lone Cloud (which is never spoken on screen), and stages the moment of death on camera. Having left Kit in a cavern beneath a massive butte, Yellowleg goes in search of the Apache:

EXT. GULLY – DAY

Yellowleg on the move, eyes alert.

> *DISSOLVE TO:*

EXT. PATCH OF GROUND

Yellowleg studying [the] ground. He looks off in [the] direction of [the] butte area in alarm. He begins to run.

INT. CAVERN – KIT

We OPEN on [the] shotgun lying across [the] coffin. The CAMERA PANS to Kit seated against the wall with [her] head in [her] arms on propped knees. Suddenly her head rises.

REVERSE SHOT – MOUTH OF CAVERN FROM HER POV

Lone Cloud is standing there, an Apache silhouette against the bright daylight.

INT. CAVERN – KIT

Paralyzed with fear – for an instant. Then she leaps for the shotgun.

FULL SHOT – LONE CLOUD

Moving into the cavern.

CLOSE SHOT – KIT

Raising shotgun to [her] shoulder and taking a bead.

FULL SHOT – LONE CLOUD

Suddenly Yellowleg appears behind him in the mouth of the [cavern].

CLOSE SHOT – KIT WITH SHOTGUN

Seeing Yellowleg behind.

KIT
Drop!

EXT. MOUTH OF [CAVERN]

Yellowleg hits the ground. Instantly – the roar of the shotgun. Lone Cloud comes spinning out into the sunlight.

CLOSE SHOT – KIT LOWERING THE SHOTGUN

REVERSE SHOT – LOOKING TOWARD THE MOUTH OF [CAVERN]

Yellowleg rises and walks toward her.

TWO SHOT – KIT AND YELLOWLEG

They stare at each other for a moment.

YELLOWLEG
YELLOWLEG
Fast thinking.

KIT
If I'd thought a little faster – I'd have
kept my mouth shut.

DISSOLVE TO:

Clearly Fleischman's extremely specific camera directions are at the behest of FitzSimons and for the benefit of his sister's performance. From the Fleischman-FitzSimons perspective, the scene is designed to show Kit having the opportunity to kill both the Apache and Yellowleg with a single shotgun blast. By shouting to Yellowleg to drop, she intentionally saves his life despite immediately attempting to deny it.

Yet in the finished film, the scene reflects Peckinpah's touch. First, the location he selects is a cave with both a mouth and a chimney opening high above. Next, he sends Yellowleg off while positioning Kit facing the mouth of the cave, holding the shotgun. Then he stages the action so that we first glimpse the Apache in the opening above Kit as he slips down into the cave unnoticed. Peckinpah then milks the moment, building the tension until suddenly the Apache appears in Extreme Close Up directly before her – a shockcut that startles both her and the viewer. Reacting, Kit pulls the trigger blowing the Apache away with Yellowleg arriving after the fact. It is an undeniably powerful scene. Thus despite O'Hara's evident dislike of Peckinpah's directorial style, he gives her one of the most memorable moments in the film. And unlike the way it appears in the screenplay, she does not have to share it with Brian Keith.

With the Apache dead, Yellowleg and Kit must make the final leg of the journey to the empty ghost town of Siringo on foot, carrying the boy's coffin between them. There they finally locate the grave of Kit's husband. But before they can bury the boy beside his father, they must confront Turk and Billy one last time. Here, the script, the book, and the film all agree on certain basic elements: After getting the drop on Yellowleg and Kit, Billy escorts them to what was once the saloon. He then sends Turk to get the money the two have stolen from the bank back in Gila City. While Turk is gone, Billy confesses that he really doesn't want to kill Turk himself, but will give Yellowleg his revolver back on the condition that he kill the old man for him. Then once Turk is out of the way, Yellowleg and Billy can settle things between them in the street, with Kit going to the winner. With cavalier bravado, Billy hands Yellowleg back his gun and turns his back to leave while grinning at Kit: "The lady's got to admit I got guts, don't she?"

From this point, what FitzSimons wanted and what Peckinpah delivered are decidedly different. As FitzSimons bitterly recalled: "I don't think Sam understood, or if he did understand, was not in agreement with, the premise of the picture: the problem of revenge for a man of moral fiber is the moment he catches up with it. I don't really think [Peckinpah] understood the morality play that was there because… what he shot was an ending for the picture I couldn't use."

In both the book and script, Fleischman gives Yellowleg two guns. However, Peckinpah and Keith found this to be too "Hollywood" and simply had him wear a single holster just as he had done in *The Westerner*. This also serves to set him in contrast to Billy who wears two. Without question, the reason behind Fleischman's two-gun approach is linked to this final duel with Billy. Since Yellowleg's right shoulder is encumbered by the lead ball still lodged there, he would appear to be handicapped in a gunfight thus raising the stakes. Consequently, as Yellowleg goes after Turk, he merely wounds him. Billy, emboldened by what he perceives as Yellowleg's poor marksmanship, then calls him out from behind. Fleischman's script describes it this way:

                    BILLY
        I'm ready any time you turn around.

                  YELLOWLEG
         You figure you're good enough?

                    BILLY
          There's only one way to find out.

INT. HOTEL LOBBY
His leg bloody and stiff, Turk is trying to pull himself back up
the stairs to escape being finished off.

EXT. BOARDWALK – YELLOWLEG AND BILLY

Yellowleg, his back still to Billy...

                    BILLY
              (grinning contempt)
     Two shots and you ain't finished him off yet.

                  YELLOWLEG
                (very quietly)
            I ain't ready for him to die.

Yellowleg stands tall and straight now. Silent tension begins to
mount. He turns slowly.

Their eyes lock. The thin buzzing of a fly is HEARD.

INSERT – YELLOWLEG'S HAND

So still that fly lands on [the] back of [his] hand.

BACK TO SCENE

The final moments. An instant before the draw, pain catches Yellowleg's right shoulder. It's enough of a movement to force Billy's draw. Yellowleg now doesn't even attempt to grab his right gun. Instead, he draws only one gun – his left – for the exchange of shots.

INT. BAR – KIT
Kit reacting to the SOUNDS of GUNFIRE. Then silence. Then SOUNDS of boots on boardwalk outside bar. Kit's eyes hold on the door.

REVERSE SHOT – BAR DOORWAY

Billy stands in the doorway.

CLOSE ON KIT

Reacting.

FULL SHOT – BILLY

Staring at Kit.

BILLY
(almost inaudible)
Winner take all…

He collapses in the doorway.

At this point, Fleischman has Yellowleg continue his pursuit of Turk despite Kit's pleas to let him go.

As the director, however, Peckinpah had other considerations. Given that Yellowleg did not carry a double-slung rig, he obviously had no left gun to draw. Therefore, Peckinpah decided to simply have Billy step forward in order to block Yellowleg's path and force the confrontation. In discussing it with Ernest Callenbach of *Film Quarterly*, Peckinpah recalled: "…[A]t the end, where Brian Keith is marching to kill Turkey, the character played by Steve Cochran steps up in front of him with his particular kind of little boy bravado, which he does quite well, and Brian pulls his gun and kills him, a brutal, realistic act...." When FitzSimons saw this in dailies, it was the last straw: "The way Peckinpah shot it, he had the Brian Keith character walk right up to Cochran saying, 'Get out of my way, Billy. I don't have any quarrel with you.' And before Cochran could get his gun out of his holster, Brian shoots him in the belly. Well, now you take ninety minutes of a movie and you flush it down the toilet. So the only way I was able to overcome that situation was to have Turk, from the top of the old mission, appear to shoot Billy in the back. Which was in keeping with Turk's character. So in other words, I had to come up with another ending, which wasn't the true ending of the true drama we were striving for. But at least it was not contrary to the drama of the picture."

Without question, Peckinpah and FitzSimons were at odds over how this gunfight should play out. But despite FitzSimons' claim that Peckinpah had failed to grasp the dramatic significance of this climactic moment in the story, it is clear that Peckinpah had a logic of his own. As Jim Kitses wrote in *Horizons West*: "As Kit had layed Yellowleg's ghost to rest, blasting down the lone Apache when he wriggles into the cave to stand above her like a primeval spirit, so internal logic demands that Yellowleg destroy Billy, a meaningful symmetry that is absurdly withheld in the final cut."

Ironically, the film still works for the viewer who is unaware of the dispute between director and producer. Early on as they approach Gila City, Yellowleg rides ahead and Turk urges Billy to shoot him in the back, to which Billy replies: "Ain't my style." When Turk presses him to do it anyway, Billy shakes his head and notes: "Any man that'd turn his back on you is just a dad-blame fool." Thus in light of the ultimate outcome, this exchange becomes unintentionally prophetic, a foreshadowing of the events to come.

Following Billy's death, Yellowleg is forced to confront his own demons as he continues to pursue Turk, despite Kit's fierce objection that his action may cost him her love. Having lived with the desire to make the drunken Rebel who scalped him on the battlefield suffer the same fate, he now takes it to the very edge. With a fistful of Turk's hair in one hand and the same knife that Turk used in trying to scalp him in the other, Yellowleg reaches the moment of revenge, then pulls back. By sparing Turk, he indeed spares himself.

As Bernard F. Dukore notes, Yellowleg's inability to consummate his revenge contains an echo of *Hamlet*. Like his Shakespearean counterpart, Yellowleg finds himself unable to act. Having finally found the man who attempted to kill and scalp him, he fails to carry out his revenge time and again despite numerous opportunities. While Hamlet's reluctance comes from a much more complex series of concerns, Yellowleg's delay is due first to his physical impairment (the minié ball lodged in his shoulder) and then to his sense of guilt and commitment in helping Kit transport her son's body across the desert to find her husband's grave and bury the boy beside it. Yet, in the end, Hamlet acts. Yellowleg does not.

While Peckinpah never would have admitted to such an interpretation, it is really the reenactment of civilization's defining moment. If Yellowleg does to Turk what Turk has done to him, he effectively enacts the ancient code of justice as described in the Old Testament: "…an eye for an eye, a tooth for a tooth." But by stopping himself and allowing Turk to be turned over to the posse and returned for trial, he is essentially reaffirming the tale told by Aeschylus in the conclusion of *Eumenides*. There Orestes, pursued by the Furies, turns his fate over to Athena, who orders that twelve citizens hear his case and decide his fate. Thus by stopping his own hand, Yellowleg ends the cycle of violence and retribution. As Dukore notes, Peckinpah, whose Masters degree from USC was in Drama, would have been familiar with Greek tragedy. And by his own admission, FitzSimons saw *Deadly Companions* as a morality tale. However, the fact is that the story originates neither with Peckinpah nor FitzSimons, but with Fleischman, whose original screenplay is the source from which the film has evolved.

Turning then to the final scene in the film, there is one last discrepancy that demands our attention. The finished screenplay titled *Yellowleg* is 115 pages and ends with the scene between Yellowleg and the posse that has ridden all the way to Siringo in pursuit of Turk and Billy, after they robbed the Gila City Bank:

...Seeing Billy lying dead on the boardwalk.

> MAYOR
> *(no pause)*
> *Looks like we found 'em.*

> YELLOWLEG
> *They figured you didn't have guts enough to come to Siringo.*

> MAYOR
> *We don't as a rule.*
> *(with a certain mild contempt)*
> *But you know how folks are. If it's their money, the gates of Hell wouldn't stop 'em.*

> YELLOWLEG
> *(to Parson)*
> *You're the Parson, ain't you?*

> BARTENDER
> *Says he is.*

> YELLOWLEG
> *(to Parson)*
> *Mead's lying next to his paw waitin' for the right kind of words.*

All eyes turn on Kit. A look of guilt.

> PARSON
> *(seriously)*
> *I'll scratch up a right fine prayer.*
> *Come on.*

And the group starts off.

FADE OUT.

THE END

However, the Thermofax Change Pages do not stop there. They continue on, ending on page 116. Instead of "FADE OUT" at this point, the transition reads:

DISSOLVE TO:

EXT. GRAVESIDE

The posse, Kit and Yellowleg standing at [the] graveside. The parson removes his hat as a cue to the others. The men take off their headgear – all but Yellowleg. Kit's eyes turn slowly to him. And he removes his hat. [We] see a faint scar running along the right side.

> PARSON
> *We are gathered here together*
> *in the sight of The Lord to deliver*
> *unto him…*

DISSOLVE TO:

EXT. MAIN STREET – DAY

The posse, mounted, stands together, ready to leave. Turk with his hands tied behind him. We have a glimpse of Kit as the posse starts off back to Gila City. They go 50 feet before stopping. They turn to look back.

WHAT THEY SEE

Yellowleg standing at the starting point. He has remained there on his horse. Kit sees him there and it's clear enough that he has changed his mind about returning to Gila City with her. She leaves the posse and rides back to him.

We HOLD them in LONG SHOT as they talk for a moment. We hear none of their conversation. After a few moments, their horses part. Kit rides back to [the] posse, trying to appear self-contained – but she is torn apart inside. Yellowleg rides away in [the] opposite direction, toward California.

As Kit rejoins the posse, they ride out past CAMERA leaving an angle on [the] empty street with Yellowleg disappearing.

Then CAMERA PULLS BACK, finally revealing [the] old sign we have seen before:

"WELCOME TO SIRINGO Pop. 873"

FADE OUT.

THE END

What is intriguing, however, is that the film, itself, ends differently than either of these versions, with the posse escorting Turk off (presumably back to Gila City to stand trial), while Kit and Yellowleg ride off together in the opposite direction. When I interviewed Charles B. FitzSimons back in 1974, he made the following statement:

"So we went ahead and we made the picture according to the original script without any of Peckinpah's changes. And as he would try to change things during shooting, we would again lock horns. When it came to the editing of the picture, of course, he wanted it edited from the material he had shot from his point of view, and I wanted it edited from the material that I had him shoot from my point of view. And being the producer of the picture and having the right to predominate, I won out."

In commenting on his experience on *The Deadly Companions* to Callenbach, Sam Peckinpah lamented:

"...[T]he whole point of the story was screwed up by the cutting... which changed the whole focus of the thing – we really had everyone riding off into the sunset, which wasn't my touch."

Given both FitzSimons' and Peckinpah's remarks here, it would seem that the ending which appears in the finished film is what FitzSimons wanted: Yellowleg and Kit riding off together, in Peckinpah's words, "...into the sunset." A truly "Hollywood ending." But that still does not explain the ending contained on page 116 of the Thermofax changes. Since this alternative ending concludes on a bittersweet note with Kit returning to Gila City with the posse, while Yellowleg rides off alone in the other direction, it would seem to be much more in keeping with something Peckinpah might have instigated. Yet when I asked Fleischman about it, he replied: "[Charles] never once invited me into the cutting room to see what mischief he was up to. At the same time, I really don't remember writing a major change, such as a full scene, at Sam's urging."

Nevertheless, the Change Pages exist only because Fleischman held onto them all these years and allowed me to examine them along with a copy of his screenplay. Since, by all accounts, he was the only writer on the project these pages including page 116 must have been generated by him. Now, nearly half a century later, it is not surprising that he does not recall the genesis of this final page. But it remains proof positive that an alternative ending was at least seriously considered.

Perhaps the key lies in FitzSimons' account of how the final picture was cut: "...[W]hen it came to the editing of the picture, of course, [Peckinpah] wanted it edited from the material he had shot from his point of view, and I wanted it edited from material that I had him shoot from my point of view..." If we assume then that the final film that exists today represents FitzSimons' view, then the ending is his. But if, as he claims, Peckinpah also shot material he disagreed with, it is possible that page 116 is, in fact, a version of the ending that Peckinpah shot as well. Since under DGA rules, Peckinpah was allowed a director's cut, this ending, along with his version of the final shootout with Billy, would have been included, only to be rejected by FitzSimons out of hand.

Unfortunately, since Peckinpah's cut of the film did not survive, all this can be nothing more than conjecture, however tantalizing it might seem. Nevertheless, when compared to the body of Peckinpah's work to follow – films filled with irony and lost love, violence and passion, missed moments and endings that fly in the face of Hollywood convention it is a case worth making.

One final thought. When I first wrote about *The Deadly Companions* and the conflict that arose between Peckinpah and FitzSimons, I was clearly biased. Fresh out of film school and filled with notions about the director as *auteur*, I had a lot to learn about actual filmmaking. While I still find it remarkable how much Sam Peckinpah's touch is visible in the finished film,

I need to say in fairness that, having now spent most of my professional life as a writer and producer and sometime director in this business, I find myself much more sympathetic towards FitzSimons and Fleischman, who labored long and hard to bring their vision of the picture to the screen.

It should come as no surprise that following this film, FitzSimons would turn his producing talents to television, which is indeed a producer's medium. As for Fleischman, a member of the Writers Guild of America since 1954, he began writing his first book of juvenile fiction, *By the Great Horn Spoon*, during the 20 week Writers Strike of 1960. Published in 1963 by Little, Brown & Company, it launched a stellar career that would bring him, among other things, the prestigious Newbery Medal for Children's Literature.

But of all those involved in the making of *The Deadly Companions*, only Sam Peckinpah would make his mark on the world stage as a filmmaker of significant note. Although Peckinpah denounced the film as impossibly flawed, it nevertheless revealed that he was capable of greater things to come. Thus when the opportunity to direct *Ride the High Country* would present itself within the year, Peckinpah was ready. Battletested and self-assured, he would accept the assignment and never look back.

The Straw Dogs
Then and Now

I t has been 40 years since the release of Sam Peckinpah's troubling but brilliant *The Straw Dogs* starring Dustin Hoffman and Susan George. It is one of those films I never expected to see remade. It seemed much too personal, too revealing both of the fictional characters at the core of the story, and the man who chose to bring them to the screen. Yet, director Rod Lurie has done just that. Sony will release Lurie's version of Peckinpah's original on September 16, in the full wake of the 9/11 anniversary media coverage, presumably in the belief that we may have reached a point where audiences are so desensitized (or perhaps addicted) to violence that the film will do well.

For the record, I knew Sam Peckinpah for the last dozen years of his life, and I wrote about *The Straw Dogs* in detail in *Peckinpah: A Portrait in Montage*. I also know Rod Lurie, though not nearly as well. As a result, Lurie recently invited me to attend a screening of his remake of Sam's film. The contrast was striking and provides useful insights into the ways in which audiences, movies, and our society have changed over the past four decades.

Each film is a product of its age. Working in 1970, Sam Peckinpah saw *The Straw Dogs* as an opportunity to dramatize two critical emerging issues that dominated the American scene in the late 1960s: the violence surrounding the Vietnam War and the burgeoning sexual revolution. Lurie's film, in my view, is an attempt to dramatize sex and violence as it exists today, specifically in the kind of closed societies found in rural small towns of the American South.

The title, originally chosen by Peckinpah, is intentionally obscure. It refers to a quote from the 5th century BCE Chinese philosopher Lao-tzu: *"Heaven and earth are ruthless and treat the myriad of creatures as straw dogs; the sage is ruthless and treats the people as straw dogs."* In other words, as Nature is impersonal and ruthless so is the wise man. Never allow your emotions to rule your head. For Sam Peckinpah, this title was meant to be ironic. His entire life—and by extension, his films—was ruled by trusting emotion over intellect. In fact, few if any in the audience back in 1970 were familiar with the quote. And for Peckinpah, that was just fine. In looking at Lurie's version, however, it seems fair to say that he is uncomfortable with such ambiguity. At one point in the current film, Lurie, who also adapted the screenplay, goes so far as to have his David (James Marsden) literally explain the term "straw dogs" in detail to his wife Amy (Kate Bosworth).

So it should come as no surprise that these two interpretations of the same material could not be more different. From the opening images, we have a stark contrast. As Jerry Fielding's darkly intense Academy Award nominated score begins, Peckinpah opens with a high angle out-of-focus shot that eventually resolves itself as children playing in the graveyard of an ancient church in Cornwall. Expanding this to the town itself, Peckinpah presents what on the surface appears to be a quiet English village, the last place one might look for violence.

Lurie, on the other hand, begins along a pastoral bayou where a deer grazes, then hesitates as it senses something in the air. A moment later without warning, the deer is shot dead by men whom we will come to know as the town bullies led by Charlie Venner (Alexander Skarsgard). Unlike Peckinpah, Lurie wants to establish right up front the violent nature of those who live in the fictional town of Black Water. He then proceeds to underscore this violence at every turn. From bar fights to the local high school football team to the brutal finale. In this part of the world, Lurie seems to be saying, violence is a learned response to the unfair realities of life.

It is also valuable to compare the way in which each director explores character. In Peckinpah's film, Dustin Hoffman's David begins as a man in denial. He has come to the town where his wife grew up in rural England ostensibly to work on a mathematical treatise for which he has received a grant. In truth, he is running away from the violence and unrest that plagued American college campuses in the late 1960s and early 1970s. What he fails to recognize is that he has brought the violence with him – in essence, it is part of his DNA.

This is a key difference between the two versions for Lurie disputes the validity of the notion of "territorial imperative" that lies at the core of Peckinpah's film. In 1970, Peckinpah read two books by Robert Ardrey: *African Genesis* and *The Territorial Imperative* which posit that in high-functioning primates, including man, there is a drive to mark one's territory and defend it to the death against all outsiders. In Ardrey's view, this is a primal urge that will surmount all others. Peckinpah's *Straw Dogs* reflects his agreement with this thesis.

Lurie, on the other hand, believes that violence in man is cultural, not innate. Hence, Lurie's film portrays David as a nonviolent man who is forced by circumstance to rise to the level of the violence he encounters. For this reason, Lurie chooses to transplant the story to the rural South where, in his view, violence is endemic, passed down to each new generation as a kind of rite of passage. In his version, David is not running away from anything. He is simply trying to work.

At the heart of the story, of course, is a notorious rape scene. It forms the centerpiece of both films. Without getting into detail, once again the contrast is dramatic. Peckinpah intentionally undermines the relationship between Amy and David revealing him as distant and cerebral, using his work to avoid contact with the rest of the world. Conversely, Amy is a complicated womanchild in search of a playmate. Into this comes Charlie (Del Henney), Amy's former boyfriend, who failed to consummate their relationship before Amy left for the States. Over the first half of the film, Amy flaunts her independence and sexuality, a modern woman confident that she is in control of every situation. The result is that the rape, while both brutal and graphic, is not straightforward. Like everything else in Peckinpah's world, Amy's motives are ambiguous. She lets Charlie into the house. She begins by resisting him, but then succumbs to the complexity of her own sexual needs and desires. Yet in a Peckinpah film, nothing is precisely as it seems. And no sooner has Amy given in to her darker impulses than Charlie betrays her, holding her down while his cohort, Norman, does much worse. The sequence is harrowing in part because of the incredibly layered performance given by Susan George. It is a powerful scene that, along with the violent confrontation at the end of the film, resulted in the film being banned in the UK by the British Board of Censors for nearly twenty years.

Lurie, on the other hand, sees no such complexity. He clearly supports the position that rape is rape, and no means no. Hence in his version, Charlie forces his way into the house and overpowers Amy, violently forcing himself upon her. Then, once he's finished, he compounds the crime by stepping back and allowing Norman to take the violation and humiliation further while Charlie occupies himself with putting on his shirt. This, too, is a difficult scene to watch. But in Lurie's version, Amy is a victim throughout. It is interesting to note that while Peckinpah's film was threatened with an "X" rating by the MPAA (the kiss of death at the box office of the time) forcing him to make certain cuts before being granted an "R," Lurie's version, according to him, received an "R" rating without a challenge. Again, each film is a product of its era.

Asked by a woman in the audience of the screening I attended why Amy doesn't tell her husband that she has been raped (the same thing is true in Peckinpah's version) Lurie offered what was perhaps the evening's most insightful moment. "Because," he said, "And this is the answer I gave to Kate Bosworth, who plays Amy: she's afraid that if she does, David will do nothing."

380

Today, violence in film is much more overt. Subtle nuances are lost on the mass audience. People pay for exaggerated thrills. And the studios of the 21st century rarely make any pretense of attempting to explore the troubling truths of human nature. Money is the name of the game, and today's films are designed to play to the greatest possible audience in order to maximize the box office grosses. Thus, it seems even more ironic that, in visual terms, Peckinpah's portrayal of violence on film is far less graphic than Lurie's. This is not to say that violence does not lie at the core of both films. It does. However, Peckinpah's intent is psychological and emotional. In the end, Dustin Hoffman's David is a changed man. In Lurie's version, David is a survivor. Moreover, the violence in Lurie's version is, in keeping with current vogue, graphically and unyieldingly in your face. By the end of Lurie's film, there are no subtle revelations. The house is awash with blood and engulfed by fire.

Clearly the final question rests with us. What, if anything, can two such different films based on the same material but made four decades apart tell us about ourselves? Sam Peckinpah's *Straw Dogs* makes no attempt to provide us with easy answers. To be human, he seems to be saying, means living a life bruised by contradictions and ambiguities. Nothing is certain. But despite this, in the end, we cannot escape the need to take a stand. Conversely. Lurie's is a world where ambiguity does not exist. His is a tale of a nonviolent man who blinds himself to the brutality around him. Finally, forced by circumstance, he briefly becomes as savage as his attackers, killing them all. Yet his actions never give rise to anything even approaching self-examination. Having made no serious sacrifice, he is satisfied with just coming through the ordeal alive. But then, in a world where our leaders are risk averse and doing nothing is the obvious political act of choice, perhaps this new *Straw Dogs* is simply a reflection of the nation we have become.

Sam Peckinpah's
Bring Me the Head of Alfredo Garcia

Looking over his brief, intense career, Sam Peckinpah's work can be divided into three unequal parts. The first is comprised of three films – *The Deadly Companions, Ride the High Country*, and *Major Dundee*. And although these works announced his remarkable talent as a filmmaker, they also provided his enemies with the ammunition to portray him as difficult, erratic and undisciplined. As a result, he would spend the better part of the next three years following *Dundee* essentially blacklisted as a feature director.

Desperate to prove himself, he eventually was forced to return to television where he had first made a name for himself directing half-hour Westerns. Hired by producer Daniel Melnick to adapt and direct Katherine Anne Porter's dark novella *Noon Wine* for ABC Stage 67, Peckinpah was once again able to demonstrate his considerable gifts. On the strength of this film and his original promise as filmmaker, Warner Brothers was persuaded to take a chance on him, hiring him to rewrite and direct a moderately budgeted Western called *The Wild Bunch*.

Shot in 1968 and released the following year, *The Wild Bunch* marks the beginning of the second and most productive period of his creative life. *The Wild Bunch, The Ballad of Cable Hogue, Straw Dogs, Junior Bonner, The Getaway, Pat Garrett and Billy the Kid,* and *Bring Me the Head of Alfredo Garcia* – seven films in less than seven years. Each a stunning original. Challenging, emotionally intense, and extremely personal, each stands alone – no two alike. Indeed, his original vision and unwillingness to conform was both Peckinpah's problem and appeal. Despite being typed early on as a director of Westerns, Peckinpah continually broke the mold defying easy stereotypes. Attempting to dismiss him, his critics labeled him as "Bloody Sam" pointing to his use of violence and falsely decrying it as gratuitous while failing to explain the simple humanity of a film like *Junior Bonner* or the lyricism of *Cable Hogue.*

As for the final four films of Sam Peckinpah's body of work, they sadly demonstrate the destructive impact of cocaine upon a creative genius. *The Killer Elite, Convoy* and *Osterman Weekend* all contain flashes of brilliance but without Peckinpah's earlier sustained vision. Only *Cross of Iron* stands out as worthy of serious critical attention. Significantly, that is the result of being shot in Yugoslavia where harsh antidrug laws forced Peckinpah to put aside his mounting addiction to cocaine and return to alcohol to keep his demons at bay while directing.

Thus, the most exceptional film in Sam Peckinpah's remarkable body of work becomes not *Ride the High* Country or The *Wild Bunch,* films which have traditionally been singled out by most critics as quintessential examples, but *Bring Me the Head of Alfredo Garcia.*

Coming as it does at the end of his most productive period, *Alfredo Garcia* is the true culmination of all his creative forces. A highly personal and uncompromising film, it is like no other. Dismissed by most critics upon its release and unfairly maligned in some quarters even today, it nevertheless demands our attention as a significant and seminal work of art by a major filmmaker. For at its core, *Bring Me the Head of Alfredo Garcia* is less an action adventure than a love story.

****

As a graduate student in Northwestern University's Department of Radio/Television/Film, I had the good fortune to have as my adviser the late Stuart Kaminsky. The author of *Don Siegel: Director*, Kaminsky had managed to get Sam Peckinpah to write the Afterword for his book in order to assuage the fears of his publisher. As a result, he was able to obtain for me the phone number for Peckinpah's bullet-riddled trailer in Paradise Cove, a beach community north of Malibu.

The year was 1973, and I called him cold. It was a little past noon on the West Coast, so naturally I woke him up. Still recovering from the aftereffects of a brutal war of attrition with MGM's James Aubrey over *Pat Garrett and Billy the Kid*, Peckinpah wasn't in much of a mood for conversation, so I did most of the talking as I attempted to persuade him to allow me to write a book on his life and films. His silence lengthened. I ran out of things to say. The silence continued. At last, he suggested that if I were really serious, I should send him whatever I had and he would let me know. Then he hung up. Obviously he had neglected to say where to send it. That was a test. The first of many obstacles designed to question my resolve and test my resourcefulness. How I met and successfully passed these challenges are recorded elsewhere, principally in the book I would eventually write, *PECKINPAH: A Portrait in Montage (1982 / Rev. Ed. 1998)*. In the end, he rewarded my persistence by suggesting I meet him in Mexico City.

We met in the lobby of the Aristos Hotel. It was midsummer, the first day of prep on what was to become Peckinpah's next feature film, *Bring Me the Head of Alfredo Garcia*. Based on what I had sent him to read along with that initial meeting, he invited me to join him as he scouted locations, met with actors and key members of the crew including Mexican cinematographer Alex Philips, Jr.

In truth, the Sam Peckinpah I met that first time in Mexico City did not strike me as someone capable of the legendary mayhem and madness generally attributed to him. He seemed fragile, not at all what I had expected. Clearly suffering from the aftereffects of his battles with MGM over *Pat Garrett*, his health was so poor that if a month or so later I had opened a newspaper to find Peckinpah's obituary, I would not have been surprised. Yet as preproduction moved ahead, Peckinpah seemed to grow stronger each day. It was as if the filmmaking process itself were the only elixir capable of restoring his health. Indeed, as I would eventually come to realize, everything else in his life came second.

A few days after my arrival, after the Mexican censors had finally cleared the film's script and given it their stamp of approval, Peckinpah handed me a copy to read. Given its provocative title, I was clearly intrigued. Cowritten with Gordon Dawson from an original story idea by Frank Kowalski, it had been sold to producer Martin Baum and eventually the studio as a dark and violent action adventure – in short, *A Sam Peckinpah Film* with all that that implied. Returning to my hotel that night, I sat down and immediately began to read. As with other Peckinpah films, the story intentionally opens with misdirection.

EXT. A WALLED HACIENDA – DAY

IS IT SPAIN – Maybe Italy – or possibly MEXICO – or BRAZIL – or ARGENTINA – or...? It is not Mexico.

In any case, we are far enough away to see the expanse of the large complex of buildings and stables, far enough not to see too may details.

Specifically, we see horses, specifically we do not see automobiles. Specifically it is a pastoral scene of great wealth...

Like soldiers who turn out to be outlaws or deer grazing in what turns out to be a prison compound, the opening ten minutes of *Alfredo Garcia* mislead us to believe we are in the 19th century American Southwest. As a young pregnant daughter is brutally forced to betray her lover's name, and her father (referred to in the script simply as "El Jefe") places a million dollar bounty literally on the offender's head, the script abruptly shifts to the present day:

EXT. HACIENDA – A SERIES OF ANGLES – DAY

THE MEN LEAVE. BUT NOT BY HORSE. MERCEDES, FERRARIS, CORVETTES...

And thus we find ourselves propelled into the 20th century. As a precondition of the Mexican Board of Censor's approval, much is made of jet planes taking off and landing as they scour the globe in search of Alfredo Garcia. Eventually, El Jefe's men arrive in Mexico at an out-of-the-way tourist trap described as:

INT. SIEMPRE VIVA BAR – NIGHT

A THIRD-RATE CLUB COMPLETE WITH FOUR GIRLS (waitresses?) a bandstand and a piano player.

THIS IS BENNIE, WHO PLAYS AND HANDLES THE CUSTOMERS. BENNIE ISN'T BIG, BUT LOOKS LIKE HE COULD BE ROUGH. BUT HE ISN'T HALF ROUGH. He's not going soft – he's gone soft. Maybe he's always been soft, but in any case he's learned to be friendly enough to talk his way out of more fights than most men can find.

He's near the wrong side of 40 and is the only gringo bartender on the Mexican side of the border who can't speak decent Spanish...

Two bounty hunters – Sappensly and Quill (Robert Webber and Gig Young) take the lead. They show Bennie a photo of Alfredo. Immediately recognizing the picture as the former lover of Elita, the woman he now lives with, Bennie plays along, promising to let them know if he sees him. After they leave, Bennie goes to confront Elita, who confesses that Alfredo was her first lover, long ago. And while it is true she was with him recently, he died in a car crash and is buried in a remote village.

Recognizing the opportunity, Bennie immediately seizes on it. There is a price on the head of a dead man. All he has to do is return with Alfredo's head as proof he's dead and the money is his. A chance at a fresh start for both Bennie and

Elita. So he makes a bargain with El Jefe's henchmen. Then he and Elita set out to on their dark and troubling quest.

Just as we begin to settle into a story we think we know, Peckinpah takes us in a totally unexpected direction. What originally seemed like a straightforward action adventure abruptly shifts becoming a complex, multilayered love story – totally unpredictable. A vivid, unsettling exploration of the true meaning of love and the consequences of allowing it to slip away.

Peckinpah starts with two unlikely lovers. Neither is young. Bennie (played by Warren Oates) is a loser described in the script as having "…gone through 40 years of life with a $1.35 in one hand and an erection in the other and now, when it's time to find out which is which, he doesn't want to look." Elita, on the other hand, is a sometime prostitute and part time actress, who loves him despite his failings. Here is how Peckinpah introduces her in the script as she spots Bennie entering the bar and brothel where she is working as a hostess:

SHE SEES HIM AND REACTS HAPPILY. Elita [once] was capable of giving herself for money, but you know now you can't buy her. Her life with Bennie is the first happiness she's had in years.

He is all things to her – a trusted friend and lover. She prays for him and herself in a clear, hopeful way. Elita is a purist. Maybe is also a little past 30 – maybe not.

Before arriving in Mexico, Peckinpah had already cast Warren Oates as Bennie. In fact, he had intentionally shaped the script to take advantage of Oates' intense, offbeat screen presence. Character actor turned leading man, Oates was not a traditional Hollywood star. His face had a livedin, worldweary quality that was more reminiscent of Humphrey Bogart than William Holden (who had played Pike Bishop in Peckinpah's *The Wild Bunch*). In fact, as has been noted more than once, over the course of *Alfredo Garcia,* Oates bears a more than passing resemblance to Peckinpah himself.

However, the casting of Elita was more complicated. Soon after settling in to the Aristos Hotel, Peckinpah met with casting director Lanca Becker, who arrived with a stunningly beautiful young Mexican actress in her early twenties. Calling himself "San Samuel," Peckinpah charmed and flirted with both Lanca and her protégé but remained noncommittal. Over the course of several hours, other young ingénues came and went. With each, Peckinpah attempted to explain what it was he was looking for. Elita, he said, was a woman of complex emotions whose beauty radiates from within. He asked Lanca about Aurora Clavel, the actress he had previously cast as Pike Bishop's lover in *The Wild Bunch* as well as Pat Garrett's wife in *Pat Garrett and Billy the Kid.* Brightening, she assured him the actress would be there shortly.

When Aurora Clavel finally arrived, Sam met her with a warm embrace. As they discussed the role, Peckinpah asked her to remove her makeup. When she did, he turned to Dawson and Davidson and said: "You see...? This is Elita." With the casting session over, Peckinpah asked Dawson to be sure to include Aurora among the actresses he would screen test with Warren Oates later in the week. Then saying good night to the others, he asked Aurora to remain. In the corridor, Davidson looked confused. Why waste money on screen tests if Peckinpah had already decided on Clavel? Dawson shook his head: "Until Sam can actually see them with Warren, nothing's set in stone." Indeed, after the halfdozen tests, it would not be Aurora Cavel but Isela Vega who could convey the earthiness of Elita that Peckinpah was after. In her midthirties and fearless, she brought an ethnic authenticity to the role. And seeing her work with Warren Oates, she lit up the screen.

The casting of Isela Vega was the first indication that Peckinpah was interested in making an unconventional love story. By decoupling love from sex, he begins to explore the true nature of the complicated relationship between a man and a woman. As their quest begins, Bennie believes that money will solve all their problems. Elita disagrees but goes along because she cares for him and believes in her heart that she can change him. It is an uncertain journey.

Stopping along the side of the road, they have an intimate picnic in a grassy field beneath the shade of a tree. As written, it is a scene where they begin by confessing their dreams and hopes for the future. It is here that Elita asks Bennie why he's never asked her to marry him. As Bennie struggles to answer, she says: "So ask me." And because he can't say no, he does. But clearly neither believes he really means it.

Changing the subject, Bennie attempts to explain why they need to find Alfredo's grave. Without explicitly saying how they will do it, he explains that proof of his death is worth $10,000, a chance for them to go away together, to make a new start. Troubled by the implication that they may have to desecrate a grave, she suggests that he could not possibly want her to take part in such an act. But Bennie insists: she already is part of it, and if she can't do it for Bennie, she should do it for Alfredo because he would have wanted her to be happy. Passing a bottle of Tequila, they drink a cynical toast to Alfredo and happiness.

As written, this is where the scene ends. But in filming it, Peckinpah, without telling Warren Oates beforehand, instructed Isela Vega to go beyond what is on the page. Challenging Bennie, she says that if he really means it, he will ask her again to marry him. Caught completely unprepared, Oates never breaks character. We see in his face the realization that despite all his procrastination and inability to commit, he, in fact, does truly love her. Thus struggling with his emotions, we watch Oates as Bennie ask her again, only this time speaking from his heart. And we see Isela, now completely immersed in the character of Elita, give in to her emotions. In this remarkably candid moment, it is no longer a scene about Alfredo or money or anything except the love between two people. She curls in against him and he holds her tight. It is as nakedly emotional

390

and honest a love scene as has ever been filmed. And in it hangs the balance of the entire film.

The sequence of events that follows is unpredictable and exceptionally complex. That night, Bennie and Elita decide to camp out under the stars only to be accosted by two American bikers, identified in the script as John and Paco, played by Kris Kristofferson and Donnie Fritts. In a scene filled with sexual tension and totally improvised, the bikers get the drop on Bennie. John then forces Elita to accompany him off into the rocks intent on raping her. Overwhelmed by a sense of helpless rage, Bennie calls after John, swearing he'll kill him. But Elita turns back saying: "No, you won't, Bennie. I've been here before, and you don't know the way."

In the screenplay, John's violent rape of Elita can be heard taking place off screen. But in shooting the scene, Peckinpah again takes things in an unexpected direction. Away from the campsite, John stops and using a switchblade, tears open Elita's blouse, exposing her breasts. Refusing to be dominated, she slaps his face hard, then does it again. When he then hits her back, she defiantly refuses to give in to tears. Denied the ability to subdue her with violence, John backs off. Brooding, he walks a short distance away, takes out his gun and sits down against the rocks considering what to do.

Sensing that unless she acts, John will turn his anger and frustration on Bennie, Elita becomes the sexual aggressor. Moving to him, she drops down before him and whispers: "Please don't... please." Then reaching out, she takes his face in her hands, drawing him into a kiss. At the same time, overpowering the other biker, Bennie grabs his gun and races to her rescue only to discover not rape but what appears to be the prelude to lovemaking. Enraged and confused, he kills both John, then his partner as he comes rushing up. Shaken by the intense emotions of these events, Elita runs to Bennie who holds her. Then turning, he leads her back to their car, and they drive away.

Playing against all of our preconceived notions, Peckinpah has turned a predictable rape scene as originally written in the screenplay completely upside-down. Instead of a helpless woman being violated who must be rescued by the man who loves her, it is the woman who rescues herself. Bennie's subsequent actions – killing the bikers – have nothing to do with saving her, but everything to do with salving his own male ego. By portraying it this way, Peckinpah exposes rape as a crime of violence, not sexual gratification. From the moment rape seems inevitable, it is Elita who is in charge. For her, sex is not love. It is simply an act to be endured as a means protecting the man she loves.

Consistently throughout *Alfredo Garcia*, Peckinpah underscores this lesson. The men may think they are in control, but without question, it is the women who literally drive every key story point. Opening with El Jefe's daughter's refusal to submit to her father's will, Peckinpah sets the story in motion. It is Elita who knows where Alfredo is buried and reluctantly takes Bennie there against her better judgment. It is Alfredo's grandmother's relentless obsession to retrieve and return the severed head that results in the senseless massacre of her family. And in the end, as Bennie holds El Jefe at gunpoint, it is his daughter who commands: "Kill him...!" Throughout the film, it is the women who act while the men react. The depth and complexity of this revelation runs counter to the common assumption that Peckinpah's work is simply a reflection of unfettered machismo. For Sam Peckinpah, nothing is simple.

Let us now turn to the darkest and most disturbing point in the film: When Bennie wakes to find himself buried alive in Alfredo's grave with Elita's lifeless body there beside him. It is at this moment that Warren Oates' performance transcends every expectation. Allowing himself to be completely buried, his clothes covered in blood and grime, dirt in his hair, his ears, his mouth, Oates delivers an astonishing transformation as he fully gives himself to Peckinpah's vision. A man now lost and beyond salvation, Bennie learns too late that he has failed to cherish and protect the one person in his life who really loved him. A sense of tragedy pervades the scene. *"Like the base Indian threw away a pearl worth all his tribe..."* Bennie has

392

nowhere to turn and no hope of redemption. And so begins a strange black comic odyssey as he takes the only course he left open to him – to recover Alfredo's head and return it while making those responsible for Elita's senseless death pay. In doing this, of course, Bennie must confront his own culpability. Thus his journey becomes one of existential self-discovery and destruction.

When Sam Peckinpah had first given me the screenplay for *Alfredo* to read that first week in Mexico City, this was the ending:

EXT. HACIENDA ENTRANCE – DAY

THE CAR SLIDES ONTO THE MAIN HIGHWAY – finally regains control and speeds away.

INT. CARLOS' TAXI – DAY

BENNIE SINKS BACK INTO THE SEAT – looks down at the bulging flight bag – pats it.

BENNIE
Relax, Al... we're going home.

EXT. HIGHWAY – DAY

AND THE CAR CARRIES HIM OFF DOWN THE HIGHWAY WITH ALL OF THE MARBLES BUT ONE – The only one that really mattered. As the car gets smaller and smaller...

FADE OUT.

The next day when we met, Peckinpah had asked me what I thought. Candidly, I said that I felt it was a potentially powerful story, but the ending had two problems. First, Bennie should not have a getaway driver (Carlos in the script) – it is his quest and he needs to finish it alone. And second, he lives.

Weighing my objections, Peckinpah shook his head. "That's because he's a survivor," he countered. "And exactly what is he surviving for?" I asked. "The one person who really mattered is dead. What's he escaping to?" "Interesting," he replied gruffly, then turned to the business of the day.

But in the end, clearly our discussion that day resonated somewhere in Peckinpah's subconscious mind. Because four months later, when he actually committed it to film, he changed the ending as Bennie completes his revenge then dies alone in hail of bullets – an existential choice made by a man with nowhere left to go.

One final observation. It's been said that great artists are both selfless and selfish. They compulsively steal time from those they love and give it to their art. Like Bennie who is blind to how much Elita matters to him until it is too late, Sam Peckinpah, throughout his life, intentionally sabotaged every important relationship in the name of what mattered to him most: his films.

On Tuesday December 11, 1973, Sam Peckinpah completed shooting the complicated sequence that takes place along the rural road where Sappensly and Quill brutally murder the Moreno family and in turn are dispatched by Bennie. The following day, the company would travel to its final location, the Hacienda de San Juan north of Mexico City not far from the pyramids of Teotihuacan. Since it would provide us an uninterrupted time to talk, Peckinpah suggested I join him in his trailer for the move. And so we spent that night drinking and discussing his life, his films, and filmmaking in general as he candidly answered every question I posed. We arrived at the Hacienda a little before midnight. In the background of the audio tapes I made at the time, it is possible to hear the constant chanting of the pilgrims as they make their way to the nearby Basilica of the Virgin of Guadalupe. A strange eerie mix of pagan and Catholic rituals. As a sign of devotion, many make the journey literally on their knees in hope of a miracle. It was dawn by the time they finally stopped. And so did we.

By week's end, Peckinpah had completed the scenes for

what would be the opening of the film – the discovery of the girl's pregnancy and her father's command that they find Alfredo and bring him his head. Having been cast as one of El Jefe's bodyguards, I was given the opportunity to observe Peckinpah at work first hand. It was an invaluable experience. He had also cast my wife, Sheila, who had flown down from Chicago, as one of the ladies in waiting. Taking Sunday off, he began preparing for what is perhaps the film's most complicated sequence: Bennie's confrontation with El Jefe and the final shootout.

Around six that evening, Peckinpah's assistant, Katy Haber, came up to say that Sam would like Sheila and I to join him for dinner and drinks in his trailer. His ex-wife, Begonia Palacios, had arrived from Mexico City, brought out by her brother, Juan Jose, who also happened to be Peckinpah's personal driver. Having prematurely given birth to their daughter and only child, Lupita, in October, Begonia had spent several weeks recuperating as Sam's guest in the home he was renting in the Zona Rosa in Mexico City. But once the baby had been discharged from the hospital, Begonia had taken her and gone to live with her mother. Since Sheila and I were the only other couple on location, Sam's invitation made sense. We obviously accepted.

Petite and radiant, Begonia was charmingly animated. And as the evening made its way towards midnight it became clear that she was attempting to invite both herself and their baby back into Sam's life. As he had been with the actresses in the casting session, Sam was both courtly and flirtatious, telling stories of how they'd met while shooting *Major Dundee,* and how he'd married her and the time they'd spent in Europe as Sam was trying to resurrect his career after the short-lived debacle of *Cincinnati Kid.*

Between the laughter and Mexican brandy, Begonia picked her moment and suggested to Sam that she not return to Mexico City but stay there with him. They could even send for the baby. Be a family again. Clearly she wanted to rekindle their relationship. Listening to her, Sam became very quiet as

Begonia continued to press her case. And then in an instant, Sam's mood completely changed as he turned on her, his voice filled with a dark cryptic edge. In a heartbeat, she knew she had crossed a line as Sam summoned Juan Jose and ordered him to drive her back to town, and never bring her back.

Later, after they had left and we were alone finishing off what was left of the brandy, Sam looked at me and said: "You understand...? Why I had to do it...? The film comes first. Nothing else matters." And the next morning in his trailer, Katy Haber took charge of his day making certain that Sam was in control of the one thing in his life that mattered most... the film he was making.

A Personal Look at One of Peckinpah's Signature Special Effects – The Squib

T iming is everything… and for Sam Peckinpah, he had the good fortune to be on the cutting edge of the developing technology that came to be known as "squibbing," the ability to more realistically capture on film the visceral impact of a bullet hit.

For Peckinpah, actions demanded consequences. Traditionally in Hollywood, a film character could be shot, tumble to the ground mortally wounded without revealing the wound. It was the same kind of game kids play.

But early in his career, writing and directing for television, Peckinpah began exploring ways to show what being shot actually meant. That it wasn't a game, it was serious and painful. In his critically acclaimed groundbreaking series *The Westerner* starring Brian Keith, Peckinpah cowrote and directed an episode titled "Hand on the Gun" (available today on YouTube). In it, Peckinpah graphically shows us the aftereffects of what it means to be shot. An Hispanic character named Oresquote, (played by Michael Ansara) attempts to dissuade a hotheaded young Easterner (Ben Cooper), who is obsessed with the mythology of gunfighting by showing him the scars he carries from being shot several years before.

Opening his shirt, Oresquote points to the small entry wound in his abdomen. Unimpressed, the kid scoffs. Then Oresquote turns to reveal the massive exit wound on his back. Unfortunately, the lesson is wasted on the kid, who doesn't think such a thing could happen to him. As a result, he ironically dies the same way, shot down in the street in the finale. Truly a remarkable moment for television in 1960.

While squibs had been used by Arthur Penn in *Bonnie and Clyde* the year before, it would be Peckinpah who truly recognized and maximized their potential beginning with *The Wild Bunch*. Coupled with slow motion camera work and inspired editing, Peckinpah, aided and abetted by cinematographer Lucien Ballard and editor Lou Lombardo, created some of the most visually jarring sequences ever committed to film. But for all their power, few in the audience who reacted to these images understood how squibs actually worked. Fortunately in my case, I would get to know them intimately.

In December 1973 on *Bring Me the Head of Alfredo Garcia*, Peckinpah decided to cast me as one of El Jefe's (Emilio Fernandez's) bodyguards. I appear in the sequences filmed for the opening and close of the picture that were shot at the *Hacienda de San Juan "Tlacatecpan"* outside Mexico City. Since my character dies in a hail of bullets in the final shootout with Warren Oates, and since I was writing a book on him, Peckinpah made certain that I was able to experience how this new technology worked firsthand.

First the wardrobe department cut bullet holes in my costume. Next, the Special Effects department took condoms filled with a liquid resembling blood and taped them behind each bullet hole along with a charge to be electronically triggered once the shooting started. Finally, behind each squib was placed an aluminum heat shield to protect my skin from the heat of ignition as each charge was detonated. As I took my position at the far end of the room near the door, the Special Effects department wired the leads to each of the charges to a master board. Then when all was ready, Peckinpah called "action" and the cameras rolled.

Reacting to Warren Oates as he pulled a gun from the basket containing Alfredo's head and started firing, I raised my Winchester and fired back. Then Peckinpah pointed to the Special Effects man at the master control board. Instantly, he sequentially ignited each squib. Feeling them go off, I reacted to being shot, spinning away and tumbling to the floor. It was over in less than a minute. However, the scene continued. And Sam, in his own perverse way, insisted I remain lying on the cold stone floor while he shot the succeeding action – take after take after take – so that others had to step around me. For Peckinpah realism was everything. And he wanted to be sure I understood that nothing worth doing could be half-done. The aftermath of the scene took a day and half to complete. An experience indelibly fixed in my mind.

To illustrate the process, here's a lobby card of the scene showing Warren Oates firing at the guards nearest the front door while I can be seen in the background starting to react to his sudden attack...

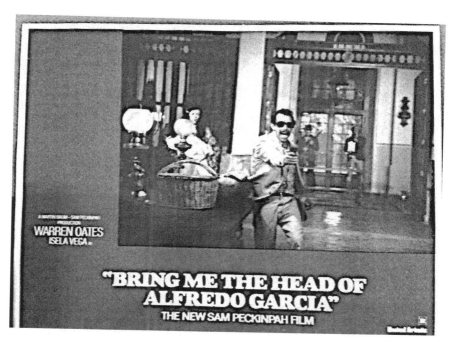

This is a production still shot of me standing guard at the door as "El Jefe" enters surrounded by his family and carrying his infant grandson.

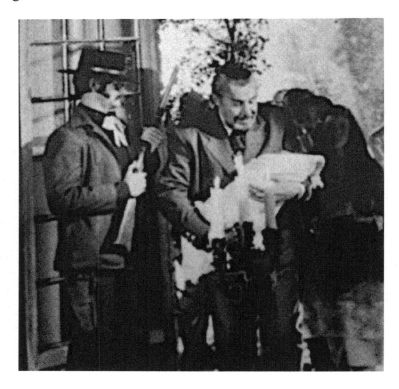

Here is a squib I liberated from the Special Effects department before leaving Mexico at the end of production. The actual condom has long since deteriorated leaving only the dried flakes of red paint and the gunpowder charge (the round dot attached to wire leads) that was taped inside my pre-rigged costume...

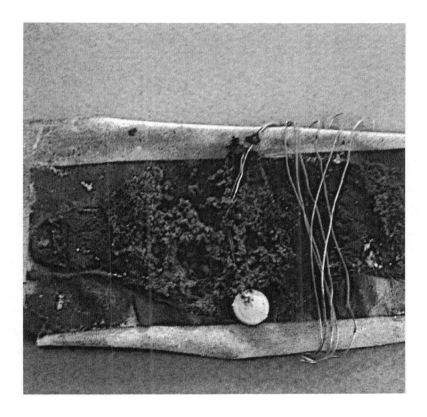

And here is the aluminum heat shield placed between the squib and my body for protection...

And finally, here is a sequence of three stills capturing my slow motion demise as Warren Oates guns me down. The chance of a lifetime and the fulfillment of a boyhood fantasy...

Two Lions on the Edge of Winter

Peter O'Toole and Sam Peckinpah
at the Formosa Café

This past week, less than a month shy of his 80th birthday, Peter O'Toole announced: "It's time for me to chuck in the sponge. To retire from stage and screen. The heart for it has gone out of me; it won't come back." But what a heart.

It's only a few years ago that O'Toole, still majestic at 74, gracefully prowled the red carpet at the Academy Awards resplendent in his brocade dinner jacket and black bow tie. Just watching him conjured up a coterie of truly memorable characters. From historical drama to high comedy, his has been a career filled with powerful performances. So it seemed hardly a surprise to find him striding into Hollywood's Kodak Theater for the Oscars, a Best Actor nominee once more for his role in the film *Venus*. As Maurice, the aging, simultaneously grand yet vulnerable British former leading man, O'Toole portrayed a man caught up in a passionate though platonic love affair with a young woman a fraction of his age. Indeed, the strength of his performance comes from the fact that it is all but impossible to separate O'Toole from the character he creates. A dancer lost in his last *pas de deux*.

Seeing him reminded me of another winter's day many years ago when I was still new to Los Angeles and working on a biography of the aging *enfant terrible* of American cinema, the late film director Sam Peckinpah.

The year was 1976 and Peckinpah had offices at what was then the Samuel Goldwyn Studios (known today as The Lot) on Santa Monica Boulevard where he was preparing a new film called *Cross of Iron* that he would shoot for a German producer in Yugoslavia. Each day we would meet in Sam's offices to talk about his films and his personal life, two subjects that were, at times, one and the same. On this particular day, we had just screened Peckinpah's private print of what is perhaps his most controversial film, *The Straw Dogs* with Dustin Hoffman. As we were returning to his office to discuss it further, the phone rang. After a brief exchange Sam hung up. "Come on," he said. "There's someone I want you to meet."

Leaving the studio by the side gate, we crossed the street and entered the Formosa Café, the venerable bar and restaurant built in the 1930s and frequented by virtually every star to work at the studio since. It was early afternoon and the place was all but deserted. Peckinpah led the way as we moved into the back room.

There at one of the tables sat Peter O'Toole in a stonewashed denim jacket and short-brimmed cap. A pastel cravat, tied with a casual knot, remained half-hidden beneath the upturned collar of his pale blue work shirt. He was nursing a Jameson and water (a world class drinker, a talent he shared with Peckinpah, water was his one concession to having had an operation the year before that removed a portion of his lower intestinal tract). Seeing us, he raised his glass.

"Samuel," he said, "welcome to my lair." His startling blue eyes caught the light. One of the most handsome leading men of his or any other age, he had begun his film career as *Lawrence of Arabia,* a role which had once caused the playwright Noel Coward to remark: "If he were any more beautiful, they'd have had to call it *Florence of Arabia.*"

"Tooly O'Pete," Peckinpah grinned. "Where the hell have you been?"

Rising as we approached the table, O'Toole embraced Peckinpah like a brother. We shook hands and sat down as the waitress approached to take our order.

One of the most accomplished actors of his generation, O'Toole, it is rumored, is capable of reciting from memory all of Shakespeare, plays and sonnets alike. He had first met Peckinpah in England in the sixties where they were introduced by Richard Harris, who had starred opposite Charlton Heston in Peckinpah's flawed epic Western *Major Dundee.* O'Toole and Harris had been friends since their days at the Royal Academy of Dramatic Art in London in the early fifties. It was a class that included Albert Finney and Alan Bates. In retrospect, they were perhaps the most remarkable clutch of actors RADA has ever produced.

Having shared many such afternoons, O'Toole and Peckinpah reminisced about their friendship, of drinking and carousing and years of living large. The subject of *Straw Dogs* came up more than once. Shot in Cornwall near Land's End on the southwestern tip of England, it had caused a tidal wave of rage among British's critics who had accused Peckinpah of inflicting the British sensibility with a peculiarly American brand of violence. O'Toole emphatically disagreed. The film was brilliant as was Dustin Hoffman's performance. Having recently spoken to David Warner, who had appeared in the film uncredited as a favor to Peckinpah at the time, O'Toole was pleased to learn that Warner had again been cast in his upcoming film.

"And James Mason," Sam added with a thin smile. "We're going to do World War Two from the German side with the Russians as the enemy. Nothing like it's ever been done.

"Mason and Warner and no part for me," O'Toole noted with indignity. "You really are a bastard. When are you ever going to cast me?"

Peckinpah held up his hand. "We'll talk when I get back. There's a script... I adapted it myself from a novel by James Gould Cozzens. Two characters. Robinson Crusoe by way of Luis Bunuel. You're going to love it. I'll send it over."

Looking skeptical, O'Toole frowned. *"Oft expectation fails, and most oft there where most it promises."*

Sam shot him with a sideways glance. "Screw Shakespeare," he said dryly.

"A sentiment I'm sure the Bard, himself, would have appreciated," O'Toole replied, pleased that Peckinpah had picked up on the reference. For emphasis, Sam expanded his suggestion to include O'Toole.

Unflappable, O'Toole smiled. "That's all right," he replied, "because I've got a picture coming up in which I'm going to play *you*."

Peckinpah stared at him for a long moment. "The hell you have," he said at last. "How can you lie with a straight face like that? God, I hate actors."

"Speak for yourself," O'Toole deadpanned.

"You are so full of it," Sam shot back.

O'Toole winked with a sly grin. "Just wait."

The picture, of course, was Richard Rush's *The Stuntman*. Filmed in 1977 and released in the UK the following year, it would not make it to American screens until 1980. In it, O'Toole plays a diabolical film director – clearly patterned after Sam Peckinpah at his most tormenting. When he finally saw it several years later, Sam hated it. Which, of course, meant he loved it. It was a performance that would again garner O'Toole an Academy Award nomination for Best Actor.

Glancing over our shoulders, O'Toole spotted two young girls hovering near the entrance to the back room. He smiled. Flustered, they looked away. Then a moment later, they slipped into chairs across the room, occasionally casting glances then quickly looking away the moment O'Toole would return them.

The talk returned to film. At that time, O'Toole had already received five Oscar nominations without winning. Always the renegade, Peckinpah had only been nominated once: with Walon Green for cowriting *The Wild Bunch*. Astonishingly, considering the power of his work, he had never been nominated for directing.

O'Toole raised his glass. *"I grow old... I grow old... I shall wear the bottoms of my trousers rolled. Shall I part my hair behind? Do I dare to eat a peach? I shall wear white flannel trousers, and walk upon the beach. I hear the mermaids singing each to each..."* He paused for effect and fixed Sam's eyes with his own. *"I do not think they will sing to me... or thee."*

"Show off," Peckinpah growled. Raising his glass, he touched O'Toole's and we drank a toast to mis-appreciation.

As we finished our drinks and paid the check, Sam spotted the two girls still self-consciously sneaking glances from across the room. Enjoying what he perceived as recognition, he nudged O'Toole and nodded towards them.

Gallantly stepping forward, O'Toole smiled. "Good afternoon, ladies. Is there something we can do for you?" Hesitant, they managed to hold out a couple of pieces of paper and asked for his autograph. Charming as always, O'Toole obliged with a flourish. Sam watched with envy as O'Toole handed back the autographs with a slight bow.

As O'Toole turned back, Sam shook his head in disgust. "I can't take you anywhere. Just once you'd think they'd ask me for mine."

Saying our goodbyes, we stepped out into the dying light and went our separate ways.

Sadly O'Toole's prophecy was to prove too true. Sam Peckinpah would die less than a decade later at the age of 59, ignored by the Academy to the end. And although they would honor O'Toole with an Oscar for his entire body of work in 2003, on this night when *Venus* might have smiled on him at last, he would be overshadowed once again, this time by Forest Whitaker's towering portrait of the Ugandan dictator Idi Amin in *The Last King of Scotland*. But then it is not the awards but the quality of the man and the work he leaves behind that matters most. And in that Peter O'Toole and Sam Peckinpah share a common fate. For they have touched our lives profoundly. And we are not likely to see their kind again.

About the author...

Garner Simmons has been a member of the Writers Guild of America since 1978. He received his BA from Colgate University (English/Fine Arts) before becoming what his father liked to call "the best educated bartender in Chicago." He served in the US Army National Guard on the streets of Chicago during the riots surrounding the assassination of Martin Luther King Jr., the 1968 Democratic Convention, and Kent State among others.

A graduate of Northwestern University's School of Communication in Radio/TV/Film, he is an internationally recognized authority on the life and films of the late Sam Peckinpah. He has spoken at various festivals and retrospectives of Peckinpah's work including Bologna, Italy (2006), the Locarno (Switzerland) International Film Festival (2015) and New York's Lincoln Center (2016). A member of the Directors Guild of America, the Academy of Television Arts & Sciences, and of the Writers Guild of Canada, he is a multiple winner of the WGA Feature Writer Access Competition (2015, 2016). As a member of the Dog Brothers, he has done the audio commentary on all of the DVDs of Peckinpah's films except *Cross of Iron* and *Deadly Companions* (both unavailable due to rights issues). A member of the Sisyphean School of screenwriting, he lives with his wife, educator Sheila McHugh Simmons, in Los Angeles, California, where he has recently completed his debut novel *The Exfiltrator*, due for publication in 2020.

Garner Simmons and Sam Peckinpah

Credits

The Wild Bunch location map of Parras, Coahuila, Mexico and surrounding area, handdrawn by Chalo Gonzalez 1967, courtesy of the Margaret Harrick Library, Academy of Motion Picture Art and Sciences, Sam Peckinpah papers File No. 82f1001.

Cover photo: Garner Simmons

416